The Akeing Heart

Also published by Handheld Press

HANDHELD CLASSICS
1 *What Might Have Been: The Story of a Social War* by Ernest Bramah
2 *The Runagates Club* by John Buchan
3 *Desire* by Una L Silberrad
4 *Vocations* by Gerald O'Donovan

The Akeing Heart

Letters between Sylvia Townsend Warner,
Valentine Ackland and Elizabeth Wade White

Peter Haring Judd

Handheld Research 1

First published in the USA in 2013 by Peter Haring Judd.
This edition published in 2018 by Handheld Press Ltd.
34 Avenue Heights, Basingstoke Road, Reading RG2 0EP
www.handheldpress.co.uk

ISBN 978-1-9998280-3-5

1 2 3 4 5 6 7 8 9

Series design by Nadja Guggi and typeset in Adobe Caslon Pro and Open Sans.

Printed and bound in Great Britain by TJ International, Padstow.

Contents

Preface   1

Acknowledgements   8

Abbreviations   11

Note   11

I. Like an astonished nervous dither bird   13

II. Entering into a dream   36

III. The new breath of life blowing out of England   50

IV. Violent and ecstatic happiness   125

V. She is like the sea   210

VI. Now and finally what love is and must be   263

VII. A last meeting must happen one time   305

VIII. The flame rekindled and abated   348

Epilogue   379

Endnotes   403

Select Bibliography   431

Index   434

About the author   456

And these are gems of the Human Soul,
The rubies and pearls of a love-sick eye,
The countless gold of the akeing heart,
The martyr's groan and the lover's sigh.

—William Blake, 'The Mental Traveller'

Preface

In the late 1930s—war in Spain, the threat of another great European war, and heated politics—the lives of three literary women became entwined through friendship, shared interests, and sex. Two were English and lived in Dorset for much of their lives, Sylvia Townsend Warner (1893–1978), poet, novelist, short story writer, and her life partner, Valentine Ackland (1906–1969), poet. Elizabeth Wade White (1906–1994), the future biographer of the Early Modern poet Anne Bradstreet, was Connecticut-born and educated. The depth of feeling in the affair between Valentine and Elizabeth caused emotional tumult for all three women, and the aftereffects of that tumult lingered with them for the rest of their lives. Blake's poignant phrase, 'The countless gold of the akeing heart', was personal for each of them.

In 1929, Elizabeth, aged 23, first met Sylvia, then 35, at a literary lunch in New York and admired her independence and witty, astringent talk. They met again in England that summer, and six years later Sylvia invited Elizabeth to the cottage in West Chaldon, Dorset, shared since 1930 with Valentine. A friendship developed between the young American and the two English women based on mutual interests in literature, the English landscape, pets, herbs, and shared political commitment in a time of looming international crisis. The Englishwomen were communists and anti-fascists committed to the Loyalist cause in the Spanish Civil War. They mentored Elizabeth, encouraged her to assert her independence from a socially and politically conservative family, and supported her efforts to raise funds for Spanish children dislocated by the civil war. The relationships altered when Valentine awoke in Elizabeth a hitherto unexplored sexuality in a passionate affair that began in late 1938 and stirred each of them deeply. Valentine expressed a 'violent & ecstatic happiness'. To Elizabeth, her lover came 'with a sharp sword and a gentle healing hand'. The affair heightened shared sensibilities, and its force and staying power seemed to take all three women by surprise. Sylvia, who had tacitly accepted Valentine's other affairs, soon found this one threatening; Valentine painfully sought to love both women; Elizabeth found herself unmoored from family and friends at home.

War in Europe left them on either side of the Atlantic, and for Elizabeth there arrived a new and quieter love, Evelyn V Holahan (1905–1985), a professional woman, introduced to her in New York City by Sylvia and Valentine in 1939.

The attraction between Elizabeth and Valentine reignited when they met again ten years later, leaving Sylvia and Evelyn in distress and themselves uneasy and unsure. 'I do not know how anyone can believe man to be mortal, who has experienced how instantly, in joy, he becomes a god', Valentine wrote after a night together in 1949. Sylvia dealt with nearly self-annihilating jealousy; Evelyn's settled and devoted 'marriage' faced dissolution. The stakes were high in personal terms, but though a break threatened, the two households held, and Elizabeth and Valentine crafted a warm and consoling friendship by letter and periodic visits for twenty years until the latter's death. But an echo of the passion remained and both Sylvia and Evelyn lived with the awareness that they had not shared these intense moments of their beloved's lives.

Elizabeth Wade White was my mother's first cousin and my godmother, a strong presence from my childhood to her death. She left a substantial archive from which I have selected for this book letters, poems, and notes from Sylvia and Valentine as well as Elizabeth's letters and journals and poems and letters to her from others. There are over 60 letters from Sylvia, almost 400 from Valentine, including poems and notes. I have concentrated on the years from 1929 when Elizabeth met Sylvia, to 1950 when all three of the women—and Evelyn Holahan—recognized that the affair was over. All but two items of the Warner materials in the archive are from these years (the exception being her notes during Valentine's final illness and death); these and the Ackland letters from this period are transcribed in full. I have quoted excerpts from the several hundred letters from Valentine in later years. With the exception of one letter to Elizabeth published in William Maxwell's collection of the Warner letters, none of this material had been available before. There are also letters from Evelyn Holahan, Elizabeth's lover and partner from 1940 onward, who became the fourth party to the affair, as well as from incidental others. All of this material is in the Elizabeth Wade White Papers at the Manuscripts and Archives Division, The New York Public Library.

The materials here add to an already rich published history. Elizabeth's and Valentine's affair preoccupied them—and Sylvia and Evelyn—for a dozen years and was an important part of their lives. Wendy Mulford's, *This Narrow Place: Sylvia Townsend Warner and Valentine Ackland: Life Letters and Politics, 1930–1951*, was published in 1988, the first biographical account to use Elizabeth's full name. Claire Harman, in her 1989 biography of Sylvia Townsend Warner, had access to letters and diary entries which she later edited and published (1993). Susanna Pinney in *I'll Stand by You* (1994), assembled excerpts from Sylvia's and Valentine's journals and letters with a retrospective narration by Sylvia in which the affair held a prominent place. In 1949, Valentine wrote *For Sylvia* (published 1985), an autobiography that dealt with the challenge of loving two people at once. Frances Bingham in her 2008 edition of Valentine's poems included extensive biographical material with many references to the affair.

It was only at the end of Elizabeth's life that she spoke to me, albeit briefly, about the relationships that the letters and notes in this book so dramatically evoke. In 1989, a review of Claire Harman's biography of Sylvia in the *Times Literary Supplement* included Elizabeth's full name as Valentine's lover. As we sat in a country pizza restaurant, I gingerly mentioned the review and my concern that she might have felt violated by the public identification. 'I was so young at the time, I didn't know what I was doing', she told me, dismissing any suggestion of discomfort. Were there letters? 'Valentine and I agreed to burn what we had'. That was the extent of what she said when her involvement became public knowledge, at least to *TLS* readers. In earlier years, she frequently told me about Dorset and the Chaldon downs, Theodore Powys and his family, and referred to Valentine as a friend. That land, its writers and people were present too in the many books and magazines in her house. When she gave me a letter of introduction to use on a bicycle trip in southern England in 1951 she told me 'Sylvia and I have quarreled recently'. She evidently thought I would be welcomed nonetheless. Alas, as I did not get as far west as Dorset, I could not use it. I now know that two years before, the affair with Valentine had reignited leaving Sylvia tormented and desperate. The 'quarrel' was of a grand proportion. I missed what would surely have been Sylvia's baleful eye.

After Elizabeth died in 1994, it was my responsibility as executor to clear out the one-time Connecticut farmhouse where she had lived for nearly fifty years. In boxes and drawers in the basement, in the library, in the study, in the box room, there were papers, letters carefully replaced in their original envelopes in boxes and file folders of various shapes, others in pigeon-holes, or piled on tables; some material dating from Elizabeth's childhood. The task of sorting was beyond one person in the time available before the house was to be put on sale so I asked friends to help. They came in shifts for one day a week. We established the dining table as the sorting point, in the small room reconstructed in 18th-century colonial style, generously illuminated by south and east facing windows. We initially sorted by year and sender and set up archival boxes as repositories. Scores of letters from Valentine had survived, whatever Elizabeth's intentions, and there were dozens from Sylvia. As we proceeded on what we increasingly saw as a treasure hunt, one of us would come back from 'the field'—the basement, the drawers and chests in the upstairs rooms, the attic—with letters, pamphlets, and books, bound and loose-leaf notebooks, menus, rail and bus timetables, Cunard Line tickets, shipboard newsletters, museum and art gallery announcements and catalogues, postcards. It took a dozen or more all-day sessions spaced at weekly intervals to complete this first sort in boxes with special allocations for Valentine and Sylvia. A quarter century passed before I was able to complete a catalog of the collection and transfer the collection to the New York Public Library.

I met Valentine for the first of only two times in 1954. Elizabeth asked me to drive her from Oxford to Salisbury where she was to meet Valentine for lunch. Valentine had antiques to show from a business that she had recently started, one that made good use of a sharp connoisseur's eye for objects (particularly small ones) and the pleasure she had from driving to auctions and visiting rural shops. I remember a strikingly tall woman with broad shoulders wearing a dark blue jacket, a tie shown off by a white blouse, and dark blue matching skirt, effectively a suit. She had an authoritative carriage, gleaming black hair in a mannish cut, pearly white skin accented by lipstick. After lunch we sat in the hotel lounge for coffee. From a capacious bag she produced items she had recently found to show Elizabeth. I admired the respectful care she used with the small wooden boxes, bowls, and odd pieces of flatware, and the precision and affection with which she described their characteristics, their provenance, and how they might have been used. In a sudden transition, she pulled up a cane beside her chair. Flashing her eyes to put me on notice, she paused, and then drew out the sword within, holding it at the ready between us. More flashing of eyes with an ominous suggestion. One of Elizabeth's favorite words was 'dramatic', which she used about Valentine as we drove back over Salisbury Plain to Oxford. In her letter about our meeting which I read 40 years later, Valentine described me as having a 'kind face' and not opinionated. I was relieved. Those flashing and searching eyes could have been more critical.

The next year (1955) at Elizabeth's suggestion, I spent the month of July as a paying guest of Elizabeth (Betty) Muntz, the sculptor, in Apple Tree Cottage in Chaldon. In the cottage where I stayed there were faint colors on the beams, lumber the villagers had retrieved from the storm-wrecked ships of the Spanish Armada in 1588. Elizabeth asked Valentine to arrange the introduction to Betty Muntz for me. I was spending a post-graduate year at Oxford and was supposed to be working up my Anglo-Saxon and Middle English. In fact, I was facing the prospect of military service and was far more interested in walking and riding along the downs to the cliffs overlooking the sea. It was a hot, sunny July; in the seemingly endless evenings, I enjoyed sitting on a bench on the south side of the Sailor's Return pub, once watching a thatcher move among the haystacks on the nearby hill, 'roofing' them to keep rain out. Betty talked to me about the past in Chaldon, the war, and her admiration for Theodore Powys, but she gave no hint of Elizabeth's tumultuous involvement with Valentine.

From Chaldon with a girlfriend, I paid a call on Valentine and Sylvia at Frome Vauchurch, their house in Maiden Newton, Dorset. Valentine was at the door, her eyes combed us as we entered, consuming impressions, I being 'kind' and polite and nervous. After a few minutes we heard a swish, the movement of crinolines as Sylvia appeared, announcing from the stairs (and adding to my nerves), that 'I've just been painting a white rose red'.

The ladies gave us tea. The one topic I remember was a reference to the Blackwall Tunnel under the Thames from Becton to Kent. Valentine told me how exciting it was to race a car through it. There was sexuality in her memory, a similar flash in the eyes at the memory of danger and thrill as I'd seen with the sword cane. Both my friend and I felt we had been scrutinized acutely.

What follows is an account of love between women. Valentine proclaimed her sexual identity in her male haircut, tie, trousers, and masculine bearing; she flaunted her maleness and was sexually aggressive, but she and Sylvia did not live in a lesbian circle and had almost no friendships with other lesbian couples. Elizabeth and Evelyn lived to the outside world as friends and companions with no explicit indication of homosexuality. Evelyn in fact denounced Valentine's provocative appearance in 1949 when fighting for her place in Elizabeth's affections. Valentine came to have an elevated view of love between women inspired by Plato's *Symposium* which she and Elizabeth read together. 'Lesbian love is, when it is in its pure state, a very strict kind of behavior-pattern, my darling: calling for control and profound attentiveness to instinct.'

I have included excerpts and references from the published material in conjunction with the letters, journals, notes, and photographs from Elizabeth's papers. There is thus a remarkably full account in their own words of the feelings and thoughts of these self-aware and articulate people in the heightened emotional circumstances of sexual passion and the response of a third and later of a fourth party. Their personal concerns played out against the backdrop of wars and threats of war—the Spanish Civil War in which the Loyalist cause united the three in the Thirties, the Munich crisis, the anxious wait for the inevitable second European war, the privations and damage of the war itself.

The locations are Dorset and Norfolk, London, Connecticut, and New York, the responses to each place experienced and articulated in the letters and journals. Elizabeth, hitherto little more than a name in published accounts of the affair, emerges in her journals and letters—and in what Sylvia and Valentine write to and about her—as someone seeking a role for herself in a period when an unmarried woman in her social circle in Connecticut was a rarity, posing for Elizabeth dilemmas of identity.

Peter Judd, Elizabeth and Wade, 1988.

I had no idea almost sixty years ago of the passions, the happiness, ecstasy, disappointment, sorrow, and jealousy that are conveyed by the letters and journals which follow. For me it has been a journey of discovery as I pieced the story together using the published and unpublished sources and my own notes and journals.

Acknowledgements

When I began to assemble my Cousin Betty's papers in The Patch, her beloved house where she had lived for over 50 years, it didn't take long to realize that there was so much material in odd containers scattered throughout that I would need help to collect and organize them without throwing out anything of value. My friends Emilie de Brigard, Alexandra Walcott, Nada Rowand, and Phyllis Johnson came to The Patch in shifts during the early months of 1995. Let me tell them again that I am grateful for their help, interest, and good company. Phyllis and my friend David Chandler gave me perceptive comments on early drafts of the book. Sandy Walcott also applied a sharp eye to the proofs.

Thomas G Lannon, Assistant Curator, Manuscripts and Archives, New York Public Library, was most helpful in working out the transfer of the Elizabeth Wade White Papers to the library in 2010. The manuscripts in this book are only a small portion of an archive that is available to researchers in its comfortable and efficient reading room. The detailed catalog of the collection is available online.

Tanya Stobbs graciously extended permission to use the Warner and Ackland documents on behalf of the Sylvia Townsend Warner estate. From my first contact with her when I began this book, she expressed her interest in seeing the project come to publication. This continued through several progress reports. I am most grateful.

In summer 1995, the year after Elizabeth's death, I brought her bequests—small items from The Patch—to her friends and godchildren in England. This journey took me from Dorset to Oxford to Stratford-upon-Avon to North Yorkshire. In Oxford, I visited Claire Harman, the author of the indispensable 1988 biography of Sylvia Townsend Warner. She had visited The Patch while researching the biography, she told me, and found Elizabeth guarded, only offering relevant dates. She encouraged me to carry on examining and organizing the papers. More recently in email correspondence, she has given this project welcome encouragement. Claire's biography was an invaluable guide.

The writer Julia Blackburn got in touch with me in connection with her interest in the Norfolk fisherman turned artist, John Craske, championed by Sylvia and Valentine. Her 2015 book on this inventive artist will certainly bring his work to wider notice. It was a fortunate happenstance thanks to the access to the catalogue of the White papers on the Internet that brought me to Julia and her husband, Herman Makkink in their house in the Argentine Valley in the Ligurian Alps.

Judith Bond of the Sylvia Townsend Warner Society read a draft and discussed the project at the Society's meeting in Dorchester in June 2012. She, and by her report, other members encouraged me to continue with the project and to self-publish. I much appreciate the interest and support of Judith and others who have considerable knowledge of Sylvia's life and works.

Chris Thomas, Secretary of the Powys Society, responded warmly to my description of a narrative and documents that connect with the lives of several members of that remarkable family. From the Society's collection, Michael Kowalewski selected the evocative images of Theodore and Llewelyn Powys, Chydyok, the house in the Chaldon downs, and Rats' Barn, even more remote in the downs. Louise de Bruin of the Society provided the photos of Katie Powys from The Mappowder Collection. I am most grateful for the use of these photographs that will enrich a reader's experience of this story.

Morine Krissdottir, the Honorary Curator of the Sylvia Townsend Warner Room at the Dorchester County Museum and the biographer of John Cowper Powys, gave me important comments on an early draft and sent me the two drawings of Valentine in the nude by Elizabeth Muntz. In past visits to Dorset, she shared her insights and knowledge for which I am grateful.

The National Portrait Gallery in London graciously permitted the use of the handsome 1934 photographic portrait of Sylvia Townsend Warner.

The late Janet (Machen) Pollock, Sylvia's maternal niece, after Elizabeth's death told me much about all three women with her particular understanding and wry humor. I regret that Janet is not alive to see this work and to continue to make perceptive comments. Monica (Hemmings) Ring, of Dorset, a lifetime friend of Elizabeth, whose name appears in these letters, was another of those I visited at that time. I was her houseguest in the charmingly named Puddletown from where she took me to places in Dorset that she particularly enjoyed. She did suggest that I should burn the letters, so this book might not have pleased her. Her love of the Dorset landscape, its remoteness and history, was kin to that of the three principals of this story and of their land and its people.

David Riedy performed a masterful job in designing the format for the first edition to present so much transcribed manuscript material and an abundance of illustrations.

Gerit Quealy helped me with the transcription of a number of the letters and applied her editorial eye to the narrative as it developed. Her enthusiasm and interest made the preparation of the first edition a cooperative effort.

Alison Bond and Joyce Seltzer of New York encouraged me in my effort to find a publisher for the book.

I am grateful to all these participants in this story and to many friends who have had to listen to me about it over the last several years.

My most comprehensive thanks go to Elizabeth herself, my Cousin Betty. She gave me her love, knowledge, and generous company throughout the over sixty years we shared. The letters, notebooks, photos, scraps of paper, theatre programs, bus tickets, pressed leaves, were a gift. Through them I came to know her sometimes uncertain and divided but always passionate younger self. She had a gift for friendship, and the abundance of letters she kept from friends, many of whom I knew, meant that as I sorted them I continued to feel part of that circle.

I am grateful to Kate Macdonald and Handheld Press for making possible through this new edition a wider distribution of the eloquence of the four women than I was able to offer. What they wrote to each other in those fraught years deserves a wide readership.

Peter Haring Judd
New York City

Abbreviations

EVH   Evelyn V Holahan
EWW   Elizabeth Wade White
STW   Sylvia Townsend Warner
VA   Valentine Ackland

Note

Letters and other manuscript material from STW and VA were transcribed in full. There are no omissions. The spelling and punctuation are as written. Brackets enclosing a blank space ([ ]) refer to an illegible word or words and do not signify an omission.

Notes on the 2017 edition

The text and images in this new edition of *The Akeing Heart* all derive from the 2013 edition. Orthographical and typographic errors have been silently corrected. The headings within the chapters, and a few less important photographs, have been removed. Long quotations from the letters in the commentary have been removed where they repeat the letter immediately following. Explanatory extended remarks by the author, originally interpolated in the text, have become endnotes. Some of the photographs have been placed in a slightly different order, to set them more closely to the paragraphs to which they relate.

I. Like an astonished nervous dither bird

On 27 January 1929 Sylvia Townsend Warner was a speaker at a literary luncheon at New York's Hotel Biltmore. Elizabeth attended, come to the city as she regularly did from her family home in Waterbury, Connecticut, two hours away by train. Sylvia, then thirty-six, was on her first visit to the US, where critics had praised her recent novels, *Lolly Willowes* (1926) and *Mr Fortune's Maggot* (1927), which had sold well in the US as they had in Britain. She was the daughter of a distinguished master at Harrow School in England who encouraged her brilliant and inventive mind. She became a trained musician and composer and was one of the editors who prepared a scholarly edition of music composed in the reign of the English Tudors, a project in which she was involved for much of the 1920s while living in London. She often entertained her many friends in her flat, and throughout the decade she had a private and heterosexual affair with Percy Buck, a musician and musicologist and the principal editor of the Tudor Church Music project. In the midst of her scholarly effort, she turned to fiction with immediate success.

Sylvia enjoyed an active life in London of concerts, opera, and friendships. A photograph of her in the 1920s shows a studious-looking woman, bespectacled as she concentrates on a manuscript, pencil in hand, an independent female scholar and writer. To Elizabeth, twelve years her junior, Sylvia must have seemed an enviable figure: an unmarried woman living on her own and a writer—just as Elizabeth wanted to do and be, though she also longed for marriage. Sylvia was vivacious and entrancing in manner, 'like an astonished nervous dither bird, with great shell-rimmed spectacles, enthusiastically discoursing', Elizabeth recorded in her journal. 'Last night was exciting and raucous

Opposite:

1. *Top left*: Evelyn Holahan, 1940; *top right*: Elizabeth Wade White, 1940s; *below*: Valentine Ackland and Sylvia Townsend Warner, 1939.

and utterly refreshing. There's no doubt about it, that sort of thing does one good, an exhilarating escape for a bit from one's own ever-present and frequently odious self. Any amount of people—all moderately established as, or wistfully and comically endeavoring to be—poets'.[1] Recalling Elizabeth at that time, Sylvia wrote '[i]f it had not been for her New England twang, her Anglophilia, her piety about literary bigwigs, she might have been any well-brought up young woman from the Shires who by some accident of pedigree had a mouth painted by Rossetti'.[2]

Elizabeth was born into a well-to-do family in Waterbury in central Connecticut. Her parents' wealth was created in previous generations. Her maternal grandfather as a youth came from rural Rhode Island to industrial Waterbury where he rose to be president of a thriving clock factory; her paternal great-grandfather similarly migrated from a country place to the factory town. In Waterbury terms, Mary Wade and William Henry White, her parents, were in the upper stratum of society, and by the 1910s their wealth could support a country house on Breakneck Hill five miles outside the city with gardens and extensive grounds; a city house for the winter, and a 'shooting camp' in the South Carolina coastal wetlands, also for winter. There were three house servants in Connecticut, travel in the US and abroad, automobiles—the Breakneck Hill house had an eight-car garage attended by a chauffeur, and a gardener maintained the grounds.[3]

On this estate, Will White played the part of the country squire in the English model; he left his last paid job in 1909 for the pleasures of seasonal shooting and fishing. Mary (Wade) White was a gracious hostess who made the country mansion a welcoming place. Elizabeth shared her father's pleasure in guns, shooting, and fishing and

Opposite from top left:
2. Elizabeth Wade White with her brother, Henry Wade White.
3. Elizabeth at age 18 in 1924. She was then at Westover School from which she graduated in 1926.
4. Mary (Wade) White in the 1920s. Portrait by Elsie Roland Chase.
5. William Henry White in 1918.

6. A view of the south-facing side of the Breakneck Hill house in winter.

had little of her mother's physical poise; people in the family often remarked that she was more her father's than her mother's daughter. At Westover, a boarding school for young women based on English models, Elizabeth's love of poetry and literature flourished. She had graduated two and a half years before her meeting with Sylvia. While many of her classmates were married (and her journal shows this is what she too wanted), Elizabeth concentrated on art classes and literary luncheons in New York, activities not calculated to attract young men of her social class. Despite her intellectual interests, like all her Westover classmates, she did not go to college.

While she was drawn to literature and enjoyed her father's manly pursuits, photographs of her in the social pages of the Waterbury newspaper show a young woman carefully posed and coiffed to match expectations of what a débutante from one of Waterbury's old families should look like, not the literary bluestocking she was within.

7. The announcement of Elizabeth's début in the Waterbury newspaper.

Without marriage and children, Elizabeth's interests became paramount: poetry, herbals—on which she became an authority—and an ancestor, Anne Bradstreet, the first published poet in the New England established by the Puritan migration of the 1630s. The culture of New England and its parent England—landscape, literature, architecture, history—became her abiding concerns, revealing the Anglocentricity if not the Anglophilia that Sylvia discerned. Elizabeth also had a gift for making and keeping friends, schoolmates, those she met on social occasions or through family, and several men with literary and artistic interests whom she met through her brother Wade at Yale College. Her brother, Henry Wade White (1909–1995) was three years younger; in the 1930s and 1940s he became a proficient painter in the American Precisionist style. He and Elizabeth had many friends in common and in later years frequently entertained together.

17

Elizabeth was always forthcoming to people who interested her, and so she was with Sylvia. After the luncheon she invited her to the hotel where she was staying; Sylvia arrived when Elizabeth's friend George Hamilton was visiting and they had been reading 'Archie MacLeish's poetry'—another indication of her interests and friendships.[4] Elizabeth and Sylvia went to Holiday's bookshop and then 'to tea at the Plaza'. 'S is a splendid person,' she noted, adding that she perceived in her 'the deep pagan religion of the earth'.[5] The next day she and Sylvia went 'up and down NY' to 'S's delightful man-hole of a bookshop'; this was 'unusually' closed, 'so we went to the Art Center and looked at Claire Leighton's woodcuts. Early lunch at the Waylin, then to see *The Kingdom of God*, expecting to be disappointed. We were not.[6] To the Waylin to collect our bags. S had left a copy of '*The True Heart*' for me, and so to the train for South Carolina, feeling quite sad at leaving NY. It has been a kind city, so full of pleasant happenings to me of late.'[7] *The True Heart* was Sylvia's third novel, just published in London and New York. A few days later Elizabeth commented in her journal: 'Beautiful individual choice of words and description, as usual deep feeling for country and understanding of personality'.[8]

Sylvia shared her lively impressions of New York and the people she saw and met there with Garnett. 'The skyscrapers,' she wrote, 'crop up everywhere, as randomly as though someone had scattered a packet of skyscraper seed. The general effect of the skyline is much like a collection of medicine bottles of all heights and shapes rising from a solid floor of little pill-boxes ... There is one large park with merry-go-rounds in it, and a small zoo, and quantities of chalets and artificial mountains and ornamental waters and notices saying Keep off, and no grass. The trees glitter with ice as though they were mica trees in a ballet, and all the children wear leather jerkins and caps with earflaps. Gentlemen walk about in shaggy fur coats down to their heels, like grizzly bears. The grizzlies wear bowler hats at one end, and light spats at the other...'[9] She found herself 'very famous' but avoided banquets and large gatherings 'and met people much like ourselves, except that they were friendlier and not so intelligent, and had some pleasant times mousing around with them'.[10] That mousing had been what she and Elizabeth had done.

Six months later, in August 1929, Elizabeth was at Brown's Hotel in London with her parents. 'Sylvia called this rainy morning to say would I go off into the country with her to see the Machens. Rather!' she rushed to record in her journal. Before their meeting she accompanied her father to Crowthers, the garden ornament place in Chiswick to find an astrolabe for the garden at home. It was just the sort of uniquely English place that she loved: 'a perfect charnel house that courtyard is, rows and heaps and tangles of garden figures, mostly old and broken; saints and goddesses, sun-dials and cherubs, busts & mantelpieces and leering satyrs, a grotesque [head] out of which at any moment might rise a dreadful sluggish creature, half leaden & half human, or a fairy ... we bought the lowly astrolabe and Daddy cut a tiny bright pink EWW in the fog-blackened copper with his penknife'.[11] The astrolabe was for the herb garden she designed at Breakneck, 'a stunning great thing' she considered it when she placed it there later in the year.[12]

> 'After lunch I was nervous & frantic, stupid! At 3:15 I went to Sylvia's house [at 121 Inverness Terrace in Bayswater]. The black chow came out on the balcony & barked & S took me into the room, which is filled with color and books and a big piano & the two carved angels.'[13]

The journey was to visit Sylvia's maternal aunt, Purefoy, and her husband, the writer Arthur Machen (1863–1947) in Amersham, Buckinghamshire, in the Chiltern Hills, a modest train ride. Arthur Machen's tales from the 1890s with their horror and supernatural themes were republished in the 1920s with considerable success. Their daughter, Janet Machen (1918–2008), ten years old at the time of this visit, was close to Sylvia in later years and became a warm, lifelong friend of Elizabeth.

> Bits of rain fell and we drove to the Baker St station & took the train for Amersham. A good talk on the train. A terrific mind S has got, and very gentle withal. From the station we walked through the pale green rain-shrouded light of a beech wood, past yew hedges & an old church, to the village of Amersham, very quiet and ancient against a whitish sky; and from there into the Manor Park, a perfect transmigration into a wilderness of smooth, sheep-cropped

hillsides and monumental trees. Certainly the minute tick of times mechanism does not measure the strangeness of such an experience, the un-continuity of suddenly finding oneself facing such unfamiliar acres beside that extraordinary person.

The brick sidewalk at Amersham was a nice colour, and pollarded plane trees, with their warm mesh of green leaves, grew outside the little alms-houses that a Lord of the manor had built in 1626 or thereabouts. A dark green door was opened by Arthur Machen, a jovially terrifying figure in a velvet jacket & floating tonsure of white hair. Upstairs in the small dingy sitting-room Mrs M appeared, vigorous but a bit distraught from sealing a hole in the water-butt. The two children, Hilary (whom we met in the street) & Janet are young & rather elfin creatures. In fact, how strange a world it is in which they all think & talk & live. Quite, quite different and fascinating.

Sylvia was an intriguing, somewhat mysterious figure to the young Elizabeth. She 'seems continually detached, not so much solitary as entirely self-sufficient, on good terms with the world, but—beyond it. Perhaps it is because one knows so little about her, perhaps because of the necessary & inevitable concentrated aloofness of the creative mind. On the other hand, there is that extraordinary, reassuring sympathy of mental contact. And more enchanting because it is dangerous.'

The conversation at the house was 'Absurd and elusive and enchanting.' After the visit, Elizabeth and Sylvia 'went to the pub, whose beams were hewn in 1500, and had glasses of Brown East India Sherry there & said goodbye and [I] went off in the rain, in an absurdly good humor, to find my way deviously to the station.' Back in town, demonstrating the relish she brought to life, 'I dined alone and on Roast Beef & Yorkshire pudding, and a glass of port.'

Two weeks later she was home at Breakneck. 'Never in my life shall I forget the glorious shining green on the lawn when I woke up early,' Elizabeth wrote on first morning back, 'I jumped out of bed and saw through the window of Mother's room the long, still morning sunlight lying across the grass, and this little dark privet hedge stretching out into blue shadows. Taffy [her Scottish Terrier] is so happy to be home. All this day has been like a dream, suddenly seeing and feeling and knowing once more the absolute, gentle beauty of this place. It is always set apart, but so soon it comes to be newly discovered, and becomes familiar again, and the wonder is taken too much for granted.'[14] When Sylvia and Valentine took Elizabeth under their tutelage in the mid-1930s, they regarded the family and its setting as restrictive; Sylvia scorned the house and its occupants in her 1939 visit. Elizabeth's affection for it and loyalty to her parents remained in spite of the views and urgings of these friends.

On trips from London in the 1920s, Sylvia spent weeks in country places to write and take formidable walks of fifteen or twenty miles. In 1921 with Stephen Tolmin, a young sculptor (always called Tommy), and two other friends, Sylvia stayed at an inn in East Lulworth. 'Dorset was new ground for all of them and they fell in love with the beautiful coast [and] the rolling chalk cliffs,' Harman writes. When his companions returned to London, Tommy explored further on foot and found a village that he immediately saw could be a retreat for him and his friends. This was Chaldon, sometimes Chaldon Herring, that 'lay in the fold of the downs, separated from the vast expanse of Winfrith Heath by a ridge on which stood five ancient tumuli, the Five Marys, and in the south separated from the steep cliffs at the sea by a mile and a half of incomparable downland.' It was 'very possibly the most hidden village in Dorset', according to another visitor at the time.[15]

Tommy rented a cottage and enthusiastically encouraged Sylvia to visit. He told her of a writer living there who had one published book, *Soliloquies of a Hermit* (1918) and the privately printed *An Interpretation of Genesis* (1911), but he had shown him a drawer full of manuscripts of novels and stories. The then unknown author was Theodore Francis Powys (1875–1953). At Tommy's suggestion, Sylvia read *Soliloquies* and, impressed, began a correspondence with Theodore and soon visited Chaldon to meet him through Tommy. She took several of his short stories to show to David Garnett in London and in turn, he successfully interested Chatto & Windus in publishing them as *The Left Leg* (1923). The favorable critical response encouraged Powys after years of neglect and initiated a productive literary career.

Theodore settled in Chaldon in 1904. He likely chose it as one of the most remote villages in Dorset, at the edge of the barren downland and away from main roads and rail lines. 'A man who rarely left home or

8. Theodore Powys in the 1930s, with his wife Violet and their daughter
   Theodora (called Susie as a child), in the garden at Beth Car, in Chaldon.
   Photograph courtesy of the Powys Society.

travelled in a car, who claimed to love monotony, and who never gave so
much as a sunflower-seed for the busy, practical life' is how his brother
Llewelyn described him in an essay quoted (without attribution) on the
Powys Society website.[16] With his wife, Violet Rosalie Dodds, he lived in
a house called Beth Car near the West Chaldon church.

When Sylvia met Theodore in Chaldon in 1922 she expected him to
'look like something hagiographical—a prophet or a hermit consumed
with the fire of god's word'. But after the meeting she noted that he
appeared more classical, 'a rather weather-beaten Zeus'. At David
Garnett's request, Sylvia provided a paragraph about Theodore he
could send to Alfred A Knopf for its announcement of the American
edition of *The Left Leg*.

> Theo is more afraid, more tunneled and worked with fears, than
> anyone else I know, even than myself. That is always why he is
> considering death. He turns to death with relief, for it is so certain,
> so reliable, so safe... His despair of the universe is an intellectual

thing, he knows there is nothing good, nothing true, nothing kind, that until he is dead, he is at the mercy of life, and that at any moment from behind some impassive mask we choose to call blessed, a blue sky, a primrose, a child, a nicely-fried egg, life, not death, will look out with its face of idiot despair, idiot cruelty. So he is always afraid except when he is writing (thinking, I should say) about death. Then he is comparatively happy and secure, so he makes these charming jokes about it. But in his writing, because one has to use other people's language and other people's thoughts to be understood by them, and because for one Theo there are fifty Donnes and Websters—philosophically, I mean—his fear of life is translated into death-symbols. But these rabbits and girls writhing in the bloody grass are horrible as reminders of what life is, when they are dead they have left off writhing. They are horrible no longer.[17]

Sylvia found Theodore's outlook as a writer an 'unorthodox version of Christianity [revealing] strands of mysticism, quietism, and pantheism, but the major influence upon him was the Bible, and he claimed that Religion "is the only subject I know anything about"'.[18] Sometimes savage, often lyrical, his novels and stories explore universal themes of Love, Death, Good and Evil within the microcosm of the rural world.' Sylvia and Valentine took Elizabeth to visit Theodore in 1935; they exchanged letters in later years, and she called on him and his wife, Violet, when in Dorset.

Outside my window above Betty Muntz's studio when I stayed in Chaldon was a lane that led up to the downs, by day a playground for the lively village schoolchildren. I looked out and saw amongst them an extraordinary figure. It was a woman with a weather-beaten face, close-cropped hair, trousers, and Wellington boots. She must have been striding through the active children, but I see her now as standing among them like a great tree in a forest of sprouts. Betty told me the woman was Katie (Philippa) Powys, a mysterious, eccentric presence to me then. I did not see her again on my walks, but I have never forgotten, and I knew instantly who it was when I found the return address of 'K P Powys' among the letters that Elizabeth saved. I know now that Valentine briefly gave her the ecstatic happiness that

9. Sketch by Elizabeth Muntz for the head of Theodore Powys placed at his grave in Mappowder churchyard.

10. Rough study for the Powys head.

Elizabeth also experienced. When it became apparent that Valentine would never commit exclusively to Elizabeth, Katie Powys counseled her with sympathy and understanding.

Philippa Powys (1886–1963), always called Katie, was Theodore's younger sister. She was the ninth of the eleven children of the Rev. C F Powys, vicar of Montacute, Somerset and his wife Mary Cowper Johnson. All of the ten who lived to maturity were 'formidable individualists', Katie among them, but she was less independent than were the others due to a highly-strung and emotional temperament. When the sister with whom she was living became engaged, the shock of the future separation led to a breakdown and six months confinement in a lunatic asylum (as it then was termed). After her release, she enrolled in an agricultural college and later worked on a farm. Years before, on a family visit to Sidmouth on the coast, she had met Stephen Reynolds, a university graduate with a degree in chemistry who had become a

11. Philippa (Katie) Powys. Photograph courtesy of the Powys Society.

commercial fisherman after a nervous breakdown. He had written a book about his life, and talked to Katie as an equal about literature and ideas. She fell passionately but hopelessly in love with him. He died in the flu epidemic in 1919, another terrible blow to Katie.

Her brother's Chaldon was a refuge. In 1924 Katie and her sister Gertrude, a painter, moved into the larger portion of a double cottage called Chydyok in the downs above the village. (The lane by the cottage where I stayed that July led there.) It was (and is) 'a brick and flint building, slate-roofed, lying in a hollow of the hills, midway between the village and the sea'. It was never a farm, always isolated. 'The wind howls round the house rattling the casements and wailing in the chimney', their brother, John Cowper Powys, wrote during a visit in September 1924. 'The view from this window stretches away down the steep valleys with a winding grassy road (no other approach except across the down turf) disappearing & reappearing over one crest of a ridge & then over another & right above them all (over the very top of the Five Maries) you can see the expanse of Egdon Heath. Three minutes' walk up the hill southward you can see the whole stretch of the sea-cliffs with the Isle of Portland & Chesil Beach ...'[19]

25

12. Chydyok in the Chaldon downs. Two houses are contained in the building. Gertrude Powys and her sister Katie occupied one from the 1920s to 1950s; in the 1930s Llewelyn Powys and Alyse Gregory lived in the smaller of the two houses; Alyse lived there as a widow to the 1950s. Photograph courtesy of the Powys Society.

Gertrude was a calm and stabilizing presence in Katie's life; the sisters would live in this remote house in all seasons and through the hazards of World War II. Katie wrote poetry and several novels, most of which were unpublished, but the novel, *The Blackthorn Winter* was a success in 1930 (reissued in 2007) and a book of poems, *Driftwood* (1930), was republished in 1992 as *Driftwood and Other Poems*.

In 1925 another Powys brother, Llewelyn (1884–1939), with his wife, the American-born Alyse Gregory (1884–1967), moved from New York where he had lived for some years to a coastguard cottage on a cliff overlooking the sea about one and a half miles from Chydyok; six years later they moved to the smaller portion of that house which adjoined Katie's and Gertrude's share. Llewelyn was ill with tuberculosis and spent much of his days bundled up in a shelter nearby to get as much sea air as he could, which is where Elizabeth met him on her 1935

13. Katie and her sister, Gertrude Powys, in 1942.
    Photograph courtesy of The Mappowder Collection.

visit.[20] His condition worsened and in the late 1930s he moved to a sanatorium in Switzerland where he died of a perforated ulcer in 1939. Alyse, his widow, continued living at Chydyok through the war and well into her old age; she and Sylvia corresponded frequently; she and Elizabeth, with whom she had a distrustful relationship, exchanged letters, and paid calls when Elizabeth was in Chaldon.[21]

William Powys, another brother, rented a semi-ruined set of buildings called Rats' Barn in the downs less than a mile from Chydyok. 'Rats' Barn is difficult to find,' according to Judith Stinton in her book on Chaldon. 'It sits on the curve of a hidden valley with a great barn courtyard and stockman's cottage, self-contained and inward-looking, half-haunted. The stone barn has doors at each end high enough for a hay wagon's entry and is still seasonally crammed with hay bales warm and round and scratchy ... Open shelter sheds face one another

14. Llewellyn Powys with Alyse Gregory, his wife, early 1930s.
Photograph courtesy of the Powys Society.

across the deserted courtyard.'[22] William Powys lived in Kenya and was rarely there, leaving its care to Katie who dearly loved the place. It was a great and poignant honor that she allowed Valentine, whom she adored, to use it for what Elizabeth described to her mother as 'a sort of camping trip' in the fall of 1938—and where they became lovers.

Katie was deeply emotional and lived with a profound sense of loss. 'I have wondered who has ever really known her heart where so many turbulent battles have raged, so many bitter disenchantments been brought to terms,' Alyse Gregory wrote at her death. She was someone 'delicately balanced, combining so vigorous an egoism with so burning a capacity for love and so great a need for reassurance.'[23] She gave both love and reassurance to Elizabeth through their common bond of Valentine.

Alyse Gregory, Llewelyn's widow, was active on behalf of women's suffrage in the 1910s. After the success of that movement, she wrote articles and in 1921 became an editor of the New York literary magazine, *The Dial*. Through that, she met Llewelyn Powys, then in America and helped him meet literary figures in the city and be published. They married in 1924, and a year later moved to England and to the coastguard cottage. Alyse was Llewelyn's nurse in his long battle with tuberculosis and tolerated his many affairs. [24] One of these was with Anne Holahan in New York; her pursuit of him to Chaldon led to her sister Evelyn coming to the village on a rescue mission. While there Evelyn met Sylvia and Valentine who years later invited her to meet them at the Cunard pier in New York when they arrived with Elizabeth.

In my 1955 stay in Chaldon, I stopped at Chydyok on my way to the cliffs overlooking the sea. I knew that Alyse Gregory lived there, this American woman living deep in the English countryside. An elderly woman came to the door on the warm day, with bees buzzing in the honeysuckle that surrounded it. She looked at me uncomfortably closely, introduced herself, but there was no word or gesture of welcome. Clearly she wanted nothing to do with this stranger whom she undoubtedly learned from village talk was associated with Elizabeth. (She was in Sylvia's confidence and sympathetic to her.) Slightly shaken, I went on my way. She was a solitary person, closest to her in-laws; Elizabeth referred to her as 'sinister' when I reported the encounter. They did exchange a few letters and visits in the years of this account.

Sylvia had met Valentine in Chaldon in the 1920s who, like her, had been attracted to its remoteness from London and to the writers and artists who lived there, including Theodore and the other members of the literary Powys family. Valentine Ackland was twelve years younger (within a month of Elizabeth's age), an aspiring poet, born Mary Kathleen Ackland ('Molly'). The autobiography she wrote in 1949, *For Sylvia*, recounts her childhood and her early artistic and sexual experiences. (Frances Bingham's narrative for the 2008 edition of Valentine's poems includes a more comprehensive account of her life and its relation to the poetry.) Molly grew up in London where her father was a prominent dental surgeon. She was educated in private elementary schools and received only a year of secondary education; her passion for poetry and ability to write well were largely self-acquired. Her parents' social ambitions led to her presentation at court before she was twenty. Straight-laced she was not. Early 1920s London was, as she wrote, 'extremely gay, and it was fashionable to commit extravagances and follies. I remember wearing a bare-backed, sleeveless bright green evening dress and screwing a horn-rimmed monocle into my eye, and walking down the steps into the Savoy Ballroom like that—at the age of 17 for—a bet.' Enjoyable as these extravagances were, it was the wild landscape of the Norfolk coast she most deeply cherished where the family had a country place in the dunes by the often stormy North Sea. Her childhood stays there were among her most powerful memories, and she repeatedly re-visited these former haunts throughout her life.[25]

Before he died in 1923, her father discovered that his daughter had had sexual relations with a female schoolmate; he savagely denounced her and never forgave her. Ruth, his widow, deferential in the marriage, subsequently put her considerable energies into Church of England activities and made her home at Winterton, Norfolk. Molly briefly took part in the conventional social scene of London, had affairs with men as well as women, and through a longer-term relationship with an older woman, floated in the bohemian artistic circles of early 1920s London. She made a hasty and unconsummated marriage in 1925 and had an abortion following a heterosexual affair. In 1926 the older woman took her to visit East Chaldon in Dorset and members of its artistic circle, which Molly determined to join and become the poet she aspired to be. By her early twenties she had assumed an appearance that proclaimed her identity as a lesbian: close cropped hair, mannish dress. She adopted the androgynous name of Valentine.[26] As a young man-woman, tall, broad-shouldered, with a pale white complexion on an oval face, she cut a striking figure. Her arrival in Chaldon in 1925 at the age of 19 with a friend, Rachel, both clad in men's gray flannel trousers, 'must have caused something of a stir', as Stinton drily observes.[27] 'She was exceptionally tall, thin, and dapper, careful of her appearance. In a letter to Katie in 1926 she describes a new golden-brown pair of corduroys and a gold and silver tie.'[28] Her fashionably long and graceful body was often sketched by Elizabeth Muntz, the sculptor, who had come to live in the village in the 1920s. One of these drawings of Valentine in the nude was kept by Elizabeth on the wall of her apartment and later her house for nearly fifty years.

At the time of Sylvia's American trip in 1929, Valentine was only an acquaintance. After renting accommodation in Chaldon for several

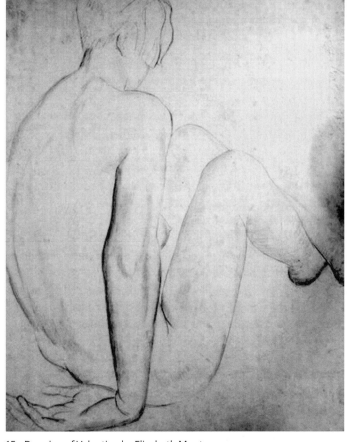

15. Drawing of Valentine by Elizabeth Muntz.

years, in 1930 Sylvia bought the cottage (always called Miss Green's) in East Chaldon that stood opposite The Sailor's Return, the pub whose name David Garnett used as the title for one of his books. It was a simple rural laborer's cottage without electricity or sanitation. As she intended to return to London for much of the time, she suggested to Valentine, who needed a place in Chaldon, that she move in and be the caretaker of the cottage, or, more grandly, as she put it, its 'steward'. Before Sylvia was to leave they spent several days together in the cottage; on the night of October 11th Valentine called out from her room 'I think I am utterly unloved.' Sylvia came through the connecting door, held her, and kissed her. In the morning Sylvia was quite certain that she had 'found love', already she was at home in 'an unsurmised

16. The Sailor's Return in East Chaldon, 1930s.

love, an irrefutable happiness', as she later recalled.[29] Sylvia shortly gave up her London flat and the two were rarely parted until Valentine's death. Upon the news that the cottage had been destroyed by a bomb in the war, Valentine told Alyse Gregory that 'in that house I was as happy as I ever have been or can ever be, happier, I think, than I have ever been—for it was the least anxious of my pleasure or joy that I have ever known.' She confided to Alyse that Sylvia 'had a wonderfully good character and almost never has black and desperate despairs.'[30] After three years in Miss Green's cottage, they spent a year in Norfolk and returned to Dorset in 1934 where they leased 24 West Chaldon, a somewhat larger cottage near Theodore Powys's Beth Car. It was in this cottage that they welcomed Elizabeth in 1935.

The two women became closely involved in the village life and were friendly with many of its inhabitants, literary or not. They became part of the Chaldon artistic circle in the 1930s along with the Powyses, and Elizabeth (Betty) Muntz, the sculptor. Theirs was an 'open marriage', tolerated by Sylvia, who even kept count of Valentine's frequent affairs with men and women. Valentine's aforementioned brief sexual affair with Katie Powys paved the way for the latter's consoling letters to Elizabeth nearly a decade later.

The late October 1929 American stock market crash triggered changes with worldwide effects. The economic depression in the US and Europe led to large-scale unemployment and the shrinkage and elimination of many individual fortunes. The depression proved to be a breeding ground for political turmoil in Germany with drastic consequences for the rest of Europe. The White family depended entirely on investments and might have faced severe retrenchment as many wealthy people did in the US, but under Will White's competent stewardship, the two houses, the annual stays at the shooting camp, cars for each member of the family, and travel remained unchanged throughout the 1930s. With her own income from inheritance—then about $4700 a year, equivalent to about $75,000 in 2010—and living at home, Elizabeth had limited concerns about money and could readily visit England to resume contact with Sylvia and her world, a part of which she had glimpsed on their visit to the Machen family in Amersham.

In her late twenties, when most women had husbands and children, Elizabeth noted unfulfilled expectations in her journal. She was unhappy with her single status, frequently confiding dissatisfaction with herself and, despite her numerous interests or perhaps because of them, a lack of direction. In politics she broke with her family, inspired by a Westover teacher who encouraged her to be aware of the problems of working people in Waterbury who then did not have the protection of unions. Later she supported Roosevelt, the New Deal, programs to help the unemployed and the poor. She argued with her father who detested FDR and the New Deal; her brother and mother on occasion fled the dinner table to find peace. Elizabeth in the midst of affluence and with interesting friends was unhappy, berating herself for lack of direction and commitment. In her journal she deplored the lack of marriage proposals and recorded hopes raised and dashed when men who interested her did not come forward. She had no relationship of any length with prospective suitors and certainly no sexual contact. She had warm male friends who were not prospects because of their apparent ambivalent sexuality.

Elizabeth was hardly confined. Though living at home; she had her own car, she was able to stay in a New York hotel regularly, to visit elsewhere in New England, and annually spend a few weeks with her parents at the shooting camp in South Carolina. But Waterbury society had its limits for her, and the hoped-for proposal never came nor was she able by inclination, training, or need to take a job and set up independent living. The disputes with her father started well before the New Deal as she noted in mid-January 1930. 'Monday 15th A shocking outbreak with Father this morning. Do not censure it, but be more careful.'[31] Occasionally she reported such incidents; more often she scourged herself for allowing her temper to show and repeated the injunction against letting it happen again. She was a long way from the bright visits with the lively, independent Sylvia; the dark mood would not fully lift until she visited England again. She was not idle in these years; she studied and became an authority on herbs, created a herb garden of her own; she learned how to construct bibliographies and in the course of that collected early editions of New England books, all pointing to research on her ancestor, Anne Bradstreet, daughter of Governor Simon Bradstreet of the Massachusetts Bay Colony. This drew her briefly to studies at Yale in the early 1930s; she also kept up with her interest in herbs and the literature associated with them, an accomplishment which later intrigued Sylvia.

On All Souls Day 1930, Elizabeth, like some of her 17th-century New England forebears, appealed to a higher power in her journal. 'Now the Lord I do pray thee take away out of my mind and lips that which is arrogant and proud and evil and unclean and let there be therein only such things that are good and true that I may see clearly and do no wrong and serve thee. For I know that the world is a good world, and I would be like until a hillside orchard of apple trees, or the kind rain falling onto the fields, or the bright pure running of a brook, in that world, thus to be instead a part of the beauty and gentleness of things that thou has made, and in nowise to be cast sorrowfully into the darkness. This I pray and also that I may remember these words to my salvation. Amen.'[32] A few weeks later she vainly awaited an unnamed man whom she hoped would love her. 'November 26th Oh God tonight I am tired and nearly desperate. If only he would come; I need him so.'[33]

Her account of an annual social event of the well-placed in New Haven and at Yale is a window on one of the better social occasions available to her. On the favorable side, she reported, Darragh (a possible suitor) and two of his friends, 'gave a well-managed, pleasant dinner-party, at which we sat down at 8:30 & did not finish until nearly 11:00 [and] my dress looked nicely'. Appy, one of the friends 'is very clever and amusing, though gloriously conceited ... the music was grand; [and] the three different people I danced with all danced very well ... George Pierson was charming.'

The unfavorable side won out in Elizabeth's view. The 'dance was thoroughly stodgy & stupid, mostly attended by very old & fat people ... D did not send me any flowers; that Appy & the Millers left the dance & went to see some people called Cosby without pretending to dance with me; that it was terribly cold & if there was any supper, none came my way ... D evidently knows I sent him that Valentine (which was really stupid) and thinks that I am in love with him, or uncomfortably near to it; he says he cannot come to the camp & got off some strong sentiments about being independent—he is still smarting, obviously, from his late misadventure [a terminated engagement]—well, he can jolly well be independent for all I care—.' She concludes, 'Oh, what the hell, I guess I can be independent too!'[34]

On New Year's Day 1934 she wrote that 'Suddenly I have wanted desperately to have a husband and children, something of my own to take shelter in and to live for, and I have looked back on twenty-seven years of being scorned and forgotten by every man I have ever cared for, few enough, and the many I have feared and almost hated for their power and their vigorous capacity for life and the awful icy lack of any sympathy or understanding between us.'[35]

Elizabeth was ripe for another vision of how to live.

II. Entering into a dream

Elizabeth gave a troubled greeting to the new year of 1935. She may have been a sociable and entertaining companion to her many friends, but within she continued to be unsatisfied and self-critical. She was twenty-eight, well past the age of eligibility for marriage among her contemporaries. The comfort she and her family enjoyed in the midst of the economic depression allowed more self-examination. 'I am sick with boredom and unhappiness, and at war with myself,' she lamented. 'I have lost (must it be true?) the blessed lonely Ivory Tower, and have got in exchange the fascinating, hysterical, hubbub of human personalities. I am miserable without them. I am confused and perplexed and excited and unfulfilled with them. I want desperately to get married, but would I have the courage, and to whom?'[1]

However, there were good times. 'Marvelous companionship, of which I would wish to be worthy ... last winter, in New York, the Opera Ball and Central Park Casino and the Spring Derby Day and our little trip to Gloucester (why is that such an idyllic memory?). Then all of August at Gloucester, and Naushon [island off the Massachusetts coast] and falling in love; and riding in the autumn, and the Yale-Harvard game and days & nights in New York and New Haven and Cheshire.'[2] There was a dark side to the self-examination. 'I want peace and serenity and to lose myself in hard and simple work. And to stop pitying myself and everybody and feeling the tragic pointlessness of life so chokingly. It must not be so, oh God, let me out of my prison, let light into my darkness, let me live and let me be good.'[3]

On her birthday in June she wrote that if George Pierson, then a young member of the Yale English faculty, proposed, she would accept. 'This is my 29th birthday, and I am in love with George Pierson, and have had no word or sight of him for three weeks.' Pierson was not forthcoming. 'June 16th Coming back from the mailbox through the

woods, with that unopened letter in my hand was a transformation, saying "All right, go ahead, strike, stab, shoot here in my breast, bared for you. I have no defense." But the blow did not fall, and he came and now he has gone away, and God knows when I shall see him again or if it will ever be anything to him whether we meet or not. He is so mysterious and detached and sure; he asks no questions, I think, of life or anything in it, and accepts from it only so much as intellectual taste allows him to.' She 'looked him full in the eye and thought "I love you".' The sentiment remained unspoken. George told her 'not to be solemn in England this summer'. In the journal she responded, 'Well, I shall go, and I shall not be solemn, & I shall try to forget him'. This she did in a matter of weeks, and it was not a solemn time.

In July, Elizabeth went to England for research, to visit her beloved Oxford, and, at Sylvia's invitation, Chaldon. She arrived there after a journey in a 'sardine-like train up with, astonishingly, Muriel Draper' [the prominent American patron of musicians and artists]. Then 'to be driven through the thatched Dorset villages and suddenly out into that wildly beautiful valley, with the green, smooth hills sweeping and rushing off into the sky; and Sylvia's stone farmhouse hugging to the side of one of them, was entering into a dream from which, please God, I shall never now completely awake.' Sylvia, well established in her partnership with Valentine, welcomed the young American to the cottage in Chaldon and introduced her to their writer friends. Elizabeth saw how they lived simply and economically in the cottage among interesting people and pursued artistic and literary interests.

Her hosts, their intellects and character, their way of life, the social and political commitments they had made, their regard for her, all a counterpoint to her sense of herself, inspired Elizabeth. 'They have achieved freedom and direction, Sylvia with her dragon-fly mind that [seems] to quiver on the edge of quaintness and then rush off to some terrific peaks of insight and her timelessly pure and courageous character, and Valentine with her clipped hair and beautifully cut gray flannels, a delicate and vibrant spirit, like one of the daggers and pistols that she loves. Right or wrong, wise or deludedly they have accepted and not denied, they are true to what they believe.' The Powyses she perceived as 'that monumental and gentle tribe, Theodore with his understanding and kindness, the mad & spiritual Philippa'. At Chydok she visited 'Llewelyn, stricken by another hemorrhage, lying in his shelter above the garden, in the midst of those sweeping hills, with all the dignity of life and death in his magnificent bearded Old Testament head'. She wondered in awe, 'why should they all be so kind to me, a stranger, and empty, among them, so kind and quiet that I could take their hands and feel a oneness with them, and look into their eyes and be comforted.'

Days later, seated on a bench at Christ Church Meadow, Oxford, she recounted 'this experience that has struck and shaken me more profoundly than I thought anything ever could again ... I am so afraid of losing that wild, simple intensity, the "terrible crystal" of those hills and their profiles, and I must keep it if I am to live.' Valentine with her rifle is an example: 'I must cast off the false values and cancerous softness of my life, as I rather frightingly shed that old sentimental idea and found in its place a primitive blood-lust to kill one of those scattering rabbits with Valentine's rifle. I must find some bit of truth in this mass of contradictions that is my mind, and cleave to it, and build up faithfully from that foundation.' She gave herself a charge: 'that I must always be one of the wild ones, that I must resist domestication, be a good deal alone, and bend myself fiercely to an ideal.'[4]

Much as Elizabeth sought to hold fast to the resolve she had set out for herself in Christ Church Meadow, time swallowed the intent. In May of the next year, she still had an expectation of marriage; after a get-together with a man identified only as 'Willard', she expected a proposal and this temporarily rid her of the 'black misery' of the winter months. When a letter came with word he was engaged, she reflected that though this was disappointing, 'marriage will come if it is meant to'. She added, 'sex taboo [takes] care of itself eventually, and accomplishment is a matter of great discipline and is a hard time, full of fear and doubt and self-mistrust, but I think out of its climactic misery something, some sort of coming to terms, will develop. And this summer's experiment is so important, I think, to either kill or cure.'[5] The 'experiment' for the next summer was research on Anne Bradstreet in England and another visit to Chaldon. But what of 'sex taboo'? Does it refer to what was then the social unacceptablity of sexual relations outside of marriage or sex between women? It is the only mention of sex in the journals. She could have had no doubt of the relationship between Sylvia and Valentine and admired the life they had made together. It seems likely that this was in her mind.

In June 1936 when Sylvia learned that Elizabeth would again be in England, she invited her for a willingly accepted visit. The prospect of civil war in Spain was a principal topic of conversation. That country had been in turmoil since a left-leaning Popular Front won national elections in February; there were strikes and anarchy which prompted General Francisco Franco to take command of army units in Morocco in July and shortly to invade Spain itself with a call to restore order and eliminate leftist—and particularly communist—influence. Just before Elizabeth's visit, Sylvia and Valentine had been in Barcelona and Madrid, where the courage of the Loyalists supporting the elected government inspired them. By contrast, they considered spineless the 'neutrality' of the British and French governments. The commitment of the Soviet Union and support for the Loyalists was one reason the two women had joined the British Communist Party; concern for laboring people at home was also a factor. They were among the many who saw the struggle in stark terms, with Stalin's USSR on the side of the idealistic and good.

As their subsequent letters show, both Sylvia and Valentine delighted in Elizabeth who shared many of their interests. They clearly regarded her as a protegée as well as a friend whom they could educate politically and wean from a constricting family influence. They took Elizabeth with them to see a house for rent in Maiden Newton, near Dorchester, to have her opinion. It was larger and potentially more comfortable than the cottage, and the River Frome flowed by it. Elizabeth joined in approval of the move; it would take over a year to accomplish and later letters about decoration and the garden show how much they made Elizabeth feel a part of the project.

In a letter after the visit, Valentine urged Elizabeth to return. Elizabeth replied from Lincolnshire where she was doing Bradstreet research.

18. A contemporary postcard view of Maiden Newton in the 1930s.

24, West Chaldon, Dorchester, Dorset.

25th June, 1936[6]

My dear Elizabeth,

(I know you are called Betty, but Elizabeth is your Chaldon name, because we always speak of you as that—!)

Here are some photographs of the house [not found], in case your single one isn't good.

These are to persuade you to return whenever you can and for as long as you can. I think they will. But I hope that Lincolnshire is being satisfying, only not so much so that you will love it better than Chaldon.

It has become very hot, and we have been gardening all the morning. Theodore [Powys] came over as we sat down to lunch, and he stayed, drinking cider and talking, for almost an hour. It was very pleasant, but we missed you.

If you can possibly manage to come to the fine wedding we talked of, it is on July 4th, at a place near Pulborough, Sussex. The place is called Apsley Farm, and the station is Horsham. We could meet you in the car on our way through Horsham, as we come from here. The wedding is round about mid-day. If you can come, do so, and let us know about it, and we'll fix trains and meeting-places.

And there is Janet Machen's address to remember—do go see her if you possibly can; she would be so very happy to see you again. Her address is: 18, High Street, Stratford-on-Avon, Warwickshire.

With love, and thanks to you for staying with us and being happy here.

Valentine

Elizabeth did not manage to attend this wedding but sent the photograph she had taken of the Maiden Newton house. Valentine suggested that Sylvia could join her on a visit to Malmesbury—which she did, and both referred to the experience in later letters.

July 2nd [1936][7]

My dear Elizabeth,

Thank you very much indeed for the photographs. They really are very fine; our house looks so romantic that I was driven out to survey it afresh, and wonder at it, and remember that it really does look like that—which it is as well to remember. For we have been busy at tedious jobs for these last days, and it is easy enough to forget even very good fortune when one gets oppressed with dull work.

If you can spare us the negatives, we would like to borrow them for a short while (about four days) to have some copies made for specially favoured friends!

I am so sorry that you can't come to the absurd wedding. We start to-morrow early in the morning, going through some new villages on our journey, and hoping to visit the place where Sylvia's grandfather preached many sermons and her grandmother sat in the front pew, shaking with laughter as her husband got mixed in his doctrine!

If only Malmesbury works out well! It looks as though Sylvia will certainly be able to go, but less likely that I shall. However, we are contriving with all our united might, and also counting on you to come here on a pilgrimage to see, ostensibly, Bindon Abbey,[8] Tess's House and a fine place we've only just found, called Woodsford Castle—and—of course—Corfe Castle. But come, anyway, and we'll find you plenty of reasons for being here!

Much love and many thanks,
Valentine

Malmesbury is one of the oldest towns in England with the still-standing ruins of the Abbey founded there in the 7th century. Sylvia was Elizabeth's guide and companion on the visit to Malmesbury. It was an encounter with the antiquity of the British Isles that greatly moved Elizabeth; it became a kind of lodestone for her sense of England. Valentine, recognizing how stirred Elizabeth was by this ruin, gave her a book on the sculptured apostles in the Abbey that Christmas.

In late October 1936, the British Red Cross invited Sylvia and Valentine to work under their auspices in Barcelona. In response, Sylvia wrote, they 'sprang into the car, and drove across France at a rate which would have been intolerable if we had not been on our way to Spain'. Barcelona, Sylvia reported, was what the USSR must have been like in its early days; there was an abundance of committees and passion, so different from 'our mealy-mouthed country'.[9]

At Christmas, Sylvia and Valentine wrote with memories of Elizabeth's visit and expectations that she would come again. There is news of Theodore Powys and of Thomas, their cat, who had welcomed Elizabeth.

24 West Chaldon, Dorchester, Dorset
25, xii, 1936[10]

Dearest Elizabeth,

The books arrived most accurately on Christmas Eve, and we thank you for them with both our hearts.

It is lovely to have Anne Bradstreet actually in the house, where she has been an endeared guest ever since you brought her here this last summer. I find that I think even more highly of her at a second reading. And I enjoy the picture of her house, and guess it is one of those, even as you told me of, with the barns joined to it, an envy that has been in my mind ever since you planted it. I continually think how secure and how romantic at once it would be to leave one's warm familiar house and walk through the cold barns, stout-built and tidy, knowing as one went, by the smell, what one was passing: the apples in tubs, the cider casks, the grain and the hay and the sheepskins. And one would hear the noise that wind has only when it blows over snow—a quite different note to any other voice of the wind,

You have given us so much of New England, you cannot guess how much. For though I had read about it, and knew about it in a book-learned way even before I met you, and had wafts of it from Frost's poems, the book-learned was speculation and a mere good memory for details, and the Frost-learned was like something which one has known very intimately in a dream, but from you I have had a kind of transfusion of New England, or infusion, I have drunk your brew of it. How strange to contrast the Massachusetts of Anne Bradstreet, and the land of Van Wyck Brooks' books: like a really splendid cake, with its ceremonial white icing of culture over its dark and solid body of prosperity. I like Emerson's aunt so much, 'not organized for a future state'; is an exquisite phrase … a cat might have made it. If I ever have a she cat she shall be called Mary Moody Emerson, It would have been a perfect name for Tom's mother, at once so prim and so passionate.

Thomas has added a new grace to all his other graces. He has taken to smelling unmistakably of violets. I can only suppose that when no one sees him he goes and rolls himself assiduously in our violet patch (Valentine picked quite a large bunch this morning). We never see him doing it, and there is not that aftermath of flattened leaves and crushed blossoms which one would expect after 15 pounds of rolling Thomas, But the only other hypothesis is sanctity, and we can't quite credit that.

He is extremely well, inexpressibly handsome, and ineffably sure of it. He has, however, moments of humanity. Yesterday, alarmed by a strange ginger and white terrier, he scratched me to the bone, and then fled into the woodhouse. The woodhouse has a door which does not quite go up to the lintel, there is a gap of about eight inches; and presently, walking into the yard, I saw Thomas hanging over the door in an attitude of really profound dejection with the front paws dangling like a seasick voyager, and the eyes full of woe. He was terribly embarrassed at having scratched so hard, and hung his head for about five minutes.

Then, quite suddenly, he hopped off the stool of repentance, and he cried into the house to be fed.

We have just come home from Beth-Car. The house was full of bright tinsel, and cracker presents, and there was a christmas tree, and a toy piano with eight notes tuned to a very modal scale, on which I played Pop Goes the Weasel to Theodore's attentive and completely unmusical ear. Yesterday we all visited the church to see the decorations. We had left the visit rather late, it was dark outside and darkness inside. We could just see the prick ears of the holly against the windows, and pale chrysanthemum eyes glaring from the font and pulpit. The effect was perfectly devilish, and gave us a great deal of pleasure.

With best wishes for 1937, my dear, and much love,
Sylvia

In a pattern often repeated in the next two years by 'S & V'; when one wrote a letter to Elizabeth, the other wrote the same day or the next. The book that Valentine acknowledges was an edition of Anne Bradstreet's poems. She, too, gives an account of Christmas with Theodore Powys and his family.

24, West Chaldon, Dorchester, Dorset
27th December, 1936[11]

My dear Elizabeth,

Thank you so much for the book, into which I plunged immediately, and in which I have been swimming ever since. It is enthralling, and except that Sylvia has a way of thieving it which distracts me, I've been happy with this present ever since it arrived. Ann Bradstreet (which I borrow from Sylvia!) is a lovely person, and I can see that she is going to inspire Theo [Powys]—he is clamoring for the loan of her already.

It is odd to think how far we have been and how much seen since last we saw you. I wish you could have been in Spain with us, because there we could have shown you exactly why we both argued so violently in favour of our political views! However, soon Sylvia will send you some photos which are good, and I am going to persuade her to copy out (or to let me copy) some of the poems she has written since then. I think you will like them and I know you will like to have them.

Chaldon is looking most lovely now, drab and gray, but the hill green and all the thatched cottages looking strangely bright, just as the hills look, under the weeping sky. It has been a warm Christmas, as it should be, and now the feast is over it has begun to rain and the wind is getting up, carrying away the faint haze that has been over us for these three days and more. There are wide flocks of birds that go over every morning and return to home-fields in the evenings; enormous companies of them, and their wings make a rushing sound most strange to hear. Granny Moxon once said that 'more'n an acre of birds' had flown over her garden—

Theo says he has rarely had a more peaceful and contented Christmas, and he looks ruddy and gay as a result. Violet is happy and Susan very happy. It is pleasant to visit them just now, and to see the house quite incredibly full of presents, decorations, streamers, holly and a little be-carded Tree. Theo brings out a bottle of port and Violet brings cake and preserved ginger, and they sit around the fire and play with Susan and her toys, in vast contentment and quietness. Please heaven this winter mood will last into the spring! And then you must come over the Atlantic again, and see us all, and be happy here.

At this present time there is a great bull which roams about in the field outside our house: last year, when he was only 3 years old, we did not take him very seriously, but this year he is really fierce, and our walks have turned into sorties to break past him—he is now lying like a large and placid beast outside the front gate, but if one or other of us was to go out he would get up and lumber towards the house, making that unpleasant and frightening screaming roar which Theo describes so well. He is not an embellishment, but he will, I think, be gone by Easter when, we so much hope, you will visit us!

Meanwhile, much love and many many thanks—and may this New Year be happy and fruitful to you—

Valentine

At the end of the year, Elizabeth was in Gilbertsville, NY, visiting Douglas McKee, Yale college mate of her brother Wade, and a lifetime friend. In her journal, she continued to deal with bleakness. 'Patience said Rilke, patience and this purity of soul which is an outflowing clear spring and not a stagnant inward seeping pool, which reserves itself forever instead of choking and poisoning the waters with the rotten leaves of selfishness and despair.' She is prayerful: 'And God help us to remake these things, and take away the terrible fear that is death in life, and grant us strength to forget ourselves and to love and live in and with the beautiful and fearful world.'[12]

19. Elizabeth and Giles at Breakneck, 1937. Photo by Harry Hard.

At Breakneck, probably in the fall of that year, a local professional photographer posed Elizabeth by a birch tree. She wore a jacket with a fox fur piece on her shoulders. Giles, her Sealyham terrier is at her side looking intently at the camera (Figure 19). Her mother framed the portrait in silver and placed it with others of the family on a table in the Breakneck living room. A comparison with the 1935 informal photo taken by her friend Prentiss Taylor witnesses the inner conflicts with which Elizabeth contended. At Breakneck, she is contained, carefully dressed and hatted, ready for the Society page— this portrait composes Elizabeth as her mother would like her to be, dignified, poised, with the accoutrements of the well to do, a purebred dog and a fox fur piece. In the earlier image in Gloucester, she is the glowing, passionate, willful young woman, close to the 'wild one' she aspired to be (and which she herself found difficult to manage). This Elizabeth had a smoldering, unbridled spirit. It was she whom Sylvia and Valentine sought to befriend and nourish.

III. The new breath of life blowing out of England

Elizabeth grew closer to both Sylvia and Valentine in 1937 through correspondence and a brief but intense visit in May when she was in England for the coronation of George VI. In Waterbury, she organized a committee to raise money to aid Spanish children displaced or orphaned by the war, an effort warmly praised by Sylvia. She gave talks on the war—controversial in America because of the antipathy of Catholics to the Loyalist cause after the Vatican had recognized Franco's revolutionary regime as legitimate.

In early March, Sylvia made another visit to the war zone with Valentine. She wrote Elizabeth from Madrid. (In later letters both Sylvia and Valentine described in more detail the occurrences on this visit.) The shortage of soap in the Loyalist areas offered a fund-raising opportunity.

Gran Hotel Victoria PLAZA DEL ANGEL, 8
MADRID 6: iii: 1937[1]

Dearest Elizabeth,

We are here, and I have seen the most magnificent people, the handsomest country; I have ever imagined. What dolts we have been not to live in Spain.

Meanwhile, there is a soap shortage ... a small misery of war, but an essential nuisance to the people who feel it ... especially these very clean people, with their passion for washing themselves. (Incidentally, when we drove here from Valencia yesterday our driver stopped at every washing-trough or fountain, sluiced himself, and climbed back into the drivers' seat, sleek and dripping like a seal).

Then, as for the soap, I am getting it in Paris next week, so that it may get here as soon as possible; but it will have to be paid for. Will you take round a collecting-box among your friends for the Soap

Gran Hotel Victoria
PLAZA DEL ANGEL 8
MADRID
Teléfonos: 12870 · 12879 · 12825
Telegramas: VICTOROTEL

6 : vii : 1937 :

Dearest Elizabeth :

We are here ; and I have seen the most magnificent people, the handsomest country, I have ever imagined. What dolls we have all been not to live in Spain.

Meanwhile, there is a soap shortage ... a small misery of war, but an essential nuisance to the people who feel it ... especially these very clean people, with their passion for washing themselves (handsome), when we drove here from Valencia yesterday our driver stopped at every washing-trough or fountain, sluiced himself, and climbed back into the drivers' seat, sleek and dripping like a seal).

Now, as for the soap, I am getting it in Paris next week, so that it may get here as soon as possible ; but it will have to be paid for. Will you take round a collecting-box among your friends for the Soap for Spain Fund, secretary S. T. W. ?

20. Sylvia's note from Madrid, 6 July 1937.

51

for Spain Fund, secretary, STW? Explain that soap is an essential in hospitals, a blessing in the trenches, and an important matter throughout the civil life of the country.

And with these short rapid words I must leave off, for there is a great deal to do, and little time, and I have to speak on the radio tonight, and must collect my thoughts for that.

Strange revolutionary situations. Here is one intellectual writing to another from Madrid—and not one word of the Velasquez, The Goyas, the architecture ... just a rapid demand for soap.

With our loves

Sylvia

At home that spring, Elizabeth raised funds and spoke to small groups. The conflict in Spain doubtless seemed remote and confusing to most in her audiences. Her notes show that she presented a short current affairs lesson stressing the legitimacy of the Loyalist cause and appealed on humanitarian grounds. She was successful in encouraging contributions in a time of limited incomes and earned Sylvia's praise the next year when she reported over $1,000 raised. She prepared comprehensive notes for her talks.

I have come to speak to you about one million children. These children are not, except in nationality, very different from the same number of American children. But one word is lacking from the vocabulary, a word which we in America still own and take for granted, and that word is security. There is no such word, no such thing as security in the lives of the children of Spain today.

As you know, Spain has been for centuries a poor and unsettled country. Feudal conditions of life existed there until only a few years ago, and the peasant and factory-working classes lived in extreme poverty. In 1936, after the overthrow of the monarchy, a Republican government was elected, which hoped to run the country according to the principles of democracy. But this meant great changes of the social order in many directions, many false steps were taken, many mistakes made, and before the government had a chance to bring order out of chaos it was faced with armed rebellion. This armed rebellion was instigated by those who preferred the old monarchical or autocratic form of government in Spain, the military leaders, followed by a very large part of the army itself, the old feudal landowners or grandees, and the rich and materially powerful organized churches.

The Loyalists in Spain are those who represent the existing government, essentially a democracy, but made up of all sorts of liberal parties including the extreme radical elements. Their army is a people's militia, hurriedly trained and equipped to meet the crisis, and consisting of working men, peasants, the best of the younger intellectuals, writers, teachers, and politicians of the country. They have been assisted by nationals and some men from Russia, and by the International Brigade, a small army of men of all nationalities who are willing to give their lives for what they believe is the right form of government.

The Nationalists, or Insurgents, are the rebellious party. They believe that lawlessness and violence will be the result of too much freedom for the working classes, and they wish to establish monarchy or dictatorship in Spain. They are led by General Franco, and their forces consist of the old standing army, the Civil Guard & the Moors, very much assisted by men and nationals from Germany and Italy.

Now, after nearly two years, the Civil War in Spain still rages, and the armies continue to destroy each other and their country.

But we are concerned with those people of Spain who do not fight, with the women, the old and sick men, and most particularly the children.

This terrible war has split a beautiful and interesting country into ragged and suffering parts. Many of the principal cities of Spain have been entirely or partly devastated by bombing from land, sea, or air, and the populations of these cities have been homeless refugees.

Our concern is with civilian populations, not with military.[2]

The occasion of Elizabeth's trip to Europe in May 1937 was the coronation of George VI. It was an event hardly of interest to Sylvia and Valentine—there was no space for royalty in their political outlook; from the Marxist point of view the pomp and circumstance was a diversion. For Elizabeth, the ceremony of the coronation had strong historical resonance, an identity with the England she loved. The same person who could raise funds for impoverished Spanish children also enjoyed the glamor of a royal occasion with the attendant dinners and dances with congenial friends. Sylvia sent an affectionate letter before she knew definitely that Elizabeth was coming. Elizabeth had discerningly sent her a children's novel by E. Nesbit, 'a most unlooked for garland into my lap'.

24 West Chaldon
Dorchester Dorset.
l.iv.1937[3]

Dearest Elizabeth.

You have tossed a most unlooked for garland into my lap. A whole Mrs Nesbit story which I did not know. I thought I had read every word of that blessed and comfortable woman, but I have never heard of the Wonderful Garden. I have just sent to the London Library for it, and when it arrives I shall unloose my cold into something serious, and go off to bed with it.

We are feeling like Noah on Ararat. The ground is just beginning to dry though still I have to walk down to the car in gum boots, and change into shoes on the road if I am going anywhere where I wish to appear elegant, I don't know if the winds blew as cold over Ararat as they do here. I cannot imagine how anything can bear to flower at all, however there is a cheerful row of polyanthuses under the shelter of the hedge, and about three weeks ago a bewildered pink bloomed.

I can only account for this by the fact that Thomas is given to sleeping on the pinks, he looks on them as so many spring mattresses. And I opine he has acted like a cloche frame. When the wretched little pink, cajoled by Thomas's genial warmth, came out in a snowstorm, Thomas did his best by lying on it intermittently, but it seemed pretty uncomfortable so Valentine picked it and arranged it in a liqueur glass.

We are much interested in Jane Amelia Moses Swinyeard Gilbert, and are learning her by heart.[4] Does she take after all of them? It must be very confusing, Thomas thinks, to have so many family trees to climb up all at once.

I wished you had been with us the other day. The Writer's Association here got up a book sale for the Spanish Medical aid. We raised two hundred pounds, the lord knows how, for it was not very well organized, and badly publicized. It would have amused you to watch the demeanour of the authors present. I was selling at the stall of autographed books, and Miss Rose Macaulay[5] has presented us with several copies of her various works, duly signed. And at intervals she came around to see how they were selling. It was terrible, for they were not selling well. She became arider and arider with each visit, until Valentine and I were reduced to sneaking volumes off the stall and sitting on them, whenever we saw her in the offing.

She is a terrifying old virago, and made it plain that she considered that we were sabotaging the natural demand for her products; nor was it possible to explain how hard we tried to unload them, that would not have been mollifying either. I collected two prizes in the auctions (oh my dear, the dangerous rapture of bidding for books!). A collection of letters written to a marriage agency c.1830—a really gratifying exposition of base passions in elegant calligraphy, and the Cresset Press edition of Crispin van der Pass's *Hortus Floridus*. Do you know this, I expect you do. It has the most romantic account of the blue narcissus, first described as the blue or unknown narcissus by a Greek botanist, emerging into real life as the choicest treasure in the garden of an amateur called Perret. Crispin drew Perret's blue narcissus; and it is the African blue lily, the agapanthus. How did it come, or the rumour of it, from S. Africa, to the ears and eyes of that greek botanist? Doesn't this please you a great deal?

I have two things to thank you for. A number of *the herbalist*, and your most enchanting christmas nosegay, which I adored. I was so pleased with the vigorous recipe among the lore.

That dark-leafed peppermint we stole is thriving exceedingly, in fact it will soon become a notorious rogue in the herb-bed. I am not so sure about the moss-rose cuttings. One survived till January, now it looks dead and sulky, but I still have hopes of its root. It has been a melancholy winter here too, long and rain-swept. Not an easy winter to write in. And with one's true mind set on Spain, all this press and wireless rumpus of abdications and coronations has been an exasperation. However, abdications and coronations have blown two hundred dollars into my purse, via the *New Yorker* and loyal mugs; so it is an ill wind that does not blow into somebody's mouth.

If you don't; write, I don't cease to think of you with love, be sure of that. But you write such charming letters that when one does come I love you even more.

Ever,

Sylvia

When she learned that Elizabeth's arrival was definite, Sylvia sent a letter to meet her in Paris.

24 West Chaldon
Dorchester
Dorset
4. iv. 1937[6]

Dearest, most unexpected, most welcome Elizabeth.

It is almost enough to reconcile one to the coronation decorations to hear that you are coming over for the coronation. And they really are deplorable, Bond Street with long white shrouds dangling from the housefronts, and the most execrable gothic wc in cement plastered to the front of Westminster Abbey.

But the public statuary is fun. It has all been boxed up in wooden cases, so that it shalln't be defaced by colonial visitors; but as in the interests of economy the cases have been kept rectangular, every now and then bits of the statuary, escaping from the rectangle's boundaries (such as a bronze horse tail, or a hand thrown out in a fine gesture, or sometimes a beaming bronze face) emerge defiantly; as though it were a form of conjuring rabbits from hats, and the technique had broken down a little; or in the case of the bronze faces, as though it were Marat in his bath.

And meanwhile Chaldon is lovely. Intensely green, after the long winter rains; and inexpressibly suave, and ringing with blackbirds, cuckoos, and amorous grunting crows.

My old London charwoman and her family are coming here on the thirteenth.[7] That is no reason why you should not come then, for she is a darling, and one of the best lesser-known treasures of England (like Malmesbury), and you would love her. If you come then I will get you a bedroom at the farm round the corner of this hill, where there is a feather-bed and/but a beautiful view to wake to, and a short walk on green turf to here. Otherwise I shall hope to put you here, where Thomas can again walk into your room and enjoy your sweet odours and share your appreciation of the vispring mattress. He grows daily in beauty and grace and dignity and affectation, is, for pomp and sumptuosity, a coronation in himself. Towzer has a hundred new ringlets in his ears.

And I have finished Valentine's patchwork coat of many colours, and she looks most beautiful in it, and I gaze on it with quite as much pride as ever Anne Bradstreet on her bed-hangings; feeling very much as she did, obnoxious—but still aware of the carping tongues which might well say—in my case—that I could have done it quite as well and I half the time by pen.

How lovely to be in Paris, in your grand address, with the chestnuts in bloom and the lilacs, and the children in the street wearing their first fine tarnish of sunburn. If this reaches you in time, will you do an errand for me? Will you go to the Association Internationale des

Ecrivains pour la Defense de la Culture, at 8 rue d'Aboukir, and ask of René Bloch or his representative if he has any information yet about the proposed congress of writers due to be held in Spain this month; whether it has been fixed yet, and where. Or if you can't go there, telephone them, but I don't know their number.

Because I am supposed to be organizing the English delegation to the congress if it comes off, and I want to know about it as soon as I can, and do not altogether rely on Bloch to remember to inform me.

If you could do this, I shall be indelibly grateful Anyhow, I am superlatively grateful to you for being about to come to England, and sweeten the coronation's cup for us.

With our love,

Sylvia

Before she sailed, Elizabeth sent the funds she raised in Waterbury for the Spanish children. Sylvia replied from Derbyshire.

NEW BATH HOTEL MATLOCK BATH SPA
Derbyshire
[Postmark 25 April 1937][8]

Dearest Elizabeth,

This is just an official receipt to say thank you for your contribution to Spain (how do you manage to possess yourself of such real specimens of English currency? I never find a pound note that doesn't look like a First Folio). It has gone to the International Legion, where it will help nourish many of your own race.

When you next come to England, you must visit Derbyshire. With us. We have found such things, all entirely unsuspected. A landscape of high green stonewalled uplands, suddenly breaking into valleys designed by Shelley—all trees and crags and waterfalls and little [ ] islets.

Lilies of the valley grow wild.

With this statement I will end for the present. With our love,

Sylvia

Elizabeth sailed 26 April 1937 on the SS *Normandie,* the elegant flagship of the Compagnie Generale Transatlantique whose maiden voyage had been the previous spring when it won the Blue Riband for fastest Atlantic Ocean crossing. With her were George Heard Hamilton, Ernest Hillman, and John Skilton, all three friends from Wade White's years at Yale, the latter two to be lifelong homosexual partners. They landed at Le Havre after five days and took the boat train to Paris. Elizabeth made notes on the small loose-leaf notebook pages she favored. There was no restraint on luxury: they stayed at the Hotel Plaza Athenée and had evenings out in style at Maxims, the Bal Tabarin, and the opera, all of which Elizabeth chronicled in spare notes.

[9]3:v:37 Paris 11:30 Parc.

4 Tu. Am Express, lunch, shop, met Ritz tea J&G; Plaza Athenée, drive in Bois; dinner Le Grenouleves.

5:W. With G.[eorge] to Invalides ... to Crillon lunch, St. Germain des Pres, walk to river & to Quai de la Moquirire, seeds Vilnique Audiux, Cooks ... haircut Guillaume, to ... Opera ... to Montmartre, to Maxims.

5/7 up early to drive to Blois, back via Chartres; Bal Tabarin on the return.

SUDDENLY APPEARING CORONATION,' Elizabeth cabled Sylvia on the 7th. 'PARIS THIS WEEK, LONDON 9TH TO 15TH THEN HOME. VERY MUCH WISH TO SEE YOU LETTER FOLLOWS. PARIS HOTEL ELYSEE PARC, CHAMPS D'ELYSEES.'

The party travelled to England by the Boulogne-Folkestone ferry, put up at the Duke's Court, 32 Duke Street, between Piccadilly and Pall Mall, and dined at Pruniers the evening they arrived. The next night they shared a gala dinner at Quaglino's, followed by *Home and Beauty,* a Cochran revue.

At the English-Speaking Union, there was a postcard from Valentine:

> 24, West Chaldon
> Dorchester
> Dorset
> May 7th[10]

> We shall be so happy to see you: please come on Thursday if you possibly can, but if you change your mind about dates, let me have a telegram. And if you can spare us more time, PLEASE do. I shall book your room now, but if you can spend more than a bare 24 hours I could arrange for you to stay at Rats' Barn (which you would love I think—). In any case, do come, and by as early a train as possible! If trains to Wool are unfavorable, I could easily meet you at Bournemouth, remember.

> Much, much love, from both of us.
> Valentine

On May 12, Coronation Day, Elizabeth and the three men rose at 4, left the hotel at 5, walked to the viewing stand on Pall Mall where they had breakfast and watched the procession until early afternoon. In the evening they went to the Savoy Hotel to hear the broadcast of the King's Speech, followed by a gala dinner at Quaglino's and a tattoo by the Argyle Highlanders.

These doings, so alien to their interests, may have amused Sylvia and Valentine in the telling. There was not much time to do so, however, as Elizabeth on May 13 spent only one night in Chaldon, putting up at The Sailor's Return.

Back in London, Elizabeth and her friends went to Laurence Olivier's *Henry V* at the Old Vic, after which, a 'ride around London in cab'. The next morning they boarded the Norddeutsche Lloyd *Bremen* at Southampton for the five-day voyage home.

On the *Bremen* Elizabeth again analyzed herself, her aims, friendships, and her relations with her 'beautiful' family that made choices so difficult. She referred to herself as having a 'dual personality' which indeed could be exemplified by the recent experience of luxurious travel and celebration of a new monarch coupled with her increasing admiration for the two active communists in West Chaldon. 'S & V' figure prominently, 'the new breath of life blowing out of England, with its terrific demands and terrifying possibilities and promises'. In an entry taking many of the pages in the notebook, she confronts what she terms her 'dual personality', pointed out to her as long ago as boarding school. 'I see myself at one extreme, sitting in church of a Sunday morning, in Waterbury beside Darragh [de Lancey] or someone very like him, with our children around us; at the other extreme, I am in Dorset with S & V, or living alone, roughly and fiercely and deeply in the country in New England. And from which of these do I take the greatest satisfaction, in which picture am I honestly alive?' She answers her own question: 'Without any question whatsoever, in the latter'. There is the dilemma: 'what should I do but cast aside, once and for all, the cloak of conventionality and live proudly as I am meant to live? But that is not, ah far from it, as easy as it sounds. For thirty years I have been tossing the ball from one hand to another, making, on the surface a fairly graceful trick of it ... I have realized that something was wrong, that I didn't fit into the small town respectable picture, that the language of my mind was not the language of that country.'

Breaking away would involve a bitter conflict with the family, 'My beautiful family, with all their mistakes and their tragedies I love deeply and desperately. I cannot renounce them ... and yet to be true to them, and to give them anything but unhappiness, I must be true to myself. And that shows me that I must cherish and protect the power to feel, for without it I am more than dead ... There are definitely two camps in my life, the enemy as Auden calls it, is so hard for me to recognize as that enemy, but for the sake of the friends and of really being able to believe and to love, I must take sides and discipline my inner self accordingly.'

Among those with access to feeling, life's necessity, are Douglas and S & V and Hoffman,[11] 'all a little dirty and uncouth, magnificently true and brave and free. Among them I feel my cringing cowardice and lack of direction, but always their wind fills my sails and gives me new life for a little time and points to the way that I should go.' She is devoted to George Hamilton with whom she shared this trip and 'whom I have persuaded myself that I was to marry and whom I know now is just across the other side, and not for me'.

On the "Brinnen"   16·V·37

Now this fantastic and very pleasant 3 weeks trip to see the Coronation with G. + E.H. + J.S. & J.C., which is all but over, and which contrasts so extremely with last year's nearly disastrous undertaking, has been as useful in its way as was last year's education in fear, for it has brought to me the problem of this dual personality, really definitely for the first time. Such a problem surely exists, and I should have become more sharply aware of it long before this, when Hilliard pointed it out years ago, though I don't think she meant it exactly as I do, but her words should be honoured, for she was, in her mad way, a very wise and instinctively understanding person. And the situation is this, I see myself, at one extreme, sitting in church of a Sunday morning, in Watertown, beside Danagh or someone very like him, with our children around us, at the other extreme, I am in Dorset with S. + V., or living alone, roughly and fiercely and deeply, in the country in New England. And from which of these do I take the greatest satisfaction, in which picture am I honestly <u>alive</u>?

Elizabeth excoriates herself, but there is promise. 'I find three separate stages to my life, the first these long years of inconsequential charming of romantic detachment in which the world outside was only vaguely disturbing and hurting, the second that sickening plunge into disillusionment of material things, the realization of inadaptability, the falling heartbreakingly in love with the wrong man; the hopeless struggle to make myself over emotionally and practically. And third the new breath of life blowing out of England, with its terrific demands and terrifying possibilities and promises.'

'Don't think so much about marriage,' Elizabeth instructs herself, and to be more socially and politically active. 'Do all in your powers for others for those who need it desperately, and remember that you neither need nor care for endless possessions, and thank God for that. Decide for political philosophy carefully, sincerely, and without prejudice, if you're to embrace Communism do it with intellectual conviction and knowledge don't, and this is very difficult, be a parlor puss carried away by emotional enthusiasm'. She recognized the conflicts this will lead to at home: 'respect the tragic intensity of Father's convictions, but believe what you believe quietly and constructively, and do what you can about it'. Follow what S & V preach (and practice) politically'. If you 'don't carry it any farther than that, you will be insulting their trust in you and making yourself ridiculous and contemptible. On the other hand, you may find in an [ ] combining of your own doubts and feelings with their knowledge and sureness, a real belief which will result in your being of service to the world in some way or other, and that is the greatest thing you can hope for.' In closing she exhorts herself to finish the Anne Bradstreet book 'as soon as you possibly can'. She warns herself to 'be firm against social and family ... with that, it is absolutely at this age, a matter of life or death, and don't forget that'.

It would indeed be easier written about than done.

At Breakneck on 20 May, Elizabeth was back with the beautiful family that she loved so much with all their faults in their beautiful estate.

Opposite page:
21. From Elizabeth's journal on the *Bremen*.

Now it is over, and I am in my own room, in my own bed, with the beautiful, gentle country whispering outside my window. After the dulled bustle of packing on that curiously lifeless boat, and desperately finishing a poem in the midst of it, and New York under a blue and white high sky sliding round us and the boat shaking in time to the ship's band, and faces, and then M's [Mother's] and W's [Wade's] faces in the gaping black dock, and the gangplanks raising their heads and fastening their jaws into the *Bremen*'s side, and then the rush of embracing and opening suitcases and goodbying and getting into the taxi, and lunch at the Plaza, and finally through train windows, this incredibly pale, holy green of the awakening country. The sunlight on those millions of uncurling tiny leaves was almost unbearable. Coming from the sea, to that physical intensity of new life was an awesomely sudden thing, and then we were at Breakneck, and I in a dizzying vision of apple blossoms and little dogs and green grass and the smell of the blessed air.[12]

Awaiting her return was a letter from Sylvia celebrating the 'the romantic, short visit' (as Valentine put it in her next letter).

24 West Chaldon
14. V. 1937.[13]

Dearest Elizabeth.

We seem to have remembered almost everything that we meant to ask you to do or to ask you to take; but we overlooked the young man called Steven Clark.[14]

Here is his permanent address

c/o The Woodlawn Trustees. Wilmington. Delaware.

I can't imagine you going to Wilmington Delaware. It is rather like Bolton Lancashire isn't it? a town of spinning sheds and hooters. But I don't think the unfortunate Steven quite imagines himself going there either. And if you would some time write him a note with the latest news of us and the developments of the River House, it would be a real kindness. I think you would like each other very much. He is a most intelligent and charming and cat-like creature—with a touch of a cat's reserve. And I know you are good at cats.

How I wish you weren't gone. I believe that you are still here as much as you can be, and I do appreciate that. But I want more. Your way of not seeming to be on a visit makes it much worse when you go, I really feel that you are plucked away from me like a lock of hair. There seems to be a bald patch on my sensations.

Come back as soon as you can. There is so much research to be done in Dorset, and as far as I can see you will have the field pretty much to yourself. All the local antiquarians that I wot of are rather badger-like old gentlemen who fill their dens with a choice selection of flints and fossils and wild birds. The human fauna seems pretty well untouched. Another thing that occurs to me is that we shall, if you research a little more, find ourselves related and yourself a partaker in the lost kingdom of the Black Dog.

But much the most important of all, beyond any layers of the past, is the present, and the present fact that we do like you so much, and enjoy you being here. So come as soon and stay as long as you can.

And we both thank you with all our hearts for coming this time, and giving us a whole day out of your narrow time in Europe.

We are all rejoicing in our presents still, Valentine with her cigarette case, and me with mine, and Thomas with his mouse—he is being very solemn about it just now, explaining that This is No Ordinary Mouse—and Towzer ogling his goodies; and the books sitting by our bed for early morning reading tomorrow; when you can fancy me bounding downstairs determined on cooking as Mother did, and telephoning unwonted orders for cream and butter to the dairy.

With our love—and I will tell you all that happens about Frome Vauchurch

Sylvia

A few days later Valentine, who had evidently mentioned the possibility that she might go to Spain as an aid worker, suggests that Elizabeth could help and be a companion to Sylvia, possibly in America. The move to the Maiden Newton house is imminent as negotiations were done with the owner, 'a small, wizened Anglo-Indian lady; bustling, autocratic and thoroughly efficient and nasty!'

24, West Chaldon
Dorset.
19th May [1937][15]

My dear Elizabeth,

It has been warm and has smelt of summer to-day, for the first time this year. The may-blossom is out and the hedges are solidly white. Grass smells sweetly now, as though it were forecasting the cutters, but it is still pricked out with daisies and buttercups. I sat on the hill and heard the cuckoos calling all the time from the far-off woods, and two partridges ran along in the wet grass, rattling out their affectionate small noises to each other as they went. It has been a most lovely, melting and compassionate day.

I thought of you with such pleasure, and wished you had been here still, although that romantic, short visit supplied us both with much happiness to remember and enjoy. It has eased my own private mind of a worry, too. Knowing that if circumstances worked out that way, Sylvia would have in you exactly the companion to solace and renew her. And I don't feel very impertinent in saying this, for you and she are alike in many things, and have the same strict intellectual minds and you will understand how troubling it is to think of her over here alone (if things worked out that way at any time) and stranded, as she would be, in spite of so many admiring friends! But America, with the chance of finding you there, is the solution to that now. And although I have every intention of staying here if luck allow it, yet IF Spain or some other similar chance materialized, I think with assurance that she would be well.

22. Sylvia and Steven Clark in Dorset, 1937.

Not that this is at all a 'charge' on you, but is actually the way things would shape themselves. I can see so clearly how you would meet sometimes in New England and in New York too, perhaps, and how the conversation would renew itself as if you'd only met yesterday, however long the break had been. It is this kind of foreseeing that is the most reassuringly permanent thing I know.

We are actually in train to get that house now. The owner is a small, wizened Anglo-Indian lady; bustling, autocratic and thoroughly efficient and nasty! She is being kind to us at the moment but she is unpleasant. However, an efficient landlord is good at all times, and in this case it means electric light switches wherever we want them, and many more than we could have afforded for ourselves! It has also meant permission to garden over there even before we take possession (which we hope to do in June) and a vague agreement that we can do 'anything' in the garden. And that MAY mean the end of the yellow privets! Anyhow it means a fine herb-bed and several fruit trees and roses. But we returned to find that the goat had escaped and had devoured EVERY ONE of our new little apple trees and pear trees and cherries ... We almost broke our hearts over that. And the goat is definitely NOT coming with us when we move!

I am reading *Mice and Men*. It is fine. There is an air of Hemingway about it, and although it sometimes breaks over into being Faulkner, which isn't so good, there are two characters which I shall always remember and carry around, and be much the richer for having known. Thank you for the book, and for the lovely case which continues to delight me.

After we had so sadly left you at the station we stopped to admire the hedges and heath and at that moment decided (both saying it at once in a miraculous way!) that we felt as though we had been visited by Artemis. And can you think of any guest you would more gladly welcome?

Artemis once sent me a little owl, when I was in [ ] Assisi. Artemis dressed as Minerva, but NOT Minerva, for directly the owl had appeared a white kid strolled down the street and the owl flew off! We think we must feed you on grey mullet next time you come, and maybe discover from this whether Diana is right, or whether Minerva is better. But Diana, I think, had an alliance with cats, and so Tom favours first notion.

Whitsun has been a mad holiday for us. Seven guests and two more liable to appear at any moment. And now the Keates are still here and my mother arrives this evening. So the two young Keates and I are going out to clean the car and make it look spruce, in preparation for a united sortie to see the new house.

Meanwhile, here is a photo of Sylvia and Steven Clark, of whom we told you. Do be sure to meet him. He is most anxious for it, and he is, beyond doubt, the most charming and the most exciting person we have lately found! He is very beautiful, too—and a delight to the eye. And that is not at all to be despised. I fancy he will need a friendly spirit to solace him, for he did not seem to feel very happy about his relations in America, and he is so completely civilised that the world can treat him roughly sometimes, but for all that he has a finely arrogant temper and is by no means defenceless!

Much love to you—Come soon again on one of these happy visits, only stay with us longer. Come and catch trout and research in and around the county. You can drive the car as you please and have any room you choose in the new house. Be bribed, therefore, and come anon!

Sylvia sends you love and agrees with every word of this, except that she rejects Minerva and holds by Artemis!

[Valentine]

In late May, Sylvia sought help for an English writer detained by the French police.

24 West Chaldon.
21. V. 1937[16]

Dearest Elizabeth.

Business first, like a good communist. It is very good of you to suggest collecting USA signatures to the Ralph Bates petition.[17] I have written to our English organisers of the thing asking them whether it would not be excellent to have a corresponding petition by a USA writer and intellectuals, rather than an appendix of them fastened to ours. Better in time, too. So if I cable your petition ahead, this will be your warrant.

And if this thing comes off, as I hope it will, I very much advise you to get in touch with Jean Starr Untermeyer[18] (101 East 55th Street NYC) She is a dear friend of mine, a charming creature, and, more to the purpose at this point, on the American Writers' League Committee which is getting up a congress of writers in New York next month. Probably she could collect the signatures of the greatest part of that congress if they are around at the time. This would save every body a great deal of postage and trouble.

I enclose a copy of the English petition, but of course the USA one should be rather different, or the effect on the French minister will be as of a flock of sheep that leisurely pass by.

Oddly enough, I have read *Mice and Men* before the book you gave me. I started in on that farmstead at once, but so, unfortunately, did my next visitor; and she shared my liking for it to such an extent that I had to let her take it away to finish. It is all right. She returns books as well as reading them.

As for *Mice and Men*, it is a small masterpiece. Small sounds condescending. Cut it out. It is a masterpiece. We both were really moved by it, it is such a book as one scarcely expected to read again.

We've got a kitten now. Tom's great nephew, grey top, white stomach, feet, and tail-tip. About 1 lb in weight and six inches long. Ruth brought him in a hamper, and he is due to go away to a good home, but far too young to go out in the world yet. So we are nourishing him for a week. It is awful for Tom is desperately madly despondingly jealous, and the kitten is madly devoted, and I am torn between the two, and whichever one I'm with I'm always thinking that the other has either died of neglect or committed suicide. I do wish this race of cats was not so damned passionate.

I only wish I could keep him till you return for you would certainly afoot him in a hatbox. But he is too young to cross the ocean alone, and the gusts of passion which result from having two of them at once are too great a strain to be combined with moving house.

For we are almost sure of the house at Maiden. The agreement came this morning, and is only delayed because it has gone back to the solicitor for an additional clause defining the riparian ownership.

There are a lot of nice things in that garden on closer inspection. Christmas Rose, and cyclamen, and a double pink hawthorn—and a short lamp-standard on the edge of the garden wall, though there is no lamp in it. We feel that this is a very stately touch. It is in a hermitage of shrub. The woman (she is odious, anglo-indian, but capable) has put in every possible electric light plug for us, even a power switch in the garage, so we can now charge our battery ourselves.

With our love,

Sylvia

A Petition to
M le Ministre de l'Interieur.

The undersigned writers and intellectuals earnestly request you, M. le Ministre de l'Interieur, to re-consider the case of our colleague Ralph Bates, a novelist of outstanding achievement, who was, in April last, served with an order expelling him from France. In view of the very great handicap to his literary work which this ban imposes on him, and in consideration of the fact that his infringement of the law was purely a technical one, we trust that you will favourably regard our request that the expulsion order may be rescinded.

In mid-June Sylvia renewed her suggestion that Elizabeth come live with them and research a Dorset parish register. This was a 'bribe', as she put it, to get her to stay longer and to focus her research skills.

24 West Chaldon Dorchester Dorset.
16. vi. 1937.[19]

Dearest Elizabeth.

I have traced one bribe (I must break off. Thomas has brought in what I believe to be a musk-rat, and I must instantly do it up in a parcel and send it to the Ministry of Agriculture to be identified, such is the law of the land and the duty of the citizen.)

This has now been done, packed in a biscuit tin, labeled Small Savouries. I hope this will make one happy clerk, whether it be a musk-rat or no. Thomas and I will now palpitate till we hear the viscidity, and know whether Thomas will go down to history as the cat who found the first musk-rat in Dorset.

To return to the bribe. There is a very fine church register at a village called Plush. It is remarkably detailed, puts in a lot [ ] births, deaths and marriages, and is being studied by a clergyman whose name I will find out.

Plush is so like a village in a nineteenth century water-colour that I never quite believe in it. It has fat green hills to shelter it, roses growing all over everything and a general air of sun-bonnet. I think you could spend some very happy days studying in Plush.

How I wish you would come here this autumn, and inhabit our spareroom with the window looking west to the river and east to the morning milk-man and the village. We have just learned that there is a hill near by, called Eggardon, with a Brito-Roman fort on it. And Steven Clark will tell you about the font at near-by Toller Porcorum, made by a rustic version of the master of the Malmesbury porch, and of the clergyman who explained it to us, saying, 'The horizontal ones are the martyrs.'

I am beginning to feel my way into that house now. I have ordered the window-curtains for Valentine's book-room, the Morris willow-branch pattern. And I am designing bookcases for my room below it. And the removal, after many unwilling tenders, no house-remover likes the position of this house, has been put into the hands of a man with the very practical name of Mr Wort. All this is very realistic.

We shall be there, this afternoon, revising more measurements, after a journey to Bridport to look into the matter of our poor Idiot, Rose Bertha, who is being somewhat of a care and trouble at the moment, having fallen madly in love with a sailor. Unfortunately, the sailor does not seem to be as serious as she. It is [a story] that would be so nice in a ballad, and is so difficult in real life. Mrs Kitchen, too, her employer, would be better in a ballad, where at a pinch one could assonate her to pigeon, than she will be on this very hot afternoon, in a lace collar held up with whalebones.

I have heard nothing more about the affair of Bates the novelist, I hope it means that he has been freed from his ban. Meanwhile, there is another thing I would like. I want a resume of the Scottsboro boys case. They have been condemned and tried and re-tried so often that like every body else I am in a complete muddle about it. If I could have the bones of the story, the dates, the various verdicts, the various sentences, I would be very grateful, as one is for anything that makes one's mind a tidier place to move around in. I reckon the American Civil Liberties could supply this data.[20]

My dear, if you want a speaker about Spain, speak yourself. It is always best to do these things oneself, there is no other way of being sure of getting across what one wants got across. Steven Clark is not a good speaker, which is a great pity, as physically he is ideal for a platform. But he lacks persuasion. At least, that was our experience here, when, on my suggestion, alas, we tried him for a local meeting for Spain, and he fell flat as a last weeks biscuit.

It makes me so happy to think that you are working like this, and that Waterbury can learn that it is possible to raise a protest against a censorship. I suppose Waterbury is about the same as Dorchester in mentality?—So sure that it is democratic that it will never open its eyes to watch what is happening to its liberties. I think of you embarking on a deal of drudgery and disappointment, and my feelings are like a brass band for pleasure; for so far, I think, the disappointments you have known have mostly been inward and spiritual, the long sighing autumnal frustrations of a splendour fading from a mind's project. And now you will learn practical and positive disappointments, that are as immediate, infuriating and challenging as a march wind combating one's intentions to do some early gardening. I have known both kinds, too; and the relief of turning from introspective disappointments to practically being thwarted, with all the entertainment of resolution, low cunning, and the resolve not to be outdone next time, is like going from embroidery to dung-spreading (that must've been a happy day!).

But yearning over you as anxiously and as proudly and any apostle, I do ask myself whether it would not be a good thing for you to have a clear start—by which I mean, a start away from home. Remember, we are here, and that at any moment we would dance if a cable arrived saying Coming. I will not dilate on the comfort of having a third head and a third pair of hands to help us. That would not be respectful to the scales. But with every scruple regarded, I can say that if you came, we would give you plenty of practice as well as theory.

This summer is so exquisite, and the news from Bilbao so agonising that I do not know how one supports the bittersweet of one's days. I don't think I could, if I had not got my eye fixed on this long project of conflict and solution. Which sends me off in a practical way, to say that there is a very good paper in your country called Fight (National Executive Committee of the American League against War and Fascism, 268, fourth avenue, New York) which you might like to read. And do you belong to the AEWF? It is a good plan to join these things, because one gets information from them that does not always come one's way otherwise, and every dollar of subscription helps. The European female section of the same League have just performed one exquisite stroke of social criticism.

They are holding a congress in Paris next month, and this is the agenda for one meeting.

La Jeunesse féminine dans le monde.

Le probleme de la femme indigène.

La prostitution.

I do not see how this could be bettered. Marx would have kissed the whole bunch of them for it. It is the second clause which is so particularly revealing.

With our love.

Sylvia

Elizabeth delayed responding to the 'bribe' until September, and then did so tepidly, an indication of her unwillingness or inability to make such a break with family and country and commit so fully to these friends, their politics, and way of life. She had come close to projecting such a course in her journal on the *Bremen*, but its potential faded in the familiarity of family life.

The day after Sylvia's letter, Valentine joined in at length, answering objections Elizabeth may have made on her brief visit. She urged her to come to England for a long stay to clarify her thoughts—as a member of their household preferably, but certainly nearby. Even if war were to come, how could she bear 'not being here'?

June 17th, 1937[21]

Dear Elizabeth,

(How fortunate you are to have that most lovely name!)

Whenever either of us has a letter from you there is rejoicing in the family, and this day Thomas, who slept with us in the caravan, shared the pleasure.

How odd it is that one feels almost agonised after sending any letter to post which is out of the usual run of letters. I had what my grandmother called 'squeamish qualms' about mine to you— thinking how this was one of the rare occasions when saying would be much more effortless than writing. 'More effortless' is nasty, but in this case the exaggeration was true. But your reply has cleared that up, & I am grateful for it and happy that it is all right.

Someone like Sylvia (another slip of the same kind—which Bain would disapprove) is worrying to the mind that looks ahead. 'Stranded' was the right word for my worst fear; but you have well and truly laid it. Actually, she is more likely than I to get into danger, but menaces of the sort that confront us all take no account of men, and you will understand how heavily a fear weighs, when it is that kind of fear. I shall never forget how lightly I felt when, sitting outside the fish-and-chip shop, I suddenly realised that that nagging might cease, so long as you and she remained alive.

What you say is true, and to preserve such a pattern is almost the most important: but poetry is more important, for both of us, and this master might order destruction, as he has done before.

I think this is obscure, but I know you will comprehend it. I don't like sending works to people! But this poem that I enclose is one that proves my words. We listened to Gerhardt on the wireless; we sat in the kitchen with the door open, at the evening, early evening, & I could see out of the door to the field where they had lately cut the hay. Happiness is so acute, almost unbearable, and the time of year makes it keener. But the needs of Bilbao had come through just before, and the intellectual-emotional pattern of awareness was positively destroyed, and refashioned. So came the poem, and so will come the auctions, later on.

'If I could fit into the small-town pattern …' But you never, never can, Elizabeth. Except for undeveloped minds, needing the ruthless staking that one gives to badly-growing plants, I dislike any kind of forcible argument: so it is not for me to argue with you about staying where you are, or moving out. But if you can decide to move I most strongly advise that you come to England, at anyrate for a spell of time. If you see the four seasons through, working here and also watching, it should clarify the confusion. I well know that fog, & it is pernicious for more reason than that its hurts your eyes. Loss of vision can result, and 'more than the average mental equipment' (this is a serious understatement) imposes a responsibility you can't avoid. And the main part of the responsibility is to SEE CLEARLY.

We have a concrete proposal, which Sylvia will amplify to you. She discovered a parish register which needs careful examination and which is apparently unique in being a description of lives as well as deaths. The time it would take to examine thoroughly would be time enough for you to live here reasonably long. You are the only person I know who can be asked to risk coming to Europe (out of your comparative safety) while things look so stormy. But if the storm broke, I believe you would find such richness that it would be worth the risk. Anyhow—could you endure it, being away?

It is partly selfish, but not so much so as to be suspect: if you can come you could either have a flat in our new house or we would find you a cottage not far away (Cerne for instance, has cottages to let which are habitable) and we would share the car with you, so that you could get across country to places useful to you. Come warm weather, you could if you chose it, move to our house, to sleep in the caravan which is very pleasant, and live not as a guest but as a member of us in and about the house. This is not intended to be a hard-and-fast design, but as a suggestion to meet the practical difficulties of removing from possessions for a length of time. Our membership of the London Library makes the question of books easily solved, & I can think of no other difficulty—because we are all three self-sufficient (I am sure of that) and the only inescapable snare is to have a member of the household who is NOT so.

The questions of furniture, if you had an empty cottage, is not too difficult: we have enough to lend, and almost enough household ware to stock you with pots and pans! I am being practical, not because I think (or dare hope) that you will decide immediately, but because I have an idea that the yeast has been added and that at some time soon you will begin to rise! And when that time comes you need not flatten at the cold draught of 'practical considerations'—but remember this letter and take steps accordingly!

I am not sure I agree about temperamental limitations: Sylvia is sure she does NOT. I think you will go much further than I shall and perhaps (but this is only because you are younger) further than Sylvia. But this is not meant 'politically' at all. I mean in intellectual development and temperamental adjustment. In any case, 'Men must be grown as carefully & attentively as a gardener grows a favourite fruit-tree'—and although Stalin said that, it is worth attention and for one's own private use!

Any subordination of your instincts to stretch is death: and the oppression you feel is a foreknowledge of death. This is true, and it is a most serious truth.

It isn't easy to grow up, and it is exceedingly painful to the conscience, but it is a charge upon all of us now. When I said to you that, childless, we must never forget that the generation of children is the generation of our children, I spoke for a certain knowledge, for when I was married (ten years ago) I miscarried of a child, and that experience of almost having makes it easier to remember. But the dictatorship of one's private and of one's household gods must be broken down, cost what it may: otherwise we cannot parent the new children, and they will perish under the Juggernaut.

I think we are too much afraid of fancies, even of the dark ones. Although this blessedly does not apply to you so much as to the people we meet of the Party—who are all too apt to dismiss truth as 'Idealism' and god-knows-what.

Mostly you must blame this long letter on my sprained ankle. It has lasted for ten days now, and has not been eased by the various activities we have had: demonstrations in London, drives to and fro, preparations for the move, gardening (slugs on the peas!) and so much else that is bad for ankles. So I am tethered to a table, and aside from poems and a most bewildering job of compiling a tear-off calendar with 365 quotations for Marxists, I sit here blissfully writing letters and reading!

But it is hard on you, and I do apologise for such a long letter. Conversations across the Atlantic are difficult and odd and tend to become recitations solo. But your letter was stimulating, reassuring, and very good to get.

Later:

I've just visited Sylvia in the pink room and found her deep in a letter to you. I hope hers will confirm you and support you.

Lastly, never doubt the flame. It allows of no doubt. I send you a book, as a kind of signature to the agreement we have made about Sylvia and as an anticipatory present for a further pact—still to be made, but surely to be made.

And Tom and Sylvia and I—with Towser who is melancholy today, send you true love,

Valentine

Moving across the field a girl in a pink dress,
over the sky white clouds shadowed with pink,
dark on my vision, near to me, your black hair;
while the viola and the voice keep
leisurely their lovely argument.
In my hand the spray of elder golden pale
And sweet with summer.

Hay in the meadow creamy-folded lies
to darken in the sun, tomorrow and tomorrow,
richening the scent already heavy
in honey loops on the cream taste of summer.

Feasting goes on all day, all night; all senses
banquet in June, and love uninterrupted
and timeless wakes in morning, sleeps at night,
rises and sets in the clear skies of joy.

Not uninterrupted. Love is not
timeless. Love is over
for thousands who went out this summer
weather
and found the feast set, and the feast was death.

And these were ours who died.
Dark on my vision your black hair,
so near to me it shadows all the sun.

A few days after these letters, Elizabeth recorded in her journal that Tom, a painter, whom she expected to propose to her had become engaged to another. The confusion of mind that Valentine had noted remained. After the ecstatic time in England and Dorset, Elizabeth was in torment.

To be surprised and hurt suddenly without warning so that the old waiting hopelessness closed in, heavily, in the old way, and then to come home and find that there cocktails and a glass of dark English ale made this lead weight slacken, the sound of the closing door not so harsh and bitter in the ears, and everything not so unhappy and uncomprehended as it had seemed, is a warning. Too many doors have banged shut, too many darknesses have frozen the warm hushing of the heart, not to make alcohol easy losing of the mind's hard tangle a refuge and a temptation. But this will not do. I suppose I didn't actually want to marry him, only I knew he was one of my people, and I loved his strong and violent gruffness and his fine, dark poetic paintings, and I wanted to hear him say, 'That's my beautiful Bett', and most of all I wanted his freedom to teach my captivity the essential secret. And that was wrong, I know it, too conscious and calculating ever to be justified, and now I am served out by that ebony haired creature with the long hard mouth. And me so pale and bright, and he always smiling a little under the reddish moustache, perhaps, after all, he belongs to me a little in a way that he never will to anyone else, and perhaps, a very small perhaps, he knows it. But never a word, never a sign for me to take and keep, that would be too much to ask.

But there were other doors that may not be shut. Elizabeth echoes the phrase she used in her confession on the *Bremen* the month before: 'keep the courage clean for those two doors and maybe a third, that have opened beautifully and terrifyingly, the discovering of what was beyond them will take all the strength and judgment and perception that you can possibly gather together.'[22]

The next year, still divided, a door would be opened for her by Valentine.

In July 1937, Sylvia and Valentine were in Madrid for a writers' conference organized by the Chilean poet and Communist, Pablo Neruda. The next month from Chaldon, Sylvia sent news of their Spanish stay. The decoration of the house in Maiden Newton is proceeding and their move is imminent.

24 West Chaldon
Dorchester
Dorset.
2. viii. 1937[23]

Dearest Elizabeth.

Your letter, and its enclosure of a begging letter for Spanish Children, came this morning. You have gone exactly the right way to work, and for exactly the right reasons. One has always to find the right approach, every town, every person, is a problem susceptible of one right-fitting solution, if one can trace it out; and the good collection shows that you have got your solution to Waterbury. I do praise and commend you. And you will be much happier having got your teeth into this sort of work.

Personally I find money the most engrossing, the most fascinating, the most enthralling subject. Having spent the chief of my life blandly unconscious of it, constantly at a loss to say which was a florin and which a half-crown, I now know all the joys of avarice. And pore over my ledger for soap and my ledger for International Brigade Dependents Fund as gayly and slyly as that little squinting blithe beast in the Matys picture of the money-lenders: the small one, I mean, like a contented teapot filled with poison.

How very artful of you to approach via RLS. I call that a superb strategy, you could not have floured your paws in a better flour-bin.

I expect we shall both live to regret that dark and gipsyfied peppermint, and future senators of the USA will curse our joint names for having introduced a pest. Mine, too, grows with a sombre determined and stealthy vitality. I find it leading an underground life in the most unexpected places. And though I mean to take a slip on to Riversdale I shall plant that slip outside the garden, probably in the waste and wilderness of rubble behind the garage. Then, of course, one fine spring morning as I look out of the sun-parlour I shall see its army of small dark spears investing us. But it will remain to be a comfort to Anglo-Indian Mrs West; she will be able to go tiger-shooting and pig-sticking through its groves.

Owing to Madrid, and having people now staying here, and one thing and another, our move has been delayed. However, three pairs of window-curtains have been contrived from Morris pattern cretonnes. Morris patterns are exactly right for that house. Valentine has the willow-branch for her upstairs book-room, and my room has a design whose name I can't remember, but it is a heavy autumnal green pattern of a sort of acanthus cum hemlock foliage. Very beautiful indeed, a poet's design.

I am sorry you won't be here this winter, though I shall continue to trim the spare-room with an eye on Elizabeth. But I think your reasons are good ones, especially that feeling of wanting to get something done and sold. I for my part, hope that I shall have the proofs of a book of poems by then. I seem to have got enough for another book, a book of decent size, I hate hors d'oeuvres poetry-books; and have a whole set on hand at this moment, jerked out of me by seeing so much more of Spain—a landscape that demands poetry, very largely, I think, because it contains this violent mixture of prose in itself—I mean that you see roads edged with rose bushes, and the rose-bushes have apparently silver-grey leaves, and when you look more closely it is because the leaves are covered with dust. All this sort of thing, this especial mixture of rough with smooth, these violent contrasts welded into a whole by as violent a sunlight, clamours for poetry.

You got my hasty letter from Madrid, I hope? I have seen such things. We were very lucky, we went long journeys by car, to Barcelona, to Valencia, to Madrid, and back again. Such things and such places. Outside Tarragona, in a rather tufty landscape domineered over by stone mountains, a perfect roman triumphal arch, massive and elegant, with the modern road enlarging to sweep round it, and as at home with it in the landscape as though the romans had laid its surface, as I suppose they did lay its foundations. Tarragona itself, with a wide street roofed right over by heavy plane-trees, and in the street, chattering like a pack of starlings light-footed in their sandals, a company of recruits, setting out for a course of training. And the curious pale towns, strung out along the main road like washing hung out on lines, with their narrow elastic-sided streets, really elastic sided, time after time I thought, No, our car cannot get past this wagon; and always the street has mysteriously widened itself, so much so that the people sitting on chairs at the pavement's edge outside the inn have not even needed to draw back a toe.

One should not go for a holiday to a country at war, and it just sounds ridiculous to say, I am feeling so much refreshed by four delightful days under bombardment. But actually, the effect is that of a wild and dream-like holiday; for the experience is so exciting, so tonic, and the people themselves so kind, and all the arrangements made for us such good arrangements, and all the things we saw so stirring and so beautiful, either of make or spirit, that I feel as though I had been dipped in some reviving river, and even now, writing this letter, begin to snuff and pine to be back in Spain once more.

I am enclosing a thing from the *New Statesman*, about the harvest, because I think it will interest you and show you one, at least, of things seen. But may I have it back again, please?

With love from us both, and congratulations,

Always

Sylvia

In late August, Sylvia celebrated the move to the Maiden Newton house and rejoiced in the Frome, the stream flowing by it.

24 West Chaldon
Dorchester
Dorset

but now FROME VAUCHURCH MAIDEN NEWTON, DORSET
27. viii. 1937[24]

Dearest Elizabeth,

You must have one of the first letters from this house, typed with a paw that totters from transplanting, book-buffetting, polishing furniture and sorting china.

We moved on Monday, and now, except for two rooms and some details in the toolshed, and a shelf or two, are straight. Oh dear, though I approve your resolve, how I wish you were coming here to share, enjoy and admire. Even though hot baths and electric light would not be quite the same rapture to you as they are to us, you would enjoy looking on at our raptures—decidedly, my paws are tottering—and could give your verdict on the question posed by me: Whether the workers on the Russian collective farms who never turned a switch in their lives enjoy it more or less than I, who had, and then had not, and now have again.

Another thing which is lovely and unbelievable. WE HAVE MORE THAN ENOUGH ROOM FOR OUR BOOKS. For we found a pair of carpenters here who have put up shelves most neatly and briskly, so much so that we now have quite a quantity of bookcases with spare room in them. They are the most entertaining pair, rather like Bouvard and Pecuchet. Just now they have been given the job of cleaning the church of Frome Vauchurch—which is minute, elderly, surrounded with a great quantity of tombs and yews. Like Bouvard and Pecuchet, they are in full flight of antiquarianism. I went to the church to ask something about a lock that didn't work, and found them just unplastering a norman dogstooth, flushed with excitement and pride. They led me around and around the interior—which measures about twelve feet by twenty-four-pointing out its beauties: a window which they felt sure, was originally a door—a cusp here and an acanthus there. Incidentally, there is a most beautiful carved Jacobean pulpit, and nothing seems to have been restored ever. You will like our church, when you come. It has one service a week, and for the rest of the time one can smoke in it undisturbed.

Via the carpenters who put up our bookshelves I come to a message of thanks from Valentine. Thanks and apologies. When we got back from Spain we found the book you had sent her. It was most appropriate, we had met Anna Louise [Strong] in Madrid, and thought highly of her for making one of the best speeches at the Congress. Between then and now, we have done everything about that book except thank you for it; we have read it, lent it, recommended it. V. says, please forgive her for being so remiss, she will write to you as soon as she has got her poetry shelf fixed as it should be, and caught another trout; and meanwhile she sends her love and thanks by me.

One trout has been caught. From the balcony, I heard a stifled yell, and hurried like any midwife to the scene, to see a silver belly lifting from the water, and to think, my God, how on earth will she land it. And in a twinkling of an eye, and like the translation of that deathbed-repenting sinner in Thomas Beston's Fourfold State, who 'jumped from the harlot's lap to Abraham's bosom', that trout, with a dexterous twitch, had been transferred from the river Frome to the roof of our coal-shed.

It was over half a pound, a very nice fish indeed.

WE LOVE THIS HOUSE. We love it just as we said we would. You are a superlative prophet.

Thomas likes it too. We had a painful journey here on the day of the move, Thomas, already umbraged by being shut up in Elsan while the removers bent to remove outside, held on my lap under a sack, muling most passionately and struggling like a salmon. I had tried him in several boxes and baskets but he was too large for any of them, he had to travel al fresco. I held his hind legs in one hand and his front legs in another and kept his head down under my elbow, and felt like Abraham sacrificing Isaac. However, once arrived he settled down instantly, and much enjoys the apple trees.

Poor Towzer is with May and Jim. His fell habit of yelling and biting his way out of captivity when alone in the house makes him too problematical for this place, where his yells could rend the village and his teeth and claws havock Mrs West's decorations. Like Simeon Mercy Bradstreet—have I got this right?—a dignified retirement seemed the best expedient for such a passionate animal. We saw him today, and he looked very well and happy, and being a spaniel and adapted to vicissitudes will most likely do well. If he pines, we shall have to have him here, in which case

God help us and God help our neighbors. One thing which is very un-expected—the Craske pictures look well in this house. I was afraid they might just forge their way out of it, being so much more vigorous than the house or the surroundings (by the way, I realized just before we moved in, who mothered this house and this garden—Kate Greenaway, dear creature!—it is hers to the life, hers to the apple-trees with their small bright fruit, hers by the green-capped conifer). But they do very well. I am not absolutely sure of the big woolwork, but the others do beautifully.

Has anything happened about those you took back? Let me know if they have been admired by anyone, because Craske would like to hear that he was admired in America.

One beautiful passage, which I am sure you will appreciate. I was explaining to the grocer which house this was (We will not call it Riversdale). I had explained for quite a while, there might have been a dozen green and white houses by the river, judging from the grocer's kind blank expression. Then a voice came from the back of the shop. 'The house where the old lady died.'

A beautiful and apparently unique distinction.

There is a new young poet. I hope there are many, but this one arrived in Chaldon from New Zealand, to visit John (Cowper] Powys, and learning that Dove and Seagull were near at hand, came on to our doorstep. He is called Douglas Stewart, and his book is called 'Green Lions,' and has some good things in it, but he had better stuff with him in manuscript.[25] A very rich and solid poetry, with a tang of Frost about it, though he has never read any Frost. A sort of Scotch bun poetry. I don't know though, if you have eaten Scotch Bun. Its other name is Apothecaries Delight. It is very hard, rich, heavy, melancholy, and tastes salt rather than sweet.

He spoke of the difficulty of writing poetry in New Zealand. All the place names and plant names were taken straight over from the Maori, and though beautiful in themselves do not assimilate with the English language. Wawapipoki, and so forth. You will see that it presents difficulties.

The green lions are waves.

With love from us both

Sylvia

Valentine's belated thank you note followed.

Frome Vauchurch
Maiden Newton, Dorset
29 viii. 37[26]

A letter of thanks should have gone to you, but so many things combines to threaten it that it would surely have been unworthy. Please forgive & understand, & allow time to go—then a letter will evolve & perhaps be nearer my desire for it! This house is as good as you said it would be—we are so happy here.

Love. Valentine

Sylvia's report that 'the Craske pictures look well' in the Maiden Newton house and that she had been 'afraid they might just forge their way out of it, being so much more vigorous than the house or the surroundings' refers to the work of the self-inspired artist John Craske (1881–1943). On her visits to West Chaldon Elizabeth had seen the Craskes Sylvia had acquired and learned about the unique circumstances of Craske's artistic development. The work fascinated her, and she came to share Sylvia and Valentine's passion for it and concern for the welfare of the artist himself.

John Craske was a Norfolk fisherman who in World War I 'was blown up in a mine-sweeper, and made an invalid, and being slightly blown out of his mind, he began to paint'. So Sylvia described it in 1932. 'He is a kind of English Douanier Rousseau but with a sort of English seriousness ... Now I hear that Craske has fallen on very bad times, and is ill and miserable. I can't afford to go there myself, and I have been trying to think of someone intelligent in his neighborhood, who would go, and look at his work, and revive him. It is attention he needs, more than LSD.[27] ... He has a very nice wife called Laura. His tariff, I may mention, is moderate. One guinea for water-colours, thirty shillings

23. Laura and John Craske at their Norfolk cottage, 1930s.
Both corresponded with Elizabeth who acquired a number
of his pictures.

for the larger needlework pictures. They are both so respectable and speechless that it is worth knowing this. The pictures really are magnificent, Defoe-like pictures, stuggy, exact, and passionate.'[28]

Craske initially experimented with making images using his wife's yarn. From this he developed a skilled needlework technique with silk as well as wool. He also became an adept water-colorist. His principal theme was the human encounter with the sea where land and water meet and in boats and ships. He also made still lifes and imaginary scenes. It was Valentine in the 1920s who learned about this self-inspired craftsman in in her native Norfolk, visited him and later introduced him and his works to Sylvia. The latter recruited Elizabeth to the cause of making Craske's work appreciated. She purchased a number of his works and interested other buyers at home. With Valentine and Sylvia she visited the Craskes in Norfolk in the late 1930s and thereafter regularly sent letters and Christmas parcels. In 1950 she was responsible for an exhibit of his work at the Mattatuck Historical Society in Waterbury. When she sold her house in Oxford in the 1970s, she donated a number of Craske's works to the Britten-Pears Foundation Library in Aldeburgh, Suffolk, adding to its already sizable collection. She treasured the Craskes, displayed prominently in her Connecticut house and a subject of comment by visitors.

Craske's art, achieved in hardship and isolation, became a shared interest of three women; it survived the bitter estrangement between Sylvia and Elizabeth. For Elizabeth Craske's works remained a link to her youthful discoveries in Dorset and Norfolk that remained with her throughout her long life.

Both Valentine and Sylvia wrote on September 7; their letters crossed Elizabeth's of the 12th (below). Valentine first:

(Tel: M.N. 76.)
Frome Vauchurch, Maiden Newton.
September 7th.[29]

Dear Elizabeth,

I wish you had seen Sylvia's pleasure when your letter came to-day, and the excitement and glee with which she received the cheque! The soap fund is going well enough for it to be most important to get more—no longer a weakling, it is such a fine child that we take intense interest in its welfare, and your cheque has brought it on wonderfully!

This house is lovelier than you said it would be: and at the time I wasn't even sure that you weren't too sanguine. As it has turned out the place is absolutely perfect and we are perfectly happy here. I am feeling basely regretful that I have just been summoned to work at a Basque Children's Home in Buckinghamshire; and even though I shall not have to be there for long, as I think, I still feel selfishly peevish when I consider how fleeting and fine these first autumn days are, beside the river and in a new and romantic house.

I am so glad you like Steven [Clark]—I don't easily like people seriously, rarely beyond the first interest of finding them work out, like base crime stories, according to surmise! But Steven is a rare and exciting person to meet, and it is sad that he has gone so far and unreachably away. But if you and he can meet and talk it is good that he has gone to America. I think you will find in him some of the things you like in this landscape. The ideal would be if you could both inhabit here and continue acquaintance in this setting, so harmonious to both of you!

It was so kind of you to send me Anna Louise Strong's book,[30] and so fortunate that I should find it waiting me when I came back from Madrid. We met her there—a queer, dumpy, tousled old woman; very dictatorial and almost impossible to converse with because she spoke so rapidly and so broadly American. She is popular and regarded with affectionate astonishment by the militia there: she interviews them and stumps into the trenches and talks Spanish in broad American and is, I think, looked upon as a lucky emblem, both of fraternization, and, more superstitiously as one might regard an elephant's foot or tiger's tooth or a stout bronze Buddha!

The book has been of great use: I have lent it to my mother, because of the chapter on religion and priests. This is a sore subject with many people over here, and the information in her book clears up

24. *Norfolk Coast* (portion) in wool and silk, by John Craske.
Photograph by Jacob P Goldberg from the Peter Haring Judd Collection.
25. *Shipwreck*, watercolour, by John Craske.
Photograph by Jacob P Goldberg from the Peter Haring Judd Collection.

a great deal of dangerous misconception. As a result, my mother has collected about £5 from various small village religious circles, and has contributed useful sums to the Basque Fund, besides being almost completely converted to the pro-Government side. Completely converted whenever she meets one of the others, anyway! So I am doubly grateful for the present. But mainly because you sent it me and I loved to get it.

Photos of the house and garden I enclosed: not very good but with a use, because they show you how pleasantly rough-grown it is in summer. [Not found.] I have caught three trout and all of them basely, with cheese! Sylvia will explain why this is in the right tradition, however low it sounds! She will tell you of the Old Lady and the melancholy story of the house. You were right to think it needed happy living in; and it will have that I think. But you must come here and judge for yourself. Truly.

Love from us all—Tom joining enthusiastically, he is spry and vigilant after mice. His coat is thick and sleek, we [] his whiskers terrific.

Love to you, Valentine

Sylvia expanded on the pleasures of the house that 'gets nicer and nicer' and is henceforth to be referred to as Frome Vauchurch, the name she appropriated from the small parish across the Frome from Maiden Newton proper.

Frome Vauchurch
Maiden Newton Dorset
7. ix. 1937[31]

Dearest Elizabeth,

I am so glad, so thankful, that you are a money-gatherer too; for so I think you will be able to understand something of the pleasure and triumph it gave me to add your most generous gift to my list of soap-givers.

The stream had dwindled somewhat this last few weeks—partly my fault, for, being taken up with the household joys I did not beg so industriously as before; and the cheque for ten pounds which I sent to Paris yesterday had taken quite a lot of scraping up. Now today, at a stroke of the pen, I can duplicate it; and the doubled amount will give them even more bargaining power, and the doubled quantity of soap travel both grandly and harmoniously together. I thank you with all my heart.

I am so glad that you have met Steven Clark. I heard from him about a week ago, he told me in his letter that he had met you; and that he, as you tell me of yourself, had the feeling that he was meeting someone who was really a friend of long-standing—only that formality of encounter somehow overlooked in your old acquaintance. I am pleased that you like him. I guessed you would, he is a cat-person, fine and discriminating and reserved I realized his private character very much from seeing him in Barcelona, and seeing how instantaneously our dear cook Asuncion took him to her bosom.

He was sick while he was there; and the entire Spanish household devoted itself to soothing his bed of pain, they even and unblushingly stole from an austere English comrade's private store of health foods in order to bring variety, beauty and plenty to his dinner-trays. I may say that Valentine and I smiled upon the thefts, and only wished the private store had been more appetising. It was for Steven, too, that Pilar made tea; boiling it piously in a large stewpan for many hours, and stirring it the while.

But he is much more than just loveable, though that is quite a lot. He is upright and discreet.

I thank you so much for the letter about Scottsboro, it told me exactly what I wanted, including the clash, which I had suspected but never been able to get properly ascertained, between the NAACP and the LLP. All the LLP people I have met have always been as grave and respectable as tea-cosies, but it seemed to me that there must be more to it than that, if only for my small personal experience of advancing behind tea-cosies in this country. And they are admirable, and keep the pot nice and warm; but have no power to brew. It is a great pity these clashes have to occur, but they are inevitable they are just another of the inherent wrangles and tangles in an unadjusted social order. We have had a minor Scottsboro affair here, in the Harworth strikers. They struck against a black-leg trades union, a mix masters and men union on the fascist lines, which was formed in the Nottinghamshire coal-field by a renegade TU man called Spencer. And there, even, renegade is not the exact word. Spencer was a timid, earnest man, he lost his head seeing the results of a previous coal strike, when the men who had struck were savagely victimized; and the english middle-class idea of compromise took hold of him, so that he worked with the owners to form this mixed union, feeling that though it would not get the men all they wanted it might save them from losing all. A most short-sighted notion, which no one with a courageous feeling about class struggle could entertain for a moment.

Well, the Harworth strike [at a Nottingham colliery] was bitter and protracted. The blackleg union men not only went on working, but fought the others, who were defended by the police of course, and the mere fact of being defended instilled in them this notion that their real enemies were the strikers and not the coal-owners and the police-owners. The village was completely split, there were shops where the scabs traded and shops where the strikers traded, rows were incessant, it looked as though there might be a general coal-strike on this issue. Finally the Government worked up one of the usual rows into being just a bit more than usual, arrested the strike leaders, and gave them such sentences that even the general public, that does not usually give a damn for such things, sat up and waved its paws.

And instantly, wielding the tea-cosies, the whole tone of the agitation changed, and instead of saying, what was true, that the strikers had been defending their rights, and admitting, what is also true, that they had been freely-fighting, the stress became exasperatingly humanitarian, and an ignominious outcry had to be made because the sentenced was a woman. Through the tea-cosies, the sentences have been reduced. But it is a very dubious victory, we feel that we would like to hit out with something harder than a tea-cosy, and the tea-cosies feel that they have been wheedled into gaining a lovely victory which nobody is in the least grateful for.

This house gets nicer and nicer. And I have learned about the old lady who died here. I got the story from the rector and his mrs, who duly called. I could see they would ask questions about us unless I forestalled them, so before they could get themselves going I demanded the history of the previous householder. Well, she lived here with a brother, considerably younger than she. They were very happy, kept themselves to themselves, fished and gardened 'and took no part in the village life'. And their money was in an annuity, and the annuity was in his name. And one day, quite suddenly, he died.Not many people came to the funeral, they had few friends and no relations. So there was no one to back up the rev and mrs in their powerful feeling that the old lady should go into an institution, settle down with a friend, anything rather than carry out her project of staying on alone in the house. For it seemed to the rev and mrs so unsuitable, so dangerous. She might fall sick and nobody know. She might break her leg and lie till the Rats' ate her; and then there would be an inquest, a scandal, everything that a rev and his mrs dread.

However, she beat them down. She even cornered their suggestion that a respectable married couple should share the house with her (the house was far too large for her) in return for a free roof, by pointing out a case in the newspaper of an old lady who was murdered by just such a trustworthy pair.

So she lived on here, no one knew how. She fished trout, in season and out of season, and the baker called. She bought her clothes, if she bought any, off a van. She let the house go to rack and ruin. She had apples, and a few vegetables, but she didn't trouble much about vegetables. For instance, there was an asparagus bed in the garden, but she covered it with pansies.

The rev and mrs called uneasily, just to see if she was still alive. They did not enjoy it. Outdoors, there was her botany. She was a terrific botanist, when the rev said placatingly, This is a pretty little pink flower, she would reply, Anacoluthon diatessaron Arbuthnotii, or something of that sort, and fell him. Indoors, it was worse. All the floors were going to pieces, it was all right for her, she was light and shrivelled as an autumn leaf, skipped over them safely. But he could not take a step without going through.

Even when she was completely decrepid, she still kept them at bay and still gardened. She used to go out of the house on all fours to get at her flower-beds. They got in the district nurse, by a subterfuge, and the old lady drove her out with harsh words. At last, when she was completely defenceless, they carried her off to the house of a woman in the village 'such a nice woman', who for the smallest possible sum of money took her in. And there, soon after, she dies.

All this was told me by these execrable skinsaving wretches with the utmost baldness and self-approval. But it is nice to think that she so stamped her will on them that this house is known as the house where the old lady died.

The apples in the garden are beginning to taste. There is a very good russet, and several queer highly scented apples, one almost like muscat grapes. And we have explored the neighbourhood a little, and found a variety of beautiful places, and one church with about the loveliest seventeenth cent. rhymed epitaph one could hope to find. We must go back again to make an exact copy, and then you shall have it.

But best when you come and read it for yourself.

With our love,

Sylvia

[Handwritten postscript:] When next you write please give figures of The Waterbury Branch, & no light-under-a-bushel-hiding dear!

Elizabeth's letter to Valentine crossed the two from Frome Vauchurch; she backed away from the 'bribe', the project to amplify a Dorset parish register and the invitation to come and live in Maiden Newton or nearby. She felt the letter important enough to keep a copy.

Breakneck Hill
12:ix:37
[carbon][32]

[To Valentine]

For a long time now, months, alas, I've been writing truly magnificent letters to you, in my head, and for the past week I've been ineffectually trying to get a passable one down in black and, under the circumstances, yellow. So many things conspire to interrupt one's trans-Atlantic conversations; every evening, at 9:10 or 11:40, marvel at the ease with which that suave voice in London tells us in America what is happening in Spain or China or Wall Street, and then I give a despairing sigh at my typewriter and go to bed.

This has been a confused and unrestful, but in many ways a gratifying, summer. Directly the wheels of our AFSC [American Friends Service Committee] committee began to turn, I went off dutifully to the sea-shore with my family, and there, in that vacuum of relaxation and self-indulgence, carried on an exhausting sort of internal awareness of Europe and remote-control of money-raising in Waterbury. In the last of which I heard that you two were in Madrid, and that Madrid was being blown to bits again. The extremes of contrast were almost too much to bear; thank God Sylvia will never see the letters I sent to her in Madrid. A series of visits in early August, with hurried committee-meetings in between, finally ended me up in Philadelphia and Temple, Univ., where I encountered a lot of inspiring Quaker gentlemen, among them, finally and most happily, Steven Clark who will come here for a week-end soon. For three weeks now I've been at home, pulling practical and temperamental ends together, helping to get 40 letters signed by six separate people and sent out to the charitably inclined of Waterbury, and barely beginning to repair the ravages to my personal correspondence. This is a beautiful September Sunday morning, still blue and green with summer, but with that curious cool calm of resignation drifting on its quiet air. A good day to write letters, important ones, in, and tomorrow I must be off to New York to see a remarkable man about our traveling around Connecticut together in an effort to start up some more AFSC committees, so far Waterbury is head and shoulders above any other local branch in money-raising.

Now it is evening (tennis and a family party intervening), with an edged wind and a small moon and millions of cricket-voices, and I am thinking how still and gentle this light must be beside the river Frome. It is splendid that you are happily and successfully settled in the new house, Sylvia's lovely house-warming letter made me feel that I had been there with you, and my God now I wish that I might be there, soon, to grow for a while in that climate where the things that I most deeply believe in are indigenous rather than exotic and to watch the light change through the long autumn and winter and spring days over those beautiful hills. But for a while yet, as you know now, I cannot come. Because, as Frost said:

The woods are lovely, dark and deep,
But I have promises to keep,
and miles to go before I sleep,
and miles to go before I sleep.

Also because I have come to believe that the real break with what is malnutritive in one's past, the real recognition and acceptance of what must be one's regime for the future, comes from a change of heart rather than a change of scene. And the latter, while it is advisable and often indispensable, depends for its success on the health of the former, just as a tremendous determination to climb Mt. Everest will come to nothing unless it is accompanied by a good deal of attention to sleeping-bags, charts, evaporated food and so on. This will probably sound too obvious for words to you, but it came to me with a painful intensity last summer, in London, in the midst of a miniature but extremely convincing nervous collapse, which I don't intend to repeat. So when I've got my heart in hand, as it were, and kept, after a fashion, the promises, and weighted my luggage with a sizable piece of literary-historical-biographical manuscript, I shall come, praying that you won't disown me when you find me sitting on your doorstep some winter or spring or summer evening of 1938. In the meantime, I live in two places at once, Dorset and Connecticut, both of which I profoundly love, and that is difficult, and a test for any mind.

The parish-register at Plush refuses to give me a moment of peace. Of course if there were anywhere in the world so indiscreetly independent a document as a register which gave a glimpse of peoples' lives, instead of leaping from the baptismal font to the headstone, with an occasional moment of time but for holy matrimony, Sylvia would come upon it, in fact I must confess that I suspected her of creating, with a little concentration and a well-chosen handful of the more potent herbs, a perfect village, complete with brown roofs and church-tower and a mild-eyed vicar guarding so unparalleled a volume. Until I discovered Plush on the blessed map in that beautiful Shell guide to Dorset, and knowing that such a place exists, believed that what you both tell me about the register must, however fantastic it sounds, be true, and live for the moment when I can gaze upon it.

Your very graceful apologies, brought to me by Sylvia and the magnificent apostles of Malmesbury, put me to shame, for what is that small (though powerful) book when you have met the original, and under such marvelous circumstances (I do envy you that trip) compared to the uplifting package for which you have had no decent thanks, over this long time, from me? The *Shell Guide* is a piece, rather a concentrated essence, of Dorset, to warm the transatlantic hand and eye and heart; and how impressive a signature Day Lewis sets to that agreement between us. His poetry is what one's own perturbed and inarticulate spirit, in these dividing days, wants and needs to say, and how beautifully he speaks now, and will speak to the future, for the awakening of our times. Do you know his prose essay, 'A Hope for Poetry'? It's a valuable signpost, I think.

I do thank you very much for both of those lovely books. I've just finished Frederick Prokocco's *The Seven Who Fled*, which the critics have hailed sky-high, it's a piece of elegant and vigorous and beautiful putrescence, as far as I'm concerned, and the thought of what even an intelligent public did with *Lady Chatterley's Lover* and now how they're lapping up this spiced brew of stagnation and death makes me rage.

Will you do something for me? tell me exactly what you think is going to happen to Spain? No one over here has the faintest idea, and most are cold or inclined to think that Christianity and civilization, under the aegis of Fascist bombers ought to win, and I am sick with fruitless arguing. You, with your wisdom and your chance for observation, ought to know if anyone does; I should like so much to have you tell me. It seems now as though only the poets want Spain to survive, but whatever the outcome, they are the ones who know the truth in the end.

Now, in return for your fine poem of early this summer, I send you a result of that curious calm interlude on the *Bremen*. [Not found.] Without apologies, for I don't believe in them, but with a hope that you will find behind the baroque frontiers what I have not even attempted to say in this letter. And with that, and my love to you both and to Thomas and exiled Towser and the new house, and deepest thanks, I will have done for the present.

In August, Elizabeth recorded what she wanted to accomplish in the autumn. 'Begin regular work on AB' [Anne Bradstreet] was the first item she put in her notebook, with work for the Spanish children, 'study Spanish, prepare yourself to give talks' second. At 31 she continued to live in the Breakneck Hill house.[33]

Sylvia did not comment on Elizabeth's decision to pass on the 'bribe' of the project to work with the Plush local registers nor on her unwillingness to come to England for a longer stay such as she and Valentine had urged. She focused on Elizabeth's successful fund-raising and left the response to Valentine.

Frome Vauchurch Maiden Newton Dorset

23. ix. 1937[34]

This is not a letter, dearest Elizabeth, Valentine is writing that. But I must for myself say how much I congratulate you on the Waterbury Branch, and how happy it makes me feel to think of you setting forth now to rouse up such new centres. And I think, too, with such pleasure, Elizabeth has a resolute mind as well as a fine one. This thing she has begun so well she will go on with and carry further.

I do think you have done marvels. I wish I could send you a brown, slender, serious, black-currant-eyed spanish child to thank you.

Lovely autumn is here. Tonight the moon wears a russet halo in a sky covered with a small regular quilting of cloud, and the garden has a cold apple-smelling breath.

The town council of Dorchester decided to build themselves a new town hall. They dug the foundations and found that the site had been used already: a roman villa, with an extremely beautiful and perfect mosaic pavement in it. Now the archeologists have got in (like the moth) and the town hall seems indefinitely postponed. However, they are bearing it with philosophy. These things will happen if one lives in a roman town. With my love

Sylvia

Reports of Japanese bombings and atrocities in China increased Valentine's awareness of the horrors at large in the world beyond Spain. She addressed the question Elizabeth asked in her letter, 'what is likely to happen in Spain?', rather than take on Elizabeth's decision not to come over for a long stay. She enclosed the typescript of an article she had written which pointed out the respect Loyalist forces and government paid to the artistic heritage of the country. She was shortly to volunteer at a school for refugee children—which she described in a later letter and postcard.

Frome Vauchurch, Maiden Newton.
September 24th. [1937][35]

Dear Elizabeth,

I do most warmly congratulate you on the Waterbury money-raising record: and I do so most humbly, too. I am so bad at personal begging that I mostly have to do it by letter and even then, I think, I make too much fuss and incline people to think they are being generous when they aren't! I cannot imagine a more difficult thing than you have achieved, and it awes me that you have done it—But your efforts are crowned with so much more than just success—there must be some lightening of load on your own heart because of this.

And of that I speak, too, with envy. To-night has been most terrible—the morning, too, was bad because our daily paper carried a photograph more frightful than any I have yet seen; as frightful as any that will ever be made. A Chinese male child, very small, very close up—lying on a stretcher with his large face contorted into a shriek of anguish that is unbearable to eye and ear and heart at once. He is burnt and blasted with explosive; one hand gone and his legs twisted and shattered, but he is alive—

Then the day went on; was fine and lovely—a slow chill mist from the river rose up and went away in the sky, becoming a blue and mild day, when the birds sang. We went to Chaldon in the afternoon, and found there too this lovely autumnal day of splendour and kindness. Then returned to meet a brilliant sunset here, and a smooth river to reflect it—and then I caught an immense trout and we ate it, and ate mushrooms picked this early morning and brought to us by a Saxon-faced child whose hands were so cold that they looked like ripe plums, and whose hair fell in light, damp golden streaks around her small neck.

After a fine supper, with quietness and books to read, and after feeding a triumphant and purring Thomas replete with two mice—we came up here to my room, gratefully turning on the electric fire and rejoicing in it, and Sylvia worked on repairing my patchwork coat and I read Swift's so-crossly affectionate letters ... then turned on the radio and heard the news. And Canton has been bombed again—a brief affair of only a few minutes, but enough to wipe out the entire working population, as it seems. They concentrated on the industrial districts and the slums—leaving alone the foreign and rich quarters and the military objectives. They smashed and burned and destroyed and killed—so that Reuter's man saw what had been long streets and broad ones filled with bodies and with maimed and living people.

And this horror so obsesses my mind that I think this may be a strange letter—the kind of letter, Elizabeth, that we shall be writing to each other increasingly often till we cannot longer write.

As for Spain—what can I say? You know that the situation is most complicated politically: that the extremists have wrecked wherever they could, whether or no they meant to—and that thousands upon thousands have died who need not have died, even under their compulsion, if only the war-machine had functioned smoothly and without these internal confusions.

I think that even yet the Government may win. It is said by people who know much more than I that they still, almost certainly, will win. But every day makes the victory a lesser one, except for glory—for the country is bleeding and the people are dying.

If the Government fails, there will be nothing left of Spain at all. There will be a mixed population, slowly gathered back and forced to stay—few Spaniards, except that the rich will return—but the rich in any country are at best 'cosmopolitan' and at worst (and truest) just The Rich. And the Spanish rich are so ignorant, so stupid and fat and lazy, that no national culture can come from them—nor do they know what that is, beyond gypsies and whores. Italians and Germans and Portuguese will be there—and a small leavening of poor Spaniards, who may or may not—in whole centuries of time—revive Spain again.

Christianity won't exist at all: I fancy that it will not even try to. Catholics there were anyhow hardly at all Christian, and after a war like this what pretence they put up won't be worth bothering about any longer. The spell is broken (was, long since, except among the Basques, who had their own peculiar and astonishing paganism which was—or so I thought—peculiarly decadent and attractive and horrible, but definitely was NOT Christian!) and the rulers won't bother to cumber themselves with old mummery. Force is the new fancy-dress, and works miracles more speedily and with more pleasure to the miracle-mongers. So far as I could judge (but we couldn't tell much, being among the enlightened) the Spanish people don't show much interest in Christianity anyway, now: even outside Catalonia they dislike the Church, and except in Catalonia they show not even the homage of fear now: no persecution, no attacks, no gibes. Just nothing.

I am going to work for a time at a Basque Refugee School near Oxford. I shall be able to see what form their religion takes. I fancy it will prove to be another form of Nationalism. That they'll hang on to the forms as they do to their language, for the same reasons. No more. But we shall see.

I'll send you some of the papers we brought back from Spain, to help in those endless, heart-breaking and back-breaking arguments one has to endure. You'll find the papers help a little, anyway. More than my scattered impressions can do, I think.

But if the Government wins—then there will be one upheaval after another, but each one, I believe sincerely, will be another wide stride towards liberty of thought: and it is important to realise that without a Government victory such a thing is totally impossible, for no one (except the imported minority of literates) will be in possession of the means to think.

I send you a translation of something which is interesting in this connection.

And the 'upheavals' won't be bloody, I fancy. They will be transfers of power: they will be bitter sometimes and they will be at first blind gropings towards something better—not more than that. But they will be towards life, you see, and not towards death. But the Fascists chalk on the walls the word, in large heavy black letters 'DEATH'. And sometimes 'Hail, Death'. Our people could not conceive of that.

Forgive me. I've done badly by something I cherish and have my hopes upon. But I wanted to answer at once, and I wanted to answer before I leave here for the Basque School. This is a long letter & I fear it is not much use. But the cloud in my mind is so wide and so black that I cannot seem to see any light through it at present. So many dead make the air difficult to breathe.

But meanwhile, life goes on and poems like your poem are written and things happen to engender them. And people like you, like Sylvia, and Steven Clark and a hundred others are still alive to keep the world alive.

And, as you say, Poets want Spain to survive. And even when the poets are killed, as Lorca was, the thousand others find tongues to speak with—Sylvia will send you (or I will if she is busy) translations of some of the thousand or so poems written by Government soldiers during this war. These are the real answers to any and all doubts. Only I do realise you can't brandish them as a final argument in Waterbury!

Forgive this letter—I send you much love and look forward with belief to that day when you will arrive on this pleasant doorstep and be greeted with a trinity of purring and rejoicing from Sylvia and Thomas and

Valentine

The typescript of the article Valentine enclosed in her letter of 13 September:

Valentine Ackland,
24, West Chaldon

In Spain

I have got a lesson-book which I brought back from Spain. It is issued especially for the soldiers, many of whom cannot read or write when they first join the Army. This book is strongly-bound, and has a little pocket in the front cover, in which there is a blank copy-book and a pencil. Every alternate page of the book has a boldly printed coloured picture and a page of print and script is opposite, with easy words spaced out, and then a line first of the vowels used and then of the consonants. Above the pictures there are suitable sentiments, not murderous and not bragging, but sentences like: 'We fight for culture'. 'The labouring people of the world are just like ourselves'. 'Work for the happiness of our State!' And in the back of this book there is a facsimile-typescript letter from Jesus Hernandez, Minister for Public Education, in the course of which he says:

'Soldiers of the People: You know how to read; you know how to write. A new world opens in front of our eyes and your understandings. This magnificent world we shall conquer if in one hand we hold the lesson-book and in the other the rifle with which we can guard our right to education ... As Minister of Public Education and your comrade, I congratulate you, in the name of the whole Government, and wish that together we may speedily have victory and together may enter into possession of a prosperous and noble Spain.'

In republican Spain to-day there is evidence that education and culture are prized above all other possessions. Jacinto Benavente, a winner of the Nobel Prize for Literature, writes these words at the back of a pamphlet showing Fascist destruction of Church treasures at Alcala de Henares (where the baptismal font of

Cervantes and the tomb of Cardinal Cisneros were wrecked by bombardment):

'History, with a high spirit of Justice, forgives and even overlooks killing, murders, any kind of violence justified by motives of the moment, in political or social commotions, but life is always inexorable in judging those who destroy Works of Art, Libraries, Historical Monuments, all that is the spiritual patrimony of a nation. Lives and material wealth have a possible atonement but spiritual wealth can neither be substituted nor replaced; its destruction is an attempt against universal culture and a theft of future humanity; it is, lastly, a sin against the spirit, the only unpardonable one for which there is no possible redemption.'

Innumerable pamphlets, posters, newspaper articles, books enlarge upon this theme, and meanwhile cheap reprints of the Classics, cheap reproductions of pictures, histories of art, of literature, of world-culture continue to flow for the publishing houses and to be bought in thousands by those people who are, we are assured, either blindfolded fools or destructive barbarians.

The Rector of Barcelona University sums up the real situation in Republican Spain, and we who attended the International Congress of Writers held recently in Madrid can testify to the absolute truth of his words: 'In the very midst of our terrible tragedy, during the most painful days of passion, all kinds of efforts have been made, and have succeeded in saving our Treasure of Art, while the Government and the people endeavour to maintain and uninterrupted life of spirit.'

There can be no prouder boast than that in the whole of history.

That autumn from Tythrop House in Buckinghamshire where she was a volunteer Valentine sent a postcard with a photo of the Spanish refugee children cared for there.

26. Spanish refugee children at Tythrop House, Buckinghamshire, 1937.

Tythrop House,
Kingsey
Nr Haddenham,
Bucks
October 17th [postmark 10 Oct][36]

Your letter came to me here & made me very happy. I am so glad I came here, & in some ways sad that my time is nearly up—but I shall be glad to see Frome Vauchurch again—

I have much to say that must go into a letter—

This house is early Georgian with a spacious Grinling Gibbons staircase & a genuine Georgian oaken stairs for the servants to use. The park is vast, & its chestnut trees now unbelievably burning in gold, the real news follows.

Valentine

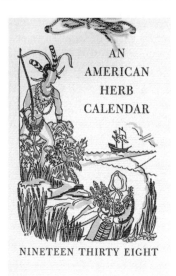

27. Elizabeth's Herb House at Breakneck.

28. Cover of Elizabeth's *An American Herb Calendar*.

That fall Elizabeth in collaboration with her artist friend, Prentiss Taylor, selected quotations and wrote text for a calendar citing appropriate herbs for each month. The twelve pages were threaded by yarn and designed to be hung on a wall, with a page for each month. It was a considerable piece of work—recognized by Sylvia who shared a passion for herbs. This project with an artistic friend was likely one of the reasons behind Elizabeth's reluctance to leave for a long stay in England.[37]

Elizabeth's knowledge of herbs and their historic uses and literary sources were put to good use. This was a project that used her knowledge of both herbs and literature, and one that she could do on home ground. Perhaps, too, it was an alternative to the work on the Plush Parish Register that Sylvia had put forward as a 'bribe' to encourage her to move to England.

In October, Elizabeth and Prentiss Taylor were in Arden, Delaware for a meeting on the Spanish relief effort. Arden was originally a summer community dedicated to Henry George's single tax policy and built in the Arts and Crafts style, largely remaining a center of progressive thinking and a suitable place for a Quaker-inspired gathering. On her return, she reflected on the mix of her interests, social activism, keeping up with friends with young children, enjoyment of good clothes and the money that can buy them, and affection for the Connecticut landscape.

This afternoon, from the train, an almost unbearable sunset, the light coming strong and deep from a horizon space under a heavy sky of clouds, striking straight across the earth and making burn with a double glory of golden fire the bright autumnal trees, the tall single maples and tulips and hickories, with trunks and branches stark black from the rain and the billowing masses of triumphant leaves against the sky's drop, mirror-gray. I was very tired after those two days of heavy and considerable accomplishment, so many people: the fine Stiphanos, Mrs I du Pont, a true person in her castle-manor in that lovely country a little like Dorset, Prentiss [Taylor] and D Minor on a gobbled dinner, the social Mrs W in her home with bad furniture and good portraits, P Malin, intense, intelligent, with dynamic oratory and a full voice, and the militantly moth-eaten Baltimore committee, then that funny train trip and New York abjectly drenched in the early morning, the vigorous young English set-ups in the white nursery school-house, Kes [(Bullock) Cole] and her new very masculine tiny contribution, Margaret [Moore] and her three children with their colds … and clothes-buying at Lord & Taylor. A black velvet décolletage with fake Victorian pearls, not too impressive until you stop to think how many small and terrified lives that $40 might save, and then you have to think, well, as long as her internal gesture of compliance is to be brought up, for a while anyhow, it must be done with a certain [style] and I don't think that is completely damnable hypocrisy.

And finally on the train for home, with which this day's scratching started, and in the car driving up from Naugatuck as always, the colours and relief, the beautiful black bark, leaf splattered road, and the thought: never fear ...[38]

In late November, Valentine wrote that she was sending Elizabeth a ring she and Sylvia had bought that summer in a Madrid shop while a bombardment was underway, she was terrified by her first experience under fire. She gave an account of her recent duty at the Tythrop camp for the Basque children and reflected on the loss of artists in the war. (For reasons Sylvia explains in a later letter, she did not actually send the ring until late December when accompanied with her own description of the circumstances of its purchase. The ring has not been found.)

Frome Vauchurch, Maiden Newton,
29 November 1937[39]

Dear Elizabeth,

I think it is probably much too early to write you a letter about Christmas, but we have been looking at presents and we had both, apart, decided to send you what we ARE sending you, as the dearest thing we could find and the most suitable and fitting and the most likely to please you. I hope it does. I remember so vividly the things that happened when we bought it. It was a very hot afternoon in Madrid; we were leaving next day, and earlier in the afternoon a party of us had already left, because the bombardment had become so heavy that they decided against staying for the extra day we had been granted. We, Sylvia and I, had seen them off—and although I cannot think that Sylvia felt it, I had felt a most unnerved sinking of my heart as the motors drove away and the guns still banged and rattled and tossed, and people still walked along the 'safe' side of the bright street—an indication that their experienced wits warned them of serious danger.

And the remaining members of the Congress (by far the majority) had scattered to various places and things, but Sylvia and I were left to ourselves for the first time in all that long visit.

I am ashamed to say (but it is, so to speak, structural in me, and so I must not let myself be too much ashamed of it) that I was scared stiff. I walked along the streets with Sylvia with my knees soft with terror, and feeling that unrighteous anger at her coolness which is hard to endure, and was also hard for her if she knew of it.

The cars departing had given us both a strong sense of being left in possession of the city and of being beleaguered there; Sylvia was enjoying it completely; I was conscious of it and excited but I was also terrified.

We walked and looked at shops. The food shops opened for an hour; the little wood shops, the paint-shops, the shops that sold aluminum cooking vessels. We went into one of these and bought a fine drinking bottle made in Berne. Then we crossed to the 'dangerous' side and went into a jeweller's shop, where they had displayed a hundred rings, with glass compartments for photographs; these the soldiers wear with pictures of their women: mothers and wives and loves-and a boy was buying one. He had a rifle over his shoulder on a sling and he wore his blanket and his little billie-can. He was just going off to the Brunete front where the triumphant attack was then being made.

We selected and bought this ring which is for you: it bears on it the hammer and sickle and also the Socorro Rojo emblem, which is revered and loved all over Government Spain and as deeply hated on the other side. It is in the little box as we bought it; and I remember very vividly (as one remembers terrifying escapes of one's childhood) how the old man fumbled as he wrapped it and snapped the elastic band around the box, and how the guns thundered and I heard some masonry fall and thought—But what I thought is base and yet I expect I shall think just such thoughts when our turn comes.

At anyrate, here is this ring for you; much more than the present we both send you with very great affection and love. I think you will be glad to have it as an authentic reminder of your own work. You should be so proud of that—

I am back from the Basque camp, from which I sent you a postcard. I could not write properly from there because we worked as hard as it is possible to work, changing that fine Georgian mansion into some semblance of a home for them, and hampered by lack of everything we needed. There were four of us at first: Janet Machen (whom you met) and 'Nurse' (an elderly spinster, short and fluffy and very talkative, who labored finely under the emergency of starting up, but failed utterly at her real job later on—a most English weakness) and Sylvia Dobson (another good-in-an-emergency person who unfortunately for it and us and herself was the Responsible, but has now resigned) and myself. We scrubbed a hundred disgusting iron bedsteads, rusted and filthy, which had come from a hospital and been SOLD to us by their kindness: we carried them upstairs, to the enormous Georgian bedrooms. We cleaned and shook and beat out three hundred square sections of mattresses and about nine hundred filthy and lean blankets: we cleaned and scoured and polished and scrubbed, and in the intervals of this we hand-pumped water into the vast cistern. The pumping was worst of all.

Then, after delays and heart-breaks and broken water-pipes and failing plumbing, the day came when the first consignment of refugees arrived: I was sent with a young and silent Englishman to meet them. At a country station five very small boys were standing, in charge of the solitary porter who kept on asking us and himself 'Can they speak?'

We put them into the back of the car and then lost ourselves in the fog. So I stopped at a village and got them some cigarettes, and after that we were all fairly happy, except that the desolation and forlornness of those children is something to remember for all time. Their first question was 'Can we play football?' and the second 'Can we smoke?'

They settled in very well and easily, and two days later about forty boys came, mixed ages from 7 to 16. They were all 'bad' boys. With them were two Spaniards, women, very good indeed.

Then came about nine girls, and finally more boys to make numbers up to 113: the full capacity and rather over that.

I am going back there in a week's time, for a week—to assist in the change-over from one Responsible to a new one.

I cannot find much to say. It needs a particular mood to tell you what it is REALLY like to have charge over these, so lost and so left and so indomitable. One child of seven was suspected of being half-witted: then it was discovered that he and two other had spent two days and two nights in a shell-hole, unable to move from it because of the bombardments from land and air. That was at Bilbao. His parents were both killed as they ran to shelter with him. He is so frantically mother-sick that he can so far only live like an animal: eating and drinking a little, but not making contact with anyone, and crying all day and hiding in corners. When he arrived in England after a sea-journey which is indescribably horrible to hear about, he immediately got typhoid. It seems a grievous pity that he did not die.

Thank you for wishing that I might have cracked a Fascist skull. It is a great kindness you do me, and yet I shall be surprised if it does not turn out to be true that I am quite as much sickened by violence and quite as profoundly antagonistic to it, as you are yourself: and I know I am as much afraid of it as it is possible for anyone to be who has not yet gone mad from fear. And the question of whether or not some kinds of people should adventure their lives, when other kinds have only their lives to give, is a question which I have often argued passionately, about such poets as Edward Thomas, in the last war, and-before I went to Spain—about Lorca in this war, as well as Ralph Fox and John Cornford ...[40]

And I always argued passionately against their going to die.

But the facts have persuaded me to a decision about this which is so contrary to my logical decision that I feel Jesuitical in telling you about it. But you ask me:

I think an artist (and this includes, for present purposes, any one of articulate sensibility and intellect) is almost inevitably driven

THE NEW BREATH OF LIFE BLOWING OUT OF ENGLAND

by his character to the extreme of what he can do, for things in which he believes. But I also think as certainly, that the other people have as strong a duty and compulsion, to prevent him if they can, and otherwise to safeguard him so far as they can. Not from sentimentality but from expediency: that the comparatively few artists should be preserved by the will of the people.

This has happened already in some cases in Spain and in Russia, and God knows in a hundred other places where persecutions or wars have visited. But for this to become a regular custom, I believe (and it is one of the deepest reasons for my main belief) that Communism must have the teaching of the people. The passionate feeling against the Fascists on the death of Lorca is not only because the Spaniards are emotional, are proud of their art: sitting in the gloomy kitchen of Tythrop House I heard two communists (very rough, very uneducated, very East End gangster class) discussing with passion the death of Ralph Fox: blaming the Party for allowing him to be exposed to danger; blaming him for going out to lead his section: blaming most bitterly the 'stupid muddle' that got him killed. And so I intervened and argued that in his job as Political Commissar he must not only talk, but must lead in activity as well, in every case, always: and that his intellectual gifts made it necessary for him to have this terrific job as Commissar—but they agreed to THAT and only reviled the soldiers who would permit him to lead them into the danger of his death. I replied that, in warfare, the long, long periods of waiting for an attack must wear down morale, and when the moment does come it isn't always that the men are ready to act at once, without leadership—and that Fox had to take that responsibility: and in war how could there always be 'someone else'.

They agreed, on the magic words Party Discipline being hurled at them: but they were not at all persuaded. And these toughs, who—we are told—scorn and destroy wantonly all things of the mind, and exalt the Common Man above every other god, were protesting till I nodded with fatigue that the Common Men should have gone without Ralph Fox ...

This is only to bolster up the argument I have put so badly to you but I do not want you to think it a weakly idealistic argument, a hope and not a conviction, I am convinced.

But this is a terribly long letter. Forgive me. I have owed you one and wanted to write it so that I should have a reply! Tell Steven [Clark] if you see this or are writing to him that we have discovered even finer roads nearby here than the road to Toller—and that Compton Valance is lovelier even than its name. And I tell you that we are waiting with increasing impatience to show you all that we have found for your delight!

America seems too far away, on this fine, cold evening when the plovers are flying round and around the meadow and seagulls are going up and down the river looking for my trout. If only war does not cut us off before the pleasures we look for—But in any case, always love to you.

Valentine

In early December, Sylvia celebrated Elizabeth's success in raising $1,180 for the Spanish children. She again warmly welcomed a visit to Frome Vauchurch and urged her to go to Spain on relief duty.

Frome Vauchurch.
Maiden Newton.
Dorset.
2. xii. 1937[41]

Dearest Elizabeth.

There are a great many things I ought to do—but the thing I am going to do is answer your letter right away. For you write that sort of letter. The moment it comes into the house it is as though Elizabeth were here; and at once I am excited, and my mind sparkling with things to say to you.

Well, we have a good habit of beginning with the weather—Lordie me, how deep in the same England we are, if we were to meet on the same scaffold I suppose one of us would be pointing out signs of rain to the other. Today, all day, our river has races past us, high out over its brim, thick, dead-leaf coloured, with a cream and coffee spume on it, whirled from one pattern to another. It is so exciting, one goes to the window and sees this flood tearing past, and it is as though one were Noah's Cat with safe dry paws. Even in spate this river is pretty silent, a secretive stream. The garden is bare, tolerably tidy. The last cyclamen has died back to the ground, there are no flowers at all except a few small russet chrysanthemums and a violet or two. But we were eating raspberries last month.

All along the windowsills are rows of medlars, laid out to blet, every one of them stolen. We were sent house-hunting for a friend of Valentine's—a silly woman, who did not like the perfect house found for her; but I did, especially its fine medlar tree standing all unappreciated by a low stone wall; so I brought back all the medlars I could carry. Not that I so wildly fond of them as all that, a medlar is not a thing one can gluttonise over; but I like to have them about the house, and it is not in my nature to leave a good thieving unadmired.

The smell of apples is all over the house. I had two shelves put up in the box-room, the darkest room there is, and there they sit, sweating slightly, and filling the house with their lovely scent. But we did not have a good crop, the trees need pruning too badly. We will prune this winter, and hope for a good crop in the summer's summer, if one can say that on the analogy of the pretty Scots morn's morn.

Your Waterbury exploit fills me with joy and admiration. You say 1180 dollars, and I see it in a long procession of black eyes burning in pinched faces. Go to Spain if you possibly possibly can. Tell your Quakers how much more money you could raise if you had been there (this is true; and more so I daresay in New England) If by any chance you go in a hurry here are some good people. In Port-Bou, the frontier town you will probably go through, Comrade Pallach of the town committee, he speaks french and is one of the rattiest and most beautify characters I have ever met, wisdom shines from him. In Barcelona, Leon and Betty Gorgas, their address is

26 Iborra, Sarrià (a suburb) but they work at the Friends depot in Barcelona. She is an Englishwoman, they are very kindly. In Valencia, Dr Max Hodann, at the Sanidad there. I forgot, in the Barcelona Sanidad, Dr. Emrich. If any of them are alive, if any of them are where they were. But never was it so true, that Walt Whitman poem that begins out of the rolling ocean, the cord; one meets and cleaves to these people, and the wind blows over the place. But the important thing is to See Spain. Then you will see, on our side of the frontier, the most beautiful sight possible on this earth, a free and proud people; whatever distress and misery you see with it is not so vital, one can see them at one's door any day of the week; but a free people is a sight to get at, by hook or crook. As for the other side—do any of the USA Friends ever get there? News comes through from the occupied territory, not much, but always the same. There is plenty to eat, plenty by Spanish ideas, anyhow; and a considerable appearance of peace and order; and they are shooting people every night, still. That is why they are calling up the women, a thing unheard of by their traditions. It is not to fight or to nurse, it is to work; for they have killed so many working-men that they feel the pinch of a labour shortage, so the widows must work in their husband's jobs.

I am finding out about Craske's things, and will let you know as soon as I can. The only snag that I can see is that lately he has been doing more needlework pictures than any other, so that the best specimens of his latest manner are likely to be in needlework. For instance, he told me in a recent letter that he has in hand, and is pleased with, a big needlework picture of the snow-sea picture you took. I will go myself to choose if it comes to choosing; but if I think the best pieces are needlework I shall send one or two of them instead of keeping to the more convenient water-colours. But I know there are some good water-colours, there may even be enough. I am, we both are, so grateful to you for managing all this. With the Waterbury exploit and the herbal [*An American Herb Calendar*], there seems to be no end to the things you can do, if for no other reason you and Anne Bradstreet should come here for a rest! Let it harden from a hope into an intention. People have so few scruples about a hope unarmatured by intention, but once they sniff intention they are much more acquiescent.

We have such beautiful family to show you, we call them the Anglo Saxons. An endless string of children, all of them with long pale faces and flaxen straight hair and long thin noses and an air of amazing melancholy and distinction, and now that the winter has touched them their blonde complexions acknowledge it with the most exquisite apple-blossom pink on cheeks and noses. They must have preserved an absolutely pure breed since the days of Edith with the Swan Neck. Everything about them is elfin and strange. They are extremely poor and ill-dressed and ill-fed (not that that is strange) and I have seen only one toy in their possession. I was walking past their house one day and one of the smaller Saxons was sitting on the house steps with a black object which I thought at first to be a black cat. But not at all. It was a coal-black, deeply-furred curly-brimmed TOP-HAT, circa about 1860 I suppose, in a very fine state of preservation. The only other family I have ever seen to compare with them for extent and rarefied beauty were my second cousins the Sandersons, who were described when they were all young and floreating as looking like 'a band of underfed angels'. There were sixteen of them and their father had fits. Those were the days.

Very very much love and admiration and congratulation
Sylvia.

At the end of her Christmas letter Valentine again urged Elizabeth to visit soon again and come with them to see favorite places in her native Norfolk. She recalled bird-shooting with her father, something which Elizabeth enjoyed doing with Will White.

Frome Vauchurch,
Maiden Newton,
Dorset.
December 29th [1937][42]

My dear Elizabeth,

Thank you so much for sending Walden—which I have not read seriously ever, and only half-read half-attentively when I was a child. This is a most charming edition, and I shall be happy with the books; their olive colour is suitable to the winter landscape here, and the picture of White Pond is especially lovely to me, so much like the wide Norfolk meres I knew when I was a child. My father had the shooting rights at a place called Rollesby Broad, where he would go sometimes in the early mornings 'flighting' the wild duck. I used to go with him, a very small child, and sit on the flat bottom of the boat listening to the reeds wagging and the water knocking, and heave my shoulders up to my ears anticipating the great noise of his gun, which always deafened me for ages afterwards. But I loved to see the black retriever spring over the side of the boat and hasten away, half swimming and half crawling on the tummocks of reeds. He never failed to find the duck, even when he was old and blind and deaf—And in the summer or early autumn we used to go for picnics to that water, and I had a small (and dangerously unsteady) green boat of my own, given me on my sixth birthday: It only held two people, and most often only had to hold me. I would paddle up and down, past the fallen tree in whose upturned roots the kingfisher built each year, and there was usually a wasp-nest there too.

Next time you come to England will you try hard to arrange it so that you can spend at least two weeks with us? This is a serious request, for we would love to take you to Norfolk to visit my home there and go over to Frankfort Manor where we lived, and visit Craske at East Dereham, and show you anyhow some of the lovely churches and the most beautiful, melancholy ruin in the world—a small chapel so old and ruined and secret that it has a lovely straight beech tree grown to full height in the center of the chancel, and long ropes of ivy hanging from the belfry, where the white owl lives. And many another place, and many people in that strange locality: Danish people mostly, with faces like foxes and who use the same strange words that old Camden listed so carefully, and Thomas Browne was proud of.

Please try hard to spare us at least that fortnight, and more if you possibly can manage it. I promise you it shan't be wasted by any of us!

I hope this New Year will be the happiest one you have ever yet known—

With love and with thanks,

Valentine

On the same day, Sylvia confessed at Christmas that an illness prevented her from previously mailing the ring she and Valentine had bought in Madrid in July and offered her account of its purchase.

Frome Vauchurch
Maiden Newton, Dorset.
Telephone: Maiden Newton 76.
29. xii. 1937[43]

Dearest Elizabeth,

Here, even too late for the New Year is our Christmas present to you. A ring, bought in Madrid, a ring of the day, with the Sacorro Rojo blazon and the CP.

It was a blazing hot afternoon when we got it. There had been a heavy bombardment all night, and an air-raid in the morning, and all day we heard the guns on the Brunete front and an occasional rattle of musketry from University City. The shop where we found the ring was in a narrow street near the Puerta del Sol, and it was its narrowness that took us there, for it was completely shaded, and down at the bottom of the narrow cañon of grey houses there was a remnant of cool. The shop itself was about ten foot square, it sold jewellery and mended watches, and changed money, and did a little pawning. There were several customers, some selling, some buying, all with leisurely Castilian grace; and because we were strangers they helped us with our purchases, pointing out the merits of this or that, and regretting the rings, being made for men, were too wide for our fingers. We spent a very happy quarter of an hour there, cool and courteous; and parted with fists and Saluds, and then we went and sat in a small square, shaded with dusty palmtrees and plane trees, and furnished with tiled benches, very soothing to the behind, and very clean and sensible, too. They would be nice in New York. A fountain was playing, and children were dabbling. And the guns got louder, and we looked at the sky-line of our hotel and noticed where it was chipped. It was hot and peaceful and dangerous, and like the end of the world. Except for the children and the fountain and the guns there was little noise. Every one sat in a heavy afternoon silence, sometimes one saw a brown hand sprawl itself out on the tiles, seeking a cool surface to rest on. Some of us looked gravely at the trees and some of us looked at our feet reposing on the fine reddish dust. Afterwards we went and had a drink at a cafe, horchera, a kind of iced sweetened barley water, and a Jewish journalist we had made friends with gave us a paper envelope with six little cigars in it: a lovely gift, for there was a great tobacco shortage, and only registered citizens could get cigarettes. He liked us because he said we were the first English people he had ever met who were not haughty.

None of this though explains why the ring comes so late. The ignominious truth is that I developed a 'local sepsis' about ten days before Christmas. At least, that is what my doctor called it. I called it a plain low ordinary boil. But in order to keep it local I had to retire to my bed and keep icily regular and completely idle. And since I am the parcel tie-er of this establishment our Christmas goodwill got considerably postponed. Every now and then in a languid way I would lick on a stamp, but otherwise I just lay there reading the *New Yorker* and eating delicious meals on trays, and hearing Valentine getting rid of the waits. We had a terrible outcrop of them, all the village children. And some damnable busy-body at the local school had taught them a series of fancy carollings, and their drawling Dorset voices, completely uninterested, reiterated Ring merrily, bells, Ring merrily, bells, till Valentine found another sixpence to drive them away with. I said that far the best way of discouraging them would be to gather on the inside of the door and sing counter-carols. But Valentine refused to gather alone.

Your presents arrived, and were the greatest delight. I adore the orphan. It seems to me that if Cobbett had met her (and I think dates would allow this), he most certainly would have married her, as he almost married that other young American, and then he would have remained in the New World, and English letters would have suffered a grave loss, and Lord Sidmouth's life would have been much happier.[44]

And I love the calendar, and am thinking of making that StrongTonic Syrup for myself, I daresay it is exactly what I need. And Valentine will have written to you about Walden. I am wrung with envy. I spend hours trying to think of books she has not got, and you score a bullseye. Well, my dear, we send you our love and our best wishes along with this ring from Spain which you are so well worthy to have. And perhaps you will even wear it there.

Always,

Sylvia

In late 1937 Elizabeth clipped from a newspaper, 'Welcome the Wrath', a poem by Stanley Kunitz. The poem concludes:

Wrath has come down from the hills to enlist
Me surely in his brindled generation,
The race of the tiger; come down at last
Has wrath to build a bonfire of my breast
With one wet match and all my descendants.

She made a note on the clipping: 'Terribly important, to get back into touch again with the feeling, the colour, the texture, the sensuous character of the world. Having deliberately let come between yourself & that the magnet, the burning glass, of love. So that no contact was possible save through that one concentrated element, now the magnet, the glass, cannot be leaned on as before, you must go back to direct contact.'[45]

IV. Violent and ecstatic happiness

During 1938, with war, and the threat of a wider war affecting them, the three women's lives were forever altered. Elizabeth's attempt to volunteer for humanitarian service in Loyalist Spain, warmly encouraged by 'S & V', ended that October in what she termed a nervous breakdown in Paris. Sylvia, passionately concerned for her protegée's mental stability and physical health, virtually commanded her to come to Dorset to recover. This Elizabeth did, in defiance of her family who had strenuously opposed her Spanish project. In late autumn Valentine and Elizabeth became lovers. 'An old year, an old life, dies, and another comes passionately and fearfully alive', Elizabeth wrote on New Year's Eve 1938. It was her initial experience of sexual love, and it stirred her irrevocably; the experienced Valentine found herself involved in a passion she could not renounce even as she could not leave Sylvia, a conflict which would persist. Sylvia, initially tolerant, experienced the gall of jealousy as she realized the depth and staying power of Valentine's passion for Elizabeth, to be bitterly recounted in her journal and notes about the affair after Valentine's death. Her role as mentor and 'priestly' confessor to Elizabeth was done.

However, before this emotional tumult, the warmth and vivacity of the 'S & V' friendship continued. Sylvia wrote persuasive, witty, and erudite letters to build her young friend's confidence; she and Valentine rejoiced at Elizabeth's arrival in London in August and were delighted to show her the Maiden Newton house now lived in; all three enjoyed motoring from Dorset to Valentine's Norfolk. Elizabeth wrote eloquently of her experience of Londoners cheering Chamberlain on his return from Munich; Sylvia denounced the deal and presciently predicted that a long war would result. 'S & V' gave Elizabeth loving care at Frome Vauchurch after her breakdown in Paris; she came to know and love Dorset and the evidences of its past.

By early 1938 Elizabeth had not taken up Sylvia's and Valentine's suggestion to settle in Dorset and research the history of an individual village. Except for a cable and a wire early in the spring, there appear to have been no letters to and from Frome Vauchurch until June, a contrast to the previous year, and probably due to Elizabeth's uncertainty about volunteering for relief duty in Spain against her parents' wishes.

It was not until June 1938 that Elizabeth wrote Sylvia, keeping a carbon. She confessed to having been living with confusion and stress; she continued to be uncertain of herself and of what she should be doing in the world. She felt shamed by not making a commitment to volunteer for relief work in Loyalist Spain. Could Sylvia bear being 'back in the priesthood' again, she asks. She reminds her of their shared love of plants and news of those she brought from Dorset to Connecticut, and in a very different context, the hammer and sickle ring from Madrid.

Breakneck Hill
Middlebury, Conn.
21. vi: 38[1]

Dearest Sylvia,

So long and inconsiderate a silence on my part cannot but have nourished in your mind anger and disappointment and distrust toward me. That I must accept as a deserved penalty, and whatever of forgiveness and understanding may go with it is for you to decide. For the real and only reason why I have not written to you in all these months is that I have simply not had the strength. That not only sounds absurd, but it is also a stupid and awful admission of which I am thoroughly ashamed. I know how you dislike such masochistic self-abasement as this but bear with me for a few words more, and then I will have done. I am in the violent toils of a struggle for psychological adjustment to a terrifying and challenging world which, in the last few years only I have been trying to face with a semblance of intellectual and emotional integrity. 'Say not the struggle nought availeth'; God knows it does avail, the serial bombers of fear, the poisoned gas of self-disgust, and the epics of weakness and self-pity must be overcome at last, but to be ill-equipped with a tin sword of intelligence and a pop-gun of will the fight is a long and enervating one. That's enough now, but how does it feel, my dear, to be back in the priesthood

29. The approach to Rats' Barn.

Photograph courtesy of the Powys Society.

after nearly six months off duty and to be hearing again, through the blue confessional curtain of the Atlantic, my whining voice? I'm sure but you must fervently regret ever having laid eyes on so wretched and exasperating a creature.

Let us now at once come to Craske. Just as your January cable arrived the English Book shop decided to devote their gallery to a permanent exhibit of international ballet material. So that possibility was out, and in a way as well, for while it would make a good entering wedge, a show there would not carry the weight of one in a regular picture-dealer's gallery. With that I started going the rounds, as much as I could at the time, and was pleased to find considerable enthusiasm for our fishermen in a tough race which generally says No with its eyes closed. But there was also much passing of the buck, at which they are adept, and a general definite stand that no committal could be made without a bigger selection of Craske's work to judge by. The man in charge of shows at the East River Gallery, a new and experimental place which has had some very good shows, was interested enough to come to mentioning details of their exhibition policies, and there are a few other possibilities which might definitely come to something if I had on hand enough of Craske's work for a show to be chosen from. So unless you are heartily sick of the whole thing and wish to have nothing further to do with so procrastinating an agent as I have showed myself to be, I suggest that when I am next in England I carry home with me, to be exhibited in New York or elsewhere if possible and if not to be returned at my expense, about thirty watercolors and a half dozen or so needlework pictures of Craske's. I would not suggest this unless I thought that there was a good chance of a show materializing provided I have the pictures actually in hand, however it is just as likely as not that a show won't materialize, so, being willing myself to go on with the attempt and do the best I can in my slow way, I leave it to you to decide if the possibility of an American show is worth the further necessary thought and inconvenience from your and Craske's point of view. In the meantime I have grown very fond of the big wolf-snow seascape through all these months of wrapping and unwrapping it and should like very much to own it. I have a timely birthday cheque on hand, and so am sending you a money order for ten pounds which I hope Craske will think is enough, also perhaps it will please him to think that one of his pictures has found an affectionate home in America. The three smaller pictures, which would not be needed for a show, I shall bring back with me when I come.

'When I come' means sometime toward the end of August. I am engaged to sail on the Europa on August 13th with Jane Cummings, who will go directly to a favorite spot of hers in Bavaria. Whether I shall go with her, for a week or so, or not is still a question, at any rate I shall be in England for some weeks chasing 16th and 17th century shadows, and need I say how much I would like to see you and Valentine and Thomas and your lovely Dorset Valley, where the trout must be biting energetically now. There is so much to talk about—and I seem to be better at talking than writing letters—, Mexico, a deeply moving and exciting and beautiful country which you must see for yourself sometime, books and herbs and cats, and the long-drawn agony that is Spain. I send you a new release of the Spanish Child Welfare Association of America, which has taken over, with an impressive committee, the money-raising end of the Quaker work; they will do well, I think and hope.

Something of Dorset has been with me through this hysterically early and then cold and rainy New England spring, for the old white pink—which must I think be Parkinson's "London Gillyflower"—though it resented its transplanting of last spring to the new world has made the best of it and blossoms this year most spicily and beautifully, and the irrepressible Black Peppermint is as firmly established now in New England as the rocks themselves. I cannot tell you what pleasure those living ties with your kind and lovely countryside bring to me, nor how deeply moved I am whenever I think of or look upon the ring that you and Valentine bought me in Madrid. Oh and another bit of herb-news: driving to New Haven the other day I nearly fell out of the car at beholding a fine patch of purple comfrey flourishing by the roadside, the first I have ever seen growing in this country, [ ] now some of it is taking fast hold in my garden to be another reminder of Dorset. And perhaps this will amuse you: I met a nice quiet domestic young woman the other evening and when we got conversationally to gardens and herbs, and witches she said 'have you ever read a fascinating book called "Dolly Willows"?' I leave you to imagine my answer

[Handwritten, much illegible] ... most particularly, and sympathetic understanding both of people who are sensitive and of people who are not, [ ] when you stop to think of it very [ ].

In a letter to her daughter in mid-July, Mary White enclosed a copy of Walter Lippmann's 'Today and Tomorrow' column from the *Herald Tribune.* In 'The Turn Since April', Lippmann noted—clearly relying on what he had gleaned from talking with British officials—that in April, with the successful annexation of Austria by Hitler, it was expected that Spain would quickly fall to General Franco and that Czechoslovakia would cave in—and these expected victories would, in Chamberlain's view, satisfy Hitler. But, Lippmann went on, the civil war continues in Spain and the Czechs show no signs of giving in. Chamberlain, he believed, was becoming resigned to the prospect that France will fight for the Czechs and Britain will be drawn in. The Lippmann clipping was one approach Mary tried to warn Elizabeth not to go abroad that summer, and certainly not to Spain. Doubtless there had been pointed family discussions.[2]

In her resumed 'priestly role'—which also had a maternal quality—Sylvia perceptively sized up Elizabeth and her fears, and pointed the way to self-confidence and independence. When the letter reached her, Elizabeth was newly returned from an enjoyable visit to Mexico with her brother and the artist Prentiss Taylor—a month-long surcease from the agonies of indecision. She was with her mother and grandmother at the latter's summer cottage on the Massachusetts coast. Sylvia wrote that the Maiden Newton house and garden go 'on getting lovelier and lovelier'.

Frome Vauchurch, Maiden Newton, Dorset
12. vii. 1938[3]

Dearest Elizabeth,

Your letter came this morning with the ten pound cheque for Craske. My first feeling was one of embarrassment. It seemed to me that I should be giving you a Craske, instead of leaving you to buy it for yourself. Then I remember that I could not afford to pay Craske such a good price; and that his bread and butter must have precedence of my feelings. So I sent off the cheque to him (I will send you his answer when it comes, he writes like a majestic wooden leg), and thank you very much on his behalf and my own. I am so glad that picture is yours. It was a beauty.

I am still very much of a mind that he should try a show in New York. I see from that invaluable *New Yorker* that they have had an exhibition of 'Sunday artists'—an absurd name—may be that would butter the slide for it. I will keep the water colours I have till you come (observe the restraint with which I introduce the first hint of the chief theme); and as for the needle-works, it will be a perfect full and sufficient reason for you to go and see Craske, I do assure you, it is a most extraordinary experience to walk into the Craskes' stuffy little parlour, and find oneself surrounded by these unaffected works of genius. It has rather the same quality of walking into an engine room and finding all the engines functioning with such savoir vivre and nobody there to give them a word of advice.

I am so glad and so much relieved in my mind that you are coming at last; I had a feeling that if you didn't come it would be one of those false steps which take years to turn backwards. One begins to attach a symbolic importance to such things as coming to England—It is probably very weak-minded to do so, but one does—and then if one belies one's intention, every superstition in one's blood begins moaning and sighing like an old house in a gale.

I have been worried about this much more than worried about you. I reckoned that your silence meant that you wanted to say you were coming and delayed a letter that would not say so. I could see a thousand practical reasons why you should not come, and one impractical reason why you should. And the impractical reason seemed to be more vital.

I heard a little of you from Steven Clark, how he had seen you on your return from Mexico, and that you had been very happy there. That you had fallen a slave to Mexican cookery. He began by saying that you had so much to say that he was consumed with wrath and envy because he had not been there himself—and that he hoped you would write the cookery book because you would be paid for it and payment is a tonic experience for the soul. Which is true, if the payment is good. I have never found the ordinary payment does much for my soul, but a cheque from the New Yorker is a cathartic every time it comes.

But though I was glad to hear all this, I am much more glad to have a letter from you, and to be back in the confession box again, my dear. It is not a time one can be happy in, and it is a most difficult time in which to make one's soul, or make it over. And the cook-housekeeper part of one's intelligence—I suppose you keep a small cook-housekeeper somewhere. I have never seen her, but on the other hand I think you to be mortal—makes it no easier by brusque rushes into one's meditations, to say, 'Really! With all this suffering [all] around, surely it is rather self-centered to be thinking about yourself'. I hope you rout her every time she puts her dull nose around the door. The worst danger of times like this is that one is under such constant temptation not to think enough.

I am glad that you are afraid. I don't mean I'm glad you are afraid, but glad you have overcome fear enough to be able to say so. Valentine, in Madrid, said to Ludwig Renn that she jumped every time she heard the noise of close firing. So do I, said he, with decision. And went on to give her a reassuring account of how to distinguish between the noises that didn't mean death, the noises that might, the noise that almost certainly does. All that while of fighting he had not forgotten how to be afraid, not how to be afraid intelligently ... a most admirable balance of mind.

Self-disgust—No, I am not so approving there. I don't believe in hairshirt for the mind any more than hairshirts for the body. Il faut etre doux envers soi; and Elizabeth is not the sort of animal who will respond to rough usage. You certainly know your faults, you have put salt on the tail of the least of them. Now I think you would do well to cultivate the poor creatures, and see what could be made of them. There must be quite a lot of unused base metal in your nature which could be tempered and wrought into value. And whoever asked if figs grew on thistles was a hasty idiot who did not pause to think of the cardoon and the artichokes.

And that is quite enough good advice to send across the Atlantic. It is much more important to tell you that you are a person I shall always think of with love, and with confidence, and with ambition. And that I have been happy all day thinking that I may see you before long. And this time, remember to come without booking your return passage. You always regret the return passage; it hangs like a millstone round your neck when you are over here. And so deal with the situation in a Marxian way, by pointing out that the state of Europe is such that it is impossible to foretell how long you can stay there. A return passage by the next boat, even, might be raw speculation. Therefore, how much more prudent it is not to book a return passage.

I am finishing a new book, which seems likely to be called *After the Death of Don Juan*. I have been writing since early spring, and now I am in that frightful state of continual fever lest something go wrong with it at the last moment. Just as a woman eight months gone with child can't see a tram on the opposite side of the street without a conviction that tram will cross the road and jostle her, I look on the butcher as a threat and the baker as a springs, and the candlestick-maker as a typhoid carrier. In fact I am really having a high old time.

By the time you see me I hope to be going about with the visionary smug smile of one who has laid her egg, cackling quietly to myself, and taking a revived interest in dust-baths and insects.

Meanwhile this place goes on getting lovelier and lovelier. We cannot imagine why we were so obtuse as not to fall in love with it at first sight, instead of sniffing round its beauties and writing calculating letters about installing a great many electric points and lowering the rent before we could consent to live in it. The garden last month was so exciting that I longed for you to be here with it; for it covered itself with lupines of every shade of sugar-pink, and with stuff-coloured irises. They had been [planted in a] combination entirely at random, on the assumption that the lupines would be the usual blue and white and the irises the usual purple. Instead, they greeted us with this intensely sophisticated aigredoux. Before that we had great fun with bulbs shooting in unexpected places—fine tulips down the centre of the path, and so forth. And the late Miss Liddon's pansies continue to grow anywhere and everywhere. I wanted some to fill up a gap so this afternoon I walk out with a trowel and collected two dozen fine young plants from under the broad beans.

We have had a great many trout—Valentine catches them and I cook them; and the society of a family of young water Rats. They sit in a tight brown nosegay on the bank—talking to each other about Wind in the Willows, I suppose.

As soon as you know your plans, you will let me know? I want to go to France for a while, after my book is finished, just to glorify, and unbend myself, but the date is completely unfixed, and will not get in the way of seeing you here.

We send you our true love.

Elizabeth did decide to go to England, satisfying her mother by including a plan to continue research on Anne Bradstreet. Mary considered this just what she should be doing, not by any means to go to Paris through the American Friends Service Committee to meet with their representative to arrange passage to Loyalist Spain. On 13 August 1938 she sailed on the *Bremen* (not the *Europa* as she had earlier written Sylvia); characteristically she had arranged in advance with Bumpus, the London bookseller, to send books to Janet's mother, Purefoy Machen (Willa Cather's *Lucy Gayheart),* to Sylvia (Rachel Field's *Time Out of Mind,* Francis Stuart's *Pidgin Irish,* Vernon Lee's *Hortus Vitae: Essays on the Gardening of Life*) and copies of *Early One Morning* by Walter de la Mare to both.[4]

Her brother Wade and several of their friends gave Elizabeth a grand send-off, a celebratory luncheon, *bon voyage* presents, champagne, flowers for the stateroom. Mary sent a separate fruit and sweets basket for each day of the voyage. Elizabeth and her friends met at the Biltmore Hotel in New York and lunched at Maillards where Wade arrived, 'looking so tall and beautiful, what an angelic creature he is!' The send-off continued from the Waylin Hotel where others joined them for drinks. She wrote her mother about the farewell in a letter taken off by the pilot before the ship left New York harbor. From the Waylin they went for dinner to a French garden restaurant for 'Charles a la Pomme soufflé'. At the pier there was 'that same old exciting, sinking sensation of lights and noise and crowds and the dark waters, and then on our way with our very nice and comfortable cabin simply bursting with flowers and packages and letters. I can't see why everybody is so terribly nice about my oft-repeated sailings, it makes me feel very suffused and very humble ... don't worry about me. I will be careful and sensible, I promise. And goodbye now for the present and my dearest love to you & Daddy & Wadex & Giles & Breakneck, from your devoted wanderer, Bet.'[5]

Separately Elizabeth thanked her father for the 'fantastically generous cheque', and offered to return some of the money later if he needed it. About her Anne Bradstreet research—the part of her venture he approved of—she wrote that her aim was to clear up 'some knotty and important research points'. Without mentioning it by name, she referred to her plan to volunteer for relief service in Spain. 'And I must ask you not to worry any more than you can help about what other things I may possibly decide to do on this trip. Please try to believe that I will not do anything without full knowledge of the circumstances and deep consideration of you and mother's feelings and of my own justification and safety.' She tenderly concludes, 'Now your problem child sends you thanks again for the huge cheque and the lovely gardenias and for your words of advice, also my best wishes and much love, from, Betty.'[6]

Elizabeth was in the midst of her 'beautiful family' at the pier on a venture intended to show independence and self-confidence.

In London she was back in her rainy, damp, beloved England at a moderately seedy bed-sitter in a walk-up on Queen's Gate, Kensington. She wrote her mother after settling in.

> No. 2 is a large old high-ceilinged house with astronautical flights of stairs and a charming landlady. My room is on the third floor, small but well equipped (h & c laid on) the rest of the pump-room facilities another half flight over my head, clean as a whistle with a starched maid with no front teeth popping in and out, & a small electric heater which may prove useful for its coolish tonight after a lovely clear day for landing ... £4 a week; a good place for a business-like and pleasant sojourn in London if only I can keep the demons of homesickness at bay and realize that it is entirely on my own responsibility that I am here without any [] person to hold my enfant gate of a hand ... And certainly it is a dear country, with the most meltingly beautiful fields and wooded hillsides, damn it, how I wish you were here to see them too.[7]

Sylvia was prompt in her welcome; she and Valentine would be in the city that week, staying with Janet Machen, her niece.

Frome Vauchurch, Maiden Newton, Dorset
20. viii. 1938[8]

Dearest Elizabeth,

It is lovely to know that you are in England, thank you for sending me that rejoicing telegram.

On Tuesday we drive to London, conveying back a carload of a family which is now staying with us. I can't fix a time to meet for various reasons; we do not know when we shall arrive; we are conveying a child who may be sick, which would necessitate an interval of cleaning ourselves before we are presentable; and so forth. But probably we shall be in London towards the end of Tuesday afternoon, and the minute I can I shall ring up your hotel. On the other hand, don't put out your own plans because of this, and if you will be busy then, go on being busy, and send a note to say so to me at this address, c/o Janet Machen, c/o Ryecroft, 4, Mecklenburgh Square:, WC 1. All this c/o means that Janet (the Machens' daughter) has been lent a flat and is putting us up for that night. And if we can't meet on Tuesday we will meet on Wednesday.

Then we will make our plans. Valentine is extremely anxious to arrange a tour for you in Norfolk, there is so much there that we should like to show you. And you must come here of course. Perhaps you could come down with us?—Wednesday or Thursday, but again uncertain as I may have to attend a committee in town on Wednesday evening—and I am wondering if you would like the run of this house while we are in France. Dates again dubious, but probably a week round the end of this month. Cat, dog, books, fishing, gramophone, car—and quite a nice woman (though she talks nineteen to the dozen and I can't vouch for her cooking) who would come in to do housework. But we can talk over all this when we meet, and how delightful, my dear, to be writing such a sloppy unbusiness-like letter on the strength of that meeting to be so soon.

With my love,

Sylvia

[Longhand] Carbon copy of book [ ] for your reading. [*After The Death of Don Juan*]

To her mother, from whom yet no letter had come, Elizabeth reported that

The weather is just as has been in England, all the year round, I think, since the mountains cooled and the glaciers melted, threatening skies, with an occasional shower and sunshine in between, and a chill which seems bent on penetrating whenever it can. I have a little electric heater in my room, which is very cozy-making, and for work in the British Museum [with its] perpetually low temperatures, I have taken in true English fashion to wear woolen undies, which greatly help to keep a semblance of circulation going ... I am having as good a time as possible in my solitary condition. This evening I had dinner at Simpsons on the Strand with a nice girl from Washington named Sara Snell and after went to see the British film *Victoria the Great*.

Sylvia and Valentine are coming to town to spend the night with S's young cousin, Janet Machen; [we] will plan a possible motor trip with them in September ... I am feeling very doubtful about Spain as I have had no definite information for a long time, and if they don't care to take the trouble certainly I'm damned if I do![9]

Although Elizabeth had written her mother that hers was a solitary existence in London, her notes show the late August days were sociable, revealing her ability to arrange lunches, teas, suppers, and theater evenings. The eating-places included such fashionable Mayfair spots as Gunther's (lunch, tea) and Prunier's; and Simpson's-in-the-Strand and The Cheshire Cheese; in addition to the film *Victoria the Great*, there was *Tobias* in Regent's Park and other amusements. London and its pleasures continued even as a war threatened which was widely expected to be one of aerial bombardment.

Elizabeth's diary entries in and near London, August 1938:

[10]**Thurs August 18** Land at Southampton, settled in London, din. with Christine at Pruniers, see. G. Smith.

Fri 19 Shop, lunch Gunthers, haircut, tea with Henrietta at Goring. Dinner Q.G. [Queens Gate]

Sun 21 To E-SU [English-Speaking Union], meet Christine & Porter for lunch, to Nat. Gallery. Dine Q.G.

Sat 20 To B.M [British Museum]. see Eric Millar, lunch E-S.U., join Bartons, Swell

& Converse, & with them to Town. Tea Stewarts, din Q.G.

Mon 22 To B.M. talk with Mrs Osler & work lunch E-S.U. home. C.& P. [at] 4:00

& to tea Gunthers. Dine Simpsons with S. Brill & to 'Victoria the Great'.

Tue 23 To B.M. lunch Q.G. to Soane Museum, Tea E-SU din Q.G.

Wed 24 E-S.U. trip to Kent 1:50. Meet Swell at Cheshire Cheese 7:00 & to Regent's Park 'Tobias'

Thurs 25 To B.M. lunch Janet Machen & see flat. Meet Mrs Rogers 4:00. E.S.U. & to Apothecary's G, tea Gunthers, din Q.G.

Fri 26 get money, pay Miss M., to PRO [Public Records Office] 10:30 Milnes for tea E.S.U. 4:30.

Sat 27 Buy suitcase. Lunch G. Ford 1:00.

Sun 28 move to Mecklenburg Squ, lunch E-SU tr to Rickmansworth [ ] 3:28 to Ned Evett's house for tea with Ned and his [wife?] & Gwen to London 7:30 supper Baker St. station

Mon 29 Buy sherry, etc. B. M. lunch [ ], E-SU C. Rycroft here meet Evetts Mrs Rogers 4:00, de Freitas 5:00 lv 7:00 for Eeling & hear C. Tathman's talk. Back to London, see Martin Pollock.

Tue 30 To Reigate 11:48 arr 12:30 lunch with Miss Rohde & see herb-garden. 3:40 to London G. Ford 5:00, [ ], with M. Pollock to 'Tobias', & talk[11]

Wed 31 B.M., lunch, License, Carlton Mansions, to E-SU 7:00 meet Allard 7:00 at E.S.U. dinner & to 'Thou Shall Not'.

Elizabeth moved to the flat at Mecklenburgh Square where Janet Machen was staying, 'Arthur's daughter, an awfully nice child, [the flat] right near the British Museum'. '[I]t seems foolish and wrong that you are not here with me too,' she wrote her mother, 'to do these pleasant things; I must say I can't reconcile myself to it, but I must admit to know what it is like to be too far away from a MAN! ... my work, incidentally, is going pretty well though nothing marvelous has cropped up yet ... I have got a mothy little woman digging up wills and mysterious documents which may help a great deal; she knows, at 5/ an hour, about sources of information which are utterly unknown to me.'[12]

Sylvia welcomed her by letter.

Frome Vauchurch Maiden Newton, Dorset
27. viii.
1938[13]

Dearest Elizabeth,

I sent off the carbon copy of *After the Death of Don Juan* today, to you c/o Janet, c/o Ryecroft the World the Universe Infinite Grace, as schoolboys write in their books. When you have finished it— which I take it will be round about the end of the month or the beginning of the next will you please do it up again and address it to B. W. Huebsch, c/o Barclay's Bank, One, Pall Mall East, and write on it to Await Arrival. And send it or leave it there, unless you like to find out from them where Ben Huebsch is staying in London, and take it to him direct and meet one of the nicest people I know even in your nice nation. He is Viking Press, and I promised to let him have the typescript when he gets back from Sweden, which he does, I think, on the first or second of September.

I am so glad to think of you in Mecklenburgh Square, with books and good pictures and those beautiful trees. It was Valentine's idea that you might like this flat and suggested it to Janet; but it is entirely Janet's idea about the Chaldon cottage. I hope you will have good weather there, though rain has a curious charm in that cottage where one hears it dropping melodiously into the tank; but perhaps this charm was strictly ownerly, and due to the sensation of owning a cistern instead of having to collect one's water from a well.

It is a sweet little cottage, and I think there is just enough of its original pink paint left to show you how pretty it looked when it was pink and white all over like a birthday cake. I expect May's cat will commend himself to you. His name is Cuckoo, he is Tom's younger brother, and a very charming animal though rather haggard and melancholy now from long absence from May whom he adored. Do not give way about seeing Theodore [Powys]. He would love to see you and it would do him good. Be firm about it, even if Violet [Powys] haggles a little.

If by any chance you change your mind and want to come over here the key is with Mrs Bartlett, and the grocer who is called Weston and Hardin, and Janet will tell you where he is, will direct you to her. If she does not answer the front door do not be dismayed but go through the little passage and into the left-hand yard and knock on her door. She sits at the back of the house usually, with a primus and a wireless, and this makes her a little inattentive to front-door knocks.

This is some Purefoy information which I have got from my genealogical cousin.[14] Not very much; but if they are your Purefoys then it establishes a link between us, though not a blood link since my mother's Purefoy connection is only an affiliation through a godchild.

George Purefoy of Hadley, Bucks (1608–1661) had a daughter, Mary, who married in 1657 Thomas Jervoise of Harriard, Herts. The Purefoys of Shelstone (wherever Shelstone may be) as well as a tribe of Jervoises, descend from this George Purefoy. The Purefoys of the Purefoy letters are also of this tribe.

As for woad, there are two sources of information. One is to write to the Society of British Herbalists (Culpeper House, 18, I think, but the tele. directory will know, Baker Street; and the other is to enquire from the Secretary, The Women's Institute, Taunton, Somerset. If it is grown anywhere Somerset is the likeliest place, and the WI who go in for that kind of thing, the likeliest to know. But I should try the Herbalists first.[15]

We start on Monday morning; and have only the vaguest notions where we are going after we arrive at Havre. This makes it seem very delightful and holiday-like. I will write to you from France and tell you when we shall be back. Probably about the ninth or tenth. And then we will have fun in East Anglia.

With our love,

Sylvia

'What a joy to have your letter yesterday,' Elizabeth wrote her mother on 30 August. 'I have been to Reigate with Miss Rohde [to see] her new herb farm and on the 10th or 11th start on a motor trip with Sylvia and Valentine [to East Anglia].'[16]

Before this, she was off to West Chaldon with Janet, then back again to London before meeting Sylvia and Valentine at Maiden Newton for the drive to Norfolk and East Anglia. In London she was occupied with Anne Bradstreet research. Elizabeth's diary entries are from in and near London, September 1938:

[17]**Thurs Sept 1** pack, etc. Lunch Mrs Rogers E-SU trip to [ ] move things. Din Ms. R[ohde]. Pruniers de Freitas 6:00

Fri 2 10:30 Wloo [Waterloo Station] to Chaldon, Wool 1:45

Sat 3 Chaldon with Janet

Sun 4 same

Mon 5 same

Tue 6 at Carlton Mansions, work in BM. din with Mrs R., E-SU & to 'Glorious Morning'.

Wed 7 Work at Genealogical Society all day. 5:30 to [Geoffrey] de Freitas's & stay for supper. Janet here late.

Thurs 8 to Somerset House work on wills with Mrs Osler; meet Mrs R. tea at [ ] meet J. Drury Lane 6:30.

Fri 9 J. left. Oxford, met Gwen [Clarkson], with her to Spread Eagle, Thame.

Sat 10 To Basque Boys Home at Eaton Hastings, Farmingdon to Little Horsley meet G. lunch Birmiston Grange, sit in field all afternoon, tea Court Farm with G. & Hugh Clarkson, back to Thame, Capt. & Nesta T. Knox for dinner[18]

Sun 11 G[wen] came 12:30, with her to Court Farm for lunch. [ ] there afternoon & walk. Tea C. F., G & Mrs Clarkson for supper Thame 6:45 to Little Horsley with Capt. Ashton to see hunt.

Mon 12 Follow with Mrs C. until 1:00 Lunch C. F., bus to Oxford, train to London, Carlton Mansions

Tue 13 meet Mrs O PRO [Public Records Office] 10:30 work there & lunch with her, to Somerset House, with Allard to 'Lots Wife' (hammer & sickle sign), din C. M.

Wed 14 Genealogical Society, shop, pack, etc. meet J. & de F's 7:00 The Book & to Unity Theatre

Thurs 15 10:30 to Maiden Newton

The crisis between Nazi Germany and Czechoslovakia intensified through August and into September 1938. On 2 September Mary White acknowledged Elizabeth's 'comforting letter', but she was 'terribly anxious ... we expect any minute you telling us that you will be right back'.[19]

In a letter of 6 September, which crossed with Mary's 'anxious' one, Elizabeth reported that she was back from the visit to Chaldon with Janet and pleasantly settled in a hotel near the British Museum. It was 'just the sort of place I think I ought to be, a pension-hotel in Bloomsbury, very English, and real and restful … here everybody talks to everybody else, and most of us are doing the same thing, practically all youngish Americans on some research job or other.' There was still no definite word from the American Friends Service Committee office in Paris on her acceptance as a volunteer in Spain. 'We must all be patient'; quoting Hotspur, 'it is from the nettle danger that we pluck the flower, safety'. (Ironically this is the phrase Prime Minister Chamberlain used three weeks later when he spoke from the cabin door of his plane en route to Munich, forever captured on a newsreel.) Elizabeth concludes: 'I think there would be a great danger in letting myself be scared out of going by my own and other's anxieties. I know you will be with me and help me in this, as always, just as I know it is a tremendous thing that I am asking of you. But it is far from decided as yet. Love to you and Daddy and Wadex and Giles and Jane Amelia [pet cat].'[20]

Sylvia sent train times Elizabeth could use to reach Maiden Newton; it was to be her first visit to the house since 'S & V' had moved in. From there they planned to motor cross-country to Valentine's family house at Winterton in Norfolk.

Frome Vauchurch Maiden Newton, Dorset
12. ix. 1938[21]

Dearest Elizabeth,

We claim you the moment we can get you. That is to say, will you come here on the fifteenth. The station is Maiden Newton, you leave from Paddington, there is a train that starts at 10:30 if that is not too early for you, and there are other trains.

It is very charming of you to ask us up for Wednesday, but the car which should make this so practicable happens to make it rather difficult. We sent it to be decarbonised when we left for France; and hoped to find it all neat and renewed when we got back. Instead we found that the bolts of its crown-wheel had been discovered in a state of extra decay, the crown-wheel had to be sent to the makers for proper riveting; the makers have only just despatched that little piece of work, the car will not be ours until Tuesday. And before we can use it properly it must be run in with a couple of short excursions at a moderate speed, and Valentine knows the road to London so fatally well that to proceed along it at a decorous speed of thirty miles an hour would be a physical impossibility.

Our tour—I might as well break it to you now—will have to include Birmingham. Because there is a congress there at the end of the week, and we should attend it for at least one day. We plan, provisionally, to spend the night outside Birmingham, and perhaps we would deposit you to meditate in some quiet country churchyard while we harden our haunches and improve our spirits at the congress. Alternatively, you could look at the Birmingham Art Gallery! Thence to Winterton, where we shall have the nice family house and the nice family cook. And from there we will drive you to London for your date.

All this—queer thought—subject to European politics. But I find it hard to believe that our government could achieve even as much bluster as yesterday's communique unless they had received a private low-down that they could do so without any serious risk of having to stand by their bond. Long threaten, long last ... If wars are like thunderstorms the next war will be a long one.

You will find the house full of Chinese poems ... in a beautiful Chinese English. The poet who is called Shelley Yang is a friend of ours. He is a great admirer of Craske. Now he is going back to China (he was a political exile) and I suppose he will be killed. And the poems are to appear in a sort of Last Will and Testament volume, and he has sent them to us for an overlooking of grammar and so forth.

Art is like a spider's web lacework that runs over the world, one strand fastened to a beam in Canton another to a grass-stalk in Dorset.

I am glad you like my book and saw beneath the wigs.

Sylvia

Elizabeth's notes from that cross-country trip from Dorset to Norfolk convey her fascination with the countryside and its villages, the enjoyment and interest all three shared, and the particular pleasure of seeing Valentine's youthful haunts through her eyes. Her hosts gave Elizabeth a close look at the land and its buildings on a largely rural route through the Cotswolds and Northamptonshire and Huntingdonshire to the North Sea in Norfolk. As Sylvia recalled, 'I know without any beating around bushes that you enjoyed the Norfolk excursion. You have a really beautiful grace of showing your pleasure, a quality beyond all to gladden the hearts of hosts and friends. I should like to think we were built on the same rig, and you too are as well assured how very very happy we were being with you.'

The diplomatic crisis intensified throughout their trip.

> [22]**Fri 16** at Maiden Newton (On the train Elizabeth wrote to Mary: 'The crisis goes on muttering but I can't think we need worry immediately with Hitler & Chamberlain holding hands! Good bye now, darling, and more anon, and so much love to you from Bet.')[23]

> **Sun 18** Lv. Frome Vauchurch with S.&V.; lunch Malmesbury. Tea Idbury with Robertson Scotts,[24] through CN [Chipping Norton], Bibury, Banbury, night at Towcester.

> **Mon 19** through Northampton, lunch Oundle, see church & [ ], across Huntington & Norfolk to Winterton. See Frankforten, St. Mary's Chapel in wood. Stay at Acklands' house.

The Ackland house was, as Elizabeth described it to her mother: 'a fine, fortress-like old place with miles of gardens and greenhouses and only a great wave-like swath of silver-green dune between it and the sea. How you would love that coast land, the fishing and its people are very New England in a way, although its geography is not, long flat swaths of country between the villages, with windmills and church towers

30. Elizabeth, Valentine, Sylvia, and Cumquat, at Winterton, 1938.

uplifting, and grey lines of willow along the Broads, and between the willows white sails pass quietly. Do you wonder that I love the country which is so constant a joy to the eye and mind and in which such marvelous people are so unaccountably kind and understanding to me?'[25]

> **Tue 20** walk on beach, to Yarmouth, lunch Winterton, drive along coast to Wells [Wells-next-the-sea] see churches Somerton [ ] and tour empty houses, Blickling.

> **Wed 21** See Winterton Church & climb tower, lunch, to E. Denisham, by Ramworth, see Craskes, E.D. church, back to Winterton via Norwich.

> **Thurs 22** Lv. Winterton, by Yarmouth & Lowestoft to Bury St. Edmunds. Lunch Angel, to [ ] ch, & Long Milford, tea & ch back to Angel for night.

> Serious news on wireless.

In a journal entry that went beyond the usual dutiful chronicle, Elizabeth acknowledged that she was in love, a momentous revelation in the context of a life tormented by its lack. The experience of motoring through the English countryside with knowledgeable and appreciative companions enlivened her spirits. In Norfolk, she saw the land, buildings, and seascape through Valentine's eyes; it was a gift, a revelation of Valentine's sensibility and feeling, her formation as a poet and person. The land, edged by the often wild North Sea, overhung by low-hanging clouds, with nearly constant wind and frequent rain was a setting that fired the imagination of both young women. Valentine was a magnetic presence, physically tall and strong, with emotions and perceptions close to the surface. She was sexually experienced and Elizabeth untried; the sexual glow added to her magnetism, and it must have been both profoundly exciting for Elizabeth and frightening too, an encounter with the unknown and feelings never before experienced. There was constraint, too, in the close company of Sylvia, her 'priest', mentor, and kindred spirit. Perhaps that is why in the entry she made in her journal she did not mention the name of the beloved.

Winterton, Norfolk, 21·IX·38

"That love is the one supreme
duty and good, that love is wisdom
and purity and valour and peace,
and that its infinite sorrow is
infinitely better than the world's
richest joy."

Standing in the dark courtyard
alone this evening, I had the
unworthy thought "what I should
like most of all now would be
to die." I have never before
had that wish so clearly and
quietly, nor known more surely
that it was not to be, for a
while yet. And I know also
now and finally that love is and
must be, that without it there is
only death, and that I am
hopelessly, helplessly, inarticulately
and everlastingly in love. With
a brave and happy dream in
the sleepless night of despair,
with a true star in the dark
uncharted sky. What I am,
what I do, what of triumph or
destruction comes to me, matters
not at all, so I am loyal in
courage and honesty to the impossible
dream & the unapproachable star, I shall
live in light & truth, and die in peace:

31. Elizabeth's diary entry for 21 September 1938.

It was a revelation and dangerous to admit even to oneself.

'That love is the one supreme duty and good, that love is wisdom and purity and valour and peace', she wrote, 'and that its infinite sorrow is infinitely better than the world's richest joy.'

> Standing in the dark courtyard alone this evening, I had the unworthy thought 'what I should like most of all now would be to die'. I have never before had that wish so clearly and quietly, nor known more surely that it was not to be, for a while yet. And I know now and finally what love is and must be, that without [it] is only death, and that I am hopelessly, helplessly, inarticulately, and everlastingly in love. With a brave and happy dream in the sleepless night of despair with a true star in the dawn uncharted sky. What I am, what I do, what of triumph or destruction comes to me, matters not at all, so I am loyal in courage and honesty to the impossible dream & unapproachable star, I shall live in light & truth, and die in peace.[26]

Elizabeth returned to London shortly to prepare for the outbreak of war and the expected air raids. She met with American friends of the Whites, and despite the threat, dined out, and went to the theater. She would shortly be fitted for a gas-mask.

> **Fri 23** lv S & V, train to London, arr 2: pm, letters, meet Henry Fuller, Am. Em, etc. tea Piccadilly Hotel.[27] See Janet [Machen] dine with H. Pruniers & to 'Paprika'.

> **Sat 24** Bad news.[28] Much anxiety see H. & Mr Fuller, get boat space from Shadwick [travel agent]. Lunch with Janet letters dine H. & Mr F. Flemings [Hotel] & to Palladium.

Discussions on the motor trip had evidently strengthened Elizabeth's resolve to continue with the plan to volunteer in Spain—and Valentine warmly supported it.

Frome Vauchurch, Maiden Newton, Dorset
24th September [1938][29]

My dear Elizabeth,

Please take this beginning of my letter as quite literally true: a greeting that will be always in my mind when I think of you.

The bookseller has been told peremptorily to send you Traherne and the Paston Letters INSTANTLY. If you are leaving at once and would like him to keep them, or deliver them otherwise than to your hotel, please let me know. He is: F J Ward, 3, Baker Street, W1.

And two books were ordered by me.

I am so glad, for your own sake and theirs, that you are going to Spain. But after our first unselfish pleasure we both grew pensive to know that we would not have your company here when, we both feel, we shall need it direly! But I am glad you will be in a country that is honest and courageous, and among friends, and able to walk into any road and any dwelling and meet people who have truth and passion in their hearts. Give our greetings to them, in your mind, all the time you are there.

But if anything happens to stop your going there, do not forget to come to us, either for pleasure (as I hope you will) or shelter.

And as for that hotel bill—I think you have only to imagine the position reversed to understand what I felt like. Meditation on the journey home cleared my mind, and a careful working out of hard facts and figures when I got here decided me. I find it almost, if not quite as hard as you do, to bend or give way! Let us both get a little more limber, for we must! But for this time, I send you thanks for your generosity and rebukes for your unwillingness to give us a chance to be generous too—and say one more thing, neither a stipulation nor a condition, but a very serious request: If you need any sort of help that we can give you (PRACTICAL help, Elizabeth!) please look at once towards us, with no misgivings of any kind. PLEASE.

It is raining and the news is grim, but it is lovely to remember how happy we were and what we saw and what we did and that perhaps fortune will let us do that sort of thing again! The Vale of the White Horse [south-west Oxfordshire], which we went through yesterday for the first time, is waiting for you to admire it.

So farewell—and blessing on you and love to you. I count always most securely on your promise about Sylvia, and more assuredly than ever, since our Grand Tour.

Valentine

Postscript:

in reply to your question in your letter to S, this morning: YES. Come when you can & as soon as you can, for as long as you can. Come in the evening or come in the morning, come when you're looked for or come without warning.

So that you do come—!

Because they must have discussed Thomas Traherne on the trip, Valentine considered it so important to get Elizabeth a copy of his poems she sent a cable:

AM SENDING TRAHERNE WITH LOVE—VALENTINE[30]

Elizabeth cabled that she had heard from the organizers that a position was available for her in Spain through the AFSC. Sylvia sent admiring support and suggested helpful people in Paris, including the poet Louis Aragon, one of the writers whom she knew through his support of the Loyalists.

Frome Vauchurch
Maiden Newton,
Dorset
24. ix. 1938[31]

Dearest Elizabeth,

I have just taken your telegram.

And I congratulate you with all my heart. It is queer that I should be so glad on your behalf for this adventure which may mean danger, which certainly means discomfort and agony of mind—for you are not one of the people who can look on sorrow and sickness and privation with a light heart; and it is news which entails an ending to all the very pleasant plans we had for your spending part of the winter here. But for all that, my congratulations are sincere and whole-hearted, and I feel a real triumph and satisfaction that you will be going to Spain. For it is a real and constructive act, and you are one of the battalion who do and should do, such acts. It is a danger and a trial which you have really earned; you have advanced to this through all the stages of the first resolve and the difficult beginnings and the even more difficult period of going on with a harassing piece of work. It is entirely by your own merit and your own steadfastness that you are now able to go as a representative—it is really so—of your country.

I expect you will be able to get everything through pretty easily; but if you have time, or if you want any particular advice I very much recommend you to try a young man at the Spanish embassy. He is called Stanley Richardson. He is a friend of mine, and knows a great many people in Spain. In particular he could give you introductions to many of the Spanish writers and artists, people like Alberti and Maria Teresa Leon, and Bergamin.[32]

I cannot swear to it that he is in England just now; but if he is he will be at the Spanish Embassy. You will find him very friendly and intelligent, and I know he will do all he can to [ ] and enrich your journey in Spain. If he is not there, and if you still think you would like introductions to some of the Alianza de Intelectuales, then, if you go through Paris, you might do well to go to the headquarters of the Association of Writers in Defence of Culture at 29 rue d'Anjou, viiie. Aragon who is the head man there is a friend of mine, and if you tell him I advised you to go to him you will surely find him helpful, if hurried. He has a great talent for knowing everybody, and doing everything.[33]

I am looking for your letter, and for more news. When did you hear? I would like [to] think the news awaited you when you reached London, that would be properly dramatic, and a superb retort to the feeling of dregs that one has after the end of a trip which one has enjoyed. And I know without any beating around bushes that you enjoyed the Norfolk excursion. You have a really beautiful grace of showing your pleasure, a quality beyond all to gladden the hearts of hosts and friends. I should like to think we were built on the same rig, and you too are as well assured how very very happy we were being with you.

I am amazed at my discipline and unselfishness that I have so little regret that our plans for meeting again this autumn now seem fading and jeopardized. No, that is not true. I have an infinity of regret; but it is definitely a countersubject to my main theme of pride and congratulation. Seeing you this year, seeing you so immensely strengthened and advanced and ripened, I could not but feel a certain glow in the thought that we may have had our part in your development; but it is the pride of the gardener, who sees the flowering tree.

We had a good trip back yesterday—no storms at all to feel, though one to look at on the Berkshire downs. I found a whole new route across the centre of England, a very artful route that avoided every single town, and embraced a quantity of water-meadows and ranks of pollard willows. Cumquat has foamed no further (pretty sweeting) and is perfectly well. It must have been an amorous demonstration, nothing more. Thomas grey and sleek and resonant was on the doorstep when we arrived.

Here is the Craske list which I promised you. [not found] But I expect you will scarcely have much time for it. If I can be of any use writing to him for you, please tell me. I am so glad you saw those pictures.

What a lot of lovely things we saw and smelled and did, and how much good talk. I am so glad we had that trip. The house is full of your gifts, and the shelves full of books waiting for you to read them, but if it is delayed, it is a delay only. And I say to myself that we shall surely see you, if only for a short while when you are back from Spain. I think with great joy that you are taking there, as well as all your other good qualities, a mind so well attuned to understanding it and appreciating its people.

With our love,

Sylvia

Later on the 24th came news that negotiations with the Nazis had broken down. Elizabeth was visiting Janet Machen and her parents, Arthur and Purefoy, in Amersham.

Sun 25 Letters. To train 2:30 to Amersham. J[anet] at station, walk thru [ ] Park; tea King's Arms; Machens for din. K.A. [King's Arms] & talk all evening.

War seemed imminent. Mary and Will demanded by cable that Elizabeth return immediately. She replied by mail from the King's Arms in Amersham leaving no doubt of where she stood on the merits of the negotiations and her decision to remain in England.

Everything is very unsettled right now, but I think that by the time you get this we shall know definitely one way or another. In the meantime I want to stay and see what happens, and I hope that you will understand rather than condemn. And of course there may very likely be no war at all, Czechoslovakia will possibly consent to being another sacrificial victim on the altar of Fascism, and even if she doesn't, Chamberlain may be able to scrape up a few final scraps of the soul of England which the devil will accept in exchange for an uneasy and transient peace. So we shall see and in the meantime I beg that you and Father will try to have confidence in my power of taking care of myself with due consideration of the many kind and helpful friends that I have in England, and that Father will not allow himself to be troubled by any thoughts as to the necessity of his coming over to extricate me from anything, any such eventuality is, I believe, beyond the probability of practical contemplation, and certainly far beyond any wish or [ ] of mine.

I came back [to Amersham] this afternoon from London and Janet Machen and I walked for miles over lovely rich-hued hills, practically wading in pheasants and rabbits … she and her fascinating mother and father dined with me under the 15th century frames of this lovely hotel, and I went back to their little flat with them, and the conversation was long and I wish I could remember every word of it.

Does this sound very mad to you, and do you really think that I should—with many Americans staying right on in England—pick myself up and scurry home like a frightened rabbit? You, alas, are far away across the Atlantic. You can only feel the ominous gloom of the situation and none of the very actual very tangible excitement and stimulation. I am not in the least afraid, only very deeply stirred and interested and anxious to see the outcome of an extraordinarily interesting situation, and I don't really think, at my age, and after the sort of life I have led that I am being unfair to you in listening to what my own spirit says in this matter. I have a very deep feeling, though I know it is asking a good deal and that you will understand my doing so. When Father's anxious and peremptory cable arrived I had just returned to London from one of the happiest weeks I have ever spent, motoring in the country with Sylvia and Valentine … in Norfolk where we stayed for three nights in the Acklands' grand house and the joy of being with those two fine, intelligent people.

Back in 'the troubled city', she rejoined Henry Fuller, 'cheerful and practical as ever, with his Father, who is an enchanting, whimsical solid, Roosevelt-hating business man, and they seem unperturbed though watchful, and don't contemplate changing their plans.'

I asked Mr Fuller directly for advice, and though he said he couldn't guess what was going to happen and couldn't advise me definitely … he seems calm and reassuring … I went to Mr Shadwick, had long talk with him, booked on the Queen Mary on October 13. He said, as all do, that if war breaks out in the next few weeks, as it may do, London is left behind for a time, and the West of England is the safest place to be, as well as the most convenient to Southampton for sailing if necessary … I will go directly to Dorset if war breaks out. I shall feel quite safe as well as happy in their house; they are as you know thoughtful and perceptive people who know a good deal about what war is and do not minimize its importance … I will take on a necessary job such as will be open to strong and interested Anglo-Saxons. I don't think I could be in a more secure or considerate place.

Love to you and Daddy and dear Granny and Janie [cat] and Giles— and tell J. that four separate cats have slept on my bed since I've been in England.[34]

Sylvia replied immediately when Elizabeth wrote of the decision to remain and to come to them for the duration if need be. The crisis was at its height. One bit of advance preparation should be to secure a supply of Horlicks malted milk tablets.

Frome Vauchurch
Maiden Newton
25. ix. 1938[35]

Dearest Elizabeth,

Your letter has just come. I think, we both think, you are doing very sensibly. When we asked you to stay with us for 'duration' we both meant it seriously, and had more in mind than safety and practical considerations. I am sure your profoundest instinct is to stay in Europe, and I believe that the instinct, like all profound ones, is a salutary instinct, and that at this juncture you would be healthier here than in the USA—or at any rate, than in Waterbury. Of course you might find fulfillment in some job in the States—but if you were to go home now I dread for you a long spell of feeling like Hopkins in the melancholy and ignominious sonnet which ends 'and each day dies with sleep'. I think it might give you a permanent crack in the heart ... the most crippling of all soul-maladies.

Of course we want you here. For an infinity of reasons, ranging from our love to our practical convenience. There is no one we would like to so well. Indeed, there are precious few we should like at all. Practically, you would be of very great help in two of the prime necessities, transport and food; for while we have a car and petrol left a second driver would be very important, especially as Valentine gets these spells of migraine when she can't drive; and you can dig and delve and have a green thumb for raising garden foodstuffs. Probably there will be a good deal to do in this locality, as we shall certainly have refugees from London and the Midlands; and there will always be work with the Friends at Street which is just over the county border. And if Valentine is ill—her tendency to influenza and its complications is my steadfast slow-burning nightmare—you can imagine what it would mean to me to have you near.

I still hope that you will get to Spain, somehow or other, and have a nous that you will. Remember, if war breaks out before October 4th, Clarence Pickett will certainly arrive in this country by one or other of the western ports, probably Plymouth or Southampton, either of which are accessible by road from here, so it might be well to lay some preliminary sketch-arrangements for getting in touch with him at his port of landing.[36]

Other things which I would recommend. To buy your ticket here beforehand: it is valid for a month, and there is no harm in having it by you. To buy any drugs you rely on now, such as that pyramidon stuff you gave Valentine. Another thing to buy, either for Spain or war, is Horlicks malted milk tablets—beastly, but sustaining—and meat lozenges. You would certainly need these either for yourself or for gifts in Spain; and they are easier to buy now than in a possible later. I always remember Valentine at Benicassim [on the Mediterranean coast of Spain], presenting Horlicks tablets to a family of naked gipsy children sprawling under an acacia, and their expressions of surprise melting into approbation as they sucked. I don't foresee any complications about your being a piece of alien baggage. I fancy that there will be so many people like yourself that this matter will be solved ambulatorily. And I assure you with my true heart that I cannot imagine any circumstances when the companionship of someone like yourself, steadfast and sensible and good-tempered and civilized would not be a help and a stay and a comfort. The thought that you may yet be with us is a real support to me. And I am convinced that you can be sure of being doubly useful, first and foremost, of course, as Elizabeth, and secondly as an American citizen. There I can speak with decent authority, having seen the effect of the International Brigade, and its subsidiaries in every walk of war in Spain. So my advice to you, unequivocally, is to follow your heart and your interior compass.

I am telling my bookseller to send you a copy of Richard Ford's *Travels in Spain.* Some passages of it may remind you, a little too powerfully for reputation of *After the Death of Don Juan.* But I whistle the thought off and reflects how very much you will enjoy the gentleman.[37]

All this letter is allowing for war. But allowing for Peace with Dishonour, remember you are plighted to come and stay with us again. There will be autumn bonfires with our love.

Sylvia

[handwritten] I do esteem your president. Even when I don't agree with him. I esteem him. & Fortunate citizen of a Republic.

Valentine the next day combined practical advice, a meditation on death, and a request for French cigarettes to bring if there is war. And come to them Elizabeth must, even if the crisis blows over, for practical and friendship reasons, and bring the gas mask she has been issued.

Frome Vauchurch
Maiden Newton
September 26th, 1938[38]

My dear Elizabeth,

With a clatter of airplanes overhead and the noise of them perfectly audible in your letter, and imitated in the rattle of Sylvia's typewriter downstairs, I write this postscript to my letter to you: We live in strange times, god help us, but among the better views I see is the prospect of your coming here.

Please decide to come and in any case for a stay with us. Even if Herr Hitler soft-pedals tonight, he may blast tomorrow: depend nothing on anything, for a while at least, except you depend on your very much admired clear-headedness and on our desire to have you here.

There is practical good, too! We have to make a shelter-trench in our garden and your long arms would be joyfully enlisted to help in shoveling, if you would do so. We have to saw and store wood against the winter developments and sort potatoes and various roots and store them. In all this squirreling you would be an invaluable help, and in return we will let you go whenever and wherever you wish, to the Friends at Street, to Bristol, to Southampton and even to America, if you must—But I think your instinct is sound and your compass-needle true.

Here is that epitaph from Wraxhall little church, near here; it is on the grave of Sir William Lawrence, who died in 1682, it says:

Welcome dear Death, let sweetest sleep here take me
In thy cool shade and never more awake me:
Like a rich curtain drawn by darkness round:
Like a close chamber, make my grave profound:
In it I'll couch secure, no dreams affright:
The silent lodger here no more dare bite.

No, I find that my copy ends abruptly here; although I did make a fair one it has gone—That (which is not a device intentional!) seems to point very clearly to your coming here. So come. Amen.

Valentine

[handwritten] Thank you for the 3d. I had not got one.

Here is a postscript more important than the letter!

Everyone seems to think it will happen to-morrow or next day; I have still a hunch that it may not: but it is very important indeed to take no chances.

We are engaged upon filling sandbags and getting mixed up in ARP, and so on.[39] We shall indent for a mask for you here; if you are offered one in London (IF) bring it along as well. Meanwhile, of course you must do as you decide best about going to Devonshire: probably it is a good plan to go, but DO GO BEFORE FRIDAY MORNING. We think there is a midnight train from Paddington which is an Express, and strongly advise you to take it. If you alter plans you can, with our most happy goodwill, arrive here at any day, any time you please.

As regards things we might need: any FRENCH cigarettes (cheapest Caporale or Gauloise preferred) a bottle of Collis Browne Chlorodyne (very useful) a small store of milk tablets. All these are usable either here or in Spain; none will be obtainable after a short while. And bring your driving licence and some soap. There will be a shortage of that, and again it is necessary for Spain as well as for here. But don't expend valuable money on getting very much—these are only suggestions!

And this is a curt postscript. I am afraid of over-burdening you. We both feel fairly selfish at the moment!

Love to you—the prospect of seeing you is a lovely and a bright one! Even if the whole world rockets into the Millennium, please don't change your plan to come to us!

The Prime Minister, Neville Chamberlain, was at Munich for the conference with Hitler and M. Daladier, the Prime Minister of France, and the Czech representatives. In London, Elizabeth was fitted with a gas mask. She heard the news of the settlement at Munich from the announcement by Ivor Novello before the curtain rose on the performance of *Henry V* on September 28. (Janet Machen was a page in this production.)

Tue 27 Am. Express get money. Tea. See Shadwick Am. Embassy. See Bill Brown, lunch E-S.U., see H. Hill Bookshop, haircut, tea E. Parker & [ ] Kelly; Plane Tree talk about Spain. Dine H. Park Lane. Hear Chamberlain speech broadcast.

Wed 28 shop, Gas mask fitted, lunch Henry Cheshire Cheese, to Whitehall, see crowds; to Westminster Abbey, Bumpus, din. H., Broadstairs, *Henry V*, meet Janet & to her flat.

Thurs 29 Crisis more or less over. Letters. Bumpus order books. Tea. Din with H[enry Fuller] at E-S.U. Helen de F. , [de Freitas] Janet 2 Fullers and 3 friends & go to Palladium. Peace announced.

Fri 30 letters Tompkins & B.[Radford] Tilney, off., tea with H & to Buckingham Palace to see K. & Q & Chamberlain on balcony. Raw & [ ] lovely sunset. Din. H. [Fuller] Frascati, 'nine Sharp' 7 to Café Anglais dancing.

The participants announced the subsequently infamous agreement at Munich between Britain, France, and Nazi Germany on 29 September. Chamberlain addressed the Commons the next day and appeared with the King and Queen on the balcony at Buckingham Palace that afternoon. Elizabeth witnessed the rejoicing with Henry Fuller and sent a vivid account to her mother.

Now that we have for want of a more critical term is known as peace, we may look back—almost as on a long past experience—on the days between Friday the 23rd and Thursday the 29th of September 1938. They were days, it cannot be denied, of violent stimulation and excitement as well as of grimness and fear.

Coming back from the completely English experience of that lovely week of motoring with S & V into a nest of frightened academic Americans at Carlton Mansions, all talking at once about what was going to happen, rather intensified my realization of what was direfully actual in the average Londoner's mind, though less wildly apparent in their words or actions. Of course, the mechanics of the situation were everywhere apparent. Gas-mask announcements, ARP Posters calling for men and women volunteers, all the parks full of gaping trenches for air raid shelters, and sand-bag brigades busily filling and stacking around the public buildings. Mostly beautiful weather, the trees still very green and just a leaf or two falling down occasionally. Wednesday was the climax of course; in the morning I had a gas-mask fitted by a gentle curate in a dingy church assembly room according to instructions posted in the hotel along with the address of our nearest bomb-proof (?) cellar accommodation, these after the comfort of eating some of the Cheshire Cheese's excellent steak-and-kidney pie with Henry [Fuller]. I walked with him to Westminster Bridge where we gaped at an indecisive-looking anti-aircraft gun, to the House of Parliament where Chamberlain was holding forth within, and orderly crowds were milling about outside, and to Westminster Abbey where we sat a whiles with an anxious multitude and heard some good music. About that time the news came that the *Europa* with Janie [Cummings] on board I suppose, had been called back to Bremen before even making Southampton and the first suggestions of the spectacular meeting to take place on the next day. We had a lovely and expensive French dinner and went to see Ivor Novello's production of *Henry V*, to hear the brave English words of Agincourt and then the cheers that greeted Novello's announcement that thanks to NC we could sleep that night without much fear of the German bomber. That is the bare skeleton of a day whose every violent and subtle flesh-tone and lineament I shall never forget and I can say quite honestly that it was a deep and a valuable experience and that I am profoundly glad to have been in London for it. And yesterday and today— when we were all supposed to have been rushing away from

London in or on any available vehicle and with 'respirators' in hand, to escape the threatened week-end bombing, we have wallowed in security, however, insecure, and covered up our—I won't put a word to it—in cheering and singing He's a Jolly Good Fellow and God Save the King to those statuesque four on the arc lit balcony of Buckingham Palace.

Henry and I and many others awaited them in the rain late yesterday afternoon and saw a most touchingly beautiful sunset and a rainbow into the bargain.

It's been fun having Henry in town; he's a capable and refreshing companion in many ways. We've done several shows, all but [*Henry V*], musicals (H's choice). And all but one of these utterly frivolous and dull, I'm sorry to say. Also we've walked about London a lot and gastronomically explored some good restaurants.

Now we're in Cambridge whose dreaming academic detachment is a joy after the gamut of London emotions. H. is settled in a lovely room, at Magdalene and tomorrow we take a car and drive ourselves—both [with] learning licenses, and I having driven Valentine's car quite a bit on our trip—to Ely and possibly Peterborough.

I shall not, as you will not, I think, be surprised to hear, set sail on the *Queen Mary* on Oct. 13th , for I still have much work to do in England, trips to Birmingham, and Lincolnshire, for wills, etc., and I want to finish all that while I am about it. And England is so beautiful now that I can't bear to think of leaving it. Don't give a thought to my health. I'm as well as a brace of rabbits, but sleepy ..."[40]

Sylvia gave vent to her scorn for 'that Hotspur Chamberlain' and the agreement in a letter that went to the post before he appeared on the Buckingham Palace balcony

Frome Vauchurch
Maiden Newton
30. ix. 1938[41]

Dearest Elizabeth,

The books came this morning. On any other morning how much better I could write to thank you for them ... but I feel just now as though only one thing could undumn me, and that, an opportunity for a face to face analysis to that Hotspur Chamberlain of what he has done and what must come of it. Nettles, quotha. Might he roll in poison ivy and prickly pears. Might I have the rolling of him.[42]

It is so disastrous, so humiliating, so dirty, that it seems impossible to find even a pebble's space of anything clean and sound on which to construct some scaffolding for hope. If we had fought Fascism and had been thoroughly beaten in that fight, if we had lost half our population, our standards of living and thinking, our works of art, our social services, it would not have been so bad as this. For out of that kind of defeat springs anger, resentment, remembrance; but put of this we shall carry not the respectable anger of the slave but the indifference of the idiot or the dead. We have not fought, so we shall have nothing to fight for. We have kept a whole skin and lost our vitality. Every one will try and forget this affair, just because it has been so shameful. There will not be a ruined building, a black cross, a bloodstain to remember this defeat by. We shall shovel it into our national subconscious where it can lie and corrupt us.

That is a queer way to thank you for a present of books, but I value culture and friendship too highly to write in any other way at this time, and I should be treating you very meanly if I did not speak out my mind to one of the few people I know who is capable of appreciating this disaster for what it is worth, a hell's fee of ruin, misery, and shame.

Frome Vauchurch,
Maiden Newton,
Dorset.
TELEPHONE: MAIDEN NEWTON 276

30. ix. 1938.

Dearest Elizabeth,

The books came this morning. On any other morning how much better I could
write to thank you for them... but I feel just now as though only one thin
could undumn me, and that, an opportunity for a face to face analysis to
that Hotspur Chamberlain of what he has done and what must come of it. Xxt
Nettles, quotha. Might he roll in poison ivy and prickly pears. Might I
have the rolling of him.
It is so disastrous, so humiliating, so dirty, that it seems impossible to
find even a pebble's-space of anything clean and sound on which to xxxxxx
construct some scaffolding for hope. If we had fought. Fascism and had been
thoroughly beaten in that fight, if we had lost half our population, our
standards of living and thinking, our works of art, our social services, i
would not have been so bad as this. For out of that kind of defeat springs
anger, resentment, remembrance; but out of this we shall carry not the
respectable anger of the slave but the indifference of the idiot or the
dead. We have not fought, so we shall have nothing to fight for. We have
kept a whole skin and lost our vitality. Every one will try and forget thi
affair, just because it has been so shameful. There will not be a ruined
building, a black cross, a bloodstain to remember this defeat by. We shall
shovel it into our national subconscious where it can lie and corrupt us.
     This is a queer way to thank you for a present of books. But I value xx
culture and friendship too highly to write in any other way at this time,
and I should be treating you very meanly if I did not speak out my mind
to one of the few people I know who is capable of appreciating this disaster for what it is worth: a hell's fee of ruin, misery, and shame.

It has rained all day. At intervals the wireless announces some new
additional flourish on our dishonour. The river is in flood, the people
who come to the house look glum and bewildered. We both have colds in
our heads. There is a war in Spain and a war in China. Czechoslovakia
is in the hands of the executioners. And we are at peace.   can/
And yet, you know, I wish you would come here as soon as you (except
forthe colds; but they will be gone by next week), I have very little
national pride; but what there is of it does get an infinity of comfort
from xxxxxxxxxxxxxxxxxxxxxxxxxxxx knowing that someone not involved
in this miserable nation realises that we are not all hallooing over
Peace with dishonour. In some way you contrive to be both a balsam and
an astringent.
As for boarding-houses, there are none. At least I know of none. If I
knew of a thousand, I would not tell you. You will kindly come here, and
stay with us as long as you care to. Anything else would be so very
silly. We have known and loved each other for so long, and spent so
little time together that I demand as much of you as you can spare.
And presently, I suppose, one will begin to work again, and there will
be many activitities to consult you about, and things we shall ask you
to do with us. So come as soon as you can, my dear, and whenever you
can, and for as long as you can.
When I think of your telegram to your father, and of how circumstances
have betrayed it into verity, I want to tear away the flesh from my
heart.
               Ever,

               Sylvia :

32. Letter from Sylvia to Elizabeth, 30 September 1938,
     front and reverse.

It has rained all day. At intervals the wireless announces some new additional flourish on our dishonour. The river is in flood, the people who come to the house, look glum and bewildered. We both have colds in our heads. There is a war in Spain and a war in China. Czechoslovakia is in the hands of the executioners. And we are at peace.

And yet, you know, I wish you would come here as soon as you can (except for the colds, but they will be gone by next week), I have very little national pride, but what there is of it does get an infinity of comfort from knowing that someone not involved in this miserable nation realizes that we are not all hallooing over Peace with dishonour. In some way you contrive to be both a balsam and an astringent.

As for boarding-houses, there are none. At least I know of none. If I knew of a thousand I would not tell you. You will kindly come here, and stay with us as long as you care to. Anything else would be so very silly. We have known and loved each other for so long, and spent so little time together that I demand as much of you as you can spare. And presently, I suppose, one will begin to work again, and there will be many activities to consult you about, and things we shall ask you to do with us. So come as soon as you can, my dear, and whenever you can, and for as long as you can.

Then I think of your telegram to your father, and of how circumstances betrayed it into verity, I want to tear away the flesh from my heart.

Ever,

Sylvia

[EWW's handwritten note on envelope] Dear Janet, I think you would like to read this letter. Hope they'll look after you properly, remember breakfast goes with the room.

Also my love,

Elizabeth

When she heard the news of the Munich agreement on the radio, Mary White wrote from Breakneck again to urge Elizabeth to return and reporting that Will shared his daughter's view of Chamberlain's capitulation and that it meant war was inevitable. 'Your father telephoned me to say he was cabling to you to take the next available boat home. This shows you how we are feeling about the war crisis … Your father thinks they gave in to Hitler too much, laying up trouble for the future but I think it was a victory for the spirit of peace, 'let them live' … Of course the radio keeps us informed, every move in this terrible game … Wade is coming with me to the dentist in New Haven and lunch at Malley's.'[43] Although she was adamantly against the Spanish venture, Mary gave her blessing to Elizabeth's alternative plan to stay and help in England and continue her research.

In her comments on the Munich agreement Valentine offered selections from Horace.

Frome Vauchurch,
Maiden Newton,
30th September [1938][44]

Oh my dear Elizabeth—Sylvia's letter no doubt will reflect to you how we are feeling, and more accurately and less selfishly than I should do. So this, aside from the plaintive opening, is a thank-you letter once again.

The lovely little solid book, the Latin Portrait, is going to be a companion and a delight to me: and the inscription too will make those dead poets speak living words. As I had written that I opened the book, fortunately at Horace, and this is what it said to me and sends to you:

Leave to the gods all else. When they
Have once bid rest the winds that war
Over the passionate seas, no more
Grey ash and cypress rock and grey.

Ask not what future suns shall bring:
Count to-day gain, whate'er it chance
To be
Nor deem sweet love an idle thing.

Perhaps Calverley is a little ponderous in this, but the advice is good and Horace is even better, and best of all, at the moment it is to be reminded by you that Horace wrote, and Vergil and Catullus—[45]

We very much want you to come, and only a little more want that you should do what best pleases and enriches yourself. I wish you all possible, possible good fortune in your Spanish arrangements but if there is delay, then I can for certain find you a pleasant bedroom in M.N., and although it is in a pub, it is in a very small, very quiet and humble pub: the room looks across the river-meadows and nothing you could do would please me better than that you should eat a meal or two or three meals a day here, and use a room as your own and the rest of our house as places where we can have your company: and our bath as a bath and our house as your house.

This is a repeat of the suggestion we made when you were here lately, and last year! Don't be like Charlotte Bronte, please: don't refuse from high principles! Both of us are wary by now, as Janet will tell you, and now don't ask unless we actively want to receive.

Yes: there is a car at Cattistock, I am almost certain, and there is a better one in Dorchester—I think we could surely get you a Vauxhall there, the same kind as mine. For local excursions you would, I hope, consent to use ours. It would be foolish not to.

As for dates and so on, they depend on you entirely. Except that I am serious in saying it would do Sylvia the kind of good she needs, if you could come even for a little while fairly soon. You will perceive the truth of this, I expect, when you read her letter. The strain was severe and now it is replaced by a heavier weight on quite other muscles. Be assured that whenever you come you will be very joyfully received, and you will achieve your desire; you will put us well into your debt!

Love to you—and thanks for the photographs too; for the other books; for Morris, whose words about Communism restored some sanity to our winds this morning—thanks.

Valentine

[Handwritten] I think there is not a lodging house here—but I'll find out—You will come to us first, anyhow—won't you?

Sylvia reinforced the invitation, and, as her notes show, Elizabeth did manage a short visit to Frome Vauchurch before she left for Paris.

i. x. 38[46]

Dearest Elizabeth

A short letter. First, to say that we shall love to receive you on the 10th, if can't come sooner. Second, that if I were you I should certainly claim your gas-mask— I am not quite sure if you will get it. They are now trying to recall them, which does not so much imply a feeling that they will not be needed as a feeling that they will—and had better be kept in good storage till then.

Today we went to Chaldon, to visit our evacuated Mrs Keates at the cottage. I mention this because of the following conversation.

Valentine: And what do you think of Chamberlain now?

Mrs Keates: Grinning hyena … feathering his own nest.

The transition is a little abrupt. Not only a cockney (as perhaps a New Yorker) could do it so well with six words and two animals.

When you come there will be a great deal to tell you. And by then I shall be talking about your lovely books. This morning I found a great deal of comfort in Trollope.

With our love,

Sylvia

After accompanying Henry Fuller to Cambridge, Elizabeth returned to London and met Clarence Pickett of the American Friends Service Committee to talk about service in Spain.

[47]Sat Oct 1 To B.M. see & pay Mrs Osler, lunch Borh with Janet & Martin; meet Henry at train for Cambridge, tea on train. Go to Blue [Boar] with H & see his room.

Sun 2 H. & I took a car took a car and drove to Ely, lunch The Lamb, Peterborough, Fotheringhay, church, din Huntingdon The Bridge, rain until late afternoon. Back to Cam. & to H's room.

Mon 3 Cambridge to London, arr. 1:00. Friends House, see Miss Thomson, Clarence Pickett din with Henry, Cumberland & to *Troilus & Cressida*.

'I must tell you, though I'm afraid it will make you unhappy, that I may within ten days or so be going into Spain,' Elizabeth wrote her mother after her meeting with Clarence Pickett. She assured her that it will be 'perfectly all right for me to go now for a short stay of observation. I shall go to Paris next Wednesday, a week from tomorrow.' Mr Pickett suggested a talk there with Levi Hartzler, who had long working ties with the American Quakers. En route to Spain they plan to have Emily Parker, a young American, accompany her. 'It all sounds very well organized.' The cable address in Paris, was Hartzler, Quak-Amis, Paris; in Spain, it was Clyde Roberts, San Nicola 25, Murcia, Spain. She had doubts and confided them to her mother:

> I'm torn apart by two strong feelings. One is my conviction that it is right and reasonable and logical for me to go and do this job for humanity that I've been given the chance to undertake; the other is the sorrow and hurt I feel in realizing that my going will make you and the rest of my dear family anxious and unhappy and undoubtedly resentful. Perhaps you are right, perhaps I am utterly wrong and wicked and selfish, God knows. But this is so definitely a challenge and a test, the first really difficult thing I have ever done in my life, that I cannot now with any hope of future self respect turn back from it, so long as I feel that the risk is not really great enough to warrant my giving it up for the sake of those I love ... remember that the Quakers are careful people ... [I will not] take blind risks, don't worry. There's not a safe spot in the world for these days for anyone, and even though Chamberlain threw one of Shakespeare's most beautiful pronouncements down into the dust, he cannot destroy its essential truth and honour.[48]

Mon 4 Friends House, Lunch G. Ford, Embassies. Meet Henry for tea E-S.U., home for din. And write letters.

Wed 5 Embassies, Friends' House, etc. Lunch [ ] de Freitas, Friends House, meet H. 7:15 din Hungana & to French without Tears.

Sylvia sent a postcard:

> I have just made up the spare room. It is ready for you any time you can arrive. Remember, if time is scanty, and the time-table to Maiden Newton unaccommodating Dorchester can also be reached on the Southern Rly.
>
> With our love,
>
> Sylvia[49]

Thu 6 Friends House, etc. Lunch Mr Fuller, Hatchetts, with him to Shadwick. Dentist, meet Henry for tea E-S.U. 5:15 home, rest. Dinner. Janet here.

Fri 7. 10:30 Paddington to Maiden Newton 1:49. With S & V.

Sat to London din Janet.

Sun 9 to Paris.

On October 8 Elizabeth left for Paris on the Folkestone-Boulogne ferry. She wrote her mother that in Spain she will be with 'fine and capable people ... Try to think of me with courage and strength, try to send that courage and strength across the ocean to me, for I shall need it.'[50]

Sylvia sent practical advice in a letter to await her at the Quaker Center. It was a mother's advice: call on me when in need. I will come to care for you if you are in distress.

Frome Vauchurch Maiden Newton
8. X. 1938[51]

Dearest Elizabeth,

You have taken your weather with you. Very soon after you'd gone, it clouded over and began to rain; and then the seagulls came over squawking, and we found ourselves talking about signs of an early, of a hard winter ... a winter that we both feel would have been less hard and less early if Elizabeth had been sharing it with us.

It was difficult and sad to see you go; for a complexity of reasons; for the single reason, that we naturally want to keep you since we love you; for anxiety because of the strain you are feeling and will feel (though I shall hold by my reading that held to that passionate heart of Spain you will find warmth and strength and healing) for the disapproving woe one feels at a state of things in which everything one loves and esteems is bound on these errands.

But when the house is on fire it is best to be awake; and for your sake and for the sake of the treasures of past and future in that house I am thankful you are awake.

It is difficult not to pursue you with practicalities. But the first one is the one you must attend to. It is this: if things go wrong in Paris, either with plans or with yourself, send a cable here, and I will come at once. I do beg of you to take this seriously and remember it, rue Guy de la Brosse may contain a great deal that is excellent; but it does not know you and love you as we do; and I should feel an eternal hurt if I thought you needed me and let a miserable Channel keep me away, if you are ill; if there is any breakdown exterior or interior; I beg of you to send for me. And I think I am only asking you to undertake what your heart would bid you do anyhow. By all my theories of following one's personal compass, one's instinct and intuition, and that profound and provident selfishness which was the fairy godmother at one's cradle, you would be making a real mistake if you wanted me and did not send for me. So remember.

Louis Aragon's address I gave you. If you have to spend time in Paris he might be able to put you in touch with some of our Spanish friends there. Anyhow he is a fount of introductions, and looks (except for the whiskers) very much like the water-rat in Wind in the Willows.

M. Thomas of the Centrale Sanitaire Internationale, 36 rue de Chateaudon, 9e, is a very good and sensible and central man. If he does not remember my name, you should remind him that in the autumn of 1937 he bought soap for Spain with money I collected for that purpose. But Spain would be password enough.

And if you fly, remember that the air is very cold.

In our tongue-tied way, we failed to say what we both thought; that you are doing an extremely brave thing. I don't mean so much going to Spain, though that is brave too, but it is the Anne Bradstreet side of this exploit that is the really taxing part of it: the departure from the accustomed, from the secure, from the seemingly-reasonable, into a new New England; and the renunciation of what is fallible in one, what is accustomed to consider failure, to say 'that's a thing I couldn't do', for an unexplored capability and sufficiency. I am thinking a great deal about Anne Bradstreet. I am dubious how far I believe in heredity; but I have a strong faith in environment, in affinity of heredity; and I am convinced that in some way, partly by thinking, partly by sympathy, you and that remote grandmother are powerfully connected, that her blood, looping over centuries, lives in you, and takes wing with you in this further migration; that if you get to Spain Anne Bradstreet will go with you.

I once that loved the shady woods so well
Now thought the rivers did the trees expel

Now take care of yourself, my dear. Remember my parting admonition to be kind to your heart. If we did you any good, it was not by severity; but long after one has learned how to treat others one fails to apply the same methods to oneself, and Elizabeth, so sensitive to every one else may not be so quick to hear the claims of Elizabeth. My heart yearns after you. But I say to myself that you will be among people of a race naturally noble and with a deep apprehension of what is good and genuine, and with living hearts. If she could meet Pallach at Port Bou, I say to myself, Asunçion or Serafin, or Alfredo at the Dos Puertas or the man who gathered and peeled the walnuts for us when the car broke down, or Ramon who wrapped Valentine's sick head in his own deal pullover, or stupid beautiful Filer who suddenly bent across the bed we were making together and kissed me—and then I remember that these are the very people you will be meeting and succouring. Give them my love, my lasting love.

And remember, that if you want me while you are in France (it might not be in Paris) you are to wire, and I will come, Maiden Newton, 276. I should like to, you know.

With my love,

Always,

Sylvia

That same day Valentine sent affection and voiced her concern.

Frome Vauchurch
Maiden Newton
October 8th [1938][52]

My dear Elizabeth,

You have gone, and taken the swallows with you: our winter birds have come—the seagulls are flying over the river and the meadows now, and it is raining and very cold. I know that you will meet the swallows in Spain. When we went there first we found them gathered like a crowd to greet us. Chaldon swallows, then, and Frome Vauchurch ones now! They will bring you many messages from both of us.

It was a very hard farewell to say: first, much sadness because you were going from here: second, concern for you: third, envy of your happy lot! I know that the actual days of getting gone are vile & totally unhappy and totally scaring, but I also know that from the first half-hour of arrival you will be in a state of suspension and fervor and contentment which I do envy you mightily.

We cursed that we are not rich! With money to spare, how we would have gone with you to the frontier (and who knows but we might have crossed it—though this would have been wrong, unless we'd been able to do something there—) and waved you across and waited to see you return. I wish most passionately that you were not getting there so solitarily. But if you can manage to endure the status of that, you can feel very well content with yourself for ever after.

Dear Elizabeth—and I haven't said thank-you for the [cuff-] links, which I love and cherish, nor for your presence here which was all pleasure, even when it was anxious and worried by the speed of time. Please take with you love and admiration and all the protection love can give—which is most considerable, most enveloping—and all the messages our hearts send to Spain. At least you are going where people are brave and honest; beautiful and almost always single-hearted. I think, if you really ever need support, you will need it when you return and breathe into pure lungs this present poison which is in England. But if you do need support, come for it and be sure of finding it: just as we shall look to you for it—thankful that for the time we are with Elizabeth-from-Spain we shall be able to take off our gas-masks and remember that somewhere there really is air to breathe.

I think I may have talked too much about my own cowardice. It is the kind of thing one hopes to get off one's chest ... but it wasn't really because of that: I'd been so afraid of being afraid, before I went, and I thought maybe you felt something of that. Everyone does, I believe, anyhow. And the one piece of advice that is worth having is this—never, for a moment, admit to feeling afraid. The admission, however modestly given, seems to make a crack—and the water gets in. Otherwise, I believe, one is very well proofed against even a heavy storm. I know you are.

Love to you.

Valentine

From home there was support too: Mary sent a 'fine comforting cable' to Paris. Elizabeth wrote her from the Hotel Commodore that it was strange to be in Paris with only a few clothes. She added, knowing it would please her, that

> Mr Fuller, Henry's father, is a rock of ages, New England brand, and it is wonderful that he is here now ... We had a beastly channel crossing on Sunday. What depths the physical system can plumb in ninety minutes! but the white wine and the good French train food were very restoring ... [Levi Hartzler, the AFSC representative] is a sturdy blond, young Mennonite who is working in Spain, waiting for me at the station. I've talked with him quite a lot since then, between meals in good restaurants and seeing some shows—*Bailalailou* Sunday, *The Flying Dutchman* yesterday with Mr Fuller, and am to go to the Quaker Club to see him again this morning... *Your Forces and How to Use Them* is with me and a great help.
>
> Goodbye my darling, think kindly of your adoring Bet.'[53]

When Elizabeth sent word of the delay in the arrangements for her travel to Loyalist Spain and that she had considered abandoning the venture, Sylvia sought to bolster her morale and delivered caustic comments on British post-Munich politics.

Frome Vauchurch
Maiden Newton
14. x. 1938[54]

Dearest Elizabeth

I am sorry you are kept in Paris. It is so exasperating, for I feel that you could have been here instead, less expense and how much more pleasure. But at any rate I can write to you again.

It has rained and rained. Everything that can hold on against the weather is a frantic green, and everything that can't has been blown into the North Sea by now. Yesterday out of the mist a majestic steam-roller appeared, and rolled our tempest-tossed drive. It had a lion on its bosom, and was driven by an old man who must have been its younger brother, he had exactly that solid and worthy and peaceable character that a steam-roller has. He was rather sad because the drive was not the width it should have been to conform to the ideals of steam-rolling. I explained that its width had been dictated by our car. He shook his head. It was obvious that he thought we should have been better advised to stick to steam-rollers.

People of this sort become extraordinarily dear to one in these bleak days. One's mental diet is so largely toadstools (and decayed at that) that a hunk of homemade bread is the food of angels.

Your lovely case of wine came, and was tenderly unpacked and laid on its rack. I am not going to say you should not have sent it. It is an Elizabeth-send, has done, and will do us, real good. We drank the first bottle of the Pope's new castle last night, with sauté kidneys and the first plant of our own celery. For some reason of the soil, I suppose, our celery is a beautiful rose-colour, and caused Valentine to accuse it of being rhubarb by mistake.

Tomorrow I am going to open an exhibition of modern pictures at the Working Women's College. This is a good institution that makes very little reclame and goes firmly on with excellent ideals. It is almost entirely free, it takes women of all ages and from all occupations, and gives them a year of college life. What is so especially good about it is that it does not take any trouble to train them as better industrial animals. No covert exploitation under the guise of classes in applied this and that.

I sent Craske his fifteen pounds. He is pleased to have it, and sends you his greetings.

I am so glad you have Fuller père. He sounds extremely reassuring, and I am glad his whimsicality includes opera. Music is so good for one's blood. If you go by submarine Valentine's envy will know no bounds. It is a thing she has always longed to do. All I know of it is that it has brought me various letters, with a grand new stamp. If you go by boat, avoid a British one if you can. I don't mean cruiser, but I don't think our hosts in those waters are likely to be good ones. Bombing in harbour must be a considerable inducement to send the second-hand. Dutch boats have a good reputation for keeping a whole skin. By the way, I forgot to tell you. If you do come into close contact with a bombardment, put a pencil or an orange stick, or something of that sort between your teeth. It makes a great difference to the shock to the ear-drums if the ivories are kept apart; and one cannot rely on oneself to preserve a gaping jaw. We never had to do this, either being so much larger and explosive so much more local than one can persuade the British people to suppose, but I have been given it as a tip of value.

Strange confidences of the contemporary boudoir. It makes me disagree with your lament for seventeenth century walls as for a lost world. I have an idea that people like ourselves are in these times very close to the thoughts of that date. It was one of the most melancholy and arduous of the centuries, full of wars and sickness and questioning. Not a portrait but has its hand on its sword. Then it was a religious, now it is a social conscience that eats the heart. Did you ever read Henry More, the Cambridge Platonist?[55] I have not read all of him, only a volume of selections. You would like him. You must read him when you come back, if you do not already know him much better than I do.

I am sorry to hear what you say about Paris and its preparedness. I suppose the Gagoulards have been putting their spoke in the wheels.[56] A couple of years ago it was supposed to be the model of Europe for that sort of thing.

England and her Hotspur? Well, people in the street are still talking about it and arguing about it, that in itself is something remarkable. The Lord Mayor's Fund for Czechoslovakia has been a considerable surprise, for it has gone up by thousands every day with the minimum of boosting, and with no official countenance. If George and Elizabeth (how I hate that woman for having such a good name!) have troubled to put their hands in their pockets, I think it must have been anonymously. The danger of it is that people may rub off the edges of their conscience by subscribing. What is interesting is the very large individual subscriptions. Spain and China at most touched the hundred pound pockets, but this is being supported by people who can add the extra zero.

One interesting thing came out last week. The government had arranged (if there had been a war) to suppress all the newspapers. There was to be one official *Gazette*, as in the 1926 strike, and the wireless. Nothing else. That this is true is, I think proved by the fact that only one paper has declared it: the *Daily Worker*, which is so independent it can say what it likes. All the other dailies are stifled by their dependence on government controlled news. But no doubt the proprietors and journalists know it, and this may be one of the reasons for the publicity they give to anti-Chamberlain news. Except, of course, the *Times*. *The Times* would become the official Gazette, though most of its special correspondents would be dismissed.

Cranborne, who was Eden's worser half, and a very knock-kneed rebel, has completely snuffed out. He came down to his constituency, S. Dorset, and assured his hearers that his loyalty to Chamberlain was undiminished, and that he never meant to wound any susceptibilities by speaking as he did in the Munich debate. He is probably betting on the formation of a national government, since Hotspur has shied at a general election. The Navy is said to be feeling extremely sour.[57]

No doubt you saw that Italy had landed a consignment of small cars bearing guns at Cadiz. A small gun-bearing car is about as much use in a Spanish battlefield as a small gun-bearing perambulator. They are certainly designed for use in towns in Nationalist territory. Taking it by and large this may be considered hopeful news.

Give my love to Paris. Remember, if you have time, the new Egyptian rooms at the Louvre. And have you ever visited the Buttes Chaumont? It has a view almost as grand as the river from Sacre Coeur, and as a piece of romantic park-planning is idiotic to a height of grandeur. It is everything that that observatory cum-crag at the end of Fifth Avenue would like to be. I expect it was designed by Victor Hugo, or perhaps Hector Berlioz. You could not fail to enjoy it; and besides being absurd it very nearly comes off.[58]

With my love always.

Sylvia

After a few days, Elizabeth told the AFSC people in Paris that she could not serve with them in Spain. She withdrew, bitterly accusing herself of cowardice. There were very real dangers and practicalities that made service in Spain at that time considerably more difficult than hitherto in the civil war. The Loyalists were preparing to hold on in an enclave around Alicante and Valencia on the Mediterranean coast; Madrid was surrounded and Barcelona blockaded. For a volunteer this meant passage by ship from Marseilles with the risk of interception by the Italian Navy—Sylvia's imagined submarine was fanciful for an aid worker. On 15 October, Elizabeth elaborated to her mother on the decision and berated herself.

> My one comfort in sending you the cable today saying that I was not going to Spain, was the thought that it would make you happy. It was not here in any way a happy experience for me; these past ten days of fear and horror and the thought of what I might be called upon to see and endure in the process of complicatedly and dangerously getting in and out of that tortured country, of the terrible dread that I might crack up either on the way or when I had gotten in and couldn't easily get out, and of finally, at the end of my endurance, going to a doctor today and being told I was not nervously put together for such a job and it would undoubtedly be fatal for me to go. So that's the end of all that hope and planning and dedication, and what a ghastly, ignominious end leaving me heartbrokenly aware of my lack of wisdom and intelligence—and stability and stamina. But it is too a beginning, the beginning, I hope, of wisdom, of knowing myself better than ever before—and perhaps starting to learn a little about my small and humble powers, if I have any, of being useful. If only I can keep myself together through this time of adjustment and discouragement, can realize that some such as I have a right and an obligation to live as decently and usefully as they can, I shall be all right, I think and hope. Oh, I am sorry the way I made one mistake after another, causing so much unhappiness to myself and to others around me. God knows, I mean, and have always meant, to do the right thing, but it seems always, in my case, to work out contrary-wise.

Well enough of such misery. You will be relieved at any rate, and I must say, I am tremendously so, too, and realize what you said in your letter about the difference of staying in England and trying to help if war came, and marching deliberately and cold-bloodedly into a strange country which is in the last and most violent and horrible phase of civil war. Oh, if only that dreadful, wicked war would end, then maybe, or so the doctor said, I could go in and help the poor tragic people and children ...'[59]

In a letter Elizabeth received some days later, Mary White enclosed a clipping from the *Herald Tribune*: 'Bitter Battle Rages on the Ebro: Many Killed as Insurgent Planes attack a Passenger Train'. She also reflected on the Munich agreement and came to the same conclusion that her daughter had: 'I'm afraid that the whole world thinks that the peace that has been brought about is very uncertain and at too great a price.'[60]

Elizabeth's distress was such that she put herself in the American Hospital in Paris. 'My heart is full of relief', was Mary's response after receiving a cable with this news.[61] From the hospital Elizabeth thanked her mother for 'putting out a hand to help', but she gave vent to her self-criticism. 'Why is it I wonder that I was born to make myself and others unhappy by consistently, and with the most well-meaning of intentions, doing the wrong thing? ... I should have known that by upbringing and temperament I was not suited for work in Spain ... I should have listened to you when you told me.' The doctor she had gone to in Paris told her 'you're not made to endure that kind of thing', and recommended the stay in the American Hospital.[62]

Valentine was prompt to offer understanding and solace.

Frome Vauchurch
Maiden Newton, Dorset.
October 19th [1938][63]

Most dear Elizabeth,

Because my heart is with you, can I say something I probably could not say another time

181

If you were to set out in a 'plane to fight fascists (I mean to use this simile) & the petrol ran short & you had to land for more; being hastily-trained a pilot of that new, unwieldy, unnatural machine, you crashed your landing. What then?

Materially: repairs, ready for the next job. Morally: blame on the construction of the 'plane, of the people who freighted it with gas and the circumstances which hurried your training & sent you out.

This is not evasion of guilt. I speak of what I know when I tell you that it is hard, and it is a duty, to refuse to blame oneself unjustly.

People of our generation were ill-designed for this generation's jobs. We have not been trained: our machines were not designed for destructive work. We meant, and our designers (parents, Society) meant us, to explore the air—not wreck the earth. It's true that now we must learn afresh, our destiny lies that way. But patience—patience—Nothing is harder to learn, nothing takes longer, than endurance. A heart conditioned not to quail even at its own temporary collapse is a heart that has been steadily, patiently, and above all kindly trained to endure. Elizabeth we've all been taught to live in dreams: we thought we'd inherited qualities that can't exist except by long separate gestation, long nurture, and care. Don't be horrified to find that you can flinch: Fall back on your second-line defence and dig yourself in. And from there repulse attacks of shame, remorse, despair. They make a big noise, but dig deep and calm your mind and nurse your heart and WAIT. It will pass.

'What!' said someone to me once, 'Did you think yourself perfection?'

This, remember, is a wound, not a disease. It's NOT that you were unsound: it is that you were hit by something launched from outside at you. I suppose it's one of the severest wounds one can get—but what then? Gingerly feeling yourself again, you'll find you are all there, all intact, still alive.

A Chinese poet said:

Never a man night-faring in hope or fear,
Hard-pressed on the face of the earth—
But still he has room to turn.
And what of Hopkins?
Patience, hard thing! The hard thing but to pray,
But bid for, Patience is! Patience who asks
Wants war, wants wounds; weary his times, his tasks;
To do without, take tosses, and obey.
And of all the best in the world for healing—which is your task,
your possible task, now:—
My own heart let me have sore pity on; let
Me live to my sad self hereafter kind;
Charitable; not live this tormented mind
With this tormented mind tormenting yet.
I cast for comfort I no more can get
By groping round my comfortless, than blind
Eyes in their dark can day or thirst can find
Thirst's all-in-all in all a world of wet.

Soul, self; come, poor Jackself, I do advise
You, jaded, let be; call off thought awhile
Elsewhere; leave comfort root-room; let joy size
At God knows when to God knows what; whose smile
's not wrung, see you; unforeseen times rather—as skies
Betweenpie mountains—lights a lovely mile.

My dear Elizabeth—if you could be here now (as would God you were) you would see no flicker of change in either of us—NOT from love determinedly steadfast, but from love unassaulted love which has had absolutely nothing to shake it. You are Elizabeth, Sylvia is Sylvia, I am I: such as we are, we remain and continue to grow and move on. Because this is real life, & love so well-founded on knowledge and understanding and veneration doesn't fail because a gale, normal to the season, blows upon it!

Sylvia and I can scarcely endure to wait to see you. Come as soon as you possibly can.

Valentine

[On a third sheet included with above letter:]

Frome Vauchurch, Friday evening

I forbore to send this letter for reasons, wishing you to get Sylvia's only if you were drafted off directly you reached Paris. Now there is a chance to write—almost a civilized leisureliness again, and I am happy for it.

The wine came. It was like a dream; or like one of the things I find my mind persists in believing. I have an ineradicable expectancy of things exciting. God knows why, most times, but you have justified it: I went into the garage on a gloomy and wet afternoon; and found this strange wooden case on the floor, Mute and heavy. Then I saw Wine and Book on it—and then our names. I was cautious and tried to lift it, scarcely believing in it then. But immediately called Sylvia from her trudge to the gate, and we hauled it in and opened it with joy and that desperate wish to thank—I do thank you! We drank a bottle. We will drink some with you, Elizabeth.

With this I had meant to send you a photograph. I shan't, though. It is probably unjust, but how can one judge except, in matters of this kind, by one's own responses: and if I had a photograph and looked at it I should be too much loosed into remembering. But Sylvia and Tom on the deck will await you when you return instead!

I'm afraid you're having a hard course of intensive hanging-about. But believe me, you are happy now—you will remember every moment of strain and hardening and of finding your intentions strong and dependable. You will remember all that with intense happiness. I envy you profoundly for having achieved your going.

No more. But here is an entrancing side-light on Janet, and as fine a piece of unconscious irony as you could have: it gave us great happiness … she is telling me a conversation with a young man who was making love to her: 'He said he didn't know what he was going to do. He didn't fancy—(a word I've forgotten. Meaning not lying with anyone). I thought it was such an obvious thing to say—"

God bless us all. But you be better blessed than that, my dear.

Sylvia the same day sent comfort.

> Frome Vauchurch
> Maiden Newton, Dorset
> 19. x. 1938[64]

Dearest, always to be dear, Elizabeth.

I should like to think that we shall have met before this letter reaches you, but I must write at once.

Your letter and your telegram reached me this morning. I was out last night, so they could not telephone the wire. First of all, do not reproach yourself. It was fatality, not fault; and only one fatality, a single blackout, not anything in the true course of your star … a finger of the cloud that moves over all of us. You are a casualty, as much of a casualty as any fighter cast on to a stretcher, whether you were hit in Paris, in Madrid, at Winterton, here, it is a flying splinter from the same bombardment. All these long days I have been cursing the delay that kept you on this rack. I didn't expect it, I didn't not expect it. But I knew what you were exposed to, and that such things as breaking-points are a matter of laws, of stresses and strains, that the mind is material as steel or timber in this matter.

Next, what your doctor said was absolutely true. And I praise you for the disciplined mind that was able to accept the verdict; it would have been so easy to go on a little further into the refuge of madness; and you did not, and that is mostly admirable, and something must stead you now.

And last, you must come here as soon as you feel fit to travel—or else you must send for me and we will come back together.

33. Sylvia's telegrams to Elizabeth, 20 and 21 October 1938.

Try to cut out London if possible until you have been here. If it is a matter of gear, Janet can see to it; and if it is a matter of formality, formalities can wait. When you see our river flowing so beautifully and our looks of true love you will—no, not forget, forgetfulness is idle, and you have an industrious mind—but you will know that life is a co-operation with living, and that you love life and are right to love it, and that the things that befall one have significance, are not the mere dead weight of catastrophe.

I think of you with unchanged love, I want with all my heart to see you here. I weep for you, but it is with compassion, not with pity. You have done nothing to add to the burden on our hearts, there is no such thing as disappointment or disillusion. You must believe this, or you would not love us as you do.

Always,

Sylvia

That same day Sylvia commanded by cable:

I WANT YOU HERE IMMEDIATELY OR SHALL I COME TO YOU SAY WHICH STOP SONNET ONE HUNDRED SIXTEEN SYLVIA[65]

Shakespeare, Sonnet 116

Let me not to the marriage of true minds
Admit impediments. Love is not love
Which alters when it alteration finds,
Or bends with the remover to remove:
0 no! it is an ever-fixèd mark
That looks on tempests and is never shaken;
It is the star to every wandering bark,
Whose worth's unknown, although his height be taken.
Love's not Time's fool, though rosy lips and cheeks
Within his bending sickle's compass come:
Love alters not with his brief hours and weeks,
But bears it out even to the edge of doom.
If this be error and upon me proved,
I never writ, nor no man ever loved.

Elizabeth cabled her assent. Later, on 19 October, Sylvia wrote the second letter of the day.

Frome Vauchurch
Maiden Newton
19. X 1938[66]

Dearest Elizabeth,

Valentine is apt to be inspired; but never better than in that axiom about travelling without sonnets. When your wire came back, it was as though you had come with it, as though I had breathed you. And instantly my faculty for joy reasserted itself and I began to plan improvements in the spare-room. Thomas has been planning them too. He has been in and out all day, not just to compose himself in adult slumbers after his wont, but walking round the room enquiringly, and coming out rather sternly, as much as to say, Why isn't she here? Why am I being kept waiting? And presently he thumps upstairs and marches in again for another look. He is a very intelligent and sympathetic and resonant cat.

I am writing because I want to, not with any particular intentions on real life. Now that all letters to France go by air-mail they all take equally long to get there, and perhaps you will have started before this gets to you. I shall send you a practical wire about a possible meeting at Southampton. This evening here was the first See how Christ's blood streams in the firmament sunset and now it is freezing hard. The holly by the back door is like a dragon, drawn up rigidly ready to pounce. Let us go for a lot of walks. Visitor's walk, for instance. Visitor's walk is a track on the large-scale ordnance map; it goes up the hill behind the railway station and comes down again further on, and on the summit of the hill it has a fine view of British villages etc. I am constantly recommending it to visitors, and one and all they return assuring me that the track in non-existent, that they have lost their way, got entangled in bramble thickets, chased by cows, and so on. I am beginning to think it is time I explored it myself just to see if they are justified in their statements. For so far, like Noah, I have remained quietly within my ark.

I have just found this exquisite stage direction in Otway's *Soldier's Fortune*. 'Enter severall Whores and three Bullies.' It is so like the next international congress that I lament the purity of the *Daily Worker*—to whose light relief columns I would otherwise send it. I am finding Otway extremely repaying. I read him in the interests of rendering psalm 37 into verse: not an occupation I should naturally choose but a good-hearted stranger whose address is The Temple, Kansas City, is compiling a psalter after this fashion, a Tate and Brady by contemporary versifiers; and he is more of a scholar than you'd think, and says most honourably. In fact I feel very warmly towards him, it is David I find allergic.[67]

This letter, so full of nonsense, should tell you, if it reaches you in time, how very happy I am at the thought you are coming here. Happy without shame or arrière pensée. I will not bend the integrity of pleasure. I tell you frankly that however much I grieve for your sorrow, yet I look forward to your arrival with delight.

Sylvia

The next day Sylvia sent another cable:

SUGGEST MEETING YOU SOUTHAMPTON IF SO WIRE ARRIVAL LOVE SYLVIA

Less than a week later Elizabeth wrote Mary from Frome Vauchurch with the news that her hosts had asked her to stay longer.

That was a nasty crack in Paris ... Valentine, it seems, has also gone through something very like this time, and has talked to me a lot about it, and that is a great comfort. They have asked me with the most insistently and welcoming manner, to stay on here, and I shall do so for a week or two at any rate, thanking God, meanwhile for such true hospitality ... I look to find solid ground beneath my feet ... Since I broke on going to Spain; I have been in the grasp of the regular old fear neurosis of the White family variety,[68] something which must be recognized ... I could be with no better people than Sylvia & Valentine, in every intellectual and emotional response to life my sort of people ... my strange misadventure and their infinite kindness ...

It is a lovely time of year here; cold at night; warm sun; the ancient country belongs as much to the pre-Roman mystery-shrouded generations as it does to our own struggling, transient pre-Fascist one. Yesterday with a tiny sliver of moon coming up we went over to the lovely heights of Maiden Castle, a great flat hill near Dorchester where some little understood race carved those great circles of fortifications on the green smooth chalk earth, to protect themselves from what? It is an incredible, awe-inspiring place.

Goodbye my love, my dearest, I'll write soon again in the meantime you know how much my love is with you and all of you and dear, autumnal Breakneck, from your Bet.[69]

It took two weeks for Elizabeth's earlier letter from the American Hospital to reach her mother. Mary's reply went to Frome Vauchurch: 'I suffer with you—nervous strain, fear, unreal fatigue .... we all think of you constantly, my dear baby ...' She urges her to return to her intellectual interests, meaning the Anne Bradstreet research, and to come home. 'It will all be worth it dear Betty if you can come to the realization of where your first duty and responsibility lies—namely in doing the job in the world that has been given you to do. An intelligent understanding and decent respect for your own physical and mental balance and well-being—a consideration and care for those who are so deeply concerned and affected by what concerns you—and going on from there to study your own very special and individual powers now to give the world what you are best fitted to give.'[70]

Over the next weeks Mary repeatedly urged Elizabeth to return. In reply to an insistent cable on 4 November, Elizabeth told her mother that she was accepting the 'curious situation' as it is, 'one day at a time', and she was being well looked after in England.[71] The pressure mounted. On 21 November Mary pulled out all the stops:

Cabled last night to say that I hoped you would be back for Christmas. It is the natural, normal, logical thing for you to do and as such should be done. It is the considerate and kind thing for you

34. Elizabeth fishing on the Frome.
35. Sylvia and her niece, Janet Machen, 1938.

to do—doing something for the comfort and happiness of others takes you out of yourself and is the healthful thing to do and as such should be done.

It will break the thread of association of ideas which have wrought upset, nerves and unhappiness to you—and as such should be done.

Your dear grandmother is eighty four years old and becoming more and more frail. Who knows how many more Christmases [she will have] … relax here where you belong, with your very own family.[72]

On Thanksgiving Day, Elizabeth wrote home, 'thinking of you all', but—referring to a 'disturbing' cable from Wade urging her to return—she wanted to stay and not to face 'all the old associations and demanding complications of life at home' until she found a new balance 'which I can do better in England'. Though she had begun to get a grip on things, 'there is a temptation to run for shelter to you who can give it more than any other'.[73]

That November, Sylvia composed poems for Elizabeth, the first of which she dedicated to her.

And how is it that I, who made
this journey solitary and afraid,
see from this raw earth rising with clatter of splintered
glass the loved and the living and the betrayed—
not as I kept them, not as I wept them,
their spring is an eternal crystal bewintered,
but rough, bold, hardy, experienced and undismayed?
And dear of greeting I can let fall,
and not smutch them,
my heart can beat as it will
and not break them,
by sight and sound and touch

they are mine, and come at my call,
and I can have them or leave them, use them or quit them as I will,
and not forsake them.

[handwritten] S T W for E W W[74]

November, 1938.

Sometimes a Christ,
sometimes a Grecian Urn I placed;
or the curt credit-note of a headstone;
Here is deposited
poor Fred
who was alive, and is dead.

In mid-November, Sylvia took the step of writing to Mary White to assure her of Elizabeth's continued improvement under her and Valentine's care.

Frome Vauchurch
Maiden Newton
19. xi 1938[75]

Dear Mrs White,

I think you will be glad of a letter about Betty. As you know, she came straight here on her return from Paris, and has stayed with us since. When she arrived she was looking extremely ill. It wrung my heart to see her so peaked and strained, exhausted with lack of sleep and that long, that destructively long waiting about in Paris. I persuaded her first to go to bed and then to see my doctor. He is a Scotchman, very skillful, and with a great understanding of highly strung people: an appreciative understanding, I must make that clear. He told us there was nothing radically wrong with her, but great exhaustion and nervous tension and that she must resign herself to a long spell of simple living and not too much thinking. This, fortunately, is something which a country house can supply.

Quite apart from the delight of having her as a guest, I am thankful that he advised her to stay with us rather than experiment in nursing-homes; for my own impression was strongly that what she needed more than anything else was to feel herself cherished and well-thought of, not a strong point in nursing-home treatment, but the easiest thing in the world for any friend of hers to supply.

Now I am glad to say, she is really better: more relaxed and confident, and not so much inclined to reproach herself—for the Puritan conscience was terribly to the fore for a while. There are still ups and downs, and will be for some time yet. Dr Gray emphasized that it must be a long business, that she could not expect to pick herself up so briskly from an injury to the nerves as from an attack of measles. But she has made the great step on of feeling happy once more, and I think that is the step that counts.

Meanwhile she has a garden, and books, and a cat (fortunately we have a very soothing cat who adores her and has been most balsamic), and country that she likes, and company (I say this with the sincerest pride and pleasure) that she loves. And, as I say, she is getting back the power of enjoying such things. So I hope that, though I know you must be anxious about her, this report will make you feel less anxious. And you can be sure that while she is here (and I hope she will not think of moving just yet) we will take the greatest care of her. She must realise—it is very obvious—how greatly we love having her and what a delight it is to have her as a companion—and I think this will help her to recover from all the unhappiness and stress she has been through.

Yours sincerely

Sylvia Townsend Warner

However, not all was entirely calm at Frome Vauchurch. On a day when there had evidently been an emotional scene resulting in Elizabeth's storming out of the house, Sylvia left a note for her return which termed her action 'flight'. She wrote on a small sheet of lined paper and turned the edges down to simulate an envelope; in the folds she placed two leaves. Elizabeth preserved the note, the envelope, and the leaves in her journal notebook.

Dear Elizabeth,

I hate hurried explanations, and I had not time this morning to say what is in my heart. I can write it quicker. It is this

36. Sylvia's folded note for Elizabeth.

First—do not think that we only love you when you are at your best. We love you without reservations.

Second; and this is harder to say, but must be said, Think twice before you leave us. Flight is a danger to you just now, you should not give your accusing angel of a conscience any temptation to say to you—Elizabeth why did you run away? As a piece of gymnastic I think you ought to consider the useful effort of resisting this impulse of flight. I think it is an echo of what you've been through—try to strip your sails to it.

Last. Valentine is very wise, and very fond of you. If you can, open your heart to her. She will do it good.

All love,

Sylvia[76]

Valentine wrote three poems for Elizabeth that November, the first a love poem.

Frome Vauchurch, 17. XI. 38[77]

Scarlet the cock-crow sound in the black dawn,
but eyes darkened to see nothing, care drowned to silence hear
nothing; body lies still, limbs long outdrawn
and pale eyes, smooth as the sea-water stone,
covered. Oh, but scarlet-clear
the sound! And love, waking in fainting fear,
bows head to listen the steady, constant heart
and with swift kisses makes closed lids apart:—
Stare at the night that's gone, but see my darling—
Day finds you not alone.

at Winterton—November 1938

O very brightly in the distance, now again the light
that only sometime rises through my night
and shines—shines small and steady and clear
over a wilderness of woe and being lost—it looks most
kindly near
Not so, perhaps, nor know I what a light
fitful and bright and distant may intend;
but as a signal, certainly, and only now in doubt
whether of wrecker, foe, or such a timely friend
as who, storm-wracked, could hope when darkness blots it out?

All yesterday and all last night it snowed
And heavy the cloud hangs
Looming with sag of snow that will fall later.
Since morning the gangs
Have laboured to clear a single track on the road
Where a man comes by, wheeling a perambulator.

Ramshackle and ungainly, it jolts and careens
Over the frozen slush.
Stiffening himself, he tightens his grip on the handle
As though he must hush
At all costs the babe asleep there, and leans
A doting gaze over the darling a-dandle.

But the hood flapped back by the wind shows a billycan,
Old newspapers tied with twine,
Foot-rags, and a mug, and bundle of fuel.
Without a sign
Of question the road-men watch as he trundles on
His little ark, his life's holding, his heart's jewel.

'[A] very disturbing and hurting letter which served to deepen the anxiety and distress of soul which I have lived in since August', is how Mary replied to Elizabeth's letter of Thanksgiving Day in which she refused to return home immediately as her mother wished. 'If you were happy and healthy and accomplishing work toward the finishing of your book I could endure the long separation and your absence at Christmas ... It seems like a nightmare from which I cannot seem to awaken. If you are feeling well, concentrate on the Bradstreet book which had such a fine beginning.'[78]

A subplot in Mary White's effort to get her daughter to return involved a potential husband. Alexander Crane, from Cheshire, Connecticut, was an illustrator who shared with Elizabeth an interest in the genealogy of New England families.[79] For over a year he had courted her, confident of Mary's support, wrote letters, and clearly sought marriage. In December, he crossed the Atlantic to, as he and Mary White would have put it, rescue Elizabeth. At lunch at Frome Vauchurch he found himself up against formidable adversaries. He 'immediately made it clear that he had come to reclaim her', Sylvia recalled. 'He was familiar and overbearing and she submitted to it. Instead of welcoming this gross Godsend, I moved in to the attack. When I provoked him into being rude to me, Valentine added her cold steel to my slings and arrows. We tossed him between us till the end of lunch, when Elizabeth took his mangled self-esteem for a country walk.'[80]

Many men would have given up their quest immediately, but Elizabeth felt she needed to make herself absolutely clear by meeting him later in London. 'He does not in any way belong in this house,' she reported to Mary after the lunch with her sharp-tongued hosts, 'and I must in all honesty face the fact I have known for a long time, that his house and mine can never be the same. I tried again to tell him so, but he still insists on believing that I can be ground down and overborne at last ... I will go to London in a few days and if possible, make the transition ... to a civilized friendship' She added that there was 'beautiful autumnal weather' and at Frome Vauchurch she enjoyed 'the companionship of people I love so much.'[81]

'I know you think I am behaving very badly,' Elizabeth wrote her mother on 9 December. "I've been living, as you must know, an inconsequential and scattered life without much central solidity or direction, now, of a sudden, I have come face to face with this central hollowness and its imperative need to be filled. Now, or never, I must establish working relations with myself.' She forcefully rebutted what

Mary had evidently written: 'get away if you can with this "nightmare" idea. I am most definitely not with strangers in a strange land. England is in so many ways, as you know, your and my real home, and as you must know, too, my emotional and intellectual contact with Sylvia and Valentine is one which has often stood the test of separation and is now well and happily standing the other and better test of familiarity.' She breaks off the letter at this point because 'Valentine and I are going off on a sort of camping trip for a day or two to an old house in the middle of the downs. It is lovely windy weather, and not very cold and we are about to start.' What they shared on this this 'sort of a camping trip' irrevocably altered their and Sylvia's lives forever.[82]

Their destination was Rats' Barn in the folds of the downs between Chaldon and the sea, for some years a building leased to William Powys. He was infrequently there, and left it in the care of his sister Katie, who lived in Chydyok, itself in the downs and as remote. Katie once told a friend 'that she would pretend it was her own home, all her own, and happy as she always was to see her brother, when he was there she felt that he had taken away her home, her refuge'. It was thus a signal honor that Katie allowed Valentine to take Elizabeth there.[83]

Rats' Barn (see Figure 29) was so named because, in the account of a friend of Katie's, 'On the bank opposite the front of the house was a huge and really lovely stand of enormous sloes ... and in that bank the rats lived in their hundreds. They were really something to watch—Rats are really most playful creatures, and very inventive— and I fancy Katie found them a most amusing change from gardening.' She would regularly spend a night there with a 'routine [that] never varied—overnight things and food in the haversack (by food I mean bread, butter and such like, anything that couldn't be kept in an airtight, rat-proof tin. The rats weren't supposed to come indoors, but there were always a few who did) and off she would go, about an hour before sunset; she'd arrive, light up the fire on the big flat hearth, light the lamp, put on the kettle for tea. It was a low room, and not that large, and the house [was] sheltered, so even in winter it would soon be pretty warm. Tea was always tea, boiled egg and toast or bread and butter ... At sunrise next morning, she'd be up and washing, almost certainly with ice-cold water from the tap in the yard ... Then she'd light up the fire again, boil the kettle and make porridge and tea.'[84]

37. Valentine, Dorset, 1938.

A brief affair with Valentine years before had cut through the solitary Katie's armor of eccentricity; its memory became rooted and enlarged in her imagination, as she later conveyed to Elizabeth. The sensual tie between Elizabeth and Valentine would have been unmistakable, so it was a generous and deeply poignant act on Katie's part to make available a place so precious to her, a gift to ease the way for her adored one-time lover. It was pouring rain throughout their stay and according to her diary, Katie 'defied the weather each evening to reach them'. Although Valentine and Elizabeth shared a narrow couch the first night, and Katie might well have questioned why Valentine needed to entertain her friend so far from Maiden Newton 'it does not seem to have occurred to her that they might prefer to be on their own'.[85]

Discovering their own and each other's body, their kindred sensibilities, hopes, perceptions in 'the violent & ecstatic happiness of these three days', as Valentine put it, propelled the women to share with each other the outer bounds of human happiness. Those rainy December days and nights together in Rats' Barn changed their lives forever. Valentine, amply practiced in physical love, had an experience that evidently took her beyond anything previously experienced and beyond the domesticity of her life with Sylvia. Ten years later when she and Elizabeth again shared a bed it was like 'being raised from the Dead'. 'Everything happened—I do not know how anyone can believe man to be mortal, who has experienced how instantly, in joy, he becomes a god.' And so it may have been at the first. To Elizabeth the time in Rats' Barn was an ecstatic end of the loneliness, uncertainty, and absence of physical love that had dogged her adult years. '[Y]ou came with a sharp sword and a gentle healing hand, and saved me and brought me out of this misery and now into a dazzle of light and truth,' Elizabeth wrote in the last journal entry of the year. Valentine uses the German 'ja' in the note she gave Elizabeth when they returned ('I love you I want you ja always'), perhaps thinking of the celebration of love in German *lieder*. But opera can also be apt—in *Die Walküre* Siegmund and Sieglinde escaped their loneliness and sorrow in an ecstatic union that showed them in a state of being beyond what they ever imagined and hoped for. And like them, and the yearning lovers of the *lieder* poets, Valentine and Elizabeth had to return to a complex reality.

38. Elizabeth, Dorset, 1938.

There was 'the work, all urgent, to be done!'—Valentine's phrase—and there would be complications, not least her tie to Sylvia, that neither could master.

For ten years the memory of what they shared in those days drove them on despite disagreements, distance, and a separation of ten years. What they shared on these days was likely the most powerful connection in either of their lives, almost beyond themselves to control. 'My darling, my darling,' Valentine wrote at the time, 'it is not possible for me to write to you as I want to do, because—for one thing I am still in a state of semi-stupor, semi-intoxication, from the violent & ecstatic happiness of these three days and the great difficulty adjusting mood & mind to present conditions—& there is work, all urgent, to be done! But—oh my dear, my sweet, my sun, my darling darling darling—I bid you remember, read, close your eyes & feel—listen, & you will hear again I love you I want you ja always: I remember our pledges, repeat them, most sensually intend them—I love you Love me always—'[86]

At first Sylvia tolerated the affair, but the combined 'S & V' concern for Elizabeth, such a characteristic of the friendship over the previous two years, was no more. Although Valentine would not leave her then or ever, Sylvia was on the outside. 'In December I removed myself to the spare room's single bed', she recalled. In the next months, she would become angered by the protégée whom she had nurtured, educated in politics and social concerns. Her affectionate letters were past, the 'priesthood' gone.[87]

There was now no possibility of Elizabeth returning home for Christmas. Mary sent an admonishing letter that reached Dorset shortly before the holiday. She told of the 'gloom of trying to adjust in my mind to Christmas without you'. Of Will she reported that 'the snowy days put him into a depression', and added, 'May I have the privilege of an old mother and say this. Don't forget the dignity and pride of loyalty to your own country in your response to the charm of another. Don't concentrate with too much intensity on the inner state of Betty … I want you to be happy and find the poise and peace that your own special temperament calls for. Don't expect too much of life …'[88]

Elizabeth sought to remain a dutiful daughter and in a letter that crossed Mary's set out her reasons for staying abroad. As soon as she read it Mary cabled:

> THANKS CABLE WONDERFUL LETTERS HAPPY ABOUT YOU NOW
> LOVING WISHES, MOTHER.[89]

She followed with a letter: 'Finally, when it seemed I was at the last limit of my endurance two letters came from you this morning. Five weeks since the last was written. It was a very great help to have your clear explanation of your state of mind and body and your intentions, and wishes, and plans … I will try to pick up my courage; it will be a lonely Christmas, but [I am] relieved; Daddy is much better, no aches and pains, and seems to be enjoying life; he plans to motor south in mid-January.'[90]

On Christmas day Elizabeth described to Mary the household and the house and how she and 'S & V' spent the holiday. It was 'the most unexpected Christmas day of my life, strange, and, of course, a homesick but withal a happy one.' Outside there was

> ... snow on the Dorset hills and meadows around this great solid house, and sea gulls and small English robins and other sorts of lovely little birds, biting all pieces of bread that we throw out of the kitchen window into and beside the river for them. A still and brooding air after a week's beginning of extreme, New England cold, and, then, a day's and night's fall of snow which made a strangely unfamiliar and yet homelike—looking England for me. It has been a quiet and detached day, no churchly or social gregariousness because S and V don't go in for that sort of thing and their friends about here have either gone away for Christmas or are too far away on the downs to be within easy visiting distance in this weather. There is holly in the house, brought by the beautiful blond child of a carpenter who lives nearby, and mistletoe and we spent the morning on presents and then ate heavenly Turkey with Jerusalem artichokes (freshly dug out of the garden!) and lovely sparkling burgundy, for Christmas dinner.

> After that we sat in Sylvia's writing-room over coffee and cherry brandy and listened to marvelous music on their gramophone, Bach's Brandenburg Concerto No 5, and took apart and put tougher again a Christmas flashlight that didn't work properly and gave each other excellent hair-cuts. All the time I kept thinking with proper mathematical calculations as to time, what you all must be doing at home. Then the short English day melted into darkness and it was time for supper, an exotic one of very small mackerel packed like sardines in white wine and oil and strange crisp Indian things called Poppadamus, and in the evening we listed to church services on the radio, and Sylvia and I played a game of chess which was terribly demoralized by the background of a wireless version of Snow-white squeaking and hooting with simpering all through it.

39. Valentine, Dorset, 1938.

The house is 'old, family built, very comfortable ... lately done over and civilized with light and water and electric heat ... it stands on a meadow (which is just beyond the substantial village of Maiden Newton beside the small and romantic river Frome.'

It has a lovely wild garden of hit-or-miss vegetables and flora and hub patches and ragged box hedges and many antique apple trees, with a mysterious, formal, stone-walled, and gated back wall which seems too old and handsome to belong with the house, but of which no explanation can seem to be found. It is filled to overflowing naturally with a fascinating jumble of books, among which appear many good old pieces of furniture, simple and business-like modern ones, garden tools, fishing rods, curtains of Morris chintz, interesting pictures, a marvelously well-toned hand-made gramophone with most beautiful records, a large and very stately gray cat named Thomas and an enchanting black

Pekingese named Kumquat. There are no domestics whatever, but an admirable individualistic system of orderliness in chaos, as it were, which works happily from meal to meal and day to day, and a grand sturdy Dorset woman living nearby who does the laundry and occasionally gives the house a thorough cleaning. Both S & V cook with the creative skill and dispatch of the creative artist, and I make myself useful in the more humble household activities. It is so interesting and informative to see how comfortably life can go on under such circumstances. Of course, I am paying my share of regular household expenses, which I am emphatically assured amounts to no more than 30 shillings a week, and altogether I feel more at home and happy here than I have especially since I am stronger in spirit and in body than I was in the autumn, than I ever have anywhere except in my own native New England house.[91]

Sylvia recalled a blot that evening, one that prompted withdrawal from her mentoring concern for Elizabeth. 'At Christmas all was duly merry until the idle of dinner, when in my too lighthearted acknowledgment of the new state of things, Elizabeth plunged into injured gloom. It was the first time I had seen her show real feeling. The sight was intimidating. In the morning she was still morose. Valentine announced that we would go out for the day.'[92]

Despite this, before leaving for a Boxing Day outing to Winterton, Sylvia again wrote to Mary White with no hint of the strain she was under.

Frome Vauchurch
Maiden Newton
26. xii. 1938[93]

Dear Mrs White,

I have to thank you for two letters. I am very glad to learn from the second that you have had mine about Betty. I am even more glad that now I can tell you that she is really very much better, looking far stronger, sleeping without any sedatives, and almost free from those fits of depression and uneasiness. The recovery has been slow; it was not a thing one could safely hasten; but I now feel that it has been sure, and that she will carry no permanent scar from all she went through. In fact, I hope she will even be the stronger for it; for it is extremely establishing to make a good job of anything, and she has certainly made a good job of her recovery. It was far more in her hands than in anyone else's. We could help; but the initial purpose and perseverance had to come from her.

She is now in what I suppose to be a completely normal state of receiving books from public libraries by almost every post. She is doing an article on Woad. I did not think that one obsolete vegetable could figure in so many sources; but it does; and she will soon know everything that can be known about it. Perhaps after that she will turn to Anne Bradstreet. Meanwhile she is teaching me a great deal about herbs, and approving of my peppermint tea, and being a most soothing and solacing housemate. You ask if I think you should have come in November. If I had thought so, I should most certainly have cabled to you; and would, at any time, if it seemed necessary. But putting truth before tact (which is usually a very weakened form of truth), I will say that I think it was better that you did not come. She was then in such a very sensitive state that any further emotional strain or sense of being an obligation must have weakened her resistance. There are times when the companionship of the people one does not know intimately is the best, the most disinfecting poultice; and I think this was one of those times. Because we did not know her with perfect intimacy it was better for her to recover her poise; and the slight discipline of living in some one else's house, and conforming to their usages, was a very valuable astringent during the first week or so.

I am so glad you have had happy letters from her. She certainly gives me an unequivocal impression of happiness now; and I hope you will have many more such reassuring letters.

Though this letter will reach you some time after the New Year I will send by it my best wishes for a happy 1939.

Yours sincerely,
Sylvia Townsend Warner.

By the way, you will have read in the press perhaps of our cold Christmas. I must allay a mother's anxiety by telling you that we saw to it, earlier in the season, that she was well supplied with suitable woollen buttress against such a cold snap.

The three women motored to Winterton to revisit Valentine's treasured house and landscape and see her mother, Ruth, who got along well with Elizabeth and was to remain friends with her until her death.

At New Year in Winterton, Valentine gave her a present. Elizabeth placed the note that accompanied it by the last page of her journal. With it was a bay leaf likely picked on a walk by the sea.

Elizabeth-

Don't be angered by this present—You will look very splendid in it, & as I love to see you.

My darling—may we [ ] New Year, loving & beloved.

Valentine

31 XII 38

1 1 39

Elizabeth made the final entry in the journal she had kept for ten years: 'an old year, an old life, dies, and another comes passionately and fearfully alive.'

Winterton 1:1:39

My darling, shall we ever see another New Year in together, with such a desperate kiss of joy and sorrow and longing as found us together breathlessly last night? Here on the edge of the sea, across these gray-green winter dunes, an old year, an old life, dies, and another comes passionately and fearfully alive. In these just past months of darkness all the old fears and mistakes have rounded upon me, first to defeat me from going to Spain, then to draw me very near to the edge of death. Then you came with a sharp sword and a gentle healing hand, and saved me and

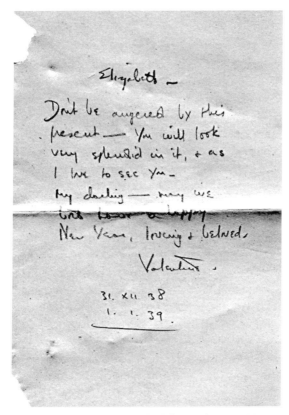

40. A New Year's note to Elizabeth from Valentine, 1938.

brought me out of this misery and now into a dazzle of light and truth. The way is a difficult and beautiful one, my darling, help me to follow it truly, remembering the bridge and Rats' Barn and the [question?] and all the lovely nights and days that now belong to us for ever. Help me to be brave and strong and alive. Valentine, I love you.[94]

V. She is like the sea

What each of the women had hoped for did not come to be in 1939: Sylvia did not regain Valentine's undivided love; Valentine's passion for Elizabeth rested uneasily with her love for Sylvia; Elizabeth learned that Valentine would not fully commit to her. What they hoped for in world affairs failed too: the Loyalist cause in Spain collapsed; Stalin joined with Hitler dooming Poland and setting off war with Britain and France. The three women spent nine months of the year largely in each other's company or close by in Dorset, New York, and Connecticut.

After the return from Winterton in January 1939 it was a strained household at Frome Vauchurch. Sylvia slept alone in the spare room— which Elizabeth had occupied earlier. 'According to the lights of the day,' Sylvia wrote in retrospect, 'I was behaving correctly in a quite usual situation. The only item by which I could have bettered my conduct would have been to take a lover. But I desired Valentine as sensually as ever, which saved me from that complication, as it saved me from any deviation into maternal kindness.' Claire Harman comments that after Christmas Sylvia was released 'from the grip of her good intentions' by the experience of Elizabeth's moods; she 'allowed herself to be unhappy—for herself and for Valentine ... [when] 12 January arrived, the eighth anniversary of their marriage, [there was] a love poem from Valentine pinned on the pillow of Sylvia's single bed, but no Valentine.'[1]

By January 1939 Mary White had accepted her daughter's absence, and thereafter her letters were mostly concerned with her own doings, the annual move to the South Carolina camp being prominent. Elizabeth wrote in early February that Chamberlain is 'obsessed with power, leading his country and the world into chaos'. She was impressed with Roosevelt's speaking out forcefully, 'even if courting the Jewish vote': 'England is watching America'.[2]

In a departure from family news, Mary replied that what 'I feel most badly about—is where you feel that Chamberlain is treacherous, complacent, obsessed with a sense of power. Not that I question the wisdom of your opinion, but that one clings to the thought that England must be right, never having let one down yet, and where are we in a world of confusion if we cannot [trust] ... England's unshakeable

41. Valentine, Eduardo Ruiz Alcaya, Sylvia, Señora Alcaya, Ludwig Renn, at the Dairy House, Chaldon.

integrity and wisdom and straight thinking & right doing. I cannot give up my ideas along these lines yet.' She enclosed an article, 'Uncle Sam Scares Europe', by Demaree Bess from the *Saturday Evening Post*. Based on a recent trip around Europe's capitals, Bess found acceptance of the Munich settlement and an expectation of peace ahead. 'England has ceded control of Europe to Germany and that should stabilize affairs'. Showing his political perspective, he added, 'The threat is from the activist US New Deal administration.'[3]

In February, Elizabeth wrote that she planned to rent the cottage called the Dairy House in Chaldon and take in two Spanish refugees, 'to give Sylvia and Valentine a respite from my company'.[4] The cost was the equivalent of $10 a week; the cottage came with two caretakers, Mr and Mrs B M Smith, the latter of whom became a regular correspondent, reporting to Elizabeth on Chaldon matters over the years.[5] With some difficulty Elizabeth took up housekeeping at the Dairy House—running a household on her own was a new experience. Like Katie, she knew how to boil water and little else. Valentine helped her to move in and set up the household and regularly visited. The move was a relief to Sylvia, freeing her from the strain of Elizabeth's daily presence, although not from her concern over Valentine's partial estrangement.

42. Valentine and Elizabeth at the Dairy House, Chaldon, spring 1939.

43. Elizabeth's notes for a dinner on 2 March 1939.

By early March, Elizabeth was entertaining at The Dairy House, with 'S & V' expected for dinner on the 2nd, Janet Machen later in the week and tea for 'Martin and Varda.' [6]

There was also unhappiness. Six days later, Elizabeth made an entry in her notebook which Valentine read and commented on.

9: iii: 39
[EWW hand]

No, the heart does not break, it turns to stone and lies cold and heavy in the breast. I know that now waiting in this Dorset village on an afternoon of sad still mist, hearing the funereal voice in the church yard, seeing the water drops hang sad and still from the cross-shaped hedge twigs. And, later, from Katie's copy of Whitman I take these words:

... wherever my life is lived, O to be self-balanced for contingencies.

To confront night, storms, hunger, ridicule, accidents, rebuffs as the trees & animals do.

On a matching sheet of paper, Elizabeth wrote:

My darling,

You have not come, and we must go now. Here is a little book for you, it's not very inspired poems. Say some good things.

[note in VA hand on the same page]

N.B. I did come.[7]

In that stressful time, Elizabeth hoped in a poem that her 'winter heart' would come unlocked.

Shall we blame Spring because the Winter stays
So long, claiming our hillsides as his own
While stone is now and the earth is stone
And no life quickens through these bitter days?

Should he not quail before the subtle ways
Of the young season—the first leaf-bud, shown
To warm him, heralding a million blown
Across his acres in a warm bright haze?
How many frozen leagues apart we stand
Why do our quiet words meet with no shock
Of soft & sudden glory in that said air?
I know the strength & kindness of your hand
And yet I know no word that will unlock
My winter heart, and let spring riot there.[8]

When Sylvia offered to leave Frome Vauchurch so Elizabeth could live there, Valentine dissuaded her. As Harman sensitively writes of Valentine and Elizabeth at this time, Elizabeth was 32, Valentine's junior by a few weeks, and naturally did not choose to 'share' her with anyone else. This was her first profound experience of falling in love, and seemed to call for a special degree of commitment. Unfortunately, it was the latter of which she reminded Valentine most frequently, and Valentine's love and lust for Elizabeth became inextricably mingled with a sense of guilty responsibility which prevented any member of the triangle from being satisfied with the situation, let alone happy. [9]

The civil war in Spain was ending in defeat for the Loyalists; Barcelona fell to Franco's forces in January, Madrid on March 28, 1939. Ludwig Renn, whom Sylvia had met in Spain when he was serving with the International Brigade, survived the fall of Barcelona and was interned in France as a stateless person. At Louis Aragon's request, Sylvia agreed to sponsor Renn in the UK and put him up. 'He had no money, he had no future, he had sat starving behind barbed wire at Angeles, he had an unhealed wound, he had seen the bitter defeat of his cause. He had kept his interest in humankind and his slightly frivolous goodwill.' His arrival cheered her up; she welcomed his way with Elizabeth; 'once when seeing her in one of her fits of gloom, he said, "Now we will dance," bowed a court bow, put his arm round her waist and waltzed with her on the lawn.' [10]

The three women spent Easter in Winterton visiting Ruth, Valentine's mother. Sylvia wished that the light-hearted Renn had been with them as he could have 'managed' Ruth as well as he managed Elizabeth.[11] In late April, he and Valentine visited the Dairy House where Elizabeth snapped a photo of them with their Spanish visitors (see Figure 41).

The Spanish refugees were Señor and Señora Eduardo Ruiz Alcaya from Valencia where he had been Director of Fine Arts in the Republican government. According to Elizabeth, they escaped by a day their execution by the fascist forces. She later recalled the challenges of preparing meals and running a household for urban people who had no interest in the rural life around them, which they associated with peasants and primitive living conditions. 'They sat about all day, quite out of their element.' The Alcayas' stay lasted about a month, until mid-May.[12]

Sylvia wrote to Elizabeth at the Dairy House to acknowledge an Easter present of a book by Vernon Lee, a sign of civil, though distant, relations between them.[13]

F.V. M.N.

5. iv. 1939[14]

Dearest Elizabeth

I think Valentine must be growing materialistic. She remembered the loaf, and the butter; and forgot to give you my message of thanks for Vernon Lee.

I think it is a book I am going to be extremely fond of. So far I have only dived around in it; and that has pleased me a great deal, with all the mysterious people called Byzantium and Helena and Johnson appearing and disappearing and appearing again, like the theatre folk in Wilhelm Meister. And I like the idea of a book on music that is not dogmatic. Thank you very much. When you come here on Monday please write my name in it.

I am so glad you are coming. I hope there will be time for you to look inside each separate tulip: they are well worth inquiring into. The large crimson ones that seem to be wholly taken up with being large and crimson have very small lancet windows where the petals join the stems and the lancet windows are a delicate French grey.

My love

Sylvia

That spring Sylvia was invited to the Third American Writers' Conference to be held in New York in June, called to discuss the decline of democracy in Europe. Despite the tensions between the three women, 'the trip offered such a good opportunity for Elizabeth to go home and yet not be parted from Valentine', that they chose to go together—Sylvia no doubt also to keep watch on Valentine.[15] In preparation, Sylvia prompted the responsible charity to find another home for the Alcayas.

Frome Vauchurch Maiden Newton, Dorset
14. v. 1939[16]

Dearest Elizabeth.

While we were in London I went to that Montagu-Pollock set-up to ask what/if they were doing about the Alcalas [sic]. As I suspected, I found they were sitting back in great tranquillity on their assurance to you that they would do something. So I represented to them that they had better start doing something immediately, since it would be very inconvenient both to the Alcalas and yourself to be left without plans till the last moment.

I hope this made some small impression. But I think it might be as well, if you have not heard anything definite from them by Thursday, to put through a call to them, reiterating that something must be fixed before the very 20th itself.

Love from

Sylvia

The Alcayas were re-settled, and the three women sailed on the SS *Aquitania* from Southampton on 20 May. Ludwig Renn came with them, passage paid by Elizabeth, and Tomas, a cat from London (found by Valentine's sister) travelled in the pet cabin. He would live to a grand old age with Elizabeth in New York City and Connecticut, his condition and activities always of interest to Sylvia. His fare was £1.0.0. [17]

On the pier to meet them was Evelyn V Holahan, a professional young woman—only a year older than Valentine and Elizabeth—born in Rochester, with a New York City job and a small apartment in Greenwich Village. Sylvia and Valentine had invited her to meet them. Evelyn had met them in Chaldon under odd circumstances. She had crossed the Atlantic and come to remote Dorset to 'rescue' her younger sister. Anne had been an aspiring actress in New York. Llewelyn Powys, then in the city, had met her in one of the Greenwich Village bohemian circles. The young girl took his fancy, as did many others, and they had an affair. (Years later Elizabeth described Anne as 'crazy ... [and the affair with Llewelyn was] causing all sorts of trouble.') [18] Llewelyn and his wife, Alyse Gregory, left the city for the Chaldon downs, and likely forgot about the fling he had with Anne. She wouldn't accept rejection, crossed the ocean and pursued Llewelyn into Dorset where for a time she would have been an unstable and unquiet stranger. Evelyn in 1935 went on a rescue mission to bring her home. While in Chaldon she met Valentine and Sylvia who enjoyed her salty sense of humor and good cheer as they would again in New York. The three corresponded and Valentine's letters suggest an intimacy indicating Evelyn had been one of her many short-term lovers.

Evelyn later recounted how she sailed to England by freighter, the sole woman, and the sole legitimate passenger, as the others were immigrants being deported for criminal activities. (The steamship company returned her fare when she complained about being exposed to this dangerous lot.) Sylvia and Valentine with their sharp eyes must have been entertained by the spectacle of the young American women, the lovelorn and her rescuer, unexpectedly arrived into the remote hamlet of Chaldon. [19]

In 1936, Sylvia had been delighted to learn from Evelyn that she was to visit them again—on the newly launched *Queen Mary*. She asked Evelyn to bring a copy of Havelock Ellis's *The Psychology of Sex*, prohibited in Britain. It was a personal request, but Sylvia was somewhat formal, signing with her full name.

24 West Chaldon Dorchester, Dorset

14. v. 1936[20]

Dear Evelyn,

I discover from Robert Benchley in the *New Yorker* that one can now buy in American Havelock Ellis's *Studies in The Psychology of Sex*—pleasant books that I enjoyed a great deal when I was young, and have always wanted to give to Valentine who hasn't read them. One can't buy them in this country, and I have failed to steal the edition that embellished my tender years ... and incidentally it had an inspired misprint, and referred to the public hair.

I wonder if you can possibly bring over a couple of volumes? The buying is easy enough. My publishers, the Viking Press, 18 East 48th Street, would buy them for you and put it down to my account with them (and I enclose an authorization, in case you don't know the firm). The best way of getting them across would be as your own property, so would you please write your name in the first two volumes, and dogsear them a bit, and underline a few passages? Then if the customs unearth them you ought to be able to explain that they are your own books and that you brought them for holiday reading; and if the worst comes to the worst, the customs should allow you to mail them back to the USA. Which would not get them any nearer Valentine, I admit, but it would save me the agony of spending money on books which my dear native land would cast into the bonfire. As for the other two volumes, they can wait at the Vikings for another chance.

I hope this is not a great deal of trouble. And if they are inordinately expensive I will leave it to your discretion—but anything up to forty dollars or so for the set I would not complain at.

We look forward to your coming. The thought that you will come by the *Queen Mary* has done a great deal to support us through the campaign of advertisement which the vessel has unloosed. I hear that the decorations are intolerably sprightly, but that the mattresses are good. Mattresses are more important.

There has been a long gap since your last letter to Valentine. I do not say this reproachfully, but a little uneasily. I hope it does not mean that you are ill, or that there is anything wrong, or imperiling your plan of coming over. We should be very sorry if it were so.

Sincerely,

Sylvia Townsend Warner

[In VA hand, with arrow pointing to 'I hope it does not mean that you are ill.'] I hope this, too!

Evelyn did not return to Chaldon. She may have started a new job as Sylvia in her next letter referred to the season being a good one in offices. As a result, *The Psychology of Sex* in its American edition also did not cross the ocean, dog-eared or not. Evelyn had compatible political views and sent a clipping from the strongly anti-fascist *New Masses.*

24 West Chaldon Dorchester Dorset
23. vii. 1936 [21]

Dear Evelyn.

Thank you very much for sending the review of *Summer Will Show* from New Masses. I should not have seen it otherwise: I find that reviews make me either too humiliatingly annoyed or so humiliatingly elated that it works out best not to collect them: but I should have been very sorry not to read this one.

We were very sorry when you could not come here. I suppose it is useless to mention that October is a very beautiful month in the country; employers seem of one mind that is a very beautiful month in the office too.

Yours sincerely
Sylvia Townsend Warner

Evelyn at the time was sharing an apartment at 26 Jane Street in Greenwich Village with Mia Frisch, who later married James Agee, the writer. At the *Aquitania's* pier in May 1939, she met Elizabeth for the first time; the two were to become lovers in 1940 leading to a lifelong partnership. Sylvia and Valentine stayed with her on Jane Street and as their correspondence shows, enjoyed being shown the city through her eyes. [22]

Louis Aragon, Sylvia's admired French Communist friend, was one of the speakers at the opening session of The Third American Writers conference, 2 June 1939, at the New School for Social Research on West Twelfth Street. The other speakers were Melville J Herkovits, the American anthropologist, who was at work on studies of American Negro culture, and Donald Ogden Stewart, the playwright and screenwriter, one of the founders of the Hollywood Anti-Nazi League.

Elizabeth went directly from the pier to the Breakneck house to rejoin her family and to prepare them for a visit from her companions. She looked forward to showing the house and grounds as Valentine had shared Winterton with her. Sylvia stayed in New York for the Congress and to visit with friends, one of whom was the composer, Paul Nordoff, with whom she kept up a lively correspondence. Valentine went to Breakneck to be introduced to Will and Mary White, Sylvia to follow a few days later.

With her long-practiced hostess skills, Mary may have been publicly gracious, but she and Will had never entertained a woman who had hair cut like a man's, wore a tie, was clearly a lesbian—an unmentionable word and concept—and who had captivated their daughter. Beyond that, she was a communist and drank too much. Valentine later acknowledged that she was 'drunken and lecherous' on the visit. Wade White recalled that she made passes at one of the maids and smoked cigars. The social and emotional equivalent of a bomb had exploded in the White household. [23]

There were letters. From Evelyn's Jane Street apartment in Greenwich Village, Sylvia counseled Elizabeth not to continue to press Valentine for a long-term commitment and to enjoy her in the present. Sylvia was briefly back in a mentor role, masking her own jealousy and unhappiness: live in the present and enjoy Valentine when she is with you, not cloud the present by trying to make a future certain. Elizabeth was unlikely to have been responsive.

26 Jane Street, NYC
8.vi. 1939[24]

Dearest Elizabeth.

I am just back from Washington; and the flat is full of your kindness and Valentine has been showing me the things you sent, but I have not yet grasped them enough to write a proper thanks for them, because what is first and chiefest on my mind is your letter. I wish I knew the answer. A theory about suffering is not an easy thing to have, one might as well have a theory about cancer. That is to say, one at once admits its existence, and desires to put it out of existence, and suspects with considerable backing of evidence, that a good deal of it, at any rate, could be abolished; but never really knows how, for what works in one case don't work in another, and so one is forced back on that irritating half-truth that it is a question of individual reactions. Some cats can swim and some cats can't. But both as myself and as a Marxist—I was myself first—I will not sit down on that half-truth. There is more to it than individual reactions; and the individual reaction of the sufferer is not the only factor, one must also include the individual reaction of the person who tries to cure. I wish more people would realize this. In cancer they do. They blame the doctor, they don't say it is all their own wretched fault that the suffering can't be cured. In cancer we are more scientific.

Sometimes I think that the question of suffering is a question of partial adaptation. Say you have a long journey, and tight boots. The moment comes when by every physical good reason those boots should come off. But a moral sense (probably based on fear, since fear seems to be the basis of all morality) says: If you take off those boots you may never dare put them on again. And you have a journey to go. And so one endures the ills one has, rather than face the sharper complication which involves the antagonism of relief and after relief an extra effort; and the boots stay on; and

44. Wade, Mary and Will White on the Breakneck house terrace.

limping and sore feet become elaborately identified with going a journey, instead of being identified, as they should be, with uncomfortable boots.

As you know, I am for taking the boots off. I am for the risk of being a hedonist, I think one should enjoy oneself exactly when and how one can, and be damned to the moment when the boots must be put on again. For one thing, one may be struck dead at any moment, and what a fool one would feel to die unhappier than one need be; and for another, every relaxation of emotional pain is a claim staked on happiness, either for oneself or for humanity. It seems to me that one is letting every one else down by being unhappy if one can possibly be anything else. It is marrying all one's daughters and granddaughters to a bad husband, just because one has married a bad husband oneself.

I suppose that is as far as I have a theory of suffering. It is a severe one because it makes one extremely skeptical towards the suffering of others. It obliges one to say, Need you have such sore feet instead of What sore feet you have. One does not deny the soreness of the feet (at least I hope I don't); but one does deny the obligation to keep on those boots.

I know you are unhappy, and have been, and have reason for being unhappy. But it seems to me also that you have had times when you need not be unhappy, when you have been with Valentine, which is your happiness; and that you have not made the most of those times; because you have tried to make of them more than the most. That is to say you have tried to make a fine day into an insurance against bad weather, you have thought more of what it will be like when it is over than what it is like at the time. And things are only what they are at the time. There are no permanent moments. Whether the clock the calendar or the dead knell end the moment it is a thing that must end. There are no roses that one can gather tomorrow.

Archibald MacLeish says the same thing about poetry when he says: Poetry can not have an elsewhere. He means that there can be no second chance for a poem, no redeeming blood can make it better than it is, no heaven can improve its rhyme-schemes. It is unredeemable. Happiness can have no elsewhere either. It is now or nowhere. The poet knows this in his blood, he concentrates on getting that poem as good as it can be. The person in love, the person in lust, the person in pursuit of pleasure must do the same thing—if he is not to be an amateur.

I am certain you were not designed to be an amateur in love. And if I say these things to you it is exactly because I am treating you as a serious artist. I have always treated you as a serious artist, that is why you first liked me, that is why I now seem to you at times extremely harsh and unsympathetic. But it seems to me this. You have the quality to be a serious artist, in loving, in living; and you have been brought up to be an amateur. An amateur in love is a philanderer. All your training has been designed to minimize the serious sensuality of your character, to make you a philanderer in love instead of a serious lover. And this conflict between character and upbringing now edges you towards that blind alley way out (but it is not a way out, it is a way to the prison, the brothel or the convent) of being unhappy, of relaxing yourself into a frame of mind which says, as your letter says: 'There seems to be such an immensity of suffering, so much energy, so much potential happiness and accomplishment poisoned at the source and rotting into waste and expense of spirit.'

But if you would speak honestly out of yourself you should by now be able to say: 'Ackland, Valentine is coming on Friday.' Just that.

Can you bear an experiment? Try this. The next time you begin to think of this cosmic suffering that makes an enormous cloudy shadow of your own black unit, analyse in yourself how much of that suffering really affects you; how much of it is a deepening of your own suffering, how much of it is on the other hand, a supporting, a sympathetic thought. How much of it, in fact, is really a thorn in your side and how much of it a trailing cloud of dark glory. You will find, for you are not a shallow person, that some of the suffering around you really and genuinely does make your unhappiness worse. But a lot of it doesn't. A lot of it either isn't there, or you don't know enough about it to establish its existence. In fact, you have been taking it on guess. And you have been taking it on guess because sorrow and weltschmerz come drowsily and soothe the wakeful anguish of the soul.

You see, I have come round to this. I am advising you not to soothe your anguish, in order to be happier, in order to have a stronger and more instantaneous hold on the joy that comes your way. It is not a council I would give to any one unless I respected them and their capacity to be more than an amateur.

With my true love

Sylvia

When Sylvia arrived at Breakneck for a two-day visit, she found Valentine 'looking gay, wicked, and imperturbable. I delighted in the beauty of her neck and shoulders (it was a formal dress for dinner hospitality) and at seeing her outside the rest of the company as a

```
                    it is a wednesday

           and all it means

                    is that on a sunday preferably and
                    probably this coming one if the sun
                    is shining and all is well

               that gordon the archangel and
                 st simeon will
                         without a doubt
                            really

                 venture to breakneck hill
                     sometime
                         during
                             the long and hot

                     summer afternoon  and
                     to remember this
                          is most
                     important for saints
                     and sinners for

            ' so much holiness will not
              have gathered since
                  a week or seven
                  days ago

            sweep well the porch of
            the church that they may
            not dash their feet
                against stones

            and prepare for us and
              until the 10th - a red
              letter day (LOOK AT THE CALENDAR)
            - be patient

                    devotedly

                        dein liebes Herz
                        ach so moglich!
```

45. 'it is a Wednesday' by Valentine Ackland.

swan outshines a duckpond'. Sylvia and Mary instantly recognized each other as antagonists, convinced 'that I was the procuress of the situation. Tall, sour-faced, white-skinned, with pale blue eyes, she was a solidly corseted threat of what her daughter might become. The house matched her; it was overfilled with cautious good taste, exhaled rapacity. It was no house to love in.'[25]

The Breakneck Hill house and the society it exemplified were of the haute bourgeois world that 'S & V' shunned, and both had tried over the years to wean Elizabeth from the social and political views of the elder Whites and particularly Mary's influence. They returned to New York, and the elder Whites chose to absent themselves in advance of their next visit.

In New York, in a poem called 'it is a wednesday' Valentine looked forward to the 10th of the month when she would be with Elizabeth again at Breakneck (see Figure 45). Valentine confirmed her preoccupation with Elizabeth (and revealed a virtuosic manipulation of the typewriter) in a poem addressed to 'dear st elizabeth'—as in 'it is a wednesday', and there is a further mention of St Simeon, he who was practiced in waiting (Figure 46).[26]

225

46. 'dear st elizabeth' by Valentine Ackland.

That June Elizabeth too wrote poems that reflected her love for Valentine, its changes and surprises.

Now that delight is known—
In its true colours, tawdry, tired, damp
And sorrow has become a grinning mask,
Which vanishes while yet we suffer;
And underneath our skulls, where used to dwell
Or so the ages tell—
Truth, knowledge, reason and respect,
Are now a jig-saw puzzle, which, making do,
To build again is harder than we asked.
One thing is left, one refuge comforting
The desert of our dearth
Ancient, incontrovertible, unsexed:
The earth.

When you came quietly
So strong, so light of foot
And stood Aside me while absorbed intent I honored
In the brown earth a yearling primrose root,
June was about our days;
And when I rose and found you there
There could not have been any blossomed ways
On earth, as my small garden does, so fair.[27]

Sylvia was with Elizabeth and Valentine at Breakneck on 16 June (the Friday anticipated in the poem). The three had the great house to themselves— 'the parent birds are away', as Sylvia put it. They were attended by the two maids, the cook, and 'Curly', George Bassett, the chauffeur, named for his hair as a youth. George Worgan, born in Wales, kept the grounds and garden. Sylvia wrote Evelyn, whose flat she had just left and with whom she had a jocular relationship.

Breakneck Hill
Saturday [17 June 1939][28]

My dear Evelyn,

I left the iron in the limp hands of your nice Mr Skinner, having had a happy farewell play with it in the early hours of Friday morning so that I arrived here with a leafy quite reputable armoury of organdy.

There is something I must tell you, because it hinges on your stay at Mr Hearst and the jade statuettes. I happened to make friends with an old man in the Parish, Watson, Watson Galleries, where they have some of the Hearst collection. He showed me catalogue after catalogue—a whole one devoted to nothing but carved staircases collected by Mr H—and so forth.

I asked what on earth would happen to the antique market with this vast collection unleashed on it. He said— 'Well, that's been taken care of—and told me that after the principal art dealers of USA have gotten together on this, and made their ring. Every thing has had a reserve price put on it—not inordinate, but pretty high, and so Mr Hearst can whistle for a quick return on his investment in art.

Isn't this a fine example of dog eat dog?

I am still thinking of the evening views of NYC. I shall never forget that frilly pattern from the observation roof. And though I was sorry that your plan of a drive did not eventuate, I hope that my [next visit] has that. This house is like nothing on earth—except perhaps a Hearst collection.

But the country is lovely, and the parent birds are away, and following your advice I sleep over the young man; so I am enjoying myself.

Valentine looks very well—but has had some misadventures with mosquitoes.

Affectionately,

Sylvia

Valentine wrote Evelyn the same day.

Breakneck Hill
Middlebury, Conn.
17th June [1939][29]

Darling,

It was good of you to write to me, & I was happy & reassured to have a letter from you. Being near you, at least in the same country, has made me feel distinctly greedy for your companionship and the slight astringency which you hand out, which agrees well with my needs at this time. THIS IS AS SELFISH AS IT SOUNDS. Have no doubts about that. But I wish I could use Elizabeth's machine more accurately!

Sylvia is writing to you because you apparently had no need to have misgivings about the evening you gave her. Indeed, so I think, for she has talked of little else, and she certainly enjoyed herself very much. I'm glad you & she get on well. Good for both. How salutary a thing is a gentle and shared malevolence!

My god, Evelyn, what a country this is! I like BEST to see the new things you are making now, but the old are good too, and the old explain a great deal to me. I am glad to have seen them. I have seen a great deal—I have talked to people I wanted to talk to, and heard some of what I want to hear, I know now that I shall be literally homesick for this land when I'm back in my own. And that is logical enough, for the settlers who came from England to this place wanted to bring all the mind and heart of England with them, and re-establish it, uncontaminated and renewed. I don't know if they've done so, for I don't know that old mind and heart and the country they loved has long since died, as they knew it would—I don't know if they succeeded in bringing it over here and rearing a true plant from that small shoot. But our poets make me think they did—although NOW America is not at all England. But I have found something very much like a home here.

47. Valentine and Sylvia at Breakneck, June 1939.

I'm not being annoying, or am I? I am not in love with New England, but I am lusting after the whole of America—I want especially to be in New York with you and to be shown the city, but by you and by no one else till I've seen it with you. Can that be? I believe so. If you will spare some evenings and if you are not too tired. I won't be a nuisance and I am depending on your truth not to let me be. For that would be bad—

In this is a little nonsense for you. It is not what I want to give you. That would be most difficult to find, but the *Memoirs of a Midget* [by Walter de la Mare] will arrive in due course (the book I did tell you about) and that will present to you a reason for liking Burton's *Anatomy of Melancholy*, which I am giving you in bits, as you know, and so you will get two pleasures, I hope, of the kind I most want to give you.

Goodbye now, till Monday or at latest Tuesday. And please don't forget me meanwhile, for I am being very happy in your country and that is more than you know thanks to you—

Valentine

Back on Jane Street, Sylvia wrote Paul Nordoff that she had stayed in a queer place. 'A country house with large grounds about it, the whole thing only about twenty or thirty years old, and already its forest primeval is getting back on it ... the kitchen garden is gone back to pasture, the pastures have gone back to woodland, little trees poke up on the lawn. Every morning when I woke I more than half expected to see this angry Red Indian woodland marching down on the house like Birnam Wood coming to Dunsinane. It was romantic and intimidating.'[30]

Janet Machen decided to take advantage of Sylvia and Valentine being in America with Elizabeth to come to New York; and was set to reserve passage on the *Mauretania* for July (paid for by Elizabeth). From her twenty-one year old perspective, she sent consoling words and sage advice to Elizabeth who had written that she was 'worried in the head' and felt put upon by her mother. 'Mummy blackmails me too—I hope you have no sense of guilt about your mother, I think unconsciously your mother will work on your sense of guilt if she can, it's so wicked!' She has had a postcard from Valentine saying 'that they hoped to stay on a little, & that they thus would be able to see me … Valentine writes so warmly about the country, that it seems likely she will eventually live there for a while'—just as Elizabeth passionately urged and desired. [31]

It was characteristic of Elizabeth's generosity of temperament to want to share those she loved with others, to show 'her beautiful family'—as she had termed them on the *Bremen*—to her lover and to her sometime mentor. Not only did a female lover for their child defy everything Will and Mary wanted, there was Sylvia who appeared to be the influence that had brought this relationship to be. As communists under their roof they were a previously unimaginable threat to people who found the New Deal radical. Add to this Valentine's drinking, the cigars, and the quarreling and tensions between Elizabeth and her visitors, the occasion was unhappy for everyone concerned. Sylvia was inwardly and perhaps outwardly, scathing, and Valentine flaunted conventional behavior as she had done in London in her twenties. Elizabeth was miserable because she could not get a firm commitment from Valentine, uncomfortably aware that it was due to Sylvia's influence. She must have been affected by her parents' dismay and surely aware of the social fiasco she created, but she evidently could not bear the idea of not showing her beloved home grounds to Valentine as Winterton had been shown to her. She seems not to have considered the alternative of letting the visitors stay in the city.

What the painful visit did not lead to was a break in the family circle. Elizabeth continued to maintain her permanent home at Breakneck, and when she did take a flat in New York, she went home most weekends. Had she persuaded Valentine to leave Sylvia and remain with her in America, the outcome could have been different, but she was fiercely loyal to her parents, whatever the differences; in later years she would quote the adage that her grandmother had repeated to her, 'blood is thicker than water'. In that June, she entertained her visitors, and continued to accept Sylvia's role with Valentine, however uneasily and unhappily.

Sylvia had expected to stay in America about a month, but Elizabeth suggested in Dorset that the three take a house in Connecticut for the summer and use it as a base to explore New England. She rented what she later termed 'a funny little farmhouse' from a family named Kibbe in Warren, Connecticut, to the northwest of Middlebury. 'Sylvia fell in with this obviously unsatisfactory arrangement,' Harman writes, 'because she was desperate to be with Valentine again and sensed that Valentine too, wanted her nearby.' Valentine recalled of the months they spent in America, 'If Sylvia had not stayed by me, then I should have been damned out and out. I was lecherous and greedy and drunken there, and yet I had two very serious loves in my heart, even then—and poems, too, in my head.' Harman comments: that '[f]alling in love with Elizabeth had brought Valentine out of a period of lassitude in her creative life, and this was very important to her, for she had an almost superstitious fear of not being able to write. This and the renewal of lust and a genuine love for Elizabeth made the affair seem worth pursuing, despite the unpleasantness of the situation at Warren and Elizabeth's increasing possessiveness.' On her part, Sylvia later noted, 'Mere fidelity could have become a bore and a reproach; it was my dependence on her which called back her sense of responsibility and steadied her footing.' [32]

'I shall be sharing a house there for the next six weeks with two other petticoats (both of them, of course, wearing trousers),' Sylvia wrote Paul Nordoff. 'It is a completely plain-headed house, no instrument of music except a melodeon in the attic, but it is lovely country, full of wild raspberries and red-haired butterflies sitting on pink flowers, and cool mountain airs, and a general feeling of Robert Frost. I only know the charm so far, no doubt when I'm living there I shall know the drawbacks too; but it promises well, and anyhow the country is lovely—so if you could come for a week-end or so, I would be a great pleasure to me.' [33]

Curly Bassett, the Whites' chauffeur, met the women at a nearby station and drove them to the Kibbe house leaving them on their own for two days, 'two long days of childish happiness'. They loved the simplicity of the house, and the surrounding forest. 'We lived on raspberries and some biscuits we had happened to bring with us—there was no store within walking distance. At dusk there were fireflies and the forest rattled with cicadas ... we fell asleep to a chorus of bullfrogs.' [34]

Elizabeth was away when they arrived but had equipped the house with linens and utensils and had left Tomas the London cat, and their fellow passenger on the *Aquitania*, to welcome them. Sylvia was delighted.

The Kibbe House
Warren, Conn.
18. vii. 1939[35]

Dearest Elizabeth.

You have no idea how uplifted I feel, writing from this address which is so very much more american and creditable to the traveler's joy than New York.

This house is so pleased to be lived in, you've no idea how it has responded to your furnishings. It was already looking happier, I gather, when you saw it last; but you won't know it when you see it again, it is so beaming and obliging. It is obviously a very simple-hearted house, with but this one notion in life, of being a thing habitable. Everything works. The water flows, and is soft water, and when it flows the automatic pump functions as busy as a sewing-machine. The water boiler heats, and immediately hot water abounds. The freezer freezes, Mrs Kibbe's oil-cooker burns with a bluer and ardent flame, and in the cellar we found a spare mirror. The butcher is charming, and the Warren stores contain everything earthly, and relays of young Kibbes appear with milk, buckets, wash-bowls, various small items which Mrs Kibbe bethinks her we should be glad of.

The only dumb note on the keyboard is the telephone, which should have been fixed this morning, by what we were told. It isn't fixed yet; and what a pity, for I want to ring you up and tell you how lovely everything is, and how happy we are, and how happy we will be.

I can't begin to thank you and praise you for all your masterly foraging and staff-work. Curly met us at New Milford, how he got all the luggage onto and into the car I do not know (he did it

48. At the Kibbe house, Warren, Connecticut, summer 1939.
Sylvia, Valentine and Janet Machen.

privately, round the corner of the stations, bidding us wait while he saw what could be done); but it was so accomplished, and even left room for a parcel of things like bread and fig-ma-jigs, from Warren Stores. When we arrived we began to unpack your box and your basket, with cries of rapture and esteem. There is everything, and more. The kitchen looks like a show-window of the Co-Op, and the linen cupboard is arranged in the traditional stripes of linen and soap, and the dresser-tops are wearing clean kerchiefs, and wherever we go there is something to announce Elizabeth (and this is not mentioning all the china now grandly arranged in the china cupboard). O Elizabeth, even to supply a cat!

He is perfectly settled, he is asleep beside me on my bed at this moment, curled up in a spanish attitude on the topaz blanket, being full of milk and meat. He had chosen his own rocker on the porch where he lies looking unutterable silent insults in reply to the cat-bird, and this morning with a yell of delight he discovered the cellar, and went round and around in it, trying on the smaller Kibbe skating boots, and experimentally preserving himself in the largest jam-pots.

We have been (I hope you will agree) decisive about the downstairs bedroom. It came on us gradually, I must say, we were darkly led along a path of treating it as the spare-room, and therefore changing its mattress for the mattress in two halves upstairs, and laying the antlers there, and moving down the battered arm-chair because it did not seem to show up so much in that rather dusky apartment. Then I added the suit-cases, and Valentine contributed the contents of the book-case which did not contain the *History of the World* by Ridpath, and then we removed the mirror. And then, looking around on it we saw that we had made of it a very tidy and reposeful box-room.

I do realise quite well what we've done. We have made what should be by all respectable New England standards the main bedroom into a box-room. On the other hand, IT HAS NO CLOSET; and again, we have two pairs of single bed sheets, loaned by the Viking Press, which would do for the single bed in the small room, which has got a closet. So I hope you will forgive us, taking into consideration that we were, as I premised, darkly led, and obeying the hand of providence, who was opportunist as usual. Now we have four well-assorted bedrooms upstairs (and at the pinch, and for a quiet-minded guest and God forbid we should have any other, the box-room could become a bedroom again).

Oh, one other improvement. By a combination of my devising and Valentine's doing, all the drawers now open. We have given them string handles.

If you suppose that I can keep my hand off that cookery book (particularly since Mrs Kibbe has bequeathed and devised us a heavy deep round pan with a short handle and a cover, all made of iron and looking as though it had been used to ballast the Mayflower) you are mistaken. But I will promise this much. I won't do any cooking except out of that book. Meanwhile, I identify wild flowers, and when I have finished this letter I shall go out to gather wild raspberries and nosegays. We found a double white pink at the edge of the wood. It had every appearance of being a wild one, if it's an escape, then it has escaped very thoroughly.

The garden reels with chipmunks, and at this moment a load of hay is being carted out of the pasture beyond the wild pasture. I am completely in love with the place, and love it so much that you may be sure that you will be in plenty of time to hear my raptures. To tell the truth, they are only just uncorked, and will flow at full force by the time you are here.

With my love,

Sylvia

I engaged rooms at that hotel. It is called the Colbourn and is in Washington Place.

When she joined them, Elizabeth planned day trips to show her visitors the Connecticut that she dearly loved, the historic houses and villages and the rural landscape. Sylvia recalled that she was a 'good pupil' but Valentine was more interested in contemporary America. In the hot, sticky weather that summer, they took long drives, and at the end of the day something often would have gone wrong, a quarrel on Elizabeth's part with a filling station attendant and on one occasion, Valentine threw a sandwich at Sylvia in the back seat of the car. Valentine and Elizabeth shared the front room. Sylvia was often kept awake by Elizabeth's insistent efforts to convince Valentine to stay in America with her. Janet Machen joined them in late July and years later recalled that with the innocence and sound sleep of youth she remained oblivious of the bitter tensions in the household.

When Paul Nordoff came for a stay, Sylvia brightened up which Elizabeth took as a rebuke. There was strain all around.[36] There was ominous news on the radio. Hitler showed himself unsatisfied and

49. (Left to right) Janet Machen, Valentine and Sylvia, with Elizabeth's roadster.

50. Elizabeth and Janet Machen.

fomented designs on Poland. On 22 August, the Molotov-Ribbentrop Pact was announced in Moscow, named for the two foreign ministers, also known as the Nazi-Soviet Pact. This sealed the fate of Poland and made it inevitable that France and Britain would intervene when Germany invaded that country. To Communists who supported the Loyalists in Spain, backed by Stalin and the USSR, and whose moral equation was Communism good, Fascism bad, this turnabout was startling. For some it prompted a re-examination and a loss of faith in Communism and the Soviet Union. This was apparently not the case in the household in Warren. In a handwritten note, Elizabeth, possibly after a political discussion with her friends, laid out a way of looking at the diplomatic turnabout while remaining loyal to Stalin and the USSR.

> 1. That the coalition of Russia with the Totalitarian states is done, not for the good of Hitler & German & Japanese imperialism but for the improvement of Russia, as the one strong soc. state, therefore not for the benefit of Fascism but for the consolidation and advancement of Socialism. The implications of this are of course terribly important.

> 2. That nothing in this war is as it appears on the surface to be therefore we must go below the surface and carefully examine what we find there.

> 3. That it seems very unlikely that England and France, even with the possible help of the US, can win this war, and to me as a person who believes in Socialism it seems in many ways undesirable that they should win.

> 4. That probably neither side will actually win, but that the course of this war will bring natural developments in all the belligerent countries, with the possible exception of Russia, which will continually change the whole nature of the struggle and will go on even after the war is finished with the result that the whole social structure of economic and political civilization as we now know it will undergo most radical and permanent change.[37]

September, 1939

The old year's youngest fire on the hearth to-night
Sharpens its claws on the first flint in the air,
And quiet the evening, book-inhabited room
Prepares itself for winter to come,
With the browning edges of fields, the early flaming-away of light;
And the cat sleeps reasonably in his accepted chair.

Suddenly a mouth that is not in this room speaking
Out of the knobbed box a harsh word, and the word is war;
And the small cat's eyes are open and afraid
As though his were the sudden seeing of man's world betrayed,
And through broken walls the wounded daylight breaking
Over the child's tin soldiers scattered on the floor.

51. 'September 1939', by Elizabeth.

At the end of the Warren stay, Elizabeth masked any tensions when she reported to her mother that 'all is as well as could be expected. The war news has made ... the last ten days very anxious indeed'. She was unsure if 'S & V and Jan will go or stay'; initially at least S & V will go to North Carolina for a bit. 'I cannot deny the fact that I shall deeply miss these people with whom I have been so closely associated for almost a year now. However, that's the way things go, and I hope I shall behave all right and I assure you I'll do all I possibly can to help you with next week's social undertakings.'[38]

Britain declared war on Germany on 3 September. The 'knobbed box' brought the news of war as their summer ended. Sylvia wrote a thank you note, not then anticipating (or admitting) her later view of the time spent in 'that hell-house in Warren'.[39]

c/o Karl Erickson
Peto. N.C.
8: ix: 1939[40]

Dearest Elizabeth

I should have written before; but we did not get here till midday Wednesday, and on Thursday Valentine was in bed with an envenomed cold (now clearing away, so that she's up again); and in the business of finding where Mrs Morgan keeps her saucepans, and trying to learn a whole new series of wave-lengths on the wireless, there was little time for a letter.

And I am so sorry that this, which has begun with an apology, must go on to condolences. I am so grieved about poor Tomas's accident—his soft dexterous fur paws. I hope it will mend, for he is so young and so healthy that there should be every chance of a good heal. Our kitten Boots, just about Tomas's age, had his leg broken under a car. We did not dare suppose he would be anything but a three-legged cat. However, he came out of his splint three weeks later with scarcely a limp. And while wearing his splint discovered that it was an ideal device to whack his co-kitten, Caspar Towser with. So I hope that Tomas will be another example of the stamina of Norfolk cats.

It is these weddings in the house, my dear. I have never yet known a social wedding not pull down calamities of every kind; but it is hard that Tomas and poor Giles, so innocent of such ambitions, and ready both of them, to ask without favours, should be the sufferers.

This is a great place: a strip of clearing and rough cultivation running up into the flank of the mountain. We are out at the tip of the spear-head, forest on the three sides of us. It is fiery hot by day, and arctic at night. There is a small river, like a lesser Kent Falls, nearby in the woods. It is as cold as though it came from a glacier. I soak myself in a pool this afternoon, and feel the noose of cold run strangling up me to my neck. The woods very dark and classical, full of rhododendrons and laurel (and bears, and coons, and deer, by reports). Last night we heard a wild-cat. But apparently a tame cat is the more improbable of the two.

I should enjoy it a great deal if I could only rid myself of this sensation of being a refugee. It is partly fortuitous. To travel 200 (700?) miles through unknown country at the outbreak of a war is like being a refugee; and the fact that we are all four of us of the same nationality doubtless adds to the persuasion. We have no plans about going back. I read in the paper two days ago that the British Consulate in New York is recommending its nationals over here to stay put. So for the present we suppose we shall stay put. It is good practice in self-control, anyhow, to be living without plans. But the transition from being a turnip to being an orchid is arduous.

I think it was more dramatic than any of us merited that the declaration of war should coincide with the close of the Kibbe House. Dear Kibbe House, I was very happy there, and almost happiest of all, I think, on that afternoon we spent among the Wilcocks graves [41] I am glad we had those hours together, it was the fulfillment of a long promise between us.

My love, dearest Elizabeth—and my loving sympathy, more than I can say. And my gratitude for New England, and all you showed me.

Always Sylvia

Janet went to New York to stay with Evelyn in Greenwich Village while she looked for a job. With the prospect of submarine attacks, the British Embassy forbade nationals to cross the Atlantic that September. However, by October it was clear that the Germans were not pursuing an aggressive approach on the high seas, and transatlantic travel by civilians was permitted. It was the period of the 'phoney war'; there were no substantial military engagements between the participants for eight months, until the invasion of France in May 1940. Sylvia and Valentine stayed at the Hotel Latham in New York while they waited for the travel ban to be lifted.

Hotel Latham
Twenty-eighth Street at Fifth Avenue
New York
Friday [19 September 1939][42]

Dearest Elizabeth.

Valentine tells me that you have arranged for our interminable luggage to be sent to New York. Thank you so much. It will be much easier to do the final resorting if I have a little more time. Now I can spend a happy animated weekend with it.

I am only sorry that I did not know about this before, for now I must be a nuisance and ask two things (which I am afraid may be bother to you). One is, I must return the two pillow-cases belonging to the Huebschs and marked E. This had to be washed when we left Warren, so that I could not pack them. The other thing is, if it is not too much trouble I would be very glad to have the muslin sheets which we got to help refurbish the Kibbe linen-closet. As the house at Frome Vauchurch has three people in it I should be glad of all the extra bed-linen I can lay hands on; and though Mr Bloomingdale's muslin will not last long, it will last a while. There are three pairs of sheets and three pillow-cases (apart from the two Huebsch articles)

I am so sorry to give you all these extra burdens just when you must have been thinking the last straw was laid.

With my love
                    Sylvia

Elizabeth could not persuade Valentine to stay with her in America, and Sylvia refused suggestions to do so. It was a bitter time for all three. Valentine was deeply divided. Sometime in late September she sent Elizabeth a note from the hotel:

Latham, Thursday night

[September 1939][43]

It is late, my darling, & I am tired & very much disappointed & feeling as though all, here & in the world, were full of horror & dismay for us, with love gone & love most terribly going—

Later

I rang you up & heard you speak. I can't write now.

My whole heart, my mind, my body, all ache & beat with love for you, desire & love—love my darling—in pity's name tell me, all ways you can that you do love me & that you will love me! <u>Tell</u> me.

Sylvia recalled seeing from the hotel window a lodging house that at night was 'a showcase of people in torments of heat and sleeplessness'. Nerves frayed in the heat. 'Early one morning I was at my own window when Valentine came in,' Sylvia recalled of the moment of decision. 'She said "I'll tell you presently," and cast herself down on my bed and fell asleep. It was partly as I had surmised. Night after night Elizabeth had tried to extort a promise to stay. With each attempt it was plainer that she had lost all conception of love except as something she could be sure of—like an annuity. But an obligation of pity and concern kept Valentine beside her, till she offered another inducement. This is what Valentine had come to tell me. "Safer as an American citizen," she repeated, "Safer! So I said, damn your bloody United States! Now we must pack and go." Suddenly we were gay and laughing.' [44]

On the eve of departure, Sylvia reflected on the sorrow felt by all three of the women. It was addressed to 42 Perry Street, Greenwich Village where Elizabeth had rented an apartment for herself and Janet. With departure came sorrow to two people, Sylvia wrote.

[Hotel Latham, New York City]
3rd. x. 1939[45]

Dearest Elizabeth,

This will be my last letter tonight. I am tongue-tied, even to a certain extent, pen-tied, in this situation when I seem to be conniving at a departure which must bring sorrow to two people, one loved so passionately and so long, the other loved profoundly, and for even longer. I can only trust you to be magnanimous enough to believe that I have done nothing to bring this about, that Valentine is going as I am going from reasons springing from a root far from love, reasons that perhaps don't even exist on the surface, or, if they do, seem such insignificant sprouts that no one could attend to them, but which are actually deep and long-rooted, and cannot be done away with. I remember that line in Marvell about magnanimous despair, and I think your despair will be of that quality.

But though war snaps, it cannot sweep away what has happened. And though what has happened now seems what ordinary people in their ordinary senses consider deplorable, and something to be overlooked, minimised, made up for, and put away as soon as possible, I hope that we are enough in our senses and far away enough from what is considered normal, to remember it in all its fullness, all its implications, and to remember it as something positive and constructive and vital.

I knew you loved me, but did not guess how. We are both of us stately and uncommunicative, it is no wonder that our relationship remained as it did—a tender and trusting friendship. But one thing in your letter I cannot agree with, disagree with strongly and emphatically. You say that when you fell in love with Valentine you betrayed my trust. You betrayed nothing. You acted naturally and properly, and as a person of sensibility and poetry should behave. There was no betrayal in that. In a way, there would have been a betrayal if you had not acted as you did. For I have always urged you, as you remember, to take chances, to accept life, to enrich yourself by experience, to be wary of the cloistered virtue that lasts for such a brief spell of authenticity. You acted as I expected you to act, as I felt you should act. So let there be no more thought of betrayal my dear, it is a false and belying word, and not appropriate to any one of us three.

When I think of you now it is with a present compassion, a sharp and haunting regret that I see you so pale, so sad, so tormented. And yet there is a deep pride and satisfaction mixed with that compassion for I see you also so profoundly enlarged that I cannot believe that when I sent the telegram to Paris telling you to come I did anything that I can feel sorry for. And when I think of you and talk of you, and meet you (for now more than ever you will haunt our house and meet me in room and garden) I shall think of you thus, a fulfilled and experienced Elizabeth however a sad one. But the Elizabeth I have always foreseen, and wanted to see—though heaven knows I had not foreseen nor wanted the sadness. My dear, I love you, and wish you well.

always,

Sylvia

[Postscript, longhand on side of page] I will write you when we arrive if I don't you will know it's because I am for the moment embedded in house or garden cares. And do you write to me.

Valentine sent a note from the *Aquitania*.

Aquitania
Saturday [46]

'Filled with her love, May I be rather grown
 Mad with much heart, than idiot with none—'
 And for John Donne to choose so is a serious matter.

Sylvia wrote to Elizabeth from a world that seems 'lilliputian' after where they had been.

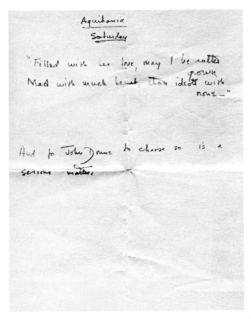

52. Valentine's note sent from the *Aquitania* by the pilot, as she and Sylvia sailed back to England, October 1939.

Maiden Newton
Dorset 13. x. 1939[47]

Dearest Elizabeth.

Valentine will have written to you and told you of our journey and our arrival. [Letter not found.]

It is queer to be back. I had forgotten how small the house is, how small everything is, the village so close, and the hill beyond the village almost within hands' touch. I had grown accustomed to the spaciousness of the states, and that is a thing I miss a great deal; and at intervals since our return I have gone round the house attempting in a foolish persistent cat's way to make it seem larger by licking some of the surface litter off the rooms. The only thing that is not lilliputian is the Jerusalem artichokes, which are about ten foot high, groves of them, terrifying. It has been a very wet summer and the garden is a jungle. I dare not look at the flower part of it yet, there is so much to do with vegetable ground and apple I will not say for certain it is our pruning, but I will maintain in a general way that it is because of that we have an enormous apple crop. Nothing else has done well, the potatoes we planted so painstakingly have cropped badly; but the apples are only to be equaled in Kate Greenaway. O God how I wish we had a good sensible cellar. As it is, they will cover the floor of the long sun-parlour (uninhabitable now because of blackout regulations) and appear with melancholy regularity at every meal. I had some hopes of help from the child in the house; but she does not like apples. It is impossible to give them away because every one here has apples to madness, and the present state of the post does not make it practicable or statesmanly to send parcels of apples away. But meanwhile they look most beautiful and are a pleasure to gather. Unfortunately one is so badly brought up that one cannot adapt oneself to looking on apples as though they were roses.

Today is a day of autumn rain. The bathing-pool is again in flood, and a damp Thomas sits steaming on my knee; he has not enjoyed himself while we were away. He has a mind above people who call him pussy. He smells of earth, so deeply that I know he must have been living a hermit's life out of doors for weeks on end. However, it has given him a sumptuous coat, and no doubt some philosophy, poor darling. Also, he has been turned out of his bedroom, which is now a Keates room. And he stands outside the door in meditated attitudes of high-minded injury.

Today we were in Dorchester (by train, because the car's battery had run down; and had to run for it, into the bargain, these are shrewd changes) where Mrs Rogers was pleased to hear of you. The pretty girl is still there, and pretty as ever. We have no news from Chaldon yet. I will visit Mrs Smith when we go. This is a short letter and a sleepy one. Its chief raison d'etre is to wish you well and bring you my love.

Sylvia

The same day she sent a more expansive letter to Evelyn, with zestful (and acerbic) accounts of the rough ocean.

Frome Vauchurch
Maiden Newton
Dorset.
13 X 1939[48]

Dearest Evelyn,

Those lovely flowers you sent to the boat lasted almost to the end of the voyage, and were a delight to us. People do not give one stephanotis often enough, I adore its scent, it is outrageously fragrant. I constantly interrogated the nosegay to find out what had happened to your interview with B and B [Benton & Bowles advertising agency], but either it did not know or the language of flowers does not include such things in its terminology. So I am still longing to hear all about it.

I wanted to ask you while you were seeing the boat off. It was a difficult question to convey by gesture, and though I could have yelled it—for I can at a pinch yell very loud—Valentine implored me not to make myself conspicuous. Perhaps it was as well. For the boat was crowded with frightful women, all longing to talk; and if I had yelled it might have given them an opening. The boat was also crowded with parsons of every kind. Three others, besides the Rev. Michael Kelly, who you saw beside us. Naturally, with such a crew, I foreboded the worst and confidently expected mines and submarines. Actually, there weren't any. But we ran into very bad weather, and the fact that the boat had no cargo, and only half her usual ballast (the ordinary pig-iron could not be taken, as it might be considered stuff of war) made her roll like a dog. There were thirty terrible hours during which all the things in our stateroom which could not be lashed raged from side to side, chairs, suitcases, the wastepaper basket, chasing each other (and us) in an incessant pendulum movement. It was odd to wake up at night and hear them still at it, jostling and shuffling hither and thither. There were several stretcher cases taken off at Cobh.

Then, when we were safely docked in Southampton, and patiently waiting in the saloon for the landing permits people to come on board the worst incident of our journey befell. For while we sat there, glum and harmless, a loud fulsome female voice began to sing in our midst, and lo, it was a stout middle-aged woman in musquash and some brown paper parcels, and the song she sang was Land of Hope and Glory.

Perhaps you do not know this air. It is sung at conservative meetings. The poet was called Louis Napoleon Parker, the tune is by Elgar at his worst, and the subject is the British Empire. [49]

This really was terrible and people who had endured the storm, and ribs and legs breaking all around them and the submarine menace with comparative calm, turned pale and trembled. When she had finished Land of Hope etc., she looked round on us in a challenging way. Then, after a short pause, she sang the doxology. Fortunately, that was all.

Our homecoming was no worse than we expected. The potato crop has been a failure, en revanche we have far too many apples, the garden is a jungle, and the house is a welter of obligatory precautions. The car battery had run out, both the animals were much too fat, and

[Missing page in the manuscript]

free leaflets on how to put out incendiary bombs (It's so easy! A child can do it) lie thick as leaves in Vallombrosa. Everybody seems very steadfast and very busy, and enduring the absence of anything to be brave about up to date with a high heart. No, that is not true. There is already one regular call for bravery—the nightly blackouts. They are so thorough that if one goes out at night one takes one's life in one's hand. It is far more frightening than in Madrid. Even bicycle lamps are dimmed, cars are invisible till they are on you, you are invisible to the cars even when they are on you, and you fall down steps with the comforting thought that if it were day you might find they had been given a line of white paint. Lord only knows what it will be like when there are air-raids, for it will be quite impossible to locate the wounded unless they happen to be still able to demonstrate where they are by steady screams. And yet I have heard people talk of the fatalism of the Spanish.

It is all very odd indeed. A recent leader in the *Times* said that the blackouts would have one beautiful result insomuch that people who used to go out to restaurants and cinemas will now stay at home and read Sir Walter Scott. Other Panglosses anticipate that it will revive the lost art of domestic piano-playing.

Personally I expect a great revival of personal experience of spectres. People must see something, and if they are offered nothing better they will take to seeing invisible objects from another world.

You can buy natty little containers for gasmasks, pink and scarlet and eau de nil; and the London shops advertise a special suit for wearing during air-raids. It is a sort of glorified pyjamas with a hood attached, and can be bought in all bright shades. One sees a number of women in uniform, but most of them keep their present day hair, and they look rather odd with flowing curls descending below khaki caps. I think the female uniform hats should have snoods attached. They could be made of string, or something serviceable and military like that. I will try to collect you some of the new advertisements, they will amuse you. But they are not very good, you could do a lot for them. In fact I see a great many things which would be much the better for you; but perhaps you had best wait [a] little for at the moment everything is so perfect that no amelioration could be contemplated.

As for the ordinary ruck of people, they are being very nice indeed, gentle and friendly and commonplace. The Keates family are very comfortable evacuates, we are lucky to have people we know so well; and my only trouble has been overcoming some of Mrs Keates's grand-mannered refusal to eat except off broken plates and to accept a reasonable quota of pillows and blankets. 'No, Miss. I'd be just as happy on the floor if it's all the same to you.' However she will soon get over that, indeed she has got as far as demanding solid chairs for their sitting-room 'The old 'un is a hard sitter and it makes me frantic to see him twiddling round on those delicate legs of yours.'

While we were still away the registration official came round. I'm afraid it may have been rather painful for him, because Mr Keates, so to call him, is not really Mr Keates. The original Mr Keates was a bad hat, and deserted Mrs Keates, and the old 'un, younger then, fell in love with this hot-tempered woman with seven children, and insisted on a morganatic match. This has gone on for years, but of course it's not possible for Mrs K. to get a divorce, any how she is both too shy and too arrogant to consider such a step. It appears that the registering gentleman came to the door and found Mrs Keates, and wrote down her name, all duly, and then asked for the Christian name of Mr Keates.

He isn't Mr Keates. Oh. I thought it was your husband here.

No. He's not my husband. But my lady knows (trumpet tones here) and she sanctions it. Do you want me to go into it, sir?

Sir, hastily Oh no, no. Pause But I must ask for his name.

Keates, loftily. Of course. The name's Reynolds.

Sir, And I think there's a little girl.

Yes, sir, there is. Christian name Barbara. Surname, Petch.

I don't know whether she told the poor man that I sanctioned that too. Actually, the child is one of these foster-children, under the LCC scheme, [50] and entrusted to Mrs K. who has such a reputation for being clean and upright and whatnot that despite her morganatic husband she really is already on one national register, that of approved foster-mothers. It appears that the poor gentleman made no comment at all on Petch, just wrote it down and went civily away.

It would be nice if you and Mrs Keates could meet. You would appreciate each other. You are just about each other's weight, I should say, you might be a little quicker in sparring but she would make up for that with her hooks to the jaw, which are terrific. It was she who described our prime minister as a low-down hyena feathering his own nest (this, I suppose, comes into the class of a quick right and left).

I am still feeling unaccustomed to my native land. I had forgotten how small it is. My Lord, this is a Lilliput. Our house is a dolls-box, and I feel as though if I put my hand out of the window I could touch the horizon of the hill while the church tower in between tickled my palm. Didn't you have claustrophobia when you first came to England? But it is a very beautiful Lilliput, and the meadows are so green I want to eat them.

Valentine is well, and dealing in a fine Robinson Crusoe way with various immediate problems like how are we to blacken the bathroom window, and live within our electricity ration (75 per cent of what we used in the midsummer quarter last year when there were two of us, and now it's winter and we're five!) and so on. She is much better at island life than I am, and it is nice to lean back and admire the new door-handle which she has just fixed in this room.

But how silly it is that you don't know this house. Blast this war, I wish you could come here and let us show a little how gratefully we remember all you did for us when we were in New York.

With her love and mine,

Sylvia

[handwritten] greetings to Anne [Holahan]

Two weeks later Sylvia wrote to Evelyn again with a continuation of her wartime commentary.

> Frome Vauchurch
> Maiden Newton, Dorset
> 29. X . 1939[51]

Dearest Evelyn.

I hasten to tell you the latest news of the struggle. The Government has just appointed two Controllers of Bird-Seed.

Tell Ripley.

Love from Sylvia

On the same day Valentine wrote to Elizabeth that 'my need for you was growing heavier and heavier'. In a long letter, she looked back on their recent troubles and sought to find an accommodation that will let her remain with Sylvia. She challenged Elizabeth to find a way for them to remain lovers without her having to leave Sylvia and analyzed the life they could live together.

> Frome Vauchurch
> Maiden Newton
> October 29th, 1939[52]

My darling,

Mark well this day, which is a Sunday and cold at that, for on it I want to write you an important question; perhaps a question second only in importance to that first one of all—to which you so certainly and beautifully answered 'Yes—I will'.

For many days now I have known that my need for you was growing heavier and heavier, and I have spent much time in wondering how possibly things could be planned for us. I have come to some decisions, discovered some certainties & suspect that some other feelings which are at present too confused to be counted upon will develop themselves into certainties. Now it is of the utmost importance for me to know from you exactly how you feel about me, what you want for us, what you would be willing and able to do—

We know enough now since you have been here with me and seen the kind of life I have chosen and prefer and since I have been with you in your country and seen some of your friends, something of your surroundings—We know enough of each other to realise that in many things we are very different and that there is conflict between our tastes, especially as regards people and social activities. It COULD be a most dangerous kind of conflict, and if we fought it out both of us would be bitterly maimed, I believe, and we would lose both love and respect for each other. Think of this, for I am sure it is true—You have already accused me of being unadaptable and unwilling to make small concessions; I'm troubled because I think you are right in saying that. I may manage to get better. There are obvious psychological reasons for my having become so, and I may manage to cure myself in part, anyway. But I DO NOT WANT to be wholly cured! I'm lazy enough as it is, and if I switched back again now to the kind of things I used so much to enjoy, I'd inevitably lose even the remnants of what I love even better, my darling, than anyone on the face of the earth. I could never promise you to become addicted to society! Mark that well—

Probably I could promise complete fidelity, because there is something beyond words precious to me in the very thing you have, sometimes, been ashamed of: your complete surrender to love, your generosity of giving, which puts it even beyond my capacity for doubt, so that even I believe quite easily that you do give me everything—I can't explain to you, at this distance, how it is with me—but that quality above all others makes me unable to imagine me loving anyone else.

But fidelity of desire is not enough to give you, because what I would necessarily be asking from you is everything you have to give. And in return I could not offer you what is probably the most important thing of all, security. It's not only the dangers which, up to now, have naturally made you flinch: the intangible perils, like the word 'Mistress' with its implication of insecurity, irritability—Perhaps there is the important point: you could not face instability. If that is so, things are better—for you would not have to face any kind of instability.

You can see towards what these words lead: the future is so hazardous, especially on this day and in this month, and during this period of the world's history that we cannot foretell our fortunes at all, but we can and must confide to each other our hope. I love you Elizabeth, and I want you. And these are two perfectly direct statements of very simple and most powerful emotions. The complications come, as always, in the actual making-real of my wishes. But I am convinced beyond a doubt now that they must be made real. You will misjudge me if you think I am being completely self-thinking in this; I wish I were. If I were we could, all three, be infinitely the better for it. But habit has got me down and I am unable to think for myself ALONE. That is where I am caught, and you with me. I am asking you, most desperately to help me now.

'I believe in you, I honour and revere and cherish you, and in all ways, for all my life, I love you ... Keep that love safe and alive if you can, and think if you want to, of how it may be.'

That is what your latest letter says to me, and if I am right in reading that important word 'may' as a promise on your part—then, my deeply loved, I have a right to ask your help now in working out a definite plan for our joint future.

Tell me, Elizabeth, very clearly and with complete candour, what you will do. I have dealt candidly with you; I have told you how it is—how I am unwilling to give up Sylvia—whose companionship is both dear and necessary to me: how she is unhappy and, I feel, cheated of what she most wants from me. I see great unhappiness ahead for her and I flinch before it. I do not think that I can deal so with her, and yet these weeks have shown me clearly that your image lies in my arms. You are wanting me and I am wanting you, and when we are together we lie down and we are happy. We have desecrated and violated that happiness NOT so much in allowing ourselves to be parted as by wasting the time we had together in useless, miserable recriminations and repining. This remembrance frightens me. I want you to understand this—it frightens me very much because I am no means sure that you would be satisfied under any circumstances with what my changing, self-willed, melancholy moods might bring you. And I know that I could not endure for half a year, again, the torments of reproaches and frustrations that I endured last year and this year.

Here is plain-speaking, dear heart; necessary now as never before. You must endure it, if you will, because of the whole of two lives' happiness at stake. I am not trying to hurt you, nor am I trying to reproach you or be severe with you. I love you so desperately and so warmly that sometimes the flames leap from me to you, and would you too. Remember, if you can, that they bite into me all the time.

You will know from the newspapers that at this moment I am writing we are expecting a violent increase of pressure from Germany, and an intensifying of the war. You know what that may mean, if it happens, if we manage between us, you and I, to make a plan of action, to arrange a method of living so that we may be together and love and care for each other (god knows it is a most difficult thing to do, but my heart tells me we may do it—) we are, even so, beset by these other dangers, and they are many—sweetheart—as you know from our conversations about probabilities. And money is another danger: I can't conceivably get across the Atlantic again, when the war stops, because the crazy taxation has crippled my kind of income, and there are no jobs for people like me ... Lovers are always fantastically hopeful, fantastically despairing, fantastically lucky, and seemingly we have cause to be all three!

You would have to leave (whether I were there or you were here) very much that you enjoy and love and have learned to count upon. Your life (even if things work out so that it is what you think you most entirely want) would be difficult and hazardous. It would not, ever, be lonely or frustrated, I believe, nor would it ever be poor in the things we both know to be what we want most. But it would demand from you an immense generosity, a measure of endurance (not endurance of me only—my sweetheart, but of other people—lack of other people—slights perhaps—and above all endurance of a state of reason dominating a state of feeling. This most difficult exercise—).

Would it be worth your while to sacrifice the affectionate approbation, the pampering, the praise and kindness of the people you have now; the comfort and assurance of being among them, the easy indulgence of your desires as whims, of your beliefs as fancies—and change to the CONFUSION of being so demandingly beloved, of being relied on, of being in all things treated as someone of first & real importance? For god's sake, think carefully about this. It is a most drastic change.

The alternative solution to the as-yet-unfound one I hope for is that we take whatever possible chances offer of being happy whenever we possibly can: that we continue in this miserable state of longing and wishing and hoping, that we try to stay true, that we tacitly allow ourselves to think of being false, that we take every chance of lesser happiness that offers itself and try our separate bests not to be crippled for ever by the weight of our separate desires. It is NOT a hopeless situation, this alternative one; it could be fairly fruitful of contentment and richness. But your letters make it clear that I have a simple want which cannot be simply attained. I want you.

Keep this letter privately and read it carefully. I ask you most earnestly not to discuss it with anyone else at all, but to have it in your own mind, against your own heart, before your own judgment only—and then to write to me as simply and truthfully as you can, giving me what hope, what help you can, telling me if you love me and in what manner you love me, if you would come to me, when that is possible, and in what way, under what conditions, you would come to me. Tell me any plans that may have formulated themselves in your mind during these long weeks, and what chances you think there are of our being together—

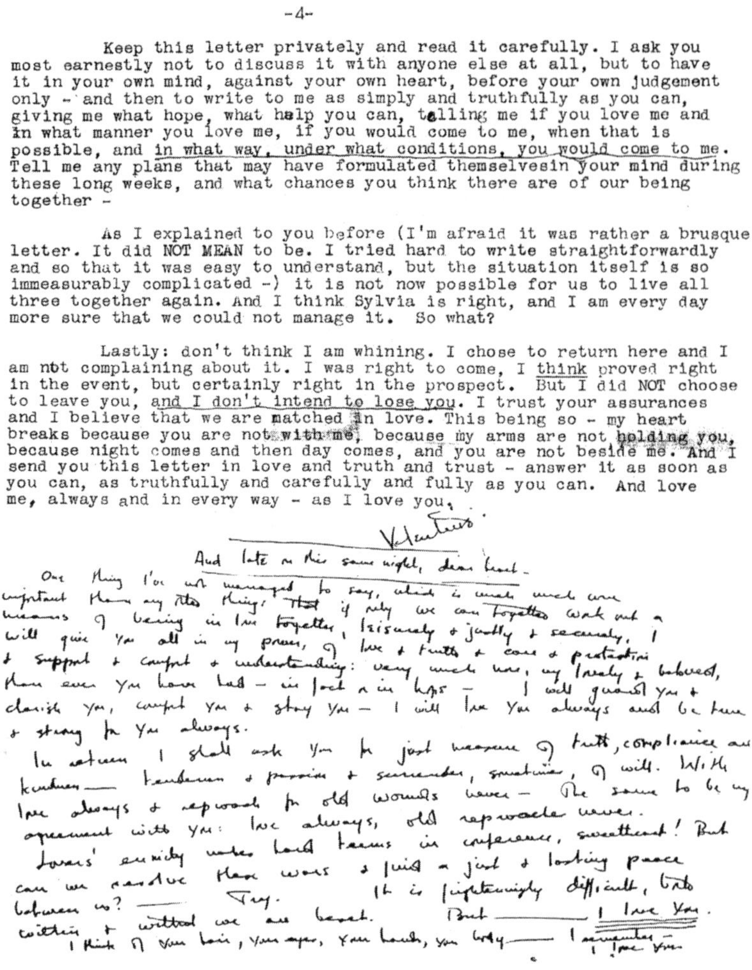

-4-

Keep this letter privately and read it carefully. I ask you most earnestly not to discuss it with anyone else at all, but to have it in your own mind, against your own heart, before your own judgement only - and then to write to me as simply and truthfully as you can, giving me what hope, what help you can, telling me if you love me and in what manner you love me, if you would come to me, when that is possible, and in what way, under what conditions, you would come to me. Tell me any plans that may have formulated themselves in your mind during these long weeks, and what chances you think there are of our being together -

As I explained to you before (I'm afraid it was rather a brusque letter. It did NOT MEAN to be. I tried hard to write straightforwardly and so that it was easy to understand, but the situation itself is so immeasurably complicated -) it is not now possible for us to live all three together again. And I think Sylvia is right, and I am every day more sure that we could not manage it. So what?

Lastly: don't think I am whining. I chose to return here and I am not complaining about it. I was right to come, I think proved right in the event, but certainly right in the prospect. But I did NOT choose to leave you, and I don't intend to lose you. I trust your assurances and I believe that we are matched in love. This being so - my heart breaks because you are not with me, because my arms are not holding you, because night comes and then day comes, and you are not beside me. And I send you this letter in love and truth and trust - answer it as soon as you can, as truthfully and carefully and fully as you can. And love me, always and in every way - as I love you.

[handwritten signature: Valentine]

[handwritten postscript, partly illegible]

53. Valentine's letter to Elizabeth, 19 October 1939.

As I explained to you before (I'm afraid it was rather a brusque letter. It did NOT MEAN to be. I tried hard to write straight-forwardly and so that it was easy to understand, but the situation itself is so immeasurably complicated—) it is not now possible for us to live all three together again. And I think Sylvia is right, and I am every day more sure that we could not manage it. So what?

Lastly: don't think I am whining. I chose to return here and I am not complaining about it. I was right to come. I think proved right in the event but certainly right in the prospect. But I did NOT choose to leave you, and I don't intend to lose you. I trust your assurances and I believe that we are matched in love. This being so—my heart breaks because you are not with me, because my arms are not holding you, because night comes and then day comes, and you are not beside me. And I send you this letter in love and truth and trust—answer it as soon as you can, as truthfully and carefully and fully as you can. And love me, always, and in every way.

Valentine

[Longhand]

And late on this same night, dear heart—

One thing I've not managed to say which is much, much more important than any other thing: that if only we can together work out a means of being in love together, leisurely & jointly & securely, I will give you all in my power, of love & truth & care & protection & support & comfort & understanding: very much more, my lovely & beloved, than ever you have had—in fact & in hope—I will guard you & cherish you, compel you & stay you—I will love you always and be true & strong for you always.

In between I shall ask you for just measure of truth, compliance and kindness— kindness & passion & surrender, sometimes of will. With love always & reproach for old wounds never—The same to be my agreement with you: love always, old reproaches never.

Lovers' enmity makes hard terms in conference, sweetheart! But can we resolve these ways & find a just & lasting peace between us?—Try. It is frighteningly difficult, but within & without we are beset. But—I love you.

I think of your hair, your eyes, your hands, your body—I remember—I love you.

On 18 November, Elizabeth ordered flowers from Rogers in Dorchester to be sent to Valentine.[53] That autumn, however tormented she was by the experience of the past months and the separation from Valentine, she took a major step: for the first time in her adult life she rented an apartment where she could live independently from her parents. She signed a lease on what she remembered fifty years later as 'a horrible little place' at 42 Perry Street in Greenwich Village.[54] The term was for one month, subject to automatic renewal, with linens included for a total of $65 per month. Janet Machen moved in, and Elizabeth was there during the week, on most weekends at Breakneck. She sought a job that would allow her to go to England in spite of wartime restrictions. Martin Pollock, whom she had met in Dorset, wrote on 7 October with little to suggest; places in the Women's Land Army (which she had suggested) were already full, and there was a three-month waiting period. 'It's a queer life in England at present,' he added, 'we live from day to day. I am gradually beginning to understand what we must fight for, but with these rapidly, surprisingly changing situations, it's damned difficult—& it's so desperately important.' [55] Elizabeth's efforts to go overseas would continue without success.

In the final months of 1939 uncertainties preoccupied the lovers as the world awaited Hitler's next move. Katie Powys understood what Elizabeth was experiencing in Valentine's absence. 'Oh! How I wish she had never left Chaldon. Even as you I expect wish she had never left New York. I don't think I know anyone who leaves such a desolation behind when she leaves—I always feel she is like the sea or rather echoes that verse in the Bible, 'Blessed is the—for he giveth yet he taketh away'. I always feel the sea does that & so does Valentine—yet what ever she may do to us—we still crave for her whether we are left satisfied in our relationships with her—'. Katie had made something of a peace, 'for out of that wild furious passion for the 1st 10 years I have reached a solid ledge at last that has stability in it. I think it is not as I have found with other love that when that wild passion is stirred in me & proclaims itself with unconstrained ferocity that instead of giving me the same response they become frightened & withdraw from me. I would have given pounds before now to have been taken some where alone with her, just for a day or two, but no it never happened & unless a chance came, all my self conscious awkwardness stood in the way— and slow response of my brain. Why I should say all this to you God knows, only that I know you have generosity & understanding through loving the same object as we do.'[56]

VI. Know now and finally what love is and must be

In the Atlantic world 1940 began with the deceptive calm of the 'phoney war', with no large-scale engagements or submarine warfare, but by June the Nazis had occupied most of Western Europe. Elizabeth anxiously followed radio and newspaper reports of air raids and a plausible threat of an invasion of England. The separated lovers wrote and cabled. Though she longed to be in England and appealed to friends there for employment, Elizabeth took a job in New York City with the Tri-State Commission, established under the New Deal Department of Labor to investigate the incidence of silicosis in miners in Kentucky, Missouri, and Indiana. She helped prepare the Commission's reports and presentations, and visited Missouri in the course of its fact-finding. It was an unpaid position, but a responsible one and a major step for a young woman who had no experience of office work. Valentine remained prominent in her thoughts. At Breakneck on weekends, there continued to be stormy scenes over politics.

When the air blitz began in the summer, Sylvia and Valentine left Frome Vauchurch to be near Ruth Ackland in Winterton. Norfolk had already been bombed, and, since invasion seemed imminent, Valentine felt it her duty to be near her mother.

By late summer the dynamics of the relationships altered. In New York, Evelyn fell in love with Elizabeth and offered herself as consoler and healer in full knowledge of the spell the affair with Valentine still cast. Valentine deemed this a betrayal; she demanded that Evelyn make her 'intentions' clear and received a curt dismissal. Elizabeth and Evelyn set up an apartment together. Nonetheless, Elizabeth continued to long for Valentine and to seek work in England and the two continued to write and cable.

Sylvia began the New Year with thanks for a Christmas present and brief news.

54. Valentine by Elizabeth Muntz (original on colored paper).
Photograph courtesy of Morine Krissdottir.

Frome Vauchurch, Maiden Newton, Dorset

i. 1940[1]

Dear Elizabeth,

The lithograph arrived this morning, much to my pleasure and much to my relief. For Valentine had said that you wrote of sending it to me and I was beginning to fear that the sea-nymphs might have got it. I am glad they haven't. It is the sort of landscape I can appreciate much better than they. Yes, Indeed, I remember the road and the hill. There was one of those family burial grounds at the bottom of it. It is a beautiful lithograph; I love the faintly false perspective of the silo.

Incidentally I was also much pleased with the packing. I am glad you sent both halves of the bisected landscape. I have long been wanting the material of another portfolio, and when I have got hold of some gum linen I shall make one out of this.

I am so glad to hear that there is a prospect of a Craske show at Levy's. I do hope this comes off. You will remember that the white needlework snow storm is not to be sold? Heaven knows when I shall see it again, but meanwhile I would rather think of it in your possession than adorning some other collector.

Ruth is here for the New Year, and to-morrow we go to Winterton for a few days. It has been deep snow there. Here it is too cold for snow. It is as cold as those knife-like days before Christmas last year, and the crows swoop down on the quarterdeck for crumbs, looking as though they would knock over the house with their wings.

What beautiful pictures in the book you sent Valentine for Christmas! Especially the Hopper of the house by the railway track. It is an eye-full, it comes at one as hard and straight as Cezanne's black marble clock.

The house is full of turmoil and packing and calls to duty. I must not let myself get onto another page.

With my love , my dear,

Sylvia

[handwritten] My greeting to Tomas. The Alcalas sent us a Christmas card. They are on Daisy Road Manchester.

On New Year's Day at Breakneck, Elizabeth was unhappy, self-critical, and profoundly aware that her life had changed. 'At the end of 1938, and in 1939 I learned first the reality of happiness, and there is nothing in imagination that can match the truth of that. I know now how it is to be in love, to be loved, to be fulfilled by the extreme, unimaginable, shared ecstasy of love.' The Rats' Barn spell held, a sharp contrast to the disagreements and mood swings of the past year that began with the great hope of the love she had found. She wrote in her childhood room and alone. 'I am torn with agony of separation, deprivation, error, and desire now because of my love. And I am steadfast and unfaltering in truth to my loved. God keep and guard and comfort my Valentine, and give me strength and wisdom and make me worthy, and bring us to each other again. God make me brave.' [2]

On 2 January in New York, it is 'like waking from a strange troubled dream into a world of reality ... It was a bad 10 days at home. I was expected to be family and happy, and I was most cruelly neither. A very bad thing was father's going into the long expected passion with me, because it was my fault that it happened and I shall not soon forgive him for what he said.' The next day Mary and Wade had come for supper in the city and to see *Gone with the Wind*, which Elizabeth found 'Almost four hours of pretentious empty film, a little moving in spots but mostly sterile and maddening'. A large drawing Betty Muntz made in Chaldon of Valentine in the nude had come back from the framer and is 'hanging now on the wall'. It would always be where Elizabeth lived. She hung it in successive New York apartments; in 1945 when she moved to The Patch in Middlebury, Connecticut, she placed it above her desk in the second floor study where it remained until her death.[3]

On the next day, she had letters from Valentine and from Katie Powys, which refreshed the memory of Rats' Barn; she lunched with her mother at The Plaza and 'wrote to V until 4:00 in the morning'.

A letter from V this morning, with notes written at Rats' in it, and one from Katie [Powys]. And this afternoon two, one just after my cable of the 18th arrived. Saying 'you must endure, you must try again, get courage from somewhere, DARE something'. And 'I love you'. Oh God let it not happen again; now that I know how it is, let me not break and fail again. Let me get through until the spring comes, our spring.

Jan [Janet Machen] and I lunched with mother at the Plaza. Lovely food, awful people, and a Fashion show. It is good to feel that I don't need that sort of thing any more ...

A meeting at the office from which I arrived home after 7:00 to find V's afternoon letters and Jan still skating. I sent off a cable directly, then heated supper ...

5 January 1940: Fortunately awaked by mother telephoning. No hot water. Posted the letter to JRS [John Robertson Scott] Please God. ... Yesterday read Roosevelt's speech and Lord Lothian's, most important, better models of sly incitement. It won't be long now, only what will happen in the meantime?; found out what I thought, that V sends it. It is very good, only said nothing about Hore-Belisha's dismissal.[4]

6 January 1940: V sends The *Knapsack,* a soldier's anthology by Herbert Read, her own copy often marked, also a hideous little false leather case marked Ration Card. The anthology is a fine thing. I had some Beowulf from it with my breakfast. Then up town to cash a check and try on my beautiful shooting-pants, which are very tight at the waist as I wanted them. Down again to get the car, suitcase & Tomas, and then to drive all the way up 5th Ave to Kes's. [5] The clutch is very bad & the car stalled at every crossing, otherwise OK. Such a wind at 96th St. A good lunch & talk with Kes; she said I looked and seemed better than ever since I came back. I said things were all right now and she said she was glad.

Then I drove through such winter light and country. Almost unbearably beautiful with the deepening and changing of sunset time. And in only a little over 2 hours. Many letters from England here. Go to NH [New Haven] with Mother & Wade & a 17th & 18th century concert which was beautiful but I was tired. A drink at George's [George Hamilton] and finally home.

7 January 1940, at Breakneck: ... W[ade] and I skated in the afternoon. It was lovely. Snow on most of the little mill pond that is my dear one, but paths swept neatly through it, and on them country children, all ages, and one tall dignified gray country man. Giles [Sealyham terrier] had an ecstatic time. All the way up the bank, to where swamp begins, was sunlit, and we went up and down, and I felt happy and thought how it would be if V was there. Wadex [Wade] looked very beautiful, in blue trousers and the pullover from Yarmouths, and we were contented together. It was a good thing to do.

At home, at a wild sunset time, I began a letter to V then was frightfully sleepy and lay down & half slept in the dark for an hour and 1/2.

8 January 1940: ... At the office, Dr. Walsh was conferring with Eleanor ... He and E. and I lunched together, much talk about Civil Liberties Union. Gallup shows CP as greatest menace by 70%, Bund 30%.

10 January 1940: ... At home there were letters from England, a sad and very touching one from Theodore [Powys], and a card from V. Drinks & talk, dinner and talk, then G's [George Hamilton's] lecture at the Mattatuck [Historical Society in Waterbury], as interesting as the subject of Abbey allowed, & well dished out. [6] And people afterward, and finally G leaving & we home and I in bed writing to V.

11 January 1940 I drove to NY this morning, a triumph of money-saving suddenly thought of. From 8:30 on the country was beautiful, near Stevenson Dam a whole old tangled apple-orchard plated with ice and the morning sun on it.

12 January 1940 Valentine's cable this morning—because of my letter of the 19th—saying 'future shall prove'.

The journal for 1940 ends on 13 January, a New Year's resolution not kept. In mid-January, Geoffrey de Freitas MP, whom Elizabeth and her brother had met when he was an exchange student at Yale, wrote recalling those days and telling her that he could not find a job for her helping refugees in England.

'Write often completely take great care. I send today all years all belief all love. EW' was the note Elizabeth made for a cable to Valentine on the 17th.[7]

In mid-January, Sylvia wrote at length to Evelyn on various topics, seemingly, as she acknowledges, for the pleasure of writing someone whose company she enjoyed. There is no mention of Elizabeth and only a reference to Valentine.

Frome Vauchurch,
Maiden Newton, Dorset
18.1.1940[8]

Dearest Evelyn,

Your conflate letter of Nov 6th Dec 11 has arrived, despite the Atlantic; and I also got the copy of the spirited interchange with the Cunard. After you had broken the spirit at your end, and I had received a cheque for the amount I (nothing if not a tactician) fell sharply on their other flank, remarking that it was sad for us all that the New York branch should be so childish; that I was returning the cheque; and that as they had acknowledged my claim to the money by sending the cheque to me I guessed they had now committed themselves to agreeing that the money was mine to dispose of; and that I wished it disposed of as I'd told them already, sent to Ludwig [Renn] in dollars. They sent a dispirited reply to the effect that their New York branch had been told to do so. If you like crowing over a fallen adversary (personally, it is one of my favourite pursuits) you might ring up 25 Broadway and ask them if this has been done.

I am very grateful to you, and I hope you enjoyed it. I was reared on this kind of thing. My father should have been a guerrilla fighter, as it was he had to express himself in correspondences like these. I remember one with a firm called Harrods, about small metal boxes, which lasted for nearly three months, my father professing to retreat and thus suavely luring them into rash statements, upon which he would pounce down on them from his mountain lair, and chew up their lines of communication, etc. I can't recollect what he wanted the boxes for; to put things in I guess. But his happiest time was when two gentlemen who had fallen out over some small matter of prestige both separately approached him for advice. He wrote the letters for both parties, working them up into a prodigious climax during which they could scarcely live in the same town, they were so irate. Thomson and Johnson would fly to him with the latest insulting missive, and one was scarcely away with the reply to it before 'tother would be in, clamouring for a fitting retort. In the end he conducted them to a balmy reconciliation, and left 'em in each other's arms. It was quite safe to do so. He knew they were too proud, either of them, to admit in the raptures of reconciliation that they hadn't been able to write these letters by themselves. I often wish my father were alive now, to manage the war.

Steam Boat Springs, Co., Three Trees N. Dakota. O happy moments with a map, what rapture it must be to be planning such a trip. You will, won't you, keep a diary, and let me see it some day? If I must travel vicariously through the west, there is no person who could do it as sympathetically for me as yourself. I am only worried because in your letter to Valentine you speak of your sister being ill. I am afraid this may dash your plans. Anyway, I am sorry your sister is ill.[9]

I very much value your account of voting in your country. We have no such mechanical joys, only a policeman to whom you show your voting card (entitling you to, I mean. It has your name on it, spelt wrong, and a number). Then, feeling that he has recognized you as the burglar he missed last week, you go into a little booth, and on a card which has the names of the various candidates, you make a pencil cross, against the one you want. Then you come out, and drop the marked card in a slot under the nose of the policeman. It is a system open to various abuses. The worst is that before the election candidates may circulate voters with sham cards, marked with a cross against that candidate's name, saying When You Vote, Vote Like This. The purpose of these advertisements is that dumb voters, women and so forth, may feel that only if they put their pens just there can they escape arrest for a state misdemeanor. The fact that there is no mechanical register of votes is also a serious potential cheat. The presence of the policeman, too, is liable to misinterpretation. He is supposed to represent the state, but in the opinion of many simple voters a policeman represents the tory candidate whose pheasant they had tried to poach last year. As a representative of the state it would be better to have some less associative figure; a clergyman, for instance. As the church is a state institution, a bishop and a constable are exactly on a par in the matter of being a representative reminder. In fact, it would be better to have a clergyman. They are more easily spared from their labours.

However, the movement for making use of our church is gaining ground. There is now an archdeacon on priest duty in a south coast town. I cannot tell you the name of the town, as it might give useful information to the enemy. As Patience Strong said in her *Daily Mirror* poem yesterday:

There is a Silent Listener to every conversion.
So let us seal our ready lips to all vituperation.

She does a poem more or less like this daily, and is a great comfort to me in these harsh times. Of course they are printed like prose, or they would seem slangy.

It was a pity of pities that you couldn't pull Lord Beaverbrook. You would be very happy over here, it seems to me. You might go and join Sir John Reith at the Ministry of Information. Now that is a public figure I feel very sorry for. He is a simple religious man, of a fundamentalist nature, never had a tail in his life; and a very good engineer. And when the BBC was started he was almost completely happy, tied up in cat's whiskers and serials, and musing on the Heavyside Layer, and getting in contracts, for he is also a fervent man of business. Just when everything was getting neat and comfortable, the idea got around that the broadcasting invention might be used to spread cultural information. And immediately Savoy Hill was rushed by a band of intellectuals, who ruined everything for poor John Reith. It was at the date, too, when intellectuals were both fashionable and powerful, and social and urbane. I know some of that crowd, and it was then that I used to see John Reith, scowling at their cocktail parties, a man of iron with damp hair, tossed from poets to psychoanalysts, no sooner escaping an educationalist than he got snapped up by an authority on Chinese painting. Naturally, he got a terrible ingrowing inferiority complex, which made him as savage as you please. But he couldn't do much, for culture had got into the BBC, and try as he would, he never really got it down. While he was demolishing the music department, another group would creep up behind him and start performing plays; and so on. Perfect transmission of pure [ ] was what he wanted; and the transmission was pretty good, but the things transmitted were not what he wanted at all. Finally, he developed persecution mania, and kept gangs of large fierce dogs, so that he could not be assassinated by oppressed intellectuals; so his only pleasure, that of having oppressed them was poisoned by the idea they might retaliate.[10]

And now, just think, the poor wretch has been slammed into the Ministry of Information, where he will have real journalists harassing him day and night. It is like that text in the bible which says: I will make my little finger thicker than my father's loins.

If it were not for going west I think you should make a real effort to get appointed somehow to work under Sir John Reith. You might make a real difference to the poor man's peace of mind, and you could use all your psychology work on him, besides the middle west housewives, who would give you a good guide to his troubles, though perhaps the most applicable would be that matron from Vermont who didn't like the advertisements of Kotex.[11]

Still, it is a good thing you aren't here now. It is hellishly cold, and has been for weeks, and everything is frozen, and everybody is cross and weary, like a hymn.

No, I am not angry with you for not writing, now that you have written. I was not really angry anyhow, why should one write letters unless one feels inclined to. And very often the people one likes a great deal are the hardest people to write to. It is very pleasant, dear Evelyn, that you do like me, I saw you did in New

York, and it meant a great deal to me. When I was with you I felt both alive and serene, as though I were sailing on a river. If you feel I could help you, it is because I felt you helped me. There can be no help that is not mutual; the reason, I suppose, why both charity and philanthropy are doomed to fall in a flat stink. Now I have spent a happy hour writing to you.

I wish you well and send you my love.
Sylvia

[longhand] You showed us a nice public letter of your composition. That is, one of Valentine's, which we are pleased with.

In February, Elizabeth made notes for cables to Valentine, the first to reassure of her emotional state.

'Darling, it's all right, I'm all right now. I have gone very deep down, since your letter came, & have come up gain. I am flesh of your flesh & bone of your bone for all my life, and nothing NOTHING can change that. And if I am to be homeless for all my days, still your heart that beats my life is burned in me forever. Remember this if ever you need to remember it come to me always from shelter & traumas & love for what you need, for what I have to give.'

That November was a month of no moment
There was not any more shedding of tears
Only capable skies
And small housewifely brown-winds sweeping away the years.[12]

Elizabeth sent a second cable from Washington. 'Yours 11th received Washington this week Hay-Adams House 16th St. for Tri-State. Keep well safe brave my love. EW'. 'Darling, I must remain for same reasons you returned do you understand accepted tentative six months responsibility writing constantly all love. Obliged against all needs but one decide accept Tri-State responsibility indefinite period writing fully please understand very lonely anxious cable if possible all love.'[13]

Elizabeth had substantial responsibilities with the Tri-State Commission as its Acting Secretary. The Tri-State Mining Area comprised Jasper County, Missouri and adjoining counties of Cherokee, Kansas and Ottawa, Oklahoma, where one half of the world supply of zinc and one-sixth of its lead was mined. Chat dust (fragments of mining waste) blew up from the mines; the silica dust penetrated the miners' lungs, resulting in silicosis that can develop into tuberculosis. The nearest sanatorium to treat the diseases was 300 miles away. In 1937, the National Committee for People's Rights investigated working conditions in the area and made a survey; out of this the Tri-State Survey Committee was created, and in November 1939 it published a preliminary report, *Living, Working, and Health Conditions in the Tri-State Mining Area.* As part of her work, Elizabeth helped promote *Men and Dust,* a film by Sheldon Dick (which was why she was in Washington at the Hays-Adams when she cabled Valentine), and the preparation for a conference in Joplin, Missouri under the auspices of the US Department of Labor.[14]

The Tri-State work was just the sort of social activism that Elizabeth had sought, but the pull of England and Valentine continued. John Robertson Scott offered a position at *The Countryman,* [15] but by then Elizabeth had accepted the Tri-State post, and in any event, permission from the Department of State to travel to Europe was difficult to obtain. On another tack, Elizabeth tried to persuade Sylvia to move to America and offered financial help.

> Several letters from V telling me that you are feeling ill (& giving a pretty good indication that she is not too well either) have substantially increased my already adequate anxiety for both of you. So I was glad to have today an opportunity to talk with your friend Ben Huebsch about my anxiety and ask him for his opinion & advice. He feels as I do that it would be wise for you to come to America, that you would really be able to do more for England, and that you would find a warm welcome awaiting you. He suggests my asking you if you would like to have either him or me talk with the *New Yorker* people & find out if their offer to you still holds good. If it does & if you decided to accept it, it would I

presume give you a certain amount of financial security and in this hypothetical case perhaps you would not mind my asking you to consider my offer to pay your passage, more in the nature of a long term loan. I imagine you would prefer such an arrangement anyway, & it would make it possible for me to give help in some other directions in which we are all interested. [16]

The first indication of what was to become a lifetime intimacy with Evelyn came in Elizabeth's entry in a briefly revived journal on 1 February.

Thank God the cold first month of this year is over, and this is the first day of the last month of the winter of 1940. There was a softness in the air today a smell of spring under cold air, and a bright but not metal sky. The good wild savage innocent feeling, which makes something without a name turn in the winter den and open its eyes and be hungry & half awake & happy and sad and nostalgic too.

Evelyn came to supper and we talked very casually because she & J [Janet] & I cannot talk in any other way together. Then J had a bath and went to bed because her cough is bad & E & I went out for a drink and had 3 & talked solemnly & at cross purposes mostly until 2:00. Well, she disbelieves in Jan's returning to England & says she can get her into a job. That is good. But she made me angry, also I made her angry. She has this intellectual curiosity about what is wrong with people & why are they lonely & afraid, then she scolds me because I am in love & unhappy & perfectly aware of unhappiness & prepared to endure it. She cannot forgive people for the waste of unhappiness. I suppose that is it. But she knows a great deal. [17]

Sylvia wrote Evelyn in February. Her intention to remain in England was firm.

Frome Vauchurch,
Maiden Newton, Dorset
28. ii. 1940[18]

Dearest Evelyn,

Your letter of Feb. 8th has just arrived. I am so glad mine came with the gas-bill, that is just how I would choose to appear, modestly and 'without any amazement' as the English church service says so hopefully of matrimony.

I had a letter from your Mr Shackleton, but fate did not allow me to fill my eye with him. He got as far as Bournemouth, and wrote calling upon your name and saying that he would ring me the next morning. Just then we were having some rather rougher weather than the resources of this country are accustomed to, and that night there was a storm which snowed up the roads and broke our telegraph wires. We managed to have a short telephone talk the day he left Bournemouth, in which we mutually regretted and bowed to the hand of fate.

His handwriting told us a good deal about his circumstances. I could discern rich and dreadful parents in it. He still seems to be rather attached to his business—or rather, to being busy at it. English men cling more to being busy than to what they are busy at—Englishmen from his drawer.

It is a form of inferiority complex, and comes from the English public school system I suppose. There is nothing to equal a classy education for breeding the i.c.

I am so glad that the 7th Avenue subway is being repainted. You are quite right, more like that will keep us happy for days. But I resent you saying that it was Mayor LaGuardia's idea. It was not. It was my idea. I can't say that I chose the colour theme but while I was in New York I repeatedly said what a good plan it would be to repaint the subway; and it is obvious that La Guardia got the idea from me, by thought transference. If it was his idea, why didn't he do it before?

I have got an idea about the new station on sixth too. I think it ought to have some animals in it. Thousands of new yorkers waiting on subway stations say to themselves how they wish they had time to go to the Bronx zoo, and yearn for leisure and baby crocodiles. My idea is that the new station should have say two violet-rayed cages and a railed tank; and that the animals should be changed once a fortnight. Then there would be something to look at, every body would be in a much better temper, the animals would get more social life; and incidentally people would then go to the Bronx zoo instead of just thinking they'd like to; for having found an affinity with a lemur, say, they'd follow it up when the lemur retired up-town. I think you might just transfer this thought to our good mayor, on whom be blessings and peace.

There's a lot I could do for New York. But not yet, Dear Evelyn, it is hard to make it sound convincing, but I don't want to move to a more back seat. My curiosity is deeply engaged by Europe. It is quite true that here I am in the depths of the country, and not so much as a leaflet has fallen on me yet, and I read censored papers, and hear less news than you do. But I can listen to what ordinary people say, and watch how ordinary people behave, and observe my own reactions, and haul my nose over the pot, guessing at the ingredients and the stage of concoction by the smells that arise. If this were my first war I would certainly find it dull as hell. But having the last war to compare it with I find endless things to muse and brood over. In fact, as I say, my curiosity is deeply engaged. And as far as one can judge oneself I think I can assure you that my intellect has never been in better shape. I have taken such strides in perspicacity during these last few months that I feel as though I had advanced from Schumann to Beethoven.

I will make no prolonged vows, nor definite statements of what I will do in a year's time, but meanwhile I am doing extremely well. You are quite right to worry, as you say, about the real devil, the atmosphere I am living in. But I can assure you that I find the atmosphere I am living in much too interesting to be unwholesome.

Still, it is a pity about the New Yorker. It's as much their fault as mine. They sent back two things, and may send back a third which is with them now. I guess they know their own business, and it is a delicate intonation to be in tune with, I have had spells before when I couldn't hit the note with them. Still, I would be pleased to see myself in that print again; and if you want to do me a service you might write them a little letter saying that it is some time since you read anything of mine there, and that you would like to read more.

However, this is mainly a financial regret. I have started writing again, and am pleased with what I do. I hope it may be a book before the year is out.

You ask what it will be like when the boy whose grandfather was a Pole meets the grandson of a real Nazi. Some of your grandfathers or great grandfathers were Irish and my grandfathers were English. We get on all right. They won't kiss and make up; but it's quite likely that they'll get on as well as we. What is so exasperating is that the grandfathers of the present Poles and Nazis may have been on quite good terms. Time and change, given elbow-room, will smooth out enmities; one's grandfather's grief is nothing like so hereditary as one's grandfather's gout. What we've got on our hands to deal with is the hereditary nuisance of oppression and nationalism which is always embroiling a current generation in misery. One of the worst problems is the problem that arises when an oppressed people begins to glory in its cross, as the Christians phrase it. Ireland and Poland both have that poison, so, as a whole, have the jews. Ireland seems getting out of the habit now, thank heaven. It is nice to listen to the Athlone radio, and hear it so full of jigs and boasts and cattle prices, and to think how twenty years ago it would have been ringing with the harp that owes, trampled shamrocks, etc.[19]

I don't forget the miseries in Poland, or make light of them. But forty years spent in Europe obliges me to know that the chief of the Polish nation has always been pretty miserable, only it was a misery that did not get publicized. Did you read that piece about Poland in the New Yorker by a woman called Sapieha? I thought it extremely revealing. She's an American by birth, I take it; yet she is describing, and as a matter of course, a country where the bulk of the inhabitants didn't know their country was being invaded, and where no attempts were being made to tell them what to do. The feudal lords move out and the cattle are left. No beautiful corn-fields or picturesque old customs can make that a happy country. And the tradition of leaving people in the status of cattle is so strong that a quite well-educated woman, and probably American by birth, is overcome by it, and takes it for granted too.

I do believe, Evelyn, that about the worst horror of war is that it gives our charlatans such unparalleled opportunities to exclaim that Peace is Wonderful.

My love,

Sylvia

Thank you so much for that cutting. Rumours of it had reached me, and I was pining for the exact text.

Elizabeth continued to long to be near Valentine despite the satisfactions of her Tri-State work. In March she wrote a two page single-spaced letter to Miss R C Shipley of the US Passport Bureau requesting validation of her passport for travel to England, the offer of the job at *The Countryman* the rationale. [20] She wrote a few days after having introduced a screening in Washington of *Men and Dust*, the Sheldon Dick film on the silicosis conditions in the Tri-State area, later recognized as one of the important documentaries of the Depression era. It was attended by her former Westover teacher, Helen La Monte, who congratulated her warmly. [21] The call of England and Valentine trumped even this important work. However, neither this nor her subsequent attempts to move the Passport Office were successful. [22]

Sylvia wrote Evelyn again at the end of March to acknowledge receipt of an Abercrombie & Fitch flashlight that required no batteries. She gave news of war preparations but made no mention of the recent events: the Finns' defeat in the 'winter war' with the Soviet Union and the German bombing of the naval base at Scapa Flow.

Frome Vauchurch,
Maiden Newton, Dorset
29. iii. 1940[23]

Dearest Evelyn,

Two letters from you, one from Vermont and one from Maine. You are improving greatly as a correspondent, or else you keep your new year resolutions rather longer than most people do.

I am so happy to think of you touring the Granite Section, and scattering the largesse of Messrs B&B (I daresay they'd rather do it by stealth anyhow), and being cherished by Uncle Tom and Albion. I would certainly prefer Uncle Tom. Did you, while in Vermont, visit that severe matron who didn't approve of Kotex publicity: God, I hope you did: She is a flower that needs gathering. I like hearing of everything except the snow and the cold and the real winter. Our own winter had been quite realistic enough for me. But I suppose it's over now. Anyhow, I'm behaving as though it were, I don't mean to lavish any more attention on it.

Valentine received with joy and awe Abercrombie and Fitch's contribution to darkest Europe. It is magnificent, and useful in so many ways. For after one has sighted the burglar by the beam one can hit him over the head with it; and then detach the dynamo and curl his hair for the funeral, or for that matter galvanically revive him, just as one sees fit. But I'm sorry to say that you haven't come to the end of it yet. One of the spare bulbs was removed by the censor, at the time we wondered why, but discovered when I tried to get a duplicate to replace it. They took it as a curiosity. It is not possible to get smooth-stemmed bulbs for torches in this country, ours are all screw bulbs. This is one of the distinctions which make it hard for Two Great Races to come together. Practically, it comes to this: will you please ask Aberfitchie for a couple of spares? Valentine will then be perfectly happy. She has a store-cupboard disposition, and pines unless she is sure of replacements.

Dear Evelyn, it is sweet of you to want to know if you can send me anything. At the moment I am unable to think of a wish in the world, except I would like a packet of thin envelopes that would approximately take this paper (here I have only been able to get thin square ones such as this letter will come in). I promise you that when I need something I will tell you, and immediately, and fully, and shamelessly. But I'd better warn you that the things I want are always of that irritating kind which sound very simple and unostentatious and which are really the devil's own bunion to produce. Like the girl in the fairy story whose father asked her what he should bring back from his travels, and her sisters said emeralds and lapis lazuli toothbrush handles and she said, Just a red rose, Papa; and the unfortunate fellow was going to Russia in mid-winter. (The result, as you may remember, was a Bear.)

Please don't think about our food situation. So far it is nothing to worry about at all. Apparently we normally eat much less of rationed feeds than is necessary to keep one alive. For instance, I told our grocer to supply us with the weekly sugar ration, and agreed with him that it would be terrible. Since then I have had to make two batches of jam just to keep level with it. Later on I suppose there will be something to grieve for; and undoubtedly things are bad for poor people in the industrial districts, but that is very largely due to the fact that many small food-shops closed down at the beginning of the war, with bad results in distribution. The real shortages are in things like animal feeding-stuffs; and this will be felt later, because one result of this had been that many food-growers, farmers and poultry farmers, have killed off young stock. But at the moment, as I say, you need not worry about us at all.

Meanwhile, you could not have sent me anything that pleases me better than the Wildlife Restoration stamps. I mean to use them intensively, it seems to me that what people in this country want is a wider interest. They are getting tired of the war and no one cares for their Peace Aims, so why shouldn't they get burned up about restoring your wildlife? English people like wild-life almost anywhere.

Later on I will come over and see the wonderful results of my simple little mission. Please I should like the mountain goat at the foot of the gangplank. I think I love him best though at times my affections meander towards the roseate spoonbill, and just as a piece of grouping the woodland caribou and the sage hen advancing on each other with remorseless strides gives me a wonderful thrill.

Incidentally, judging from the new Republican programme your future generations will have their rightful heritage of timber wolves all right.

Meanwhile, I hope you are doing something reciprocal about protecting Bertrand Russell from all those wild mothers who seem to be so umbraged with him. What do they object to, that he is a pacifist or that he has spent the last twenty years trying to make children healthier. Mothers are difficult to understand.

My last letter about the difficulty of relinquishing a ringside seat even if you don't so far feel much about the show will have done something to answer your questions about the trip. As for financial difficulties they would appear at first sight more impressive than the moral one, but I have always gone on the assumption that the Lord won't provide and this has made me very resourceful and placid about such things. It would be nice to know the truth about it all. Undoubtedly our papers understate the future prospects. Equally undoubtedly, yours whoop them up excessively. Mankind is considerably more adaptable than mankind's pastors and masters see fit to let on. Just as moralists say that it's a sin to steal a pin and pin-taking is a sure sign of moral ruin, economists say that you'll be in a pickle if you inflate a nickel, etc. But one has to remember that both moralists and economists make their modest living by conserving morality and remember that I cannot wholly forget that the alternative title to Mr Keynes's little book which is selling so well, How to Pay for the War, is How to Pay for Maynard Keynes.

He is a nice man. I used to see him in London and in his stately home at Cambridge. He has a very fine taste in art and did a great deal to raise the standard of college claret. As for his scheme, it seems to me by his own economic standards to be just damn silly. If thirty million, say, people whose purchasing power has been restricted during a war period, are suddenly given purchasing power at the end of it, they will make one simultaneous rush for the civilian goods they haven't been able to buy; boots, blankets, and so forth. Meanwhile the boot and blanket industries will have been restricted too, they won't be able to compass the demand. A five dollar pair of boots will cost twenty dollars, and if that isn't inflation what the hell is? And if the purchasing power is let out in bits, as it will have to be, then x worth of purchasing power will mean one thing at one period and another at another. And people notice that kind of thing, too. I don't mind any of this. I am not an orthodox economist, like Mr Keynes. But such considerations should give him a bowel-ache. But I am glad his little book is selling so well, because he is a good spender, and will buy some pictures and so on with the results. Which shows, cher Pangloss, that there is a soul of good in things evil, would men industriously sniff it out.

You have heard, of course every one has heard the story of the air-man who dropped his leaflets in parcels, and was rebuked for haste. Have you heard the other end of the story? One airman came back hours late from a leaflet expedition and was asked why he'd been so long over it. He replied, well, sir, they don't seem to have many letter-boxes, so quite often I had to ring the bell and wait for them to come to the door.

I heard the other day from dear Ludwig [Renn] that he has had the refund from Cunard. So now we can ascend into heaven and relax.

I can't tell you anything else except that Lord Beaverbrook is improving the nation's food supply by growing water melons in the Highlands. As far as I know this is not true,

With my love.

Sylvia

In April, Elizabeth was inspired to write a poem; Valentine was far away, the shooting war imminent.

APRIL IN ENGLAND, 1940
Bird says, and knows:
Now all is well again;
Spring comes, winter goes,
With the young straight rain.
Underground destined food
Stirs for our summer need
Between root's longitude
And the unsealing seed.
No bird but reckons best
To remain alive,
Busy to build a nest
And rear, and thrive.

And man says, knowing too well
Where last week's late snow fell
Soon the green will spring;
And pale as the new season's morning sky
In copse and meadow corner the secret primrose lie.
Emphatically the blackbird will sing
Between sky deeper-colored, warmed through,
And the wood's answering floor of blue.
Oh will this April bring
Me, watcher, praiser, sight of primrose and bluebell sound of
bird's call,
Before the bomb's fall? [24]

On 9 April, the Nazis invaded Denmark and Norway—the latter triggering the unsuccessful British intervention at Narvik on Norway's Atlantic coast. Katie Powys referred to these dire events in mid-April.

My Dear Elizabeth-

I hope you are alright—This is a year ago since you were down with Mrs Smith with Spaniards. —I wish you were there now, with Valentine's car out side & plenty of petrol in it. How I would love to come down & find her there again with you I could feel I could talk with, you who always understood—and since then what terrible things have happened—We absolutely are horrified by Hitler over running Denmark & trying to seize Norway too, with all the terrible consequences that it involves—I feel so upset for Norway—It makes one wonder what will happen at the last & am amazed at seeing my life going on as usual—I have not heard from Valentine since it happened, but we had just arranged that I should go and stay there next Wed: week-April 24 to 27th—This will be a great joy to me, so give me a thought when if this letter reaches you in time—And when I am sitting in her room I shall think that I am not the only one who feels really happiness there within—What an amazing power Valentine has over the ones who love her—To me sometimes she is like a queen who rules her destiny—her hearts destiny of her followers—Never do I cross a street with such safety & assistance as when I feel her hand on my arm. She is the only person I know that asserts that right over me—Her influence always makes me yield my personality to her—Yet I am never false to myself when I am with her, but I am always candid, & like sunshine among flowers enjoy my confidences with her.

I wish the War did not make everything so difficult, even as it seems to do, enlarging the distance of the Atlantic between us— To walk—to read are the only defenders against the awful threat of the moment.

I hope it won't be too long before we meet again.

With every best wish and love from Philippa[25]

Evelyn fell in love with Elizabeth. In mid-April when Elizabeth was en route to Joplin, Missouri, Evelyn concluded a letter, 'It is late and I am very sleepy—and I wish you were here because you see Elizabeth, I do love you.' [26]

Valentine responded to Elizabeth's news that Evelyn had fallen in love with her by pledging herself to Elizabeth and challenging her to pledge likewise.

F.V.

17. IV. 40[27]

My beloved—(that is a very beautiful word, Elizabeth—solemn & serious, & meant to be so, from me to you.) My beloved—No one can tell what will happen to us, I well know that, but if you come to me I want you to understand what will be constantly in my mind, what will be my hope & my intention. Perhaps you will make it yours too—

But it is difficult to know how far I may go in absolute candour to you, without committing the great offence of seeming to pledge what I cannot, yet, absolutely honestly promise you. Understand that I am telling you now what are my dear hopes, my most deliberate intentions when you are here with me.

I want & I intend that we shall be together as belonging to each other; I shall do everything in my power to make you happy; I shall be faithful to you (I know, now, that I can promise that without fear of breaking my word to you) & I shall consider you as owning my pledge of faith, & myself as owning your pledge of faith; we shall be each others' property & possession.

I will give you constancy of care and of protection. I will not leave you nor will I ever fail you, as lover, as husband, as companion.

Opposite:

55. Photographs of herself included in Valentine's letter to Elizabeth of 17 April 1940.

In return, you will give me constancy of love, of companionship and loyalty. I will give you all you ask of me so far as I can always, asking you only that, in major decisions, in any conflict of opinion between us (short of a really violent clash of moral convictions) you will follow me.

I know that these ideas can only apply, at first, to an experimental situation: but if that is ever to be changed into what we hope, the best way of giving it every chance of success is to have its skeleton built & to allow love, time & intimacy to put its spirit & blood & flesh upon it. For—my loveliest, my most beloved & worshipped, treasured & desired—you must come to me as mine, & that must be happiness & joy, enchantment, content to both of us.

I want to put this new ring, this most solemn, most lovely of all, upon your finger. I want to bend over you as you lie naked, & I want to take your hand in mine & with this ring to claim final & absolute possession of what, so far, I have held by your grace. For this to be as we both want it (I believe you want) you might brave all the dangers & come to me & I must meet you & take you to myself & never let you go again.

Do not feel mistrustful of me because I have been honest, always, with you. I have not bound myself when I did not know if I could stay. I have not pledged till I could know I could perform. Now I KNOW that I can continue to give you the absolute physical constancy you asked & promised.

I will wait for you. I have, these few days past, rejected a love that, heaven knows, I needed. I sent you a cable about it because I did not know whether you having E might not have [reservations in?] your own belief—& because, too, I was afraid I might have to do it. For I did want to—I thought her very lovely & I do not easily reject its chance of love & relief. Never mind. No more of this. It's done with. I did not. I want you, Elizabeth.

Later

It is so late. I am not well. I've got some kind of a throat infection & a fever. It's epidemic just now & I've caught it. This letter will go with a soldier, [ ] to D [Dorchester] where it may catch an earlier mail than if it went from here. The posts are VERY uncertain just now. I've heard nothing from you since the letter about E [EVH] being in love with you. My darling, lying here in bed I wonder (forgive me) whether you can maintain your own standard of fidelity—& yet I do believe, yes. I do.

I've been thinking the important thing about love—about being in love—is its image of the beloved. I know perfectly well that you are not all I have you in mind to be; just as I am different in some ways from your vision of me. But with both of us, BEING loved TRULY—have created within in us by the other one, those very qualities which otherwise are lacking. I—because of you wishing it from me—am become faithful in heart & body to you, because by that I am duly your lover, & what you wish me to be. Yes—because I must have it so in the woman I deeply love—am trustworthy in body & mind, am able to lose the world for love, & am candid & brave in love. You are not these things necessarily, any more than I am constant. But TOGETHER IN LOVE we are good! I love you—MINE

Valentine

On 10 May 1940, Germany invaded the Low Countries and France. Within three weeks, the evacuation of Dunkirk was completed, and the Germans were about to enter Paris. England was alone; Churchill replaced Chamberlain as Prime Minister. Elizabeth was even more anxious to get permission to travel to England: 'England is where I belong at this time.' Sylvia replied with strong counter arguments that June, and pointed out that she could not stay at Frome Vauchurch in a mènage a trois: the 1939 experience was not to be repeated.

Frome Vauchurch,
Maiden Newton, Dorset
12. vi. 1940[28]

My dear Elizabeth,

I was sorry to hear you were moving out of Perry Street because I supposed—your letter tells me I supposed right—that you would find it irksome at home. I imagine a disproportionate fist thrust through a window and a tinkle of falling glass, as in Alice. And I congratulate you sincerely on having outgrown so definitely a setting where you have for so long been a bad fit. If it is not too late I congratulate you too on the Tri-State. I read the reports in the Joplin Whatnots that you sent to Valentine; and as far as I could judge it looked as though the Inquiry had been just about what was wanted; and not so resplendent a success as to cancel itself out and lead to nothing but a scattering of humanitarian roses after it was dead.

I can sympathize with how you are feeling. I feel that way myself—about France. Part of my mind is forever walking about in Paris—streets I know, the other streets where I have said to myself, I'll go down there some day. People seen casually and for an instant rise up in my memory, a man in a wineshop, a serious child in a school overall, a woman behind a street stall handing me a bag of green almonds, two middle-aged argueing men walking down in the Alley of the Observatory as though it and their discussion could never end. These feelings are inevitable; though I think they are considerably false and sentimental. It is a symptom of social maladjustment that makes one feel so passionately attached to countries where one is 'on a holiday', where one can be freed from the sense of social responsibility. If we were more satisfied with our own countries, if we were not so ashamed and so uneasy about the deficiencies there, we should not be liable to sentimental idealisations of countries not our own. Such idealisations are only the other side of the canvas of an indiscriminating patriotism; and just as much the sign of an uneasy conscience. Nobody who truly feels himself a citizen of the world would develop these peculiar attachments; they are a nationalism perverted, nothing to do with real internationalism.

Still, that doesn't make it any less painful to be haunted by such preoccupations; and, as I say, I can well understand how you are feeling about England, as the same bug is biting me. Nevertheless, I am so sure that is a bug that I question your justification for saying that 'England is where I belong at this time'. In the largest sense, one 'belongs' to the world (since science has not yet demonstrated to us how we 'belong' to the solar system); and people of exceptional ability can really achieve this position of belonging to the world. For practical purposes one belongs where one has most responsibilities, and is best equipped to understand and fulfill them. One sees this tidily demonstrated among people who acknowledge no responsibilities whatsoever and achieve a kind of bogus internationalism which makes them perfectly at home in identically artificial Hotel Splendide conditions; very expensive two-headed calves whose cages transport from Biarritz to Honolulu. The outside of the cage is plastered with more and more labels of coasts each bluer than the last, and inside sit the monsters.

Your will to see Valentine seems a much tougher and more unassailable reason for coming, a reason that I cannot and do not feel inclined to debate. But I think you should start—if you do start—without illusions. I know that Valentine has told you that already conditions would make it very difficult for you to have more than fits and starts of each other's company; and such conditions are likely to be even more exigent as time goes on. But apart from these practical wartime impediments you must in justice to Valentine realise that spirit as well as circumstances is subject to and that a meeting at this time is likely to be quite as painful as pleasurable, is as likely to result in distress and embarrassment as in consolation. In advising you not to come she is not merely considering your feelings and your safety. She has considered (as she is right to do) her own; the probability of a double distress, the distress of her own disappointment in finding that she can take no comfort from your being here, the distress of disappointing your hopes and intentions of being a comfort.

This is not anything to do with Evelyn. It is inherent in the effect of war on all personal relationships. What she felt, and what she said about Evelyn is not modified; it is side-tracked, cut-out, to all intents and purposes invalidated by what has happened since. The question of Evelyn, so to speak, is at this moment, inaudible. The guns are too loud. And similarly, you must take into account the probability that if you come to England the guns may be too loud for Valentine and yourself to be able to hear each other's voices; that the situation will not allow you to retain enough private individuality to work out any settlement, any temporary amelioration even, of your individual problems.

I find it very unpleasant and difficult to write all this: partly because I too am subject to this same strain, and find it an effort to discuss a private situation; partly because I am so circumstanced that to be advising you not to come must almost certainly make that advice seem either self-regarding or malicious; and partly, please believe me, because I don't want to make you any unhappier than you are, and hate that our old peaceful and confident relationship should become all snarled up with explanations.

If you reckon out all these reasons why I don't like writing this you will realise that I have a good and serious reason for to be able to overcome all the reasons *against*. One other thing I ought to say. I don't think it is a factor that should affect your decision to come or not to come, since it is not anything that would essentially concern you; but to put all the cards on the table I must include it.

If you come, I would prefer not to meet you. Circumstances may make it impossible for me to carry out my preference, that is a thing that would be perhaps beyond my decision. But as far as preferences goes. I am sure of my own mind, and if it is possible I shall abide by it. I do not feel that we can do each other the slightest good by meeting. Our past does not provide a foundation for our present because our present has developed at such an acute angle from our past that the relationship of the two is a geometrical impossibility. Any present contact between us must be a strain on us both, we should inevitably become entangled with all those varieties of compromise, making-allowances-for, adjustments, considerations, uncertainties, misapprehension, that beset us last year and that this year would make both more acute and more inadvisable.

I wish it were not so; I wish it were not so particularly because I can realise that in this last interval since October you have become so much more the person I long ago knew you could, and hoped you would, become. It is sad and taunting that the mature Elizabeth I looked forward to should be the present Elizabeth I don't want to see.

But it would not do. We should not be enough our own mistresses to meet. Everything would be vitiated by the fact that we are unwilling opposites, that Valentine and you and I cannot be long together without all causing each other doubt and misery. Both you and I are obstinate and theoretical characters, and the combined obstinacy with which we tried to carry out a theory of ideal conduct must at times have been a very edifying spectacle. Indeed, I would say we did pretty well. But not well enough to do justice either to our intentions or to our theory. And not well enough to compensate for the incidental lacerations all round.

I wish I could say to you: At least, if you come you will be the better for me being out the way. I wish I could promise that I should so easily be out of mind by being out of sight.

But I don't pretend to anything like consideration, tact, self-effacement. I can't even claim that I suppose I should ease Valentine by being out of the way. My reason is based on something quite plain and crude; that having suffered a great deal and seeing no one a penny the better for it I don't want to suffer that way again. I don't suppose any expedient will make me suffer less, but I will try a variant, spike myself on a different sort of thorn. Probably it will be just as bad, may be it will be worse. When I think of it it seems obvious that it will be worse. For if you come, and if I won't remain with you and Valentine, then clearly I expose myself to all the special twists of torment that war can inflict on the person who is absent from the only thing they love. In fact, I shall just change partners with you, shan't I, since that is what you're feeling now?

Don't think (I don't) that this frame of mind is for ever. It is much more in the nature of some remedial process, a water-cart policy. But for the present it is certain. It is not because I have changed my feelings for you, or resent what has happened. It is much simpler and more imperative than that, it is just that I know that I cannot, this year, endure a repetition of last year. Even Mithridates, I suppose, varied his poisons.

And one other thing that I must say to ward off a possibility of mental torment for you. Valentine now knows how I feel. But while there was a possibility that she might decide to go to USA I said nothing at all of all this. You can't think me reasonable, tolerant, magnanimous, any of the things you might like to think me. But think me sincere; and not ungrateful, nor unloving.

Sylvia

In this acute period of the war there was no prospect that Elizabeth would be allowed by the State Department or the British government to travel to England, much less live there. In New York, when the Tri-State work was done, she volunteered with the Red Cross and became a driver in its Motor Corps, driving homebound people to and from hospitals and doctors' offices. In Waterbury, she was active on behalf of intervention to save England. This was not a popular position when the 'America First' movement was at its height. A brochure she distributed laid out the reasons for intervention. [29]

Despite Elizabeth's attachment to Valentine, she and Evelyn became close. Evelyn sent love and support in a special delivery letter to Breakneck in mid-July. 'I love you Elizabeth and hope that I can be with you very soon. It is useless to ask you to be happy but try it. Think about your lovely countryside & not about the people in your house; be in the sun and go to bed early and have faith that your life is going to be as you want it.' [30]

In August, as the danger to England grew acute with Nazi air raids and the prospect of invasion, Evelyn offered comfort and reaffirmed her love: 'I should like very much to be able to do or say something that would lessen your fright about Valentine's safety. It is no help to you to tell you to have faith but there is nothing I can say other than that—unless to tell you I understand the particular kind of hell you are living through. The only use this can be to you is to possibly lessen the lonely fright you feel. If you will believe and remember that I am watching over you with loving concern you will know the only comfort one human being can offer to another during the times when we walk alone.' [31]

Sylvia and Valentine had moved to Winterton to be near Ruth Ackland. They knew it was a more dangerous location than Dorset because it was closer to what would soon be German airfields across the North Sea, but they felt it their duty to support Ruth. The Battle of Britain had just begun in the skies, an invasion seems likely. Sylvia shows no fear.

The Mill, Winterton, Norfolk
18: vii: 1940[32]

My dear Evelyn,

You are the only person who gives news of Sixth Avenue and I can't imagine how nice it is to hear news of trees being planted. Then, instead of receiving condolences on the removal of iron railings from Hyde Park. I say with unwavering faith in Mr [Robert] Moses that I expect it is a good plan to remodel Washington Square ... though I like it very well as it is. I wish it could be remodeled to suit its local population; with quantities of cypresses, and a lemon grove, and perhaps a small model of Vesuvius, and an opera-house in the place of that Baptist or whatever it is edifice at the corner.

I wish I could thank you for those envelopes. At any rate I thank you for sending them. But don't send any more. I think the British Government are taking a circuitous way around the paper shortage by just discouraging any attempt to write. For instance,

56. Evelyn Holahan, summer, 1940.

one lot of paper did get through to me; but I was learned better by having to pay a customs duty on it that must have been about two-thirds of the value of the paper. Similarly, I expect those nice thin envelopes have just been nicely and parentally sequestrated. Meanwhile, with the natural perversity of an island race every soldier I set eyes on is writing a letter. It is all very disconcerting. Kindly hearts start canteens for soldiers, and supply them sandwiches, doughnuts, light literature, hot sweet tea, and manly indoor sports. Soldiers march in and demand writing paper and salads.

We came here about three weeks ago. Partly because Ruth [Ackland] was representing herself as an overworked Britannia guarding the Norfolk coast single-handed, and partly because we felt we could do more than address silver paper for the Red Cross, which was the sole activity in Maiden Newton. Ruth was not quite so overworked as she made out, but there is more to do here, and I am not sorry we came, though I miss a garden of our own and wonder if our tenant is really doing her duty by the sweet-corn and the potato crops. (Ruth, by the way, is Valentine's mother.) I like Norfolk people anyhow. They have a snarl in them.

Ruth is very religious—Anglo-Catholic, covered with medals of St Christopher and what-not, to which the war has added an assortment of voluntary badges. She adores idols; but being both heavy-handed and un-sure footed, no idol stays intact in her possession. There are at least six plaster Jesus's in the house, and not one of them but is minus an ear, or a foot, or is somehow the worse for Ruth's devotions. Perhaps the best is the crucified Jesus which she keeps for her prayer circle. He hangs from the cross by one arm, the other arm, broken off at the shoulder, dangles independently, as though it expressed some theological schism. She is also very fond of china rabbits, in short could describe her as ikonophile.

If she didn't trust in God and believe in human nature she'd be all right. But as a mother she might easily be worse. She might be Mrs White. Your desire to put idle land into cultivation is too good an idea, I'm afraid, to be worth going on with. It is impossible to make people see what stares them in the face. For that matter, there is plenty of idle land in this country—but you can look long over it before you see a trace of anything being done to it. On the other hand, if you started a campaign for growing more mustard and cress to send to starving Europe, and pointed out that it can be grown on a damp blanket, and then issued an appeal for blankets, I have no doubt you would get a magnificent response. You must follow this up by a scheme for growing turnips in chamber pots and lilies (for war graves) in Park Avenue. But the trouble about you is that your ideas are so idealistically practical.

Kindly observe my [prescience] about Wendell Willkie. I will now go to my real Sibylline leaf, and, maintain that if he gets in you will soon have a fine and flourishing variety of American Fascism … something really home-grown, and far more appealing than the Bund or Father Coughlin. [33]

I was very sorry to hear that your father is dead. It is so rare, so difficult, to be on terms of any sort of sympathy with the preceding generation, and yet, when one can achieve this, it is such an interesting and valuable relationship, that to lose a friendly father is to mislay the key to a large part of one's background, as well as being a person one loves. Later, already perhaps—you will begin to meet him in yourself. It is a queer and ghostly encounter but nourishing if one can keep sentiment out of it, and you will do that, I think.

If we are short of money I will bear your promise in mind. It is a very kind one, and I am very grateful. To show that I take it seriously I will say that if I later ask you for money it would be best to send it in English currency. It takes months to disentangle dollars over here. Banks are short of everything except tape, and dollar cheques are about as immediately appreciated auriferous nuggets: indeed, the nugget might well have it. But at the moment we do all right. As far as I know it is still allowable to the dollar-pound exchange on your side.

We are sending you a few auriferous nuggets ourselves, I see. Do not fail to meet at least Mr Reid [Samingham]. If you try hard you might even get a drink off him, and the story of his hard sad life, which proves, as plainly as any religious magazine story, that Gold is not all.

Time still comes, though intermittently and belatedly. And I can't express how pleased we are with it. One of the items I relish most is the pages on Science. I hope there is some science going on here (during the last war Rutherford and the atom had a secluded but fruitful life together); but there is no news of it. It is interesting how soon science can be forgotten. As you know, during the evacuation of Dunkirk the sea was unusually calm. I heard this fact mentioned the other day, with the rider that it must have seemed like an answer to a prayer to Mr Churchill. On my remarking that Mr Churchill and the Admiralty still could avail themselves of the services of the meteorological bureau I was frowned on as one who spreads rumours likely to 'create alarm and despondency'. Answers to prayer are more patriotic, and the vision of admirals telephoning in voices choked with tears urging the premier to pray some more is of course less bleak than the impartial face of a barometer. But personally I still like a little science, and hope that Time and Mr Luce won't be so carried away as to discard it in favour of the latest things of tidings of Bundles for Britain.

I can't send you any news I 'm afraid. For one thing, it would be coals to Newcastle. But I beg you to remember that the mass of people in this country are not really represented by the people now leaving it for yours—or by the counter-irritant reports of populations joyously frolicking round bomb craters. We are, in fact, not such damn fools as we are made out to be. So don't be misled by what rises to the top. Scum constantly, as Mrs Beeton would advise.

I hope dear Raymond G Swing is not really ill. It was a great blow to hear him say he was obliged by reasons of health to give over broadcasting on the BBC.[34]

With love ever,

Sylvia

Please let me know your back is better. I insist that it be better.

PS Can anything be done about Craske? He has no chance of a market here now. I would be deeply grateful if you could get his affair going.

At the end of August, Valentine demanded of Evelyn an accounting.

Winterton, Norfolk
August 30th, 1940[35]

Dear Evelyn,

I hoped that, from one or another reason, I should not write this letter; it seemed to me possible either that you would send me what I have now to ask of you, without the asking, or that the necessity for it would be smothered in sharper necessities. The first didn't happen & the second was a miscalculation. Simply, as things here become daily more uncomfortable and ill-balanced, so the discomfort of the ill-balance in our triple-alliance is, for me increased. It is certainly not my business to enquire into your private & separate feelings, but I have a right to know them as they concern Elizabeth.

Will you try to tell me, as simply & candidly as possible, how you stand in regard to Elizabeth? This question seems to fall into two parts: First, it enquires about your present estate; Second, it asks you to define your wishes. I know it is a queer way of asking you your 'Intentions', but most unfortunately it is the only way open to me at present.

I have urgent reasons for needing to know, which are so easy for you to imagine that I needn't go into details. The urgency may not be so easy to understand, but it is partly due to the sharpening of the general sense of urgency over here and partly to the fact that the likelihood of my seeing Elizabeth in the near future is much lessened now.

Elizabeth has told me, obviously with care & accuracy, how she conceives matters to be between you. I have of course told her that I am writing to you. It's ridiculous to use the future as a 'threat', & I don't mean to do that when I tell you that so far as I now can see it Elizabeth's future in some measure and my own to a considerably greater extent, depend on your accuracy and candour now.

I wish I'd written to you three months ago; more still I wish you had written to me directly you knew which way you were taking yourself. In any event, it is impossible to foretell such strange shiftings of character & relationship as seem to be taking place among us just now. The immediate concern is that the immeasurable violence of the times (together with the results of it upon people like myself, fortunate enough only to feel its by-products so far—such as lack of sleep, lack of liberty, increased tension & so on) demand a great deal of self-control and clarity. It has become really urgent to straighten out emotional tangles & to clean out & disinfect the places in one's life which otherwise would become plaguespots. In sober fact it is impossible to keep integrity of mind (sanity, I suppose) if, besides the attack from outside, one's own life shelters a Fifth Column, or suspects one.

Please believe that this letter hurts me more than it hurts you— probably the first time in history the phrase has been justified!

Yours,

Valentine

Using her office stationery, Evelyn sent a brisk reply and kept a carbon.

Benton & Bowles, Inc. letterhead
Sept. 9th [1940][36]

Dear Valentine:

I too, am sorry that you felt the necessity to write such a letter. Either I am inexcusably naive or, inexcusably brutal, but at any rate it had never occurred to me that I should write and tell you the things you demand to know. However, I am perfectly willing to answer your questions.

From the beginning and up to the present date, my purpose with Elizabeth was to offer whatever help and comfort I could to one who was not only desperately unhappy but in a definite danger as a result of this prolonged unhappiness. This is something which to a degree, I would do for most any good human being. In her case I have tried to a greater degree because I believe her to be an exceptionally fine character and to my standard of values on human beings, one who deserves as much help as it is possible to give. This always has been, is, and I expect will continue to be, my only purpose with Elizabeth.

As to my 'intentions' I cannot answer that question because I have no intentions as you mean the word. You seem to doubt the fact that the only person in this world whom she truly loves is yourself and that her one consuming desire is to be with you again. If I have any intentions it is to do anything I can to help bring this about for if it does not happen, I assure you it will be tragic for her. What my innermost feelings are for her are quite my own business for I make very certain that they in no way influence our relationship. This may seem odd to you but I am a much thicker skinned person than either one of you. Under the circumstances (and by that I mean the knowledge of where her heart and soul belongs) it could be an extra piece of folly for me to have intentions—so called.

From my point of view there is no question of a 'triple-alliance'. I am sorry (for you) if you conceive it as one for I assure you, you are using a ghost for the third member. Also, Valentine, I most solidly deny any responsibility—as a result of my actions to date—for the future relationship of you and Elizabeth. Very frankly, I believe this is something you are responsible for.

If after reading this you feel that you cannot believe what I have said and that you do not trust me as your friend, I would greatly appreciate it if you would do me the favor of telling me so.

I am very sorry that I have not written to you and Sylvia for such a long time. The combination of hard work, not too good health and anxiety over events happening in this mad world, seem to destroy my confidence in having anything worthwhile to say. After a month of comparative ease and rest I am feeling quite myself again and don't expect to go off any more deep ends.

Janet Machen, who had been sharing the 42 Perry St. flat with Elizabeth wanted to return home to be near her family now that the war was on. 'I'll never forget the sight of the girl on the blacked out dock as we put her on board the ship,' Elizabeth recalled. 'She broke down and cried and cried. She was rescued by two determined women, one of whom was a Mrs Simpson who going to England to become part of the Army nurse corps there. They took Janet under their wing.' Valentine later sent news of Janet who was working in London during the worst of the war, but often visiting in Dorset.[37]

In September, Evelyn and Elizabeth took a flat together at 519 East 19th Street in New York. At Christmas, Evelyn committed herself to Elizabeth. They were both 34 years old (as was Valentine).

Dec. 23rd [1940][38]

There is nothing I could give to you, my dear Elizabeth, that would be any measure of the deep pleasure and gratitude in my heart on this Xmas day. If it were within my power to do so, I would give you that which you want most for I love you Elizabeth and your happiness is my single wish. I would like you to take heart about this coming year. Please try to believe that it won't be too difficult and that it may be a better year than you anticipate. Also, remember my darling that you will not be alone. God bless you and keep you.

Evelyn

Elizabeth replied in gratitude from Breakneck the day after Christmas.

I have thought a lot about you. You as a part of my life intermittently from last February to September and every day since then, you in the note you sent me with your present. And it has made me feel very humble and grateful and curiously certain that I am alive, not a lost ghost any more. And I am Happy in the midst of much anxiety and unhappiness near and far, to think that you will be here with me tomorrow night, and I can put my arms around you and feel you close against me and lie down beside you in bed. I want you to find this when you come, if possible, so you will know what I should have written before I left New York, but was too ragged to do so directly: that at this season of thanking for gifts and benefits received I am full of deepest gratitude to you, my dear friend, for the companionship, the shelter, the kind and patient understanding, the true home and the wise and gentle love that you have given me. I seem to have managed very well with my life, to have accomplished so little and to have brought too much unhappiness to myself and to others—those I have loved but among them—and I guess I am not a very good person or at all a wise one. But I have the power, thank God, to honor and recognize goodness and wisdom, truth and purity and courage, when I see them, and I have found them in you, my darling, more dear and abundant than in any other person I have ever known. And since we have been together I have seen you happy. I have felt you happy, and to be a part of that happiness has made me feel that [was a] form of goodness.

I don't in the least know about the future. Things have happened to me suddenly and violently in the past two years, and have shaken me deeply and permanently, and who can say what the next will be. But I know with serious knowledge what you and I have found together, what we have now, and I know how important it is, in all ways, that I should make and keep myself worthy of what you have given me for us to share together, and so, at this ending of our first year, I give you, my dear, my great thanks and true love, from

Elizabeth[39]

VII. A last meeting must happen one time

Valentine probed the nature of their past relationship in letters to Elizabeth from May to August 1943. She wrote from her desk at the Dorchester County Council Office of Civil Defence, often interrupted by the noise of bombs. These intensely thoughtful and searching letters are all of hers that survive from the seven-year span, 1941–1948. Other letters are from Sylvia, one to Evelyn to whom, as before, she wrote expressively. Her letters to Elizabeth were shorter, but cordial and informative in response to presents at Christmas and food parcels. In late 1943, probably in response to a request from Elizabeth, she reported on Valentine's poor health that caused her to leave the Civil Defense Office.

Elizabeth and Evelyn continued to share the apartment on East 19th Street and usually spent weekends at Breakneck. After the invasion of the Soviet Union in June 1941, American supporters organized relief committees, which in 1942 became a nationwide organization, Russian War Relief. Elizabeth was chair of the Waterbury chapter, and went on to work for the national organization. In 1942, she spent several months in Minnesota and North Dakota organizing local committees for the organization. Nevertheless, she continued without success to seek overseas positions with the Red Cross and later with the commission that former New York governor Herbert Lehman was heading to aid refugees in Europe.

In January 1941, Sylvia sent New Year's greetings to Evelyn with an account of wartime conditions and her and Valentine's service to soldiers on duty on the coast.

Frome Vauchurch
Maiden Newton, Dorset
5. i. 1941[1]

My dear Evelyn,

I am delighted to say that your Christmas present reached us (it is gloomy to think what a lot of Santa Claus's boxes are now making coral.) And thank you so much for it, it is lovely to have such delicious tea, and tea so fresh that one can appreciate how delicious it is. And it is also very pleasant to know that the China Aid is also the better for it. What a ridiculous and fantastic set-out, tea sold to aid China at war arriving in this beleaguered island! It is a sort of mad and bloody version of the Scilly Islanders living by taking in each other's washing.

Tea means a great deal now, when food is getting progressively scantier and nastier, when wine though nice as ever is definitely rare, when one's clothes get shabbier and shabbier, and conversation becomes more and more belittled, and wolves sit patiently smiling on every doorstep. Even when it is almost a necessity, tea still contrives to keep an air of being an amenity—real tea, proper tea, like yours.

Heaven knows, we have nothing to complain of, beyond the inherent nastiness of war. Our roof is still over our heads; though every night we hear aeroplanes going over on their way to strip roofs of other people's. We keep our health, and—what is a much more remarkable achievement—our tempers. And though of course one can't expect Mr Chamberlain to die every week we usually contrive to find some agreeable incident to meditate on; or else something to be angry about which also stimulates one's juices and keeps one going.

It is hellishly cold. Snow on the ground, and a hard frost, every thatched roof has a set of long icicle fangs, and the only colour in the landscape is the various shades of crimson, scarlet, purple and dull lilac of faces and hands in various states of cold. The BBC recently broadcast some advice to householders which included a recommendation against allowing one's incendiary sand to freeze.

The destruction of the Wren churches is hard to bear. And I have felt a particular pang about Trinity House, one of my favourite buildings. It was so small, so sober. That kind of thing never gets replaced, if there is another Trinity House it will be a great civic monstrosity like the Port of London building. One of the most galling sidelines in the situation is the number of disgusting buildings that still remain unharmed, but I have to remember that, up to the loss of the Wren churches, the worst piece of destruction in London was carried out in peace time and in cool blood when the crown rent authorities demolished Regent Street. Amidst the howls of Goth and Hun which are just as loud, I suppose, on your side of the Atlantic as on mine, it is interesting to remember this forgotten fact. But I expect you had better mention it with discretion, facts are always so unpopular in war, and the voice of reason is unpopular at any time.

Three days a week Valentine and I take out a YMCA van. We have a round along the coast, the stretch of mainland so oddly called the isle of Purbeck. All its bleakest and most inaccessible and solitary places have little groups of soldiers, and our van is about their only contact with the world. They are in this beautiful scenery, the sort of places holiday-makers would give their eyes to be in, or else in the purlieus of the grandest parks, only ordinarily enjoyed by dukes and so forth. And of course they are bored to perishing point, and extremely cold. At one of our stops there is a pure negro, whose father, he tells us, was Portuguese and his mother English (odd mingling of two great colonial powers). He looks so odd against the background of snowy parkland and Palladian stables. His vitality is a great comfort to us, he strolls about bareheaded and with no extra clothes and never seems to feel cold, and addresses amorous remarks of a purely conventional nature in Spanish and Portuguese ... at least, when we understand them even worse than we understand Spanish we presume it is Portuguese. He is very popular, I am glad to say. I suppose his fellows feel much as we do about him, and warm their hands at him, so to speak.

It would be very nice work indeed if it weren't voluntary: We neither of us take kindly to blacklegging; and if it did not smell at once of charity and of profit-making (though that's no novelty, I have never smelled a charity that did not also smell of profit-making, it is an economic law that if you wish to help the poor you have to make enough money from them to have money to spend on the pursuit); and if the tyres weren't so bad, or could be renewed, but they can't be, for of course there is a shortage of rubber and if the hours weren't so long, and if the van didn't joggle so. It is a Ford V8, a lovely engine, and Valentine drives it as though it were a private car, suave as a Béchamel; but jolts are inevitable on such rough tracks.

As for the look of the country, it has been indescribably beautiful during this spell of snow. A white sky, and white and gray world, and a seal like a blue moonstone.

We have had an AFS worker [2] from London down here, sent for a spell of rest. He told us some of his working adventures, he has been on since the first Blitz, and one of them was how a collapsing riverside building shot him into the Thames; but the stories he most enjoyed telling were long intricate departmental rumpuses on small points of procedures and etiquette, and how, arraying himself in virtue and argument, he had persuaded a superintendent or worsted some libertine proposal to revise a button. It has long become a wonder to me how any donkey in the British Isles has a hindleg left on it. I can only suppose that in the course of ages the breed has developed a peculiar resistance. I marvel, and am just as bad. For instance there was the day when Valentine mislaid me for half an hour at the fishmongers, and coming at last to fetch me away, found me locked in earnest discussion with the fishmonger's wife as to whether or not the fact that bluebottles afforded a food for spiders was a justification for the existence of bluebottles.

This is too late to wish you a happy New Year, so I will chance it and wish you a happy Lincoln's Day.

Ever,

Sylvia

Valentine put her typing and organizational skills into service at the Dorchester County Council Office of Civil Defence from where she wrote on 8 May 1943. It was the first of long and remarkable letters written in between what she described as arduous duties. In the later of these letters, she explored her past relationship with Elizabeth, what went wrong, and expressed doubts about the future. The American troops that would participate in D-Day thirteen months later were already in evidence.

Frome Vauchurch
May 8th evening [1943?][3]

Since your decision and our circumstances—and by your decision the implied adjustment in your own mind (you see how I am learning the words! That is Provincial Diplomacy) I think I should begin letters My dearest Elizabeth—which is true to fact, since the Possessive is purely formal, and neither intrusive nor provocatively 'national' (as being an under-statement ... which, come to look at it, it is not).

My dearest Elizabeth,

There is a great gale blowing again; it has come at a bad time—the fruit blossom was just 'setting' and the early spring had encouraged blossom on every kind of fruit and the first vegetable. All this is now strewn on the garden ground, and when I go to work I walk over long lanes of chestnut and lime-flowers and the lilac in Hugh's garden is torn off and scattered on the ground.

There have been other gales too. Janet is staying for the first part of her holiday in the cottage Sylvia and I own, and Steven [Clark] is accommodated nearby.

[Section apparently cut out by censor]

And we? Nothing much, but I am kept busy on my job. Janet comes here next week. I'm staying with Monica [Hemmings Ring] for a night on Monday and I think Janet will not arrive till Tuesday but I don't know. Steven (Clark] and she, so far as I now know, will be married very soon & you know as well as I do how it will turn out. I think (as usual!) that far too much has been SPOKEN and WRITTEN on both sides, and so they will never be able to forget, and never as able to forgive. However, maybe it will be all right. They have the last remedy to hand: if Janet has children she will be happy.[4]

I travelled to work in a train opposite to a little, dusky American officer who was asleep. I gently and unobtrusively kicked him awake and then we conversed. He gave me a cigarette. He had come from California, but he'd been brought up in Pennsylvania and he knew places I'd been with Steven et al, and so we had a pleasing journey and I was able to tell him about the people he was going to & give him an introduction to the gardener, which should mean some fine fruit for him later on! We could hardly endure to part and only managed it after exchanges and invitations and so on. He wasn't very nice; he was what we'd call 'a regular' that's to say: he'd been in the Army for some time before the war, & he despised the Draftees & called them 'Boyscouts'. I thought of Franklin and scowled at the little man. But he'd had a long tough journey and he was very tired. I think he found the going hard, although he had two thousand cigarettes and paid 2d for twenty— he told me. Maybe that was just Californian reckoning.

There is intense activity in my business just now, and for once it is justified. Single-handed in the office, with my boss 'in' only 3 half days a week, I am hard beset and now the duplicator has broken down, just at the wrong moment, and so I had to type by hand no less than 166 notices of an urgent meeting ... And then cut the slips separately and send them off in old envelopes with stickers ... it took, for interest's sake, just six hours to do ... To-day I was allowed off an hour before my time, to get to Weymouth to do a small piece of essential shopping: I got there and raced to the shop and back to the Station and caught the train in just exactly twenty minutes, against the gale and the rain ... and meeting Hugh by mistake and so having to walk politely instead of a jog-trot as I'd been doing!

I've never carried so much in so many shopping bags in my life! We do lead strange lives now—but I complicate mine by choosing to re-read the Webbs' 'Soviet Communism', in two fat volumes. For the second time. It is a good way of staying fresh in one's mind.

Anna Seghers' book never reached me (no reproach intended; I know you did send it, but it must have been drowned and I'm trying to get a copy here; it is printed here now but the supply is very short & probably I'll have to wait a while, but don't worry any more about it—I shall get it one way or another. [5]

Your birthday present: I have tried to get you one of the very nice leather bags in which at present people choose to carry their money and/or belongings; they are very pleasantly made and, very fashionable—and very rare! If I get one and send it, do be sure to buy some saddle-soap (I don't know if you call it that? It is yellow and soapy but in a block and used for harness and so on) and then work the leather about when it is wet with soap— that makes it pliable and it becomes a very beautiful honey-colour which will please you.

No more now. I hope that you and Evelyn are getting on well and that your spring is being a happy one. You were right to stay there & I wish you happiness and peace—and I do this truly.

Love always,

Valentine

Two weeks later Valentine wrote Elizabeth.

Whitsunday
[May 1943][6]

I hope this will please you. I'd be glad to have it back, if times allow which is very unlikely. It is the second good one I've had [possibly a poem, not found]—the second was better & drew a reply (written in mid-winter when I was ill, I hurry to say!) and apparently what I let slip about my countrymen (always excepting some of them: Auden and so on) must have been quite lucky, I can't remember much of all that except that when Winifred [Duncan] had remarked that she had started to send off a parcel and then stopped because she realised that Britain was getting most of the US food & that she understood the townspeople were doing nicely on oranges. I believe I said temperately that they weren't and that while we were happy enough in the country people we knew in London & Glasgow & Birmingham were just in the mood

311

for oranges. But however I said, evidently it annoyed her and I am so very glad of that.

But I am sure I did not imply that she was wallowing in my lap. I'd not have thought of it. Her letter had been full of sorrow because she had a nasty idea that Mexico might enter the war. I believe she misunderstood my sympathy.

This is a holiday here as you won't remember because you were not here for Whitsunday, I believe, and anyway every day was a holiday, so to speak. But it is being a pleasant one, although the wind shifted to the North and we were very cold as we slept out on the lawn. I lay and watched our searchlight for hours, dancing patterns with the sight of ten others in the visible sky; some Germans came over and we got one of them down, but I did not see that—nothing more than the sudden bright light behind the stately hill which you will remember—and then, long afterwards, a heavy sound.

We have been eating strawberries; no one can buy them now and so many have to be given away and instead of dishes we eat them singly with grunts of appreciation. However, they are exquisite anyway and so the slugs thick too. The garden is overgrown; we neither of us have much time for we are both writing at top speed as well as both, now, working full days all the week. The house is a mat of spiders' webs, but they serve to catch the moths which otherwise would eat our clothes. IT IS UNBELIEVABLE LUXURY TO HAVE A NEW SHIRT & STOCKINGS & SCENT... I am most deeply grateful for these—I am so very shabby. I believe your parents would feel even deeper distrust of me if they could see me now!

A real letter follows. I expect you will defend Winifred Duncan to the top of your bent, but it'll be too late anyway—she will have gone Galloping Off Over the Hills.

I send you my very true love always.

Valentine

Five days later Valentine reported that Winterton had been hit by bombs.

Envelope stamped 'Opened by Censor
May 24th 1943[7]

A parcel of books arrived from you, so cleverly arriving on the very day after my birthday—thank you so much, and especially for the Anna Seghers one, which I am very glad to have.

My mother did manage to come down for the day, although her village—our village—was subjected to a violent blitz at 7:30 in the morning a few days before she was due to come to me. Luckily, she and Mary escaped, although not one house that <u>was</u> left standing had any glass or doors left in it. My mother, of course, behaved superbly and is looking, on the whole, the better for it, although she is remarkably thin and pale and apt to become very excited when the Alert goes, for instance. Unfortunately a nearby town had a terrific pasting yesterday and she has gone there today to visit what may be left of my relations who live there. The place is still in the state of chaos that is left after such a sharp raid and I'm afraid Ruth will get a shock—But I was too late in hearing the news to prevent her starting, and I am not allowed to leave my job here so I can't follow her! War-time work is extremely taxing sometimes, and never more so than when one wants to leave and may not.

I'm sending you a rather strange present but the one I hope you will like. Treat it with saddle soap and wriggle it about and knead it hard and the fashion here at present [is] to wear these things and keep pennies and oddments in them, and this one is particularly well made, I fancy. I have one for ammunition and so on.

I wish you would manage to write to me and tell me how you are both getting on and what jobs you are doing and how you like them. Will Wade be affected by this new call-up? I suppose he will—Franklin is getting on very well & writes extremely interesting letters. I made friends with one of your officers on the train the other day and we got on well. He gave me a cigarette and caused me much anguish by assuring me that he got them for 2½d a packet—can this be true?!

No more now—you will have heard from Janet I daresay. She IS being so maddening! I've got to write to her now, if I can squeeze a minute more out of my lunch-hour.

I hope your new year will be a very happy, safe and peaceful one, and I send you, always and for ever, My love and blessing.

Valentine

Three days after this Valentine gave news of her duties and of the effect of the war on Sylvia and her mother, Ruth, in reply to a new letter from Elizabeth.

27th May 1943[8]

Your long letter came to-day, my darling; it has taken a considerable time to get here and I wish it hadn't. I thought you had stopped writing to me.

I've just sent off the formal acknowledgement card of a food parcel which came at exactly the right time—they always do come at the right time anyway, but this was especially good because Ruth had just arrived from her very untoward experiences and she was looking incredibly thin and strained. The fact that she had been proved to be so necessary to the people there had been a shock to her, actually; she was glad but it oppressed her because she is very unhappy now at W [Winterton] and this has clamped the chains on harder and it scares her. Well, anyway—I opened the butter and fed her well, and she looked much better—and I sent her home with a supply of stuff, mainly from the lovely things you've sent us. We are being cautious, with good reason, and we are storing what we can, and distributing when we should, so that there is something against the leaner times to come. As you know, we are still almost shamefully well-fed and it is difficult to remember reason when one's conscience remembers Europe. But this has been a hard war, even so far, and a long one, even so far, and I think this country has made out as well as it has done very largely because our food has been adequate. But there are sometimes considerable difficulties to overcome and the food you have sent us has been beyond words welcome—I can't tell you how deeply thankful we have been for it more times than you could know.

It is hard that I can't send you some coffee—I have tried to get permission but I'm not allowed to. It isn't too easy to get and one can't, of course, just live on coffee as we used to do—but I'd got two pounds of it saved for you and then the post-office refused to take it and apparently it is absolutely forbidden to send food out—I am so sorry, I'd have been happy to send you some, even though I expect you'd have thought it very odd tasting!

My work is going on well; I've been extra busy recently because of more responsibilities put on the Civil Defence hereabouts, but we're managing to carry just about treble the work we started out to do, and to do it with about half the staff! Everyone is being very fine. I've just been interrupted in this letter by a long session with a Medical Officer, Home Guard, who came in to see me and whom I had to persuade of the necessity of our people being issued with more First Aid equipment ... it took a long and solemn conversation. I am alone here, as you know, on 2 whole and 4 half days in the week, and the Controller only puts in his half-days at letter-writing. I do the negotiations and adjustments and so on, as well as the issuing of stores and all the (INNUMERABLE) 'Returns' and so on. It is very hard work and I like it. I see a great number of people and I like that: they range from our three local Peers to the village carpenters and carters who are the ARP [Air Raid Precautions] Wardens, and in addition I have a number of parsons and their wives and the unidentifiable sandwich-filling which in every village lies between the workers and the drones—That is a fine mixed metaphor to please you.

Tomorrow I am meeting an American, Redwood Anderson, for lunch. I don't know him but he has told me to recognize him by his ash-stick and the fact that he looks like a countryman. I don't much like the sound of that and I didn't at all like his poetry, but I am glad to meet someone like that.

Hugh (my before-this boss) comes in to see me very often. He lives near this place and passes it every day. He is very charming and we seem to get on pleasantly, or so I often think until suddenly it appears that all the time we have not been getting along well really! Sylvia dislikes him, but she is wrong: he is lazy, stubborn, gentle, ugly, enormously tall (I have to look up even to see his chin—or his sister's chin or his mother's chin, come to that!) and probably he could be unpleasant, but he is very nice to me and it is always very comforting to be thought well of.

I believe that is what went wrong with us, you know—In love it is absolutely that each should KNOW that the other really respects and admires and thinks highly of—You never believed that I thought like that about you; I did believe you thought that about me, at first, but later it became painfully clear that you didn't, and I believe that was what turned the whole thing bad. It is not as trivial as you will think it—it is profound ...

The fact that you are glad you did not come does prove that you have found solid ground under your feet and that you know it at last, and that you are walking with assurance. I am deeply glad of that and I am sure that it was shrewd as well as sound common-sense that made you decide as you did. But I don't agree at all with your theory of a 'last meeting'. That will never happen deliberately ... a last meeting must happen one time but never, I think, by arrangement beforehand, so far as we are concerned.

It is probably better that we never meet again; much better for Evelyn and the Elizabeth who lives with Evelyn. I think I am not different—I am not nearly as limber as you are—with Sylvia, with you, even with Monica and Janet and Hugh, I am Valentine and what wounds and loss and disfigurement I suffer show as plainly however I am housed or bedded. So there is not so much to be lost, you see—it is a steadily losing all the time—For you there is the likelihood of a total loss, and of the loss of something which you have new-created and which is, because it is created to fit a certain frame, quite undistorted by the pull and stress which wrecked the one before. By this I mean that you are a different person with Evelyn, and that what you are with her is unaffected by what you were with me—but if you saw me, which Elizabeth would be there? Either way, both would suffer and you might easily lose what you have so properly & sensibly made for yourself. But though it may be better that we do not meet again I still feel in my bones that we shall meet again. But I utterly reject any kind of arrangement that it shall be the last time. Neither you nor I are in a position to dictate terms.

Sylvia would understand. I shall not tell her since you tell me not to. She has always understood very clearly from her own point of view, of course, as all of us must understand like that—it's the only way; the process of 'putting yourself in someone else's place' isn't in fact possible. The thing that people who are in love are usually closely together and so they see from approximately the same angle, and things look approximately the same—I don't know why you always assure me that I don't understand you—but I know that I often tell you that you don't understand me and we may both be right. I incline to think we must be when I read your 'You will be disgusted at this or you will laugh at it and turn away—' That does not sound to me at all like anything I do. I don't react like that, ever.

I do not hate you at all—neither bitterly nor passionlessly nor passionately. I do not hate you at all. (Naturally I do not 'hate' Evelyn either. I used to feel a spirited kind of rage with her which would have been very happily used up if I had been able to throw her into the river or something quite small like that! Naturally, that kind of nonsense fades out and time just obliterates it. In fact 'naturally' is the opening word to any remark I might make about any feelings I find in myself about Evelyn now. I don't want to see her again because we were mutually disappointed when we did meet and that is always depressing and burdensome. Now, naturally, we would have still less to talk about. But in regard to her, with or without you, I think everything is in a healthy and natural condition and healing up nicely.)

... I was interrupted.

I have got Le Creve Coeur and it goes around with me always. The poems are most lovely and I can scarcely hear, or dare, to read them. I wish you had not quoted the one you copied for me, but I thank you for it. [9]

The work that you are doing is very hard but obviously worth it and I am very glad you [are] doing the tracing job. I hope you will pass out successfully from the course and get a decent job. [Bo Foster's] Scottish friend is doing the same thing and finds it entrancing. She is fortunate because she's allowed to do it at home. She puts in a solid 9-hours a day at it. And the RWR [Russian War Relief] seems to be your other most useful work—I wish I had been at that party—

What IS Evelyn's work?! Janet tells me that she has mysterious indications that E is being something very fine somewhere but without any information about where! Is it still B&B? I hope you won't both go into the same factory—I am sure that is a very bad arrangement. One shouldn't work with the person one lives with except on one's own life-work, which is a (very) different matter. These routine jobs are so trying anyway that the distraction of having a lover around is the last straw—or so I've found. But the attraction of having your grandmother's house [The Patch] is certainly a strong argument and I hope you will get it, although I think it is dangerous for you to be so near your parents' house—

I cannot tell you how happy I was made when Holderlin's poems arrived—that was a very important day in my life and I can't thank you enough for sending them—

If this letter is disjointed it is because people keep on interrupting me just now I have to go and assemble some gas-masks and issue them to the people who've come several country miles to fetch them.

... One of the nastier minor deprivations we endure is the lack of scent! Every stuffy room and office, usually overcrowded anyway, smells heavily and inescapably of HUMANS. Monica, who sleeps two nights a week (and has done since war began) in a large underground room with 10 other people, on ambulance duty) says that is becoming unbearable, and try as I may to conquer my extreme dislike and disgust I cannot bear to go into the main-office room—which I ought to do every day from here—

The Labour Exchange has sent me another notice and we fear that all is to do again. Now that I am in uniform there is a chance they will not snatch me. Sylvia meanwhile, in addition to WVS twice a week, [10] to housework and garden and to her own work (a new book just coming out) has taken a daily job, 2 hrs a day, as dispenser and general help-meet to the local doctor. She does it very well and adores it. If I had been called up, or if I am now, she will not come with me—you were wrong about that: She argued that she would, but I said certainly I would not have her and in fact she would not have come. But we could not afford to keep on the house & so she would have gone to London & lived there and I shd. have done my best to get to her if ever I got a day off. But the 'individual code of convenience and pleasure' that you talk about is not just something one 'should' sacrifice for a rather mystical 'public good'. Everything is vastly more complicated than that and while we work, at our private or/and unofficial jobs as a team we must keep at any rate in close touch, or else nothing will get done at all and that would be a pity. Meanwhile, we are all, as you know, on tenterhooks about what and when and where we shall attack and so everything just goes on working as hard and fast as it can in preparation for when the balloon goes up. It stands to reason that then a lot of other things will come down on our devoted heads, and so we've got to get on with drills and practices and plans and what-not as fast as we can. A neighboring town, as you'll have read, got a hellish pasting the other day—a Sunday, at lunch-time. Ruth went there next morning early (not knowing what had happened) and found it still burning. Our great friends, Kate (like K Cornell) and Christopher were there: Kate is a Warden. They both survived. I'm glad: they are both excellent and C is a fine scientist.

That is really all—I wish you would manage to write to me more often. I know how you feel about it and this isn't the kind of letter to make you want to write back, I'm afraid. I send you for your birthday my dearest, dearest love: this is really a 'new' year for you and I hope it will prove your choice right and happy as well as wise, and I hope your years will be rich and sheltered and that you will enjoy and be made happy.

Valentine

Two days later Valentine wrote briefly with thanks for a gift and suggested a birthday present she would give to Elizabeth.

Letterhead: Dorchester Rural District Council
May 31st [1943][11]

My darling,

A wonderful parcel came from you yesterday and has left me gasping—it had in it my most needs—I am really limp and lame as regards clothes, and uniform (as I have it) comes very slowly and only provides positively exterior covering: no shirts, no stockings, ties and so on, although they allow a grand 'freedom' about these—if one can get 'em! I am overwhelmed by what you've sent me. I wish you knew how much good it does to me to have something new that makes me feel once more as if I were C L E A N and not deplorably frowsty (an English word you will not, I hope, ever know the meaning of!)

No more now: office hours and the hell of a day. I sent you off a letter which, in its course, deplored that we have no SCENT to mask—not so much our own, accustomed smell but the smell of the others we have not elected to live with! You sent me that too—and God bless you for it. I am quite maudlinly thankful ... tho' why poor Mary Magdaline should be the type of a grotesque and overdone thankfulness, heaven know—she had the main reason for tears and for thanks—she had RELIEF.

I send you for your birthday all I can find of what, modest or not, I know will please you if you remember what mutually, of the things we could obtain outside of ourselves, gave us pleasure ... We are very short indeed of things to buy (of things I would ever buy for you, I mean) and I have done my best, by diligent searching, to get you the things you may enjoy—and though they are—My love goes with them, & with or without them would go to you, but I hope it will carry them safely. It will if it possibly can.

Have a happy, a fulfilled, a contented and a SURE year, Elizabeth, my darling.

Valentine

Oh—and the RWR insignia—I love it. I can wear it without offence even here & under my Boss, and that is a small, inestimable salvation to me—as things are here. And the chess & draughts ... and the funny book of pictures—and the splendour of soap that is fat & in paper, & that smells sweet.

Next Valentine offered more deliberate reflections on their relationship and a summing up, interspersed with references to nearby explosions. Elizabeth had written from St Paul, Minnesota where she was organizing local committee support for Russian War Relief. She too, despite her settled relationship with Evelyn, kept probing the nature of the affair with Valentine. Almost four years after they had seen each other, this is Valentine's most elaborate evaluation of the affair. She considered this letter a major statement about their relations and asked Elizabeth to save it.[12]

20th July 1943[13]

My darling, your long letter from Minnesota reached me this morning. In it you ask me many questions and make many statements, all one question and all one statement really. I do not know how to answer so that you will understand me truthfully—it seems to me that you often, ever since 1940 maybe, reject my words in case you should find them truthful—I hope that is not so, I hope you will understand.

I have thought you faithless: I believed it true to say so then; now I realise clearly that—while I still think you committed an act of unfaith, the moment you felt your life to be separate from mine nothing that you did subsequently could be faithless to me; only I did not have that feeling so soon as you did—I did, believe it or not—feel quite sure that however terrible or horrible our love might be it was completely binding. You can easily say that I took it for granted that, once mine, you would be mine for ever—whatever I did or did not do. Maybe it was like that for a while but only in the happiest days, days which I can scarcely remember now because the fearful days and hours of interrogation, reproaches, accusations, and despair do—now—seem to me to have been the sum total of our companionship. Very soon, therefore, I lost the easy, untormented faith that all was well because we made each other happy. But I did keep a strange conviction that the kind of love you had for me was worth your having as well as being worth my having. Thus I came to trust in it as lasting and so I ran on for a long, long time—charging you with infidelity and offences which you certainly were not able to commit after—say—summer 1940. During the time I was at Winterton in that year I was very nearly out of my mind and that has altered me very much—inside and out. I think you should understand that.

You write to me because sometimes you remember that you loved me. I write to you for the same reason, I suppose and because what I thought you were to me is still very vividly impressed on my mind, although I know now that most of it is wholly of my creation and the rest has ceased to exist for me, although it is alive and on the earth and seen by other people. I am both by chance & by intention a poet and that means that any form of beauty that comes near enough to be caught is caught, is consumed and does become part of myself. What I thought I knew when I loved you was astoundingly beautiful—what I thought we did, what I thought we felt, together and separately, what I thought we made—It was really beautiful, and you and I looked beautiful in the light of it: I do not have to 'remember' that; I am that, it is part of me now, and must be.

You loved a person you 'knew and worshipped and honoured and trusted without question'—and while you felt that the person

TELEPHONE No. 500.

DORCHESTER RURAL DISTRICT COUNCIL

CLERK,
H. O. LOCK.
SOLICITOR.
ASSISTANT CLERK.
A. E. SYMES.

53, High West Street,
Dorchester.

was so, and I hope n thing will ever be so bad again for either of us.

And that is all I can say, because it says all there is I think, except that after a time perhaps the bad parts of this will sink and we shall see again the best of it – and then we shall lament the loss of that, it is true, but we shall be better for having at last lost sight of the disgraces.

Valentine.

22nd July

Please will you keep this letter — I do not suppose I shall ever write another such & I have read this over carefully & find it still to be accurate & true, so far as the written word, can accompanied by please a tone of voice, can ever be exact in matters of so much moment. Please therefore keep this letter because if ever again you question how & why things fell out as they did something said, a recognisable although not said, in this letter will explain to you, I think.

57. Valentine's request to Elizabeth to keep her letter.

existed and the love existed, I was slow and anyway absorbed in the adventure and discovery and joy of creating 'you' and 'me' and I did not realize, at once, when you lost what now I suppose you think of as illusions. They were not illusions while you believed in them they were truth; but because I did not realize when you stopped believing, I was completely astray when I found that suddenly (as it seemed to me) instead of seeing me and ourselves as gods you were seeing a whole variety of monsters, and that where (I knew) you had found goodness and beauty in me you found baseness and a shoddy sort of exhibitionism. That is why, in America, I scarcely knew myself at all and that is why I must often have seemed to be 'putting up with' a great deal of scolding and reproach. To our outside viewers, you know, it looked like that and that, too, I used to realize sometimes—and it bewildered me to find myself there. Like the woman in the nursery rhyme, whose skirts were clipped—'this is none o' I ...'

It is no use trying to recapitulate, except that you must not still—at this distance—accuse me of being stupid and stone-cold. From the excess of passion I had for you I became perfectly indifferent and dead, and for two years or more I had no life except in head and heart. Now I am right again, I think, and that is all there is to it. I must often have been very slow and awkward in my dealings with you while I was crippled, but I ask your forgiveness and kind understanding for that. I could not help that, although I tried very hard to help it very often.

I loved you very very violently and very deeply also—In temperament we were, I suppose, perfectly unsuited and I did not look ahead at all. I would not have come to this, if I had looked ever so keenly—

I do not want to blame anything unfairly on this war, but the very great horror of 1940 (so far as it was our year, I mean) was that the total confusion of mind, surprise and shock that I had from your letters about E was horribly matched, gigantically enlarged, by the things that happened across the Channel, and in this country. There was a madness, a lunatic neatness of pattern which did overset my balance and took away my judgment for a while. I made too much fuss and I felt too sorry for myself and not nearly enough for you. I felt overwhelming compassion for you it would overwhelm me suddenly and if I had not been 'padded', so to speak, with my own almost-madness I should have died because of the grief I felt for you. You could see, if you looked, if you believe me (and how can you not when I am speaking so truly to you?) that this madness and sorrow and desperation of desire for you and you only, with the staggering lunacy of the world & the merely physical results of sleepless nights, terror, apprehension & menace, all these things combined to make me commit excesses of fury and pain, which caused you pain and caused you to lose sight of what I had been. I often blamed you for it then, but now I do not at all blame you for losing sight of me as I was, in the constantly changing, increasingly unpleasant visions of what I did become. Only, I am still sore when I remember that you accepted those as truthfully what I would always be & sometimes—often—you seemed to say that I had always been as vile—

However, all that is over, it cannot happen so again although since it has happened it has a kind of immortality. But let us try to forget it, & then it will diminish and perhaps die forever.

As for how we are towards each other I did not mean to condescend to you. I have never in all my life felt condescension towards anyone, and it is unlikely that I would experience it for the first time towards someone I have loved as much as I loved you. But I seriously apologise to you for having given you any reason to suspect this of me. It was not 'kindly meant'; it was a statement, I thought, of fact. And I did feel glad that you, as I thought, had found safety and something, at any rate, of what you most wanted. I meant no insult to you or to myself—it would be a violation of myself, indeed, if I condescended to you.

My own circumstances are not quite as you picture them to yourself and me, although there is an approximation. My job is not important, except that whatever work is done (only a little of it NEEDS to be done) I do without help. Our lives here are very odd just now, as you can imagine: (As I wrote that something went off somewhere and my chair bruised my backbone! God knows what it was, though.) We are all rather on edge & becoming very tired; there is a sense of very great strain and it shows either in sharp resentful tempers or—much more commonly, I'm glad to say—in a rather over-elaborate politeness. For instance, Monica let herself be carried past her station & lost about 2 hours of a holiday because she wouldn't push and fight her way out of a crowded train. She explained that she hadn't dared to start to push, because she'd not have been able to keep her temper if she'd once let go! It is like that for all of us. I think what you say is true and that fortunate people like myself feel a sort of 'grim contentment' but I don't quite agree with the second word! I am occasionally, very rarely, extremely happy; I get moments of rapture and of being aware: most other times I'm hanging on because I must hang on and there's nothing else to do. My uniform is still only a fine topcoat and a rather rakish beret—not much to boast about and I don't, even now, much like being dressed up, although I do find it useful because it makes one anonymous and soldiers aren't so attentive as they are when one is more noticeable. My 'grand rejected suitor' (Hugh would be surprised at that! If he thinks about it very much at all I don't believe he quite believes it) is very nice as an addition to the people I know and has provided me with a great embellishment to my life in his mother of 80 and his quangly six-foot blonde sister; both of these women I like very much and feel happy with, the old one especially. And I enjoy the occasional luxury of lobster and family silver and very beautiful portraits, and the melancholy garden. So that Hugh has been very lucky to me, so far as that goes, but you will admit that it doesn't go VERY far! But never do I tell you that you do not exist in all this. We are all what we are, and what we are at this moment, it seems to me, is machines that keep on running as well as they can. The rare moments of being ourselves are very precious but quite unforeseeable. (Another HELLOFA bump. I often wish I were not alongside a church in this office; churches do seem to get hit. But the noise was miles off.)

Winifred Duncan: I do not cultivate her. I have written her two letters and a postcard in four years, and I have not answered this letter, nor shall I, although I wrote an answer which gave me relief! She is not, I think, very unhappy; she is not too badly off (it is not true that she is living on practically nothing, unless you mean mentally and spiritually) and she is sufficiently irresponsible and well-padded to be able to believe in her importance: there are elements of comfortable living in that list of possessions, surely? I think she is not too badly off. I would LOVE to keep a fungus-garden, but I shall never strive officiously to keep Winifred!

People come in here to see me; Betty Muntz came yesterday—the first time I've seen her since 1939, just after I got back here. She looks exactly the same. Katie [Powys] comes sometimes, and occasionally Alyse [Gregory] or one of them will send a friend of theirs to meet me here. I had lunch with a funny little scholar the other day—who subsequently sent me a copy of his very learned book on prosody, of which I understood one word in twenty and none of the graphs. Otherwise I meet the one or two people I would choose to meet, out of the very many that I have to see because of my job. Monica lunches with me here quite often and we play chess, or walk and explore the little town in which I show her many things she, living here all her life, has never seen.

(later)

I was interrupted so many times that I stopped this; now my boss has gone home to his lunch & all is well. He is a DEVIL to work for & it is very unpleasant indeed while he is around. I'm awfully bad at bearing to be bullied!

You did ask me very seriously, as it seems to me, WHY we write to each other; later in your letter you say (as you have said before) that you will see me when again it is possible to move, and that it will be to see me once more only—and so on. I think I am not being unreasonable or unkind when I ask you please to tell me plainly that you do not love me. It is still a considerable pain to me to probe like this into a wound which so nearly did not start to heal. It is true, as it seems to me, that we well might feel the old violence of passion and desire when we meet again, but what virtue is in that now? It would be wrong, I think, to allow it. You have hated me and abused me; I have hated you and abused you. We have not behaved as we should have behaved to each other and it would not be seemly to make love when we cannot be in love together. And for you to come as you say here ('... I have developed a sort of animal instinct of self-preservation by now, and when I come I shall not come alone') for you to have that in mind is grotesque— you must see that. Perhaps, as you read it (except that I used to know E) it really makes no odds to my side of it whatever you come with; the important thing is that you have this crazy situation in mind—a kind of Browning 'Last Ride Together', travestied and put out of reason by this bringing of an anonymous second-string to be a what? Spectator? Witness? Refuge? Reading this again and again, with care and so far as possible detachment, I can only find in it yet another way of telling me that, long ago now, everything ended and closed down.

But I wish you would tell me without guile. I have tried to write this clearly and in candour. Do you the same by me, so far as you possibly, possibly can.

Lastly, I have wanted you to write to me because a heart loves to think that it is beloved and, I suppose, I have not wanted to let that go so long as I could believe in it—however dreadfully it was told to me. But, I have had such profound misery for you, as well as from you, that I would (except in my worst moments) accept anything that would make you happier and do almost anything in the world that might bring you to see me as I am and not as (you persuaded me? Or wholly was it that I persuaded you?) I have seemed to be. It seems, from your letter & all our recent letters, that we have nothing at all to give each other now except woe. You tell me, in a kind sort of way, that in the end it will be worse for me than you—For some time it was so, and I hope nothing will ever be so bad again for either of us.

And that is all I can say because it says all there is I think except that after a time perhaps the bad parts of this will sink and we shall see again the best of it—and then we shall lament the loss of that, it is true, but we shall be better for having at last long sight of the disgraces.

Valentine

[Longhand] 22nd July Please will you keep this letter—I do not suppose I shall ever write another such & I have read this over carefully & find it still to be accurate & true, so far as the written word, unaccompanied by glances & tone of voice, can ever be exact in matters of so much moment. Please therefore keep this letter because if ever again you question how & why things fell out as they did [,] something said, & recognizable although not said, in this letter will explain to you, I think.

Valentine wrote next in August, without reappraisals and with, among other items, news of bicycles and bicycle-riding and of Janet who might marry Steven Clark.

Civil Defence Office
Dorchester Rural District Council
August 13th, 1943[14]

I thank you at once, the very day the book arrived—for the new stories by Dinesen, who I know as 'Baroness Blixen'—they are, so far as I have read, equally good as the Gothic tales, which I thought really outstanding as work & as artistic truth. I am very happy to have this book, Elizabeth, and I do give you most hearty thanks for it.[15]

I read throughout lunch, which I have sometimes now in the restaurant you and I had supper in, the evening we attended Sir Oswald Mosley's unpleasant meeting in this quiet town! Now you would not know this eating-place. It was always shabby and provincial and unpretentious, now it is packed full of people, one stands in a queue to get a seat; the meals are served on one heaped plate, mainly potatoes and carrots, but always with a two-shilling-diameter piece of meat or fish triumphing on top of the vegetables ... It is essential to read at meals nowadays and I was fortunate to-day to have this book—it seemed to me so palatial a book, so spacious, grand and noble. I read 'The Heroine' and now I am reading 'Alkmene'.

The Aragon I had, as you will know by now because I have quoted from it and told you about it, I have travelled with my copy so often that its cover has come off and now the pages are becoming detached and soon it must be put lovingly away; this new copy I am very happy to have; the poems are a part of life now, as timeless and essential as Keats or Handel—though neither of these is, at any rate superficially, like Aragon! If ever any contemporary English music is to be heard, listen to Benjamin Britten's St. Cecilia's Day, with words by Auden. It is very, very fine.

I have been very busy lately; we have quite a lot to do and so much that is unexpected and which has to be done in a hurry. The man I work for is responsible for all Civil Defence matters in 55 villages, some of them very remote and unenlightened and one or two of them not really villages at all, but suburbs of towns and so especially to be looked after. He is only on the job—that is to say, in this office, during 3 half-days a week and I am the only hireling he has. It is pleasantly various, as a job, because I do the usual work of typing, taking down letters, telephoning and so on, but in addition I handle equipment and issue it, issue First Aid and such-like stuff, assemble and fit the various kinds of gas-masks and so on and deal with the VERY odd, assorted people who are our Wardens, First Aiders, Firemen, and so on. It is a most mixed job and so it is good for me and whenever (as yesterday) I have a free stretch of time I settle down and continue with the copying and revising of my book, which takes ages and is very tiring.

The days I eat in town are not really so good as the picnic days when, except for the times Monica comes here, I can read and eat in peace and solitude. To-morrow, which is Saturday, if it is at all fine, Sylvia and I will take the train half-way home and get out and prowl in the woods until the next stopping-train passes and takes us on to home. That is the only way of getting out into another part of country without unduly laborious journeying beforehand.

Janet arrived in to see me, without warning, on the Saturday before August Bank Holiday; it ought to have been a holiday for me, too, but there was a sudden urgent piece of work to be done and I had to open up the office. I was half-buried in envelopes and duplicated papers and whatnot when Janet arrived, and she was sullen and disappointed because I'd no time for pleasantries but instead impressed her to work for half an hour or so—which was not at all what she'd intended; She looked very well but depressed and heavy—you know that look?—I don't think things are going too smoothly with Steven [Clark] and Charles [Ring] and the whole set-up. She has got herself into a habit of dissatisfaction which is very hard to break and neither of these gallants is the one to break it for her, I fancy. But on the other hand it is perhaps true to say that it doesn't so much matter who or what she marries as it matters that she should marry someone as soon as she can—because she is scared of not being married and that is a dreadfully heavy fear for a young woman to carry. I hoped she would find herself able to make friends without staying only in one set of people—the war has leveled things out a good deal; in the towns anyway, and yet Janet has become much less able to mix than she was—She is quite genuinely uncomfortable, uneasy, with most people she meets just now and I do not think, from that point of view, that the job she is in is very good for her. But it suits her because it is not very strenuous and it is safe—that is to say, she won't be called up and no one interferes with her. I sometimes wish she had never asked me to get her that job! I wish fervently that she had never fallen in love with Steven—if ever she did—and that when she was so obviously determined to love SOMEONE at Warren [Conn.] we had contrived someone else—anyone bar Steven!—It is difficult not to say impatiently OH GET ON WITH IT AND MARRY! When they go back and forth about to be or not to be—but I believe it would be disastrous. But how can anyone know?

Meanwhile, a long letter from Paul [Nordoff] with the good news that he is again composing and that he has set two more of my poems (the last were very beautiful, I thought—did you see them?) and that he is hard at work and doing well. Franklin writes often; I hope he will do well now; the army seems to be using him wisely at last. He has an earnest, very gentle and courageous character and he knows a great deal about living. Paul is not earnest and is bullet-headed but not courageous and knows nothing at all except how to survive the most impossible and fearful crises, the most violent assaults from fate and people and his own imprudence and folly, but he is almost too obviously a genius and so intolerable except to a very few people—but luckily he doesn't dream of that and most times feels himself to be universally beloved—the rest of the time he is in despair and out of just that kind of tempest music comes as clean as a whistle!

After you had told me that I had a lovely uniform, & I had replied bitterly that I had a damnably heavy top-coat only, I was issued with a very noble pair of trousers (called SLACKS when they're female!) and a funny little jacket which is cut with a riotous swagger at the back and which has capacious pockets: His Majesty's shoes, which he also gave me, are singularly uncomfortable. I remember Hilary, Janet's brother, telling me that Army boots were fine once your feet had become unconscious inside them, so I wear my shoes hoping to faint within them, but so far I've not managed it. However, since the clothes problems is really extremely acute now (WHY didn't I buy more shirts in NY? I'm wearing one of the funny little linen ones now that I wore in Warren, so long ago—) this uniform is a blessing. Coupons have to be given up for it, of course, since I am a whole-time worker, but it's worth it. Only they don't supply anything to wear on top of the trousers or underneath 'em either, which is strange [ ] when you consider the high level of our public morals.

Ordinary people are becoming nicer and nicer: manners are really more frank and friendly than they were and everyone chats easily and readily to everyone else and—what is perhaps more important, people aren't affronted if one doesn't talk. But this applies only to common people: the others are getting worse and worse! But there aren't so many of 'em as there were: that process of 'absorption' we talked about has got well under way.

Tell me if that book I sent you ever did reach you?

No more now. I am already wondering what I can send you for Xmas, since there is positively NOTHING in the shops except, as always so far, the most handsome selection of things made of leather—but all of them things which, while you would undoubtedly like them, would not be of use at present: a saddle, for instance, or a fine bridle, or a Sam Browne belt ... and a very splendid 'bus conductor's money-wallet!

Have you got a bicycle yet? I am very happy with mine, which is a wartime one but has a back-pedal brake, an old-fashioned device now revived again and most excellent for these hills and for town riding where one needs a free hand for signaling and so on. It hasn't got quite straight, Parish-Worker-Style handlebars but neither has it the kind that suggest a fox-tail tied on behind! It is a nice little creature and gives me considerable pleasure although I hate going for long rides because it tires my knees. I could think New York will be enormously improved when everyone tears about on silent bicycles like they do in London! Janet has got an upright one, on which she looks very prim and stand-offish. She and Steven side by side on bicycles look most extraordinarily funny. Conversation is (quite seriously) very often concerned with the vintage or otherwise of one's machine, and Monica is very haughty because her's is one which was second-hand when she was given it in, I think, 1930. It is very tall and massive and erect and the shabbiest of any in the district; I hate going out with her because it rattles and scares all the birds and beasts which otherwise are my delight when I'm out: they don't mind at all so long as there is no rattle, and I believe that if one could ride without handlebars and without staggering it would be a fine way to bird-watch.

I watched a lovely young dog-fox crossing a field when I was out once, and I could follow him for some way over the smooth down before he suddenly turned and saw me and was off in a flash. It was the nicest hunt I have ever had!

No more—Sylvia's new book is out over here and is sold out (the small War-time first edition) already. It is good but I expect you know all the stories already. [*A Garland of Straw*, 1943]

I always send you my love, Elizabeth. I am glad to know that Evelyn has joined you and very glad to hear that she is well out of B and B; I am sure she will be glad too, really.

Valentine

Sylvia wrote at the end of 1943, in response to Elizabeth's concern over Valentine's health, worn down by the commute, wartime food shortages, and the office position that she had been forced to resign.

Envelope 'Opened by Censor'
Frome Vauchurch
Maiden Newton
December 1943 [16]

Dearest Elizabeth,

Your letter of Dec. 5th came a few days ago. So far, there has been no definite advice of an operation for Valentine. Indeed, it is not certain whether she really has gallstones. The local doctor thought so, and the treatment he prescribed, a pill called Cholelith, seemed to apply. But he is not her natural doctor; Gray of Weymouth, whom you saw, is still that, only war-time reasons of time and space make him less immediately available. However, she did see Gray later, when he examined her, and said that he could not be sure. The only thing that was certain was that her liver was larger than it should be. He put her on a regimen, and asked her to wait a little and he would see her again. Meanwhile, the influenza epidemic intervened. Gray was tied down in Weymouth, doing his partner's work as well as his own; then he had it; then Valentine had it; so the second meeting was postponed, but I hope he will see her this week. Meanwhile, she goes on with the regimen, and seems to me considerably better, and has not had any more bouts of pain like the first one which sent her to the local man.

Gray said he was averse to operations in war-time. That in any case he would not wish to operate on her till she had a considerable spell of preparatory rest. I think he is only partially convinced that it is gall-stones, and very likely would not have thought so at all if it had been for the previous diagnosis, and the Hypocratic oath or whatever it is that compels doctors to uphold each other. To me it seems possible that this may be a glandular upset. Valentine's glands have always been extremely sensitive, her work is frequently exasperating, other glands have reacted to strain by swelling and pain. It seems likely enough that this is an example of the same thing. And she has never had any of the usual pre-conditions of gall-stones, like constipation.

I will let you know what Gray thinks when he sees her again, and if an operation is needed I will bear your kindness in mind. But if we do avail ourselves of it, it won't be suddenly, so there will be time for you to make your adjustments. I can always borrow from my amiable publishers if our own capital won't stand the racket. As you guess, a fifty per cent income tax does become noticeable; and as I pay the USA tax on any money I earn in your country before my own native land snatches half of what's left, the remainder is dwarfish. On the other hand, there is nothing to spend money on, or very little, for the things one likes are unobtainable, one can't travel, books and gramophone records are extremely difficult to get—it would take more time and more ingenuity than we have to be extravagant. So one shogs along, and remains solvent more by compulsion than by intention.

Two fine boxes have come from you this morning. I hope it doesn't seem that we accept them as a matter of course. It's not so. We are thankful for them, and they make a very great difference to our daily bread and our daily graces for bread. The butter is a particular god-send just now, for the winter milk ration is small and severe, and if it were not for your butter we should grow very parched and papery. And the noodle soups were a blessing during our spell of influenza. Mine was nothing, a mere fleabite, and Valentine's nothing compared to what she can do in that line: but for all that it left us feeling the usual melancholy lethargy, and to be able to have a restorative soup with none of the preliminary trouble of making it was a great consolation.

Another delight about your parcels is being able to have something to distribute to other people who need extra cosseting. You have raised a great many heads, I assure you.

I am so glad you have this job for Russian War Relief, because I imagine you like it, and I am sure you will have the pleasure of doing it well. I remember how well you managed the Spanish

Relief in Waterbury. If you were a prophet in your own home-town Dakota and the rest of them must be childs-play in comparison. I envy you having a moving-about job, and such possibilities in your own country of seeing unknown places. Claustrophobia is the worst thing here, and almost every one suffers from it. One of the most unpleasant phenomena of claustrophobia is the accompanying growth of morality. When people see the same people day in and day out their boredom develops into censoriousness, all the hideous handmaiden of morality. I don't mean that behaviour is particularly moral. There is just as much thieving, whoring, drunkenness, as ever, maybe more. In the case of whoring, certainly more. But it arouses nothing but morality, and so is entirely unproductive. No one seems to be any the gayer, or any the more enlightened for it. I hoped this was merely provincial, but we had a letter not long since from Nancy Cunard in which she said the priggishness of London is unbelievable. She ought to know.

One is never certain whether letters get across. So I will duplicate Valentine's thanks for the Christmas parcel. Everything in it was something that she wanted, or needed. I wish you could have seen her unpacking it.

With my best wishes,

Sylvia

After her mother's death in 1943, Mary White inherited her country place at the foot of Breakneck Hill. Martha (Starkwether) Wade, whose city house was next to the Whites' in Waterbury, had converted a small farmhouse, a fifteen minute drive from the Whites' Middlebury estate, into a comfortable retreat, named by her 'The Patch' because of its modest size. After the war, Mary made it available to Elizabeth, and she and Evelyn gave up the East 19th Street apartment in October 1945 and moved in. From there they started a business in old books, 'White & Holahan Books', travelled about to auctions and sales, carried on an extensive correspondence, and made what they referred to as 'whiskey money'. Elizabeth moved her herb house from the Breakneck

58. The Patch, Middlebury, Connecticut. Elizabeth's grandmother modified this 18th-century farmhouse and gave it its name. Elizabeth and Evelyn moved there in 1945.

59. The covered walkway at The Patch.

60. Elizabeth at The Patch, 1940s.

grounds and improved the flower and vegetable gardens. She had returned to the rural Connecticut that she loved. In the care of the two women, The Patch became a hospitable place for family members, a wide circle of local friends, and out-of-town visitors.

A great change in the White family came in 1947 when Will White at the age of 71 suffered a disabling stroke; Mary set up twenty-four hour care for him at Breakneck. He lived another five years and survived Mary's death two years later.

Elizabeth attributed the widening rift between the US and the USSR in 1947 and 1948 to US belligerence rather than to actions of the Soviets. In 1948, she and Evelyn actively supported the Progressive Party presidential candidate, Henry A Wallace, who had broken with the Truman administration's increasingly militant response to Soviet actions in Eastern Europe and the Balkans. Elizabeth served on local and state committees for Wallace, setting her apart from her family and most of her neighbors.

In 1946 Sylvia and Valentine purchased Frome Vauchurch in Valentine's name. In the late 1940s Valentine became increasingly self-critical and melancholy, preoccupied with perceived past misdeeds. A major crisis in her life came to a head in 1947 when she faced her alcoholism.

From 1945 to 1948, Sylvia sent thanks to Elizabeth for parcels of food and other items, much appreciated in austere post-war Britain.

Frome Vauchurch,
Maiden Newton, Dorset
16. ix. 1945[17]

My dear Elizabeth,

After rather long last I had a letter from Roger Moline to say that the vitamins you sent him arrived safely and have been distributed through the Service Special des Jeunes. And that he is extremely grateful for them. He was slow to write because he has been, like every doctor in France, swamped with the mass of prisoners returning from German c. camps and the incessant struggle and scramble to find the things needed for their treatment. Part of the delay, however, was not his fault. Your parcel got entangled in the customs and he had to spend some time disentangling it. If—I say if—you feel inclined to send any more, apparently it is best to send in small parcels, which are handled by the postal services, with more expedition and fewer formalities.

It certainly shows official integrity carried to great heights of abstract purity when the customs of a starving country hold up supplies of vitamins: but I can believe anything of a customs official—in any language.

Your parcels to us arrive, and are extremely joy-bringing: do you remember the dutch bulb-growers catalogues?— will be a long while before we see them again, they ate all the daffodils last winter. We are extremely grateful; I think it is very largely thanks to you that we have both remained healthy and spry.

Janet, as I expect you know, is in Italy, on a Red Cross do. She thinks pretty poorly of the people she is with—they are of the usual missionary kind, all knowing their way about and keeping up the prestige of the organization by moving from luxurious villas outside Naples to equally luxurious flats in Rome. But she has made a lot of illicit lower class Italian friends, and been to a christening party, and if she goes on like this I daresay she will be sent back for fraternizing.

We are still here—but the lord only knows on what tenure or how long it will last. Every one is in the same state, it is just a case of musical chairs, and when the music stops another one is out. I wish we could have a barge on the East River like the gentleman in a recent *New Yorker*, recent to me, that is. It would suit us very well; but I gather one has to be a gentleman. There are also said to be some unoccupied Round Towers in Ireland only it is difficult to get there. As it is a universal quandary one takes it very lightly.

The girl in Rogers' fruit and flower shop—the pretty black-eyed one is back again after four years in a factory. She asked after you and sends you her regards.

And so do I,

Sylvia

Elizabeth continued to send food parcels and small luxuries to friends in England, much appreciated at Frome Vauchurch. Sylvia replied to her at The Patch, where Tomas the one-time London cat, remained in residence.

Frome Vauchurch,
Maiden Newton, Dorset
10. 1. 1946[18]

My dear Elizabeth,

Thank you so much for the box of Christmas candies. They are so pretty, as well as being delicious. I eat them as much with my eye as my taste. Though a few vanities are creeping back coloured cellophane is not among them. When I gave a piece of yellow cellophane which had wrapped the prunes in your box to a little girl and told her to look through it she handled it as cautiously as though it were a viper and after one glance at a golden world stuffed it into her packet in case I should want it back again.

If we followed Valentine's advice and had a Minister of Grace as well as a Minister of Works little girls would not be as unadorned, and everybody would be in a better temper. I assure you the sugared almonds which came in your parcel have done us much more good because of being lilac and pink and sea-green, and teasles, which until this year have not been more than a rather moderate pleasure to people who like life forms in nature, were adored by thousands of Londoners this winter because the hawkers had the brilliant idea of dying them purple and crimson and bottle green, and arranging them in bouquets all over their barrows. Rosamund's purple jar was not more passionately gazed upon. I like to think of you domesticated in your grandmother's house. I remember it very well, especially the dining-room and the sugar maple in the garden. Does it keep the furniture? Houses grow to depend on their furniture, and it would be a pity if the two were separated.

Mrs Craske in her Christmas letter asked after you. I hope I may see her when I go to Norfolk next month. At any rate I mean to find time to see Craske's Dunkirk—his last picture—which is in the Norwich Art Collection.

I am delighted to hear that Tomas is so well and handsome. He will enjoy sharpening his claws on that sugar maple. He will probably come to think that it is all his doing. Tom—who is much older than I care to reflect on—is well and carries his years with great suavity.

Please give my love to Evelyn. I hope you will both have a happy 1946. I daresay it will turn out none the worse for beginning when most of us cherish few illusions about how rosy it will be.

With love,

Sylvia

Sylvia wrote again at year's end 1947. Monica Ring had returned from America, where she had visited Elizabeth and Evelyn at The Patch.

Frome Vauchurch
Maiden Newton, Dorset
29. xii. 47[19]

Dear Elizabeth,

I should have written you before to thank you for your kind and enlivening parcel, but my mother became ill and I had to go down to Devon to look after her. To a doctor, to her doctor at any rate, there is nothing simpler than senile decay. I did not find it so simple. It was strange to sit in that dusky house under the shadow of the moor, hearing the wind howl and the rain beat against the window while my mother went riding on her pony past the Madras Jail and along the Adiah at six in the morning because afterwards it would be too hot to ride. Finally she became well enough to be moved into a nursing-home, and I came back the day before yesterday, to wait for what the next step may be—for I don't think she'll settle down in it. I wish I could send her back to India, it would be less strange to her now than anything she has seen in the last seventy-five years.

It was very fortunate that your parcel had a tin of guava jelly. She liked it very much, and it did a great deal to appease her wish for Indian fruits. I was very grateful to you.

Monica Ring wrote about her visit to The Patch. She liked it very much. I think she was happier in Connecticut and felt more at home there than anywhere else she has been. I was very sorry to learn from her letter that a maple tree had been broken by the gale. Was it that maple in the garden? I should be very sorry if it were. It was one of the trees I remember.

Here we sit with a bright sun shining and a north wind blowing, and every appearance of the oncome of another spell of last year's cold weather. Thomas wears an enormous coat, a prophetic one, I'm afraid. He has grown very frileux with old age, last winter almost finished him. But he is as nimble and as supple as ever, and plays Devil in the Dark with the young Pekingese with benevolent malevolence, so to speak, pouncing out on him from corners or rising in the air just in front of him till Shan is overwhelmed with religious excitement. They are devoted to each other, and we have scarcely needed to educate Shan at all, Thomas has attended to all that.

Monica spoke of Tomas and said he was enormous and most imposing. He seems to have struck her as a sort of Dr Johnson.

I suppose you are all be-snowed, though I hope the New York snowfall did not drop its 25.8 on you. How lovely the George Washington Bridge must have looked, suddenly embonpoint with snow: I wish I had seen it. Other people's snow is much more interesting than one's own.

You will have seen that Arthur Machen is dead. I am glad. The shock of Purefoy's death in the spring (she died quite suddenly, and he was alone in the house with her when it happened) wrenched his hold on life and made a noble ghost of him, and his life since has only been an exercise in fortitude. But it has been a cruel year for Janet: a childbirth and two deaths in just over a twelvemonth; and now the child is ill. I wish I could find it possible to think better of her husband. He appears to me to be made of very cheap material—bakelite, or something of that sort, and I have a feeling that he is a young man without a single recess in his character. I cannot like characters with no cupboards, can you?

I hope you will have a very happy new year. I still hope, too, that you will be summoned for u.a. [Un-American] activities. You would make such an excellent appearance, and I think you would enjoy yourself. [20]

Ever,

Sylvia

In January 1948, Sylvia was dealing with her mother's 'cascading tumble into senility'.

Frome Vauchurch
Maiden Newton, Dorset
24. i. 1948[21]

Dear Elizabeth

I have to thank you for that most satisfyingly ample letter—knowing how you are about letters I feel doubly satisfied and ampled—and for the christmas present of fruit which came yesterday. We got to work on it at once—and oh, those apricots! It is so charming of them to be on stones, it makes them so much more dangling than the gutted ones which really have nothing to dangle for; and the difference in flavour is extraordinary. I am still rolling my eyes as I remember them, and I reflect on that great resource of parcel in the storeroom.

I hope you are still enjoying otium cum dignitate, not that there is ever any otium when one has once set up housekeeping—but at any rate you have not so many committees in your hair. But I suspect you will be representing Connecticut yet. I hope so; you would do it very handsomely, and on a good stout cushion of warrant, for I cannot believe Wallace would have had any following at all in your state if you had not taken it in hand as you did. Long before a Wallace campaign was born or thought of, I mean, when you were collecting and working for Spanish relief. It is curious how almost everything of value at the moment in Western Europe or USA has a spice of Spain at the bottom of the pot. It is like Charles I's four Arab horses still dominating the stud-book.

How is your mother? I feel with a fellow-feeling for you, though our respective fixes are so unlike each other; but there is something profoundly shocking in the child having to admit the mother as a responsibility.[22] Quite apart from affection or the surface feeling of family, it is a biological rupture, and jars through all one's set-up. As far as her scattered wits allow her to be anything, my mother seems happy in her nursing home, and is certainly well looked after. But I hope she will not be stretched out much longer, even though she has so little consciousness of her particular rack. It is a curiously ghostly, morbid, and impious-feeling experience to visit her, as I have to do ever so often, and witness this obdurate vitality scrabbling about in its ruins, fishing out little scraps of 1880, 1920, all at random, turning them over and over, and dropping them like cherrystones.

The decayed sprightliness of Torquay makes a horribly suitable background for it, too. I think it would quench even your brother's enthusiasm for victorian gothic.

I am glad that Tomas has turned into such a ripe and Raeburnian country gentleman. I suppose he has a glass of port after dinner and keeps a record of the rainfall.

Ever

Sylvia

Frome Vauchurch
Maiden Newton Dorset
31. iii. 1948[23]

Dear Elizabeth,

March is going out a lion in a mackintosh, the wind howls, the rain is beating the hyacinths into a pummy—and still I have not written to thank you for my Christmas book. I read it with great pleasure. What a comfort it is to find a novel that is historical without being period. I hunch my shoulders every time I hear the latter word. There were some scenes in the book which gave me a feeling of true actuality: the raid on the village particularly, and the flat matter of fact roll-call of the dead and surviving. I think that was the chapter I liked best of all, then there were fine things in the journey, too, and I believed very strongly in the trappers tidy light warm house—the respectable basis, no more, of American isolationism.

Valentine gave you my message, so you know why I have not written before. My poor mother's cascading tumble into senility was a great shock and strain. I knew theoretically that it, or something like it, was probable; but theory is not so taxing as practice; and there were times, especially the first time when I was down there alone, when I guessed I was pretty near the edge of a breakdown myself. I am still feeling rather like the day after the earthquake. When I was a child I was always pretty much afraid of her (she was not unkind, but she was alarming with a pouncing tongue for deficiencies and a flailing determination of purpose); and when for the first time in my life, so to speak, that I could have no reason to fear her, all those old terrors came ramping out of the wood.

I thought so well of your letter in the Waterbury paper: and I hope there were some people to read it to a purpose. By the same post Monica sent me some cuttings. It really looks as if Wallace had shaken that odd wall between Republicans and DemocRats' and as if they might coalesce against a new political party. It would be a more natural deviation, I suppose. It would certainly be a much easier one for Europeans to grasp. Now we have a witch hunt too: openly, it has gone on under cover for some years now. The BBC has been the first department to act. It has fired three people from its European broadcasts section. But the previous under-cover hunting has been practiced there too. They unloaded all their Spanish republican people from the Peninsular section about two years ago, and replaced them with trusty franco-catholics.

If I were one of the Nobs of Reaction I think I would be a little pensive about the witch-hunt being openly on the programme. They won't gain very much in the way of heads, heads came off pretty much as they wanted before in the sacred names of efficiency, redundancy, and coincidence; And by doing it openly they will annoy quite a lot of people who wouldn't care in the least about just or unjust dismissals, but will care a great deal about copy-catting USA. I should suppose that that old crocodile Churchill is charmed, for the chestnuts are got out and the paws burned.

Did you read (it has been rather soft-pedaled, as blasphemous) that the Italians, god bless them, are having a state sweepstakes on the results of their election? It is as refreshing as a cuckoo opening up in the middle of church congress.

Ever,

Sylvia

VIII. The flame rekindled and abated

In spring 1949, the affair between Valentine and Elizabeth was rekindled when they met in Dorset after ten years. Sylvia's tormented and resentful response was elaborated in her journals and in the narrative she later provided for *I'll Stand by You*. Evelyn remained devoted and accepting until her forbearance was exhausted. The next spring there was another brief reprise of the affair, to the distress of all four women, but the fire did not persist. The two households remained intact. For the nearly twenty years remaining to Valentine, she and Elizabeth maintained an affectionate correspondence with meetings carefully planned not to hurt Sylvia or Evelyn.

Elizabeth and Evelyn, now in their early forties, visited France, England, and Scotland from late March to early May 1949, an opportunity for Elizabeth to see friends and familiar places after ten years and the ravages of the war. Their trip—as followed through Mary White's letters—included Paris, London, Oxford, Norwich, and Edinburgh. Mary White was then in remission from the cancer that would return in June and result in her death in July.

Elizabeth visited Dorset by herself. 'It was such a pleasure to see you the other day if only for such a short time,' Alyse Gregory wrote from Chydyok where she had lived through the war, 'for I felt very much like a wraith looking across the dim, distant years to a country still so dear to me yet so infinitely out of touch.'[1]

It was on this brief mid-April visit that Valentine reluctantly agreed to a 'last meeting'. Even though it was ten years since they had been in each other's presence it turned out to rekindle the long dormant flame. 'E arrived at Yeovil and I met her. We scarcely spoke and when at last we did it was with the utmost formality. But after we'd had tea and driven around the country, and returned to her bedroom at the Acorn Inn at Evershot [between Yeovil and Dorchester] she gave me the signet ring

she had made for me, many years ago—and then she kissed me. And at once the love flowed back, like a stream returning to its old bed—and the river has run unusually smoothly and deeply ever since.'[2]

This renewal of their passion took them by surprise. Elizabeth had just been on a satisfying visit to old friends in Paris and London with Evelyn. In her journal Valentine expressed apprehension and deep ambivalence about Elizabeth. 'Towards her I feel a violent desire to possess, a profound obligation to love, a feeling of assertiveness and a dangerous excitement because of this. I can look at her with dislike, and feel bored by her; I can find time drag when I am with her and feel perfectly alien to her—and then at a touch all that is blown away and all I need in the world is to know that she is mine. I could readily kill her, obviously; but not kill myself because of her—and I would die, I think, without Sylvia.'[3]

When Valentine returned to Frome Vauchurch, Sylvia saw that she had been made 'suave and handsome by love', the dread sign that the affair had resumed. She knew that Elizabeth had to return shortly to her ill mother but anticipated that when she 'was free to come to England, she would, and from then on they would live together'. An even greater shock came when she understood that Valentine meant for them to live together 'all three. V and E as lovers, S as companion'.[4]

In Dorchester on this visit, the lovers spent three nights 'in the large dark bedroom' of the Kings Arms Hotel. 'On the first night everything happened; we were completely and irrevocably restored to each other, with greater happiness and completion than we had ever imagined. Everything happened—I do not know how anyone can believe man to be mortal, who has experienced how instantly, in joy, he becomes a god.' Valentine considered she had been 'raised from the dead' and told Sylvia that 'she entirely loved Elizabeth, that Elizabeth needed her, that it had been settled between them that Elizabeth would return and that from then on they would live together.'[5]

In early June, Sylvia wrote Alyse Gregory of a proposed ménage. '[In] a month or a couple of months Valentine and Elizabeth will be living together. Here, in this house, I hope. It seems much the best plan.' She had reluctantly accepted the plan, although unwilling to remain at Frome Vauchurch as 'companion', and she held the hope that it would not last.

It will assure Valentine a continuity of work and trees growing and books, some of her roots will remain in the same ground. It will settle Elizabeth with a certain degree of responsible domesticity, which will be much more settling to her nerves than flitting from hotel to hotel; and for my part, I would rather have the sting than the muffle of staying. Practically, too, it is much easier to find a roof for one than for two.

But the main reason I am telling you all this is that for the first time I have been able to feel a living and in-my-flesh belief that Valentine may one day return to me. Till now I have assented to this belief with something more calculating than hope and more tremulous than reason; and chiefly because I love her [and] cannot bear to disbelieve her assurances. But yesterday, I saw her not only more shaken by the news in the cable than I (that could be accounted for by her doubled state of mind, and the burden of two loves she has to keep her balance under) but—what is the word?—the word is very nearly appalled. It seemed to me as though this was the first time she had realised herself as living without me, that, until now, solicitude had always presented it to her *as me living without her* .... I cannot tell if it will make the immediate future easier ... But it was there and I saw it and want to tell you ...[6]

The prospect of a trial period of cohabitation with Elizabeth—now planned to begin in September depending on Mary White's condition—prompted Valentine to write an autobiography that affirmed her devotion to Sylvia. In *For Sylvia* she termed the test of living with Elizabeth and of loving two persons at once the second greatest crisis in her life, akin in gravity to when she faced her alcoholism two years before. In late June, as she prepared for Elizabeth's return she set down her thoughts.

I write this on a day when I have heard that any time now another one I love will come to live with me here, in this house where Sylvia and I have lived for twelve years together, through bitterness of private woe, through war, through my degradation and shame and the almost two years accomplished of my heavenly rescue and our increased happiness and peace. I do not know how this new thing has come about, nor whether it is the work of heaven or hell. I cannot, for more than a moment at a time, realize what it will be like to be here without Sylvia—or anywhere without Sylvia. But I have a conviction that this must be tried; although it is so dangerous I can scarcely measure it even in my fancy.

Whether I have been set askew in my judgment by those long years of drunkenness and waging useless warfare, I do not know; or whether I am as I feel myself to be: so made that I really can, in truth, be in love with two separate and most alien people.[7]

Valentine completed the autobiography on 4 July 1949 and inscribed it to Sylvia, from 'Valentine—who loves you'.

'If this is infatuation,' Sylvia wrote in her diary in late June, '[I]t is the wariest, the most long-sighted infatuation the world has ever seen. No, no! It is generalship before a crucial engagement. But it is strange & bizarre et elévé, that I should be her Chief of Staff.'[8]

While she waited 'subduedly' for the uncertain date of Elizabeth's return, Valentine detected a lump in her breast, adding to her stress; for a time she concealed the news from Sylvia. (It was, however, non-cancerous; the breast cancer that would prove fatal developed later.)

The prospect of the trial cohabitation became imminent sooner than expected. Mary White's cancer had been in remission but in June became active and led to her death at the age of 71 on 3 July. A few days later, Mary's will of April 1948 was shown to her two children—'read' would be the Victorian term, and the surprise and shock was similar to that in novels of that period. Mary provided that her daughter would have no control over assets in the estate. Though the securities were shared evenly between the two children, Elizabeth's share was left in trust with her brother, Wade, as trustee. Even more hurtful to her daughter was the provision that all of Mary's personal property, jewelry, clothes, and most importantly, The Patch, Elizabeth and Evelyn's permanent residence, were to go outright to Wade.[9] The will was published in the Waterbury paper, and one view at the time was that Mary White had wanted to insure that not a penny of her estate would go to Communists and their sympathizers.[10] In light of what its postwar aggressiveness had revealed about Stalin's Soviet Union,

Mary and other relatives looked critically at Elizabeth's wartime efforts on behalf of Russian War Relief; when the will was drafted Stalin's aggressive moves in Eastern Europe were in the news. The brutal Communist takeover in Czechoslovakia had taken place in the spring when Mary had her will drawn up. In that same season, Elizabeth was campaigning for the Progressive Party, whose standard-bearer, Henry Wallace, favored rapprochement with the Soviets. However, behind Mary's draconian will may have been another motive: disapproval and rejection of her daughter's sexual relationship. While Mary sought to protect her assets from Communism, she also may have wished to preclude any use of the assets by Evelyn, the female lover of the daughter whom she had intended for a conventional marriage. Whatever the motivations, the will was an implicit slap at Evelyn as well.

Will White had no part in the matter of his wife's estate. With limited speech and mobility from his stroke in 1947, he was an invalid under twenty-four-hour care spending his days on the Breakneck second floor.

The revelation of her mother's lack of confidence in her and contempt for her interests and activities deeply affected Elizabeth; that it became public added to her distress. She sought comfort and support from Valentine and made reservations for her first flight across the Atlantic.

At the end of July—when correspondence between Elizabeth and Valentine had firmed up the dates for the trial cohabitation—Sylvia wrote in her diary, 'Four months so happy, & three so wretched. It is a strange thought that in time to come I may yet turn back to it for record of better days ... for ill or well, I have been with her, slept by her, heard her voice, felt her hand. What she did, she did unwittingly, in innocence & too great trust in me; & since then she has still been the light of my darkened eyes, & the core of my heart, & my strength& comfort, & raison d'etre, and all I have.'[11]

Valentine was aware that she could not live without daily contact with Sylvia; she was alarmed about the lump in her breast; but told herself she had to go through with the trial cohabitation. She believed that 'God had ratified the pledge between Elizabeth and herself,' Harman writes, and 'now she must try the spirits, if they be of God.'[12] Another cause of anxiety were the frequent changes in commitment from Elizabeth. Initially the trial was to have lasted four months, but, despite the urgency of her desire to have Valentine's support, she pared down the period to one month from four—exacerbating Valentine's inner conflicts and uncertainty. 'It was a come-down, and an affront—such an affront that I could hardly look V in the face', was Sylvia's acerbic reaction to Elizabeth's abrupt changes in plans, and they did deeply upset Valentine. The project altered from the ménage a trois to a month in which Sylvia would stay in a hotel 'instead of moving out entirely'.[13]

With less than a month to go, Valentine was in 'a state of suspended animation'. Her letter indicates that she had shared the news of the possible cancer with Elizabeth (although not then with Sylvia). Elizabeth was also resuming her research on Anne Bradstreet to be done in London, for which Valentine suggested useful contacts.

Frome Vauchurch
Maiden Newton, Dorset
August 8th [1949][14]

My darling, it's early morning & I want to get this off quickly before I go to work. Your two letters of 3rd and 5th came this am, with enc. from R unread as yet. Thank you for yours, & for the confirming cable, my sweetheart. Forgive that I don't reply to the cable suitably, but there are good reasons for this apparent neglect. It is NOT neglect—heaven knows (and you shd know it too?). R telephoned me to say that you shd write to Revd. Canon Anson, Master's House Temple, London and say you were told to do so by Mrs Neligan, wife of Bishop Neligan of Auckland, NZ. Anson is his chaplain or something and Neligan was my uncle. Apparently this will open whatever sesame there is to be opened. I'll note the address and then if you don't get round to doing it before you come, you can while you are here.

Not much more than 3 weeks ... it seems an endless age of time, I know it is shortening every hour. My darling—for pity's sake take care of every moment of time and do not hurt yourself or get ill or abandon yourself to any demons between now and the 2nd September, no matter how reasonable and human-formed they appear to be!

Could you tell me WHICH AIRPORT you come to? No one seems to know, hereabouts; I've asked Joan to inform me, since she commands an office staff but I doubt that she does not know much! I would need to know (and can find out from Cook's of course, I'd forgotten that!).[15] Don't be alarmed, if you were, about my lungs. Maybe I didn't have occasion to tell you at the time. It was May 1948 when they discovered it, after a scare of TB. And it is precisely the same as silicosis in its results, and not anything that gets worse—it merely means, as you say, some kinds of care.

No more now except, my own darling, my most beloved—I am in a state of suspended animation mercifully: but only suspended. All the life of the whole world, past present and to come, is lying in wait, just below the smooth surface of these quiet days and nights. God keep you; God bring you—

Valentine

In mid-July Valentine wrote Sylvia, away tending to her sick mother, to explain how profound the feeling of 'everything' that she had experienced with Elizabeth had been, how much she loved her, but that Sylvia was her 'whole life'. 'I love Elizabeth, but the whole truth—all the truth I have ever seen and known and all the loves and desires and recognitions of my life, and all my happiness and endeavours to be good (in the sense of being whole) are all planted in you and growing out of you ...'[16]

Sylvia made plans to stay away from the house when 'this baleful Eliz.' arrived.[17] On 12 August her dread intensified: 'In three weeks time she will be here. Her foot trailing on the stairs, her glance dawdling over our possessions, her voice & smell filling the house. I feel a curious defencelessness when I think that while V is at work she will be here alone, with house & garden to herself. It is not hate that I feel. It is loathing—as though I saw a frightful never-quite forgotten sore re-opening in my flesh.'[18] Three days later, 'sitting in our newly painted chairs on the porch ... [Valentine] began again about the problems of Evelyn'—the fourth party to this involvement who was to be left behind during the trial cohabitation.[19] Was she to continue as Elizabeth's partner? For her part, Sylvia made it clear that she could not remain at Frome Vauchurch during the 'trial'. Three days later she had fallen 'morally low by misfortune. I wish I could lay emotional booby-traps for Eliz. and it is an effort to put roller-towels with my large red initials on them...'[20] On the 21st the 'date that seemed only a little while ago, so inconceivably far away now seems appallingly near', and she had a dream of 'Eliz.' breaking into her room at the hotel.[21] The next day: 'Brown is the madman's colour. I had a bad night, seeing a beggar's coat with long skirts hanging on a bare thorn-bush, and Eliz. lying on me like an incubus, and at the end of September lying in wait.'[22]

On 31 August, Valentine settled Sylvia at the Pen Mill Hotel in Yeovil and on her return to Frome Vauchurch telephoned that Mozart and Winterreise were on the wireless. In the hotel 'I feel idiotic with grief,' Sylvia wrote, 'with care, with bewilderment, with exhaustion of spirit. This is where I have travelled since May. Yet my love left me swearing I was her love, and that it rested with me to save her if again she is whirled away.'[23]

Elizabeth's friend Douglas McKee—years before nominated as one of the kindred spirits in her notes made on the *Bremen*—understood why she chose to go to Valentine. 'When one is wounded, it is best to go where one's instincts lead one. People are like the animals in this respect, for we generally know what place and what associations can most gently heal us. And I think that you have need of healing, and to spend time where you will not be buffeted.'[24] At that point Wade had made no move to alter the arrangements set up by their mother.

But what of Evelyn? She drove her partner to Idlewild airport in New York to fly to be with another lover for a month. There was no doubt that she was aware of the trial cohabitation plan; she addressed her letters to Frome Vauchurch. At the airport they were joined by Kes (Bullock) Cole, Elizabeth's close friend from New York who wrote warmly to Elizabeth of the good humor of the departure and 'talk of the transcending beauty you were about to see'.[25] Evelyn returned to The Patch to tend to Tomas the cat, and Daisy the dog, and make regular visits to semi-paralyzed Will White at Breakneck.

The next day Evelyn reported to Elizabeth that

> After a usual Merritt Pkwy passage I arrived at the grape arbor at 3:35 and was frantically greeted by Daisy. We sat on the bench until after four and although I didn't see anything—even a bird—that resembled a DC-6, I knew you were close to me and comforted.

> After a small wash with a fresh up to see my second favorite father & had a pleasant ¾ hours with him. He looked very dashing in dark blue ...

> It is a lovely moonlit night and though you cannot know until this reaches you, I am thinking about you my very dear Elizabeth & asking God to bring you safely back. Tomas sends his love (at the moment he is very cross because I stopped his exertions on the chair) and believe me, my Elizabeth, so do I.
>
> Evey[26]

The next day she sent a postcard with a photo of Calamity Jane (see Figure 63); the point was obvious and it also evoked the memory of their happy visit to the Black Hills in 1942 when Elizabeth was in South Dakota organizing for Russian War Relief.

A few days after Elizabeth moved into Frome Vauchurch, Valentine took books to Sylvia at Pen Mill. 'She is much more tired than she meant me to know,' Sylvia recorded, 'all her movements, slightly sleep-walking, spoke of deep fatigue. She even admitted she was tired. Yet Eliz. is being quiet and reasonable, and, as far as she can be, helpful. And there is pleasure; but between the pleasure, tedium, and the oppression of talk in idleness.'[27]

On 4 September, in the first of her daily letters to Sylvia at Pen Mill, Valentine was positive. 'White, Elizabeth Wade is being extremely virtuous and willing and hard working, within the limits of my patience telling her how to be! She makes the big bed and carries the coal ...' Valentine was dealing with her own 'sense of violence of various kinds about Evelyn. I have said definitely that she must return to Evelyn ... although she does not, perhaps, feel able to think of it as anything final'.[28]

Calamity Jane
when a Scout
for Gen. Crook
in the Black Hills
S.D.
127 ℋℰ

Friday - Sept 2

Lovely day. Tomas tossed
up what seemed to be
mouse. Speaking of mice,
Mrs Grey is, at the moment,
nibbling at our history
books.

Berry Elizabeth.
Evelyn

AIR MAIL
15¢
UNITED STATES POSTAGE

MIDDLEBUR
SEP 2
1 PM
1949
CON

Miss E. W. White
% o Warner - Ackland
Frome Vauchurch
Maiden Newton
~~Dorst~~ Dorset
England.

From The Patch, Evelyn kept Elizabeth informed in detail of people and activities at home.

Sunday, Sept. 5/49[29]

My dear Elizabeth,

This has been an unusual Labor Day for me as it has been (1) the very first Labor Day I have ever spent alone in the country and (2) the only one I can remember indulging in pure manual labor. 'We' arose at 8 A.M., had a substantial breakfast, swept around a bit and then begin to polish. We polished silver on dresser, lion glass ware, mirrors, etc., and then took a half hour off to rush up and see your Daddy. Then we rushed down again to cleaning out closets, drawers, medicine cabinets and what not until it was time to take a bath, put small chicken in oven and rush up to see Mr White. The self established routine calls for 20 minutes in the A.M. and 1-2 hours in late afternoon...

As Mary Martin sings: 'You can't light a fire when the wood's all wet'. Instead of all this chit-chat I could have told you about these past three days that were warm, blue, and gold; the garden never more enchanting, and the long nights of bright stars and brilliant moonlight. There are pages to be written about the sudden experience of intimate living when you walk around your own house and notice for the 'first Time' the amount of the intimate collection of living. Just the process of collecting summer laundry is a love story within itself. My whole instinct is to write you a most passionate letter but it is no longer my privilege. (But still my right.)

Evey

Opposite:
63. Evelyn's Calamity Jane postcard to Elizabeth at Frome Vauchurch.

When she next wrote, Evelyn was at the Algonquin Hotel in New York where she and Elizabeth regularly stayed.

[Algonquin Hotel, New York letterhead)
Tuesday, Sept 6/49[30]

My dear Elizabeth:

I have been thinking so about you and would give anything to put my head on your beloved shoulder for just a few minutes.

This morning when the alarm went off I made the fatal mistake of not getting up & next I knew it was 8:50 so I flew into my clothes, grabbed my bag, drank some orange juice, said good-by to Tomas & Daisy & headed for NY. It was a ghastly trip as the parkway was crowded with Labor Day weekenders who had decided to go home Tuesday & avoid the crowds. I arrived here at 11:45 & flew into a taxi for Dr M. [John F. X. Murphy, DDS] who for once was waiting for me. After a rather harrowing session, I staggered uptown to meet Lucy & by the time I met her I had the shakes—couldn't drink a cocktail which appalled her. I have been resting all afternoon & after I get some supper I am going to bed. What I need is a lot of sleep.

Darling I hope you are feeling better and are getting lots of rest. Having you alive & well is the only thing that matters to me.

I meant to tell you, we are simply awash with vegetables and I have sent out SOS's all over the place. My god, those squashes! I took Barbara a basketful—tomatoes, squashes, cabbage & cucumbers. I am trying to keep up with the little cucumbers but the damn things seem to spring to full size in one night. I am going to make T. juice on Thursday.

Paul Robeson sang again last Sunday at Peekskill & the results were far worse than the previous week-end.[31] Dewey [Gov. Thomas E. Dewey) ordered 1000 troopers & and other 1000 special police to guard the concert. They did & everything was OK until just as the concert ended the troopers & police departed leaving the audience to come out alone & face this vicious mob who stoned them, burned up cars, & beat up hundreds. It is a hideous thing. The streets of Peekskill were hung with banners which said: 'Wake Up America—Peekskill Did!'

My Elizabeth, don't forget me & the love I have for you. I miss you darling. These have been such beautiful days & it seems incredible that we aren't standing hand in hand to live in them.

Evelyn

Returned home, Evelyn found two letters from Frome Vauchurch and responded tersely with a postcard.[32]

'She is being good and very kind. She truly loves me and while she is with me she trusts me almost completely.'[33] So Valentine reported; the exiled Sylvia was in torment.

I understand that this evening, lying in deep misery, thinking of a passage in Valentine's letter how she in her love with Eliz. can live innocently—and that it is because I am steadfast and completely 'without guile or reservation'. Recht sich auf erden. [Law on earth.] She lives and loves innocently with Eliz. because I am shaken with fears and doubts, ravished with physical and mental jealousy, and steadily murder myself in concealing it. But she tells me she is feeling well, and poor tired, tousled Janet, with grey hairs on her forehead said how beautifully she looked. I know. So she did by me once. Alyse said it was by being sure of me that she was able to love Eliz which is strangely akin to that enigmatic and shocking remark of hers that it was with the me in her that she loved Eliz. I cannot understand it. I am a Manichee far from my home.[34]

The next day 'my love came. She looked as beautiful as Janet said yesterday … It numbed my heart to think that I must have made her look lifeless and almost plain—and, thinking of a passage in Valentine's letter that it is Eliz. whom I hate and strive against who renews her beauty'.[35]

'This morning a letter in which she writes of the duality of her mind,' Sylvia wrote a day later, 'which can reconcile my belief in her truth of love, and Elizabeth's corresponding belief, and feel in herself both loves compatible and not conflicting, though to either of us in total war. It is a difficult letter, written in great fatigue and melancholy—and I have been perplexed all day, both how to understand it, and how to act on it.'[36]

Elizabeth had written Evelyn 'things will work out'. After news of pets, Will White, and friends, Evelyn made it clear that there would be 'no working out'. In a passionate rebuke, she gave vent to her opinion of 'the Dorset Sappho' and what she considered Valentine's posturing as a male. By contrast, she and Elizabeth together had established a different identity in community around them and among family.

Wednesday, Sept. 14/49[37]

My dear Elizabeth:

Tomas is on his foot-stool, Daisy is on her pillow, the darkness is full of small singing and chirruping. I went to NY today by train and after a rather long session with Dr. M [Murphy], I had my shoes shined and came home again. It was good to be with Dr M today for he is now an old friend. He was very sweet and quiet today and it was a kind of comfort ... I received your letter of Sept. 9th before leaving this AM and was glad to see your handwriting. I am glad you are happy and having a rest and I hope the rest of your stay will be so.

My dear Elizabeth, I note that you are still talking about working things out. We have talked about this subject several times but I suspect you either half listen or won't believe what I say, so perhaps if I put it on paper you will really read it. I beg of you to put your mind at rest about working things out for I assure you you can't work this out to suit yourself. I ask you to forgive me if I seem unreasonable, unfair, or quarrelsome. Also, I want you to understand I am not pleading for your love. As I told you last May you cannot plead for that, and I told you then there isn't any question of it for the wonderful life-giving warmth and light in my life is gone. You must stop tormenting yourself and kidding yourself and accept the situation for what it is and will be, as far as I am concerned, for always, and there just isn't any question about 'working things out'.

First of all please understand that I never will accept, trust, or respect V for reasons I have very definitely and clearly told you. On this matter, any possible doubts I might have had (and I assure you I had none) would have been more than confirmed this past summer by the selfish histrionics she burdened you with at a time when you were already most sadly burdened. However, there is no point or need to discuss this subject as I am sure you know how I feel.

Secondly, I cannot and never will, be able to regard your great love with the degree of respect such a love of yours should have. You have rightly censured me for speaking of your relationship with the Dorset Sappho in 'vulgar terms'. The grotesque is usually vulgar, and when you have had sexual relations with a man you are more aware of how grotesque it is for a woman to try to act like a man. All the wedding ring, collar-and-tie, strutting and talking, business is pathetic and grotesque. It is absolutely impossible for me to reconcile my knowledge of you—my wonderfully dignified, intelligent and steadfast Elizabeth—as being a partner to such a spectacle and grotesqueness. In view of our past relationship this may appear as hypocritical talk but such is not the case for I am expressing an opinion about a type of woman and not a subject. You and I loved each other as two women, and every thing about our relationship was based upon that of two women—with no pretenses to the world or to ourselves about one being the 'man in the family'. We sought and found active love in the only ways two women could. In the eyes of God whether we were immoral or not we will have to wait to find out (I don't believe so), but whatever, we reacted naturally and not with the grotesqueness of trying to pretend we were anything but two women in love with each other. I don't doubt but what many of our friends—both liberal and conservative—speculated about our relationship but because they were not challenged by absurdity in our behavior, we were able to have our life together, with many friends and the most solid test of all—our families.

In saying this no doubt I have distressed you for which I am sorry but Elizabeth, you and I—and everybody concerned—are in deadly danger and the sanest thing we can do is to speak honestly, and above all, not delude ourselves or each other. As I have told you in talking to you, and as I am now telling you in this letter, you can't 'work this out', so relax and go with what has been done. Eat your cake darling and be philosophical, for that is the quietest thing for you to do.

In view of the things you have said to me, and in the two letters I have had from you, I feel that you do not (or will not) understand what has happened to me—the being I have always known and lived with—or to the Evelyn you have known. My dear Elizabeth, I am not fighting for my life for that has been taken away but I am fighting, and desperately, to get my feet on solid ground, to grasp on and have the courage to pick up what is left. I realize time is the 'great healer' and that countless people have suffered this experience, but I never knew how long this kind of dying took. There is no rest from the burden of thoughts—day or night. For me the nights are the worst for I cannot sleep and when I do the brief hours are torturously dreamed—so it is better to be awake. Realizing this un-natural Evelyn state, and while trying to get back to myself, I ask you, as a friend, to bear with me. Also, I ask you to forgive my recent social misdemeanors which have caused you embarrassment and anxiety (also myself—but not until later!) which—I trust—will not re-occur. If you, my very good friend Elizabeth, would come to my aid NOW (and just put aside the double-talk about 'working things out') I believe and know you could help me to work out our briefly remaining time together in the best possible way for both of us. If you know anything on this earth you must know that I love you with my whole heart and being, and that above all things I want you to have a good and happy life.

Take care of my beloved Elizabeth.

Evelyn

'A letter from Evelyn this morning precipitated a profound and miserable gloom,' Valentine reported on 19 September. 'My offer of Dexedrine was refused ... I don't know what Evelyn has said, but that the letter is furious, abusive of me and pleading and threatening with Elizabeth ...' The relationship between the two had 'not ever been clearly defined, and it is not that kind of a relationship. This would not matter except than in a crisis it means that neither is quite sure of what position to take ...' Valentine was hopeful that 'this cloud will pass'.[38] Sylvia recommended giving Elizabeth more Dexedrine. 'It is not a serious likelihood of bringing on an obsession. The obsession is there already. She is an addict to her melancholy.'[39]

Ruth Ackland visited Frome Vauchurch when the 'trial' had run nearly three weeks. It was 'such an immense joy to have that time together, dearest,' she wrote Elizabeth. 'I loved every minute of it ... further friendship leading to increasing happiness for me. I do think Elizabeth darling, that you are being quite splendid, the fine way you have taken this horrible blow. The victory you have gained over bitterness is indeed a lovely thing. I admire [you] my dear.'[40] (Sylvia called this 'bawding' on behalf of Elizabeth who had exercised 'her sesquipedalian tact and charm on Ruth'.)[41]

Valentine had tea with Sylvia at Yeovil on the 18th, eleven days before Elizabeth's departure. 'She looked extremely tired, and the pain in her arm has come back, but Eliz.'s melancholy was dissipated by benzedrine. What a pity we didn't know of this useful drug ten summers ago, when it seemed as though only dynamite could perform that office.' The horror of the summer in Warren remained a recurring memory.[42]

Evelyn made plans for Elizabeth's return. She assumed that life would continue at The Patch as it had before the 'trial'. (Of this letter Valentine wrote that she hoped 'it was all about practical matters. They are having a very grand new car and I expect it is about that', and she affirmed that she didn't in the least envy them.[43])

Tuesday, Sept. 20th [1949][44]

My dear Elizabeth:

... I should not be writing letters at this moment but I had to tell you about your beautiful new car which I collected today. It seems to me this particular car is the handsomest thing on wheels and I felt most superior driving it home. I am sure you will be pleased with it and enjoy driving it but I don't see how we can ever keep it down to 40 M.P.H until the first 500 miles are accomplished for if you barely touch the accelerator the car just zooms. I took it up to show it to your Father and he seemed very pleased with it.

This past weekend the Agees and Martha were here.[45] Jim, Mia and child departed Monday morning and Martha stayed until this morning so we had a day of peace and quiet together. My god-child is a monster! She won't be three until this November and she is the size of a seven year old. She talks like an adult, makes her bed (perfectly), and wiped the dishes for me. I tell you it gave me the willies! Fortunately I had bought a ham for Jim's arrival was unexpected and as I have told you, his appetite is monstrous. Almost the entire ham disappeared for Saturday dinner and a small pork roast—which I had expected to use this week—went on Sunday. Mia and Jim certainly are a pair but were very sweet guests this weekend.

The other night when I was playing some records the radio suddenly gave forth with ungodly noises which frightened me so that when I rushed over to shut of the record player I pulled the arm so far back so now the record player and the insides of the radio are away for repairs. It seems one of the condensers gave away which accounted for the noise—and the smoke! It discouraged me a great deal.

The garden continues to be utterly beautiful and full of flowers. It has turned quite cold today and I fear we have a frost lurking around, waiting for the night. I am sorry you have missed this spectacle.

Wade is off to Boston and Gloucester this Thursday until next Monday at which time he is returning with John Alden in his pocket. I saw the Hamiltons for a brief moment and am going to have dinner with them this Friday when I go to New Haven to collect the pictures. Next Wednesday is a Murphy day in NY [Evelyn's dentist] and while there I am planning to go to Bronzini's and get Wade a present and also one for Helga [Chase] which we both can give to her.

I had your postal card of complaint about the lack of letters which I don't understand as I have written—aside from the S. Dakota cards—at least five letters to you, which for me is nothing short of miraculous.

Need I say my darling Elizabeth that I am looking forward to seeing your beloved face next week.

Evelyn

From Paris, Douglas McKee saw a resolution of the issues raised by Mary White's will. 'I do hope your sojourn in England has been as reassuring and fulfilling as you hoped. And as I said, I'm not hurt that you shan't be coming here. A letter arrived from Wade yesterday. He's feeling intensely lonely in that big house, and said that next year he may follow me here for our birthday reunion. I can't help thinking that time will straighten out your extremely delicate relations with him. His attachment to your mother was certainly strong, and although he's remarkably sensitive and emotionally confused, I think he has a nice sense of justice and rightness. After all, he and I are both children of Libra.'[46]

Valentine accompanied Elizabeth to London for her return flight at the end of September. From Ruth Ackland came a note wishing 'courage' and that it will be 'not goodbye but only a little "au revoir" for you will come back to us I know dearest & will find just the same love & welcome awaiting you from us all who love you so dearly. I shall think so specially of you on your journey [and] when you reach home & face all the various problems I know ... Godspeed to you this time will have so refreshed and enlivened you that you will be able to face everything with a new courage [and] a fresh outlook, when things unessential to real life will take their minor place ...'[47]

On 29 September, Sylvia was back at Frome Vauchurch, talking to Thomas the cat and Shan the Pekinese, 'combating my feeling that I should find Eliz. upstairs. But the poor thing has gone on this misty autumn-smelling morning I wandered about from room to room looking out the windows. Kitchen, bathroom, small sun-parlour, cupboards all as tidy as they could be.'[48]

Elizabeth flew back in time to celebrate her brother's birthday on October 1. The day Valentine returned from seeing her off she mailed an image of Tobias and Sara in bed as a reminder of their time together and reflected on what they had found out in the trial (Figure 64).

Frome Vauchurch Maiden Newton, Dorset
[2 October 1949][49]

I feel a kind of fellow-feeling for these two, for all he is so ugly, my darling—because they were lying together on the night that we were, and because I think they were happy. So here are some pictures (she is lovely in the large one?) and I like the marriage register because of her proud 'pianist' under his mute-looking 'peer of the Realm' ...

How long does this take to get to you? It will be posted on Oct. 3rd. Try to remember to tell me.

Mr Ward is sending you, from me, the Waddell trans. of the Desert Fathers and her stories of their lions and so on. I permit you to enjoy them but ask you to remember that there is, as I think, a little too much sweetness about in the books! (But do enjoy them: do READ them: what is happening to your solitary hour? Hold on to that, dear love, and may it be blessed to you.)

Do not despair if things are very difficult at first; keep on trying for a pattern and do not be sold into multiplicity. For you, with me, there is a firm, clear pattern, surely and deftly drawn, within which our joined lives must move in grace and as it were classically. We found it so and we shall always find it so, and with God's grace we shall prove together that I am right. But it should be so even

64. Tobias and Sara in bed. Postcard from Valentine, explained in her letter of 2 October 1949.

when we are in body separated, and even when our lives become, from time to time, cluttered up and confined and seemingly without form or void. The pattern is there all the time and we are set for ever, now, within it: like figures on a Greek vase—Move to the inward pattern, my beloved, and as you can, make your life conform to the rhythm, and especially inside your lovely mind. It is a simple, clear rhythm, not calling for acrobation or for any sort of austerity or deprivation. But it does demand attention & a good balance and a knowledge of how to attend to its laws—lesbian love is, when it is in its pure state, a very strict kind of behavior-pattern, my darling: calling for control and profound attentiveness to instinct. All that, really, is in the Symposium ... I bless God that I found that little copy for you, and there could not be a clearer sign of how it is meant to be with us than that we went to Salisbury and found that little book. Abide by it, sweetheart, and love me—

Who am your own

Valentine

Sylvia recorded her torment in her journal throughout the fall of 1949 and into the next year when Elizabeth came again. She conveyed not only her suffering but Valentine's fluctuating confidence that something could be worked out so that she could love and be loved by both women.

October 11[50]

the disease of Eliz is working in her far more deeply than in 1939—when she often resisted it, and tried to throw it off; and in me, I know, it is working like a malaria; and if I am not helped soon I think I shall lose my last power to hold out, it will becomes such an obsession of helpless anxiety, of impotence, of insignificance. And still, though I have lost all affection, all respect, for Eliz: I am visited with pity for her, for what must be some spark of real feeling amid all that sprawl of emotional verbiage, self righteousness, and chicanery of argument. And in that real feeling there must be an element of horror at all she has brought about. I who have brought about nothing, but merely struggled to retain my integrity of love, feel horror. But also, and worst, deep shame at my consenting in 39 in that hell-house at Warren. If had stood up then, this would not have happened—and I did not—and it has.

October 16[51]

She talks of Eliz. Constantly—no, it is more accurate to say that Eliz. Is constantly in her talk. Sometimes I bat it back, but I cannot be forever batting.

Elizabeth made an all or nothing demand:

October 24[52]

> another frightful letter came this morning, saying it must be all or nothing, and full of threats of renunciation. And all that morning we talked of it, and she is rent between us. But Eliz. will certainly destroy her with possessiveness thwarted, and I may be enabled not to harm her if I go away. So in the upshot a clear letter was written, saying that there must be a year's trial in which she lives with Eliz. and after that it may be possible to work out some future expedient. She showed it to me, and I agreed.

November 18[53]

> She [EWW] has shown, as far as I know, no shame on either side about Evelyn: for taking to her, for leaving her. She left that unabashed parcel for me at the end of Sept. (after I had injured her feelings by going to a hotel); the letter from Evelyn in May [September?] that shook her to the core did not shake her into answering it—or remembering it, when she got a similar one while she was here. Again she was shaken to the core. And with this assiduity to collect her dues, Vénus toute entière welded into a tax-collector or bailiff, she can perfectly well be shaken to the core one day; and go bravely on to collect her dues the next [...] Such woe, such foreboding, and such nausea fill me that I can hardly contain myself ...

On 21 November, Valentine wrote Sylvia that she sensed from Elizabeth that 'something has changed and enabled her to "accept" some new manner of living. I think she is en l'air, and has a notion that her proposal of coming over here at more or less regular intervals is the same as my earlier suggestion of her living here ... She's had a talk with Evelyn, who has said that she doesn't think Elizabeth could possibly separate herself from me, and has said that she will stay in America for 3 months next spring while Elizabeth comes here.'[54] Valentine was not certain of the 'change of heart', as the cohabitation plan had been altered so often from what had originally been planned.

On 30 December, Sylvia recalled the events of the past months:

> When I look back at May and see how Eliz. had, it seemed, all the cards in her hands, body, renewal of lust, reparation of what had been wrong, romantic quest, twelve whole years, money, novelty, beauty, a surface undaunted by war, two large new cars, the spring, instinct at its liveliest, and determination; and I am old, familiar, the worse for wear, and stupid with shock. How comes it then? Partly Eliz.'s fatal rapacity, get-sure-quick, poor wretch; partly my truth, which stayed when everything else I had tattered away; but mostly my Love's love, her innocence from all calculation. But no river could be more astonished; after a deluge, to find itself in its familiar bed.[55]

Sylvia's torment and Valentine's uncertainty and ambivalence continued into the new year of 1950, which in mid-January 'turns towards Eliz.'s determined new assault'. Two days later: 'Valentine came back from work with a letter from Eliz. I think it must be about coming in the spring, for she suddenly looks aroused, and combative, and decisive.'[56]

Then there came an intervention on Elizabeth's behalf by Kes (Bullock) Cole. In late January, while at the Hôtel Vendôme in Paris, she wrote Elizabeth that she had arranged a visit to Frome Vauchurch. 'I want to tell you that Valentine wrote such nice letters, and I am going, with pleasure, to see her next week. I will write you when, just as soon as we work out the dates. I feel very sure something constructive and real will come from this meeting.'[57] (She was also pleased that Elizabeth, like herself, was seeing a psychiatrist. 'I am so glad that you are looking into your own depths with the trained creeturs beside you.') From London, Kes telephoned Frome Vauchurch and reported that

> Valentine was out but Sylvia answered, and was very nice indeed as we arranged the dates. Valentine will write what train to take on Saturday, the 29th. I will be there until Monday morning. It seems a right and reasonable thing that the people who love you should meet quietly. Usually it is not what one person says to the

other that is important, but what the conversation stimulates the person to say to himself, clarifying his own thinking.

Bet darling I have thought of you so much. Yesterday when the white cliffs came closer and closer & thought so hard of you ...

I'm very tired, but I cannot ever tell you how glad I am that I came.[58]

On 28 January at Frome Vauchurch, Sylvia commented on Kes and the visit of conciliation. She deemed her a

kind crow, and very amiable, and with beautiful brows and extremely sure honest eyes. After she had got her strength up with a solitary walk, she came in—and so I learned—tackled Valentine on Eliz.'s behalf. I knitted by the dining room fire—dissembling the shock more than I had expected—of an American voice twinned with Valentine's overhead and got dinner and dawdled ... Kess had asked what chance of a solution that would not havoc V's relationship with me. She had said that torments and reproaches made holes in our life together, through which life was lost; but that if she were happy with Eliz. it would be all right with us. This was such a shock to me (for it seemed to me the most out and out denial of any validity or meaning left in my love as it appears to her and was said with shining confidence in May) that I think I showed nothing at all.[59]

To Kes, her mission was a success and it resulted in an arrangement that would be 'all right' for Evelyn too.

That Valentine loves you there is no shadow of doubt and she seemed to feel absolutely that there was a solution to your problem if you both approached it very quietly. As for myself, my relief knows no bounds that you love such a rare spirit.

We did get through to each other from the beginning and throughout she showed the greatest kindness and responsiveness, as did Sylvia. Rather than your thanking me, I thank you ...

It is much better to tell you about Dorset rather than to write it. Suffice it to say for now that it was beautiful—& good. I think don't say anything to Evelyn about this change of heart about V. This situation can work out all right for her too. I would like to tell her face to face & it might make her feel better. I am sure this is right.[60]

There is no indication of what Kes conveyed to Evelyn when she returned, but clearly Evelyn stood her ground, did not leave, and accepted Elizabeth's need for Valentine. She and Kes were at the airport to see Elizabeth off on the second of her flights to 'work things out' with Valentine.

When Elizabeth wrote that her plane would arrive on 19 March, Sylvia began a countdown to the dreaded day. However, all was not smooth between the lovers. Valentine received a letter that she 'found hard to endure. This she told, that evening, and spoke of all the discontinuities, the pains and embarrassments of this affair, and how she is divided in her mind as to how to meet Eliz.'[61] But Valentine refused to take Sylvia's offer to go with her to Paris instead.

After Elizabeth's departure Evelyn wrote

Sunday March 19th [1950][62]

My darling Elizabeth, it is now 4 P.M. and no cable from you. I tell myself you must be safe for bad news travels fast and I have been listening to news broadcasts during the day.

Darling, it is such a lovely, warm day. I am being St Francis today, with all the animals and birds just egging me on. As per your instructions Daisy hasn't focused her eyes away from me for a minute, while Tomas is melted butter and doing every trick in his repertoire. (To be sure much fish is changing hands.) I fed the birds before my own breakfast (the halo formed then) and the beloved chickadees have been so sweetly heard from all day. To complete this beatific role I watered those things in the laundry and everything else around the house that looked green and dry. I was so errant in the role that I most graciously forgave Ruth Northrop [Middlebury neighbor] for being so crass as to ask me to Sunday dinner and granted Miss Hunt [Marion Hunt, Waterbury friend] an audience at 5 P.M. But my darling everything is so full of you. It doesn't seem possible to endure six weeks of this along with the sorrow in my heart. However, when I get my plans for brooming, hoeing and visiting underway, the time problem will dissolve.

After we left you yesterday we went up on the ramp and watched your departure. It was a curious sensation to feel so 'removed' and watch your beloved figure struggle across that gale swept runway, up those final stairs and disappear into a silver tube which, when the door was shut, seemed so hermetically sealed. Whatever it did to your insides I assure you the take-off was a poetic dream. Once that 'tube' started down the runway and left the ground, it became a silver bird that soared through the brilliant sunset light. It was so beautiful, and mechanically perfect, that as I watched you disappear into the sky I felt assured about your safety.

As there was a bus starting back to NY immediately after your departure, Kes quite firmly refused to have me drive her back so we had but a few minutes conversation before parting. (I will keep in touch with her and let you know how things are going.) As you were in it and part of it you know there was a beautiful sunset, so my drive home—2½ hours—was enlightened by pink colored clouds and early evening stars. Being very tired I had a brief supper and went to bed and slept soundly until 7 AM at which time I arose and donned my St Francis robe.

Under separate cover I am sending a review of Eliot's 'Cocktail Party'. This reviewer seems to think that the Trinity Holy Ghost and what-not are mixed up in it.

My darling Elizabeth, I love you.

Evelyn

'Teach me not to number my days' Sylvia concluded in her diary the day Valentine left for London to meet Elizabeth's flight. However, the outcome of the meeting in London was the reverse of what she had feared. 'She came back yesterday [23rd]. "I can't promise," she said, "that I won't fall into pits of depression. But it is at an end."'[63]

The meeting was a decisive anti-climax, 'an unmitigated disaster' as Harman put it. 'Valentine saw that Elizabeth's moods were so unpredictable and so often draped in black, that there was no point in deluding herself any longer: "It is not love of her. I loved, I still love, my fancy, nothing else." Elizabeth came down to Dorset, lingering out the last few bars of the piece, but the affair, that had been so much more than an "affair", was over.'[64] 'I think Valentine has never loved or needed me as much as she does now, or I her,' Sylvia wrote Alyse Gregory on the day she returned. 'We hold on to each other like convalescents.'[65]

Elizabeth remained in England for a few weeks. She resumed her Anne Bradstreet research and arranged to enroll at Oxford to gain academic credentials for the work. She then returned to The Patch and Evelyn. At about the same time Wade renounced his role as trustee of his sister's securities and made The Patch over to her, so eliminating the draconian provisions of Mary White's will.[66]

In the early summer, Evelyn was in Rochester to care for her sister, Betty (Elizabeth Holahan) who was recovering from an operation. The affection she and Elizabeth shared for the formidable London-born tomcat, Tomas, in the form of a kitten that resembled him, was a talisman that caused her to pour out her renewed love.

Friday, July 7/50[67]

My beloved Elizabeth:

This evening Betty came down to sit in her garden and I thought you would be pleased to know that while we were sitting there—at the far end of the garden—I suddenly heard an approaching, emphatic and familiar Tomas sound. As I looked toward the house I saw a small edition of HIMSELF whisk around the corner, up the steps, poke open the not-too-closed screen door & disappear into the house. I stood the suspense as long as I could & then said to

Betty: 'What about the kitten now in your house?' She was very airy about it & told me it was a stray kitten that she had fattened up. Finally I went in and found a charming, long-legged, skin & bone character sitting at the foot of the stairs and bellowing demands. Much hamburger & milk passed between us after which he joined us & lay purring on the cool grass between us. I will tell you more about him when I see you. But I tell you this because in that familiar context the whole knowledge of my love for you, and the intensity of missing you, flooded over and swept me away.

My beloved Elizabeth I pray to God that the sun will never rise on the day when you are not the greatest part of my life.

For me, whatever sorrow or unhappiness we have had between us has no meaning in comparison to the rich happiness, companionship, and love I have had, and have with you. I consider myself among the favored mortals to have found a person with whom I am in harmony. I regret that I cannot enrich your life in the many ways that you enrich mine but my Elizabeth please know that I see, understand and so admire the strength of your character, the richness of your mind, the beauty within you and the goodness of your heart.

I truly believe my darling that if we will hold fast with ourselves & each other that we will know a good life always. It is a fearful world now and at the moment a terrifying one but what ever good or bad is to come, may my hand be in yours. Never forget my beloved Elizabeth that as long as I live you are not alone for I love you always.

I am distressed about my situation here for I so want to go home & yet I cannot bring myself to leave Betty at this moment for she is as weak as a kitten. Her arm is getting better but she still cannot completely dress herself. I know I am a comfort to her & she has begged me to stay but I told her today that I have a home & obligations and that I cannot & do not wish to remain away indefinitely. She understands that but being emotionally upset she cannot bear to ask 'strangers' to help her in the bath or in dressing. I hope I can be with you again on Tuesday but if I have to remain until Wednesday, please believe my whole wish is to be with you and I regret every day that passes without you.

Please take care and don't worry or be frightened, or be unhappy. I think of you constantly and my arms are around you always. Goodnight Elizabeth.

Epilogue

There is not one but a number of epilogues.

Elizabeth matriculated at Oxford in September 1950, a course she had set following the abrupt rupture with Valentine that March. She was 44, and it was a tribute to the work she had already done on Anne Bradstreet that the English faculty accepted her candidacy without a previous degree. She and Evelyn rented a flat in North Oxford during term time and returned to The Patch in Connecticut during vacations.

Elizabeth was in her second year at Oxford when I visited in June 1952. I had been on leave from my junior year at college and, after a solitary time in Italy, was eager for company. I was warmly accepted into the widening circle of friends she and Evelyn had made, as, led by Elizabeth, the doors of the university and its community opened to them. I didn't have a hint of it then, but now know it was only three years since the 'cohabitation' trial with Valentine had nearly resulted in Evelyn's departure. To my youthful eyes, there was no sign of discord that June—quite the reverse. Ironically, however, in my very first journal entry on that visit there was a reminder of that tumultuous time. My hosts, I noted, had just left to drive 'the voluble Mrs Ackland' to her Norfolk home. This was Ruth, Valentine's mother, who, to Sylvia's disgust, had 'bawded' for her, favoring Elizabeth at the time of the cohabitation. This energetic lady had bemused me when, in coat and hat, with minutes to go before her departure, she dashed off a dozen short letters, for her work with the Mothers' Union she told me. Ruth was being looked after by Evelyn as well as the favored Elizabeth. It would have provoked a caustic outburst from Sylvia.

I stayed briefly in their flat, then moved to student digs, a modest walk through redbrick North Oxford. My notes convey the flavor of the transformed lives of 'E and E' (or 'B & E' as I put it, for Cousin Betty), Elizabeth in her beloved England and the Oxford she had so enjoyed on a long stay in her early 20s. Their acquaintances were broad, neighbors, dons and their spouses, fellow students of Elizabeth, eccentric adjuncts, even some undergraduates who became companions for me in my theater- and concert-going. A smattering of journal entries:

65. Elizabeth after receiving her BLitt at Oxford, 1953, with Evelyn and Wade.

[1] **June 13**: At the King's Arms for lunch, usual scotch ale and ham rolls …

June 15: Discovered Cousin B and Evelyn walking to 10, Charlbury [their flat] fearing to be late for our supper. Good supper as usual with Mozart after (C major symphony and Solomon again in a wonderful gay concerto).

June 17: Party with Evelyn & Cousin B at 10, Charlbury, morning spent in aiding shopping, afternoon in preparing & nibbling various crackers, cheeses, pickles, etc., cashew nuts. The party itself was a large jammed affair …

June 19: Evelyn & I at supper at the Kings Arms Woodstock and after listened to Gluck's wonderful Iphigenia overture and Harold in Italy.

June 25: Very pleasant supper with B&E; discussed war situation in England.

66. Elizabeth and Evelyn in the sitting-room at 52, Park Town, Oxford, 1960s. Oil painting.

Late in her life, I asked Elizabeth if she regretted not going to college after graduating from Westover. 'Oh no,' she replied, 'the parents offered me a stay at a finishing school in Rome, but if I had gone to an American college, I never would have had the experience of Oxford.'[2] She took hold of it, enjoyed the academic whirl and spectacle, the beauty of the buildings, their connection with the past; they and the English countryside remained potent memories.

Elizabeth received a BLitt in English in 1953 with a dissertation on Anne Bradstreet, certainly the first dissertation at Oxford on that subject and an unusual award for someone in her late 40s with only a secondary school education.

The England that so attracted Elizabeth as a young woman continued to do so, and she lived in that dream from 1950 through the 1970s, alternating in the course of a year between months in Oxford and Middlebury, no longer confined to the academic schedule. At Oxford she and Evelyn made many friends among her teachers, including Dame Helen Gardner, scholar of Donne and TS Eliot and one of the

67. Elizabeth and Evelyn at 52 Park Town, Oxford.

luminaries of the university in the 1950s and 60s. Dame Helen became a lifelong friend and stayed at The Patch on her American visits. It was Elizabeth's custom to invite professors, researchers, fellow students, spouses, friends of friends, to drinks and dinner at home or in a hotel or pub. She swept people of different ages and backgrounds into her orbit, treating them to a sociable time and establishing friendships. The two were a team—a beguiling combination of seriousness (Elizabeth) and disarming down-to-earth American humor (Evelyn). After renting places for a number of years, they finally bought a row house on Park Town Crescent, part of that notable example of Victorian residential development. They entertained American friends in Oxford and English friends in Middlebury. In both places, their ever-widening circle grew to include the children of these friends as well.

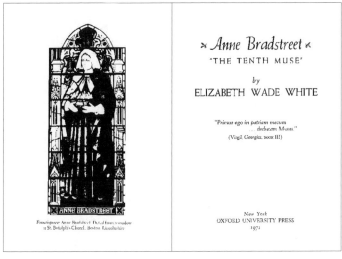

> ↗ *Anne Bradstreet* ↙
> "THE TENTH MUSE"
>
> *by*
> ELIZABETH WADE WHITE
>
> "*Primus ego in patriam mecum
> ... deducam Musas.*"
> (Virgil, *Georgics*, book III.)
>
> *New York*
> OXFORD UNIVERSITY PRESS
> 1971

Frontispiece Anne Bradstreet. Detail from a window
in St. Botolph's Church, Boston, Lincolnshire

68. Elizabeth's dissertation on Anne Bradstreet, the first biography of the
poet, published by Oxford University Press in 1971.

Elizabeth had found an element in which to thrive, one with intellectual stimulation, a congenial society, and most of all a framework. She had been right not to take on independent research as Sylvia had suggested—the 'bribe'—or carry on her Bradstreet work alone. The 'team' had found a métier in which they thrived, with an eclectic and varied circle of friends, and expeditions throughout the British Isles that helped to cement their relationship—radically different than any imagined life with Valentine.

The 1950s and 60s were good years for investments; the steady rise in the IBMs and others in the 'nifty fifty' then favored by trust officers, meant that skimming would not matter, growth would soon replace what had been taken out, or so the advice went until the steep dip of the early 1970s. This allowed for trips to Greece and to Egypt with Wade, countless overnight visits to friends on both continents, explorations of the British countryside, regular stays in London and New York. These appealing activities distracted Elizabeth from expanding the

69. Wade, Evelyn and Elizabeth in Greece.

dissertation on Anne Bradstreet into a book. She would make resolves, but it was not until Helen Gardner whipped the manuscript into shape while visiting The Patch that it could be successfully submitted to Oxford University Press. It was published eighteen years after the BLitt degree. No matter the tardiness, Elizabeth accomplished what she had set out to do forty years earlier. *Anne Bradstreet: The Tenth Muse* (1971) was the first full-scale biography and helped spur a growing interest in America's first female writer and published poet in the years since.

In the context of the unresolvable affair with Valentine, Elizabeth's choice of scholarship and a life devoted to family and friendships became the 'solid ledge at last that has stability in it' that Katie Powys sought after her experience with Valentine.

But there was a price, paid by the steady and stalwart Evelyn, whose life's purpose was expressed through Elizabeth. By the early 1980s, geriatric conditions had largely immobilized Evelyn. She died at The Patch in 1985, leaving Elizabeth for a time almost speechless with grief.

At the reception at The Patch following Evelyn's memorial service, I was briefly alone in the front room off the crowded living room. This was where coats could be left on grandmother's settee; over the fireplace was the John Craske seascape showing a section of the Norfolk coast with its associations with Valentine; on the opposite wall was the oil portrait of 'B and E' in their prime, seated in their Oxford house on a summer day. With no preliminaries, Evelyn's sister came in with what she, I suspect, had been holding back for years. Coming directly to the point, she told me that Elizabeth 'killed' her sister, turning Evelyn into 'a housewife'. So, she became an alcoholic and victim of its antecedent ills. I was not surprised. For at least the previous twenty years on social occasions and at home in the evenings, Evelyn became unsteady, her slurred speech leading to bickering and arguments. She was hospitalized twice for bones broken after falls at home under the influence. In Oxford, years after that happy visit in 1952, I heard Helen Gardner warn Elizabeth not to do so much entertaining, 'remember Evelyn, Elizabeth'. Elizabeth was powerful and energetic, and prided herself on holding her liquor. Evelyn told me more than once how she enjoyed 'following this one' who brought her to friendships and experiences that she enjoyed. But she did not have the same level of physical and psychic stamina, and what she did have waned as she grew older. She enjoyed the social whirl, and that, surely, was the gold in her life, but sorrow attended her inability to keep up. Evelyn was also aware, as her letters showed, that Elizabeth had been more deeply attracted to Valentine than to her; after the 'end of the affair' she saw the frequent letters come in from Valentine and forced herself to accept the periodic meetings, not secret but excluding her. She had entered her relationship with Elizabeth as a helper, one who could deal with a beloved who had a greater passion. Elizabeth's break with Valentine in 1950 was a clear choice in Evelyn's favor, but over the ensuing years the continuation of relations with Valentine seemed to have had a subtly corrosive effect.

In the family there was a collateral effect from Elizabeth's successful Oxford venture. When her first term there began her father had been confined to the second floor at Breakneck since 1947; three daily shifts of nurses cared for him. Although there was no dearth of funds to support Will's care, Mary White, burdened by the tasks of running the operation in the large house, pressed Wade to leave New York to keep her company. He had been studying sculpture in the city, 'which he loved'. But he was closely tied to his mother, her ally in marital disputes and in relations with her headstrong daughter whose opinions and behavior were provocative. He had shared none of his father's manly pursuits; it was Elizabeth who enjoyed them. For his mother's sake, he returned to help run the household for a father he resented. After Mary died in mid-1949, he had the full responsibility of keeping the vast establishment going for the invalid on the sun porch, a plight he bitterly recalled in later years. Elizabeth, in shock over her mother's will, was away on the trial cohabitation that September, and again the next spring, and for longer periods when her Oxford matriculation began in autumn 1950. What was a turning point in Elizabeth's life, meant the absence of any practical backup to her brother for extended periods.

After Will's death—two months before my June 1952 visit—it was Wade who had to empty the huge house, find places for the furniture and decorative objects, the one-time target of Sylvia's derision. Many of these had descended in the family, which Wade conscientiously distributed to relatives. It was a massive, lonely, and numbing job. Elizabeth helped on her weeks in Middlebury, but the greater burden was on him. During this evisceration, Wade came to detest Breakneck— it lost for him any of the enjoyment he may have felt in the past; for Elizabeth it remained in her mind as it was on her return from England in 1929, lyrically recorded in her journal.

Wade sold the house and its extensive grounds to a local attorney at a fire sale price, or so—from a distance—Elizabeth asserted. The buyer found no use for the house and had it demolished. It stood for just 40 years, built by Will to provide enjoyment by later generations; there were no grandchildren and in the 1950s no one in that area had use for a house of that size. Will had lovingly landscaped the grounds, laid out several gardens, activities that Elizabeth followed closely as she grew up. Like fishing and shooting with him, these of her father's interests became hers. As an emblem of her connection to Breakneck, she moved the astrolabe to The Patch; with it, too, came the memory of selecting it at Crowthers in London the day in 1929 that she and Sylvia met to visit the Machens in Amersham, and a reminder of Will inscribing a 'tiny bright pink EWW in the fog-blackened copper with his penknife.' She and Will had created a herb garden, overlooked by a small prefabricated house in which she put an old apothecary set of drawers and a counter on which to prepare the herbs for drying. She had the Herb House re-assembled and placed overlooking the driveway entrance to The Patch.

Thirty years later, in leafless late winter, a friend and I set out to find what remained of the Breakneck house and grounds. I knew that the buyer had not carried out his original plan to subdivide the property; it was still undeveloped so there could be traces of the past. On the long curving driveway up the hill we found the road broken up by saplings and brush that thrust through the tarmac; closed for years, it was impassable by cars, and difficult enough on foot. At the top, once open with views all around, the forest had taken over, saplings and brambles made a dense cover. The maple shoots sprouting in the lawn that had amused Sylvia in 1939 had conquered, the Puritans' fearsome wilderness was back. Pushing through the thicket we stumbled on the foundation. That was all that was left now, in effect the cellar had become a sunken nursery for scrubby trees. It was a forlorn relic, probably only visited by neighboring boys. It also seemed far too small to have held so vast a house above it, but that is the nature of foundations seen without superstructure.

Claire Harman told me that when interviewing her for the Warner biography in 1983, Elizabeth was guarded in her responses, explaining that she 'wanted to protect her brother Wade from the story'. He had joined their mother in deploring Elizabeth's refusal to come home for Christmas from Frome Vauchurch in 1938. To see the 'English women' in person was far more shocking. Their visit was a scandal among neighbors and in the family. In later years Wade would recount Valentine's pursuit of one of the maids, and certainly her and Sylvia's communism and her (unmentionably lesbian) appearance appalled him.[3]

Despite her deplorable friends, the abandonment he felt when Elizabeth removed to England was acute. Brother and sister remained loyal to each other, regularly in touch, they shared holiday gatherings, travel, and parties. The damage was beneath the surface and revealed itself in occasional outbursts of temper.

While attending to family affairs, Wade served as Art Curator at the Mattatuck Historical Society in Waterbury, and organized shows from the works of the many artists who lived in western Connecticut, several of them European refugees with major reputations. After he disposed of Breakneck and its bounty he found a satisfying role as Archivist of the Fogg Art Museum at Harvard. Some years later, with his friend Tibor Kereces, he moved to Fairfield, Connecticut where they restored a Victorian house. In his 80th year in 1989, in a remarkable set of circumstances, Wade was re-discovered as the painter he had been fifty years before. The Mattatuck Museum (formerly the Historical Society) in Waterbury, unbeknownst to him, had de-accessioned several paintings he had given them years before. At a New York gallery, which appraised them, they were admired, but there was no record of a painter named Wade White. By chance, a visitor overheard mention of the name; he had been a student at the Fogg Museum, knew Wade as the former Archivist, and that he was alive, and living in Fairfield. The work went to a gallery that specialized in 1930s American art; its owner visited Wade in Fairfield on the Fourth of July 1989. Wade unrolled the canvases that had been stored for years in his attic. The paintings are in the Precisionist style practiced by a select few artists in the 1930s, portraying flat surfaces, sharp shadows, and precise detail. In this near-fairy tale story, the paintings were exhibited in New York accompanied by a handsome catalogue, and several sold for five figure amounts. 'It feels like a dream', was Wade's refrain. Age and increasing dementia meant that he was unable to take comfort in this belated success and confirmation of his talent.[4]

The affair between Elizabeth and Valentine ('if you can call it that', in Harman's apt comment on the inadequacy of 'affair' to describe the complex relationship between the two), transformed after 1950 into frequent exchanges of letters and meetings carefully planned not to include Sylvia or Evelyn, though with their knowledge. Valentine's letters indicate that the two shared a quiet and abiding love and concern for each other. Copies of her letters to Elizabeth in the nineteen years after 1950 fill over six hundred pages. Elizabeth's letters do not survive, but Valentine's comments show that there were substantial reports from her.[5]

70. 'Gloucester Churchyard' by Wade White, oil. Photograph by
Jacob P Goldberg from the Peter Haring Judd Collection.

Valentine began an antiques business in 1952, specializing in portable,
usually small, objects she found on rounds of village shops and fairs;
she later converted a shed at Frome Vauchurch to make a shop. Her
letters recount the pleasure she took in the finds and placing them
with visitors to the shop—though she often gives Elizabeth first pick
for herself and presents for others. When Elizabeth relates illnesses,
Valentine sympathizes, suggests remedies, often inquires about
Evelyn's health; she shares news of her own ailments, increasingly
serious over these years, heart trouble, a cancerous breast tumor, a
mastectomy and a removal of the adjacent lymph glands (among other
discomforts, making it painful to type). She suggests books, shares
news of Janet Machen and her family, the Powyses, Alyse Gregory,
Dorset friends. As her mother's health declines, the letters tell of the
complexities of treating and caring for her and of the memorial service
and the memorial monument in the Winterton church. Invariably and
frequently the two exchanged presents, each fitted to the taste and

interests of the other and amply described. The anxiety, uncertainty, and conflict are gone; she barely alludes to the raw passion that once drove them. Once or twice a year they would meet.

Elizabeth never again saw Frome Vauchurch and Valentine never saw the Park Town house in Oxford, but they shared news of these places. The bond that connected them was strong and discreet from those to their partners. While the turbulence of 1938-1950—the 'troubled years', as Harman refers to them in the context of Sylvia's life—never returned, the reunions were an affectionate and perhaps melancholy reminder of what had been and what might have been.

Elizabeth and Sylvia never met again and communicated only during Valentine's final illness and at her death. Evelyn did not see either Sylvia or Valentine after 1939.

A 1952 letter from Valentine touched on many of the themes of the later letters. They had recently met in Silchester in Hampshire where there was a 'horrid' shop, and not long before they had visited the antique market in Salisbury. Elizabeth and Evelyn were soon to return to the US.

October [1952][6]

Thank you for your letter, my darling; you will have got mine by now, or by the time you return to Oxford after Silchester, & know that it was very much the same for me as for you, which is so good.

I've just remembered the Scottish address & I'll give it to you, though I don't expect you will have any time for writing: from about October 8th to 15th we shall be at Amulree Hotel, by Dunkeld, Perthshire. An odd address, but correct, if you should have any spare moment; but I think you would be wise to spend any time you have in resting: you looked very tired.

Monica [Ring] has actually sailed—so probably you will just see her. I hope you will. She is said to be very well, & Carola [her daughter] too. Charles [Ring] seems to be already here, or just-about-to-be-so.[7]

When I was buying buttons for it to-day, I remembered that I had not told you that the first suit of clothes you gave me—the gray one that is the god-parent of my Galashiels tweed, has been dyed the darkest conceivable brown & looks all set for another ten years! Isn't that remarkable? As you share, among other things, my feeling for long-lasting clothes, you will be pleased to hear this & I MEANT TO TELL YOU OF IT. (The BLUE suit is a lovely one & I cherish it & bless you for it.)

I meant to tell you of quite a lot of things I never got near to remembering, but never mind—they will keep, or you won't be much the poorer if they don't.

It is very late at night. I have been polishing a very touching object I bought to-day: it is a 'frying-pan candlestick' made of thin, very pale brass: it could be almost any age & has certainly seen several generations to bed—probably in a stone farmhouse near Sturminster Newton, where I found it. It was so dirty that I did not know in the least what it was made of, and now it shines like sun on water & feels as smooth as satin. A darling little object, both practical and delicate. I hope it will go to a very charming pair of people who live in the hinterland of Wales & are poor and uneducated, but with a great tenderness for things that are truly old and plain.

I sold the little brass jug I bought while we were in the Salisbury market, and I am becoming attached to the sardonic fish with ferocious spines and a single blank eye ... What about the ivory seal? It was extraordinarily generous and noble of me to tell you to get it, but I'm afraid like so many of my truly noble actions it passed unobserved. If you really find you have no feeling for it (the seal, not the action) I will send you 8/6 and the postage ...

To-day was tiring but most pleasant: I took Bo [Foster, friend and former lover of Valentine] (with whom, after long uneasy years I have now managed to establish a very happy companionship, thank heaven) to a remote place called Marnhull, where there are some splendid stone houses & quite a good church. There she gave a speech and I prowled about evading friendly people & finding a wonderful junk-shop kept by a wizard who favoured me most kindly. Then we had a disgusting tea in a frightful shop in

Sturminster and I got back very late in a blinding rain-storm, richer by some very lovely junk—notably the brass candlestick and a fine blue bowl of the earliest Worcester, and an unidentified cup-and-saucer in the most fantastic Chinese-Gothic style I have ever seen.

This letter is dull for you, my darling, & dull for the cats who are sitting like graven images on either side of me, willing me to go downstairs and find them some food. And I must go, for they and you compel me.

If we are not in touch again before you start away, know that I shall think of you on your journey & wish you well & a happy arrival, and a flourishing Tomas—

Love to you always, Elizabeth
Valentine

'Evelyn & I at supper at the Kings Arms Woodstock' was the entry in my journal on 19 June 1952. Where was Elizabeth? I suspect she had gone that day to Salisbury to meet Valentine, where, 'I meant to tell you of quite a lot of things I never got near to remembering ...' and went to the antiques market where she encouraged Elizabeth to buy an ivory stamp. I surely knew where Elizabeth had gone, as Evelyn did; but then I had no inkling of the affair. In retrospect it seems evident that Evelyn, if not accepting, had resigned herself to the continuing contact between the former lovers. After turmoil, the two loves co-existed, Evelyn's with Elizabeth, and Valentine's, if at a physical distance and at a radically reduced intensity, with Elizabeth, Sylvia at Frome Vauchurch with Valentine, physically close, but emotionally and, after Valentine's conversion to Roman Catholicism, to some extent intellectually, apart.

Coexistence, in love as in international relations, does not imply without stress. There can be a toxic effect in repeated awareness that a beloved once had a stronger emotional connection with another and that it is still alive, albeit modified. It may have been one of the factors that sapped Evelyn's confidence. And Sylvia, brooding after Valentine's death over the affair with Elizabeth, retaliated with the collection of letters, diaries and a narrative that revealed her vehement rejection of co-existence. She never escaped the power of that hurt. Valentine's letter to Elizabeth and the others that followed illustrate that, for them at least, there was a *modus vivendi.*

A lump in Valentine's breast in 1967 proved to be malignant. An eminent surgeon performed a radical mastectomy, leaving her shoulder and an arm in pain; but despite the surgery, the cancer recurred the next year. In July 1969, Valentine wrote Elizabeth, 'I'm perhaps in trouble again—having had my shoulder treated, they think they found signs of a recurrence of cancer "elsewhere", by X-Ray. I'm to go [back] on July 29. Think of me that day if this reaches you in time. I can't write more, nor more legibly, because my left hand does not anchor the paper properly!'[8] In late September she was still able to type, though not with her usual accuracy.

> I cd not write before, my darling, but the news is not so good that you need urgently to hear it: there is, as I could tell myself, a further spread of the disease, & I'm to go back to the massive dose of hormone as soon can I & I am to go to Guy's [Hospital] again for some day's check-up of the strange collection of drugs I've been given trying to cut them down, to give the hormone the maximum chance. This kind of General Check-up is always very trying, as no doubt you know, so I do not welcome it, even if they don't find anything more to make things worse. [...] There isn't anything much to say, is there? Such a situation has its peculiar nastiness for the victim, but I'm quite aware—too poignantly aware—that it wounds most bitterly those it is not engaged in killing. But still there is nothing profitable to be said and so I won't try.'[9]

Four days later Valentine could no longer write. Elizabeth sent fruit. Sylvia responded with unflagging politeness despite such deep resentment. 'Valentine thanks you very much for the figs—engagingly inappropriate to November, and delicious. There is little change in her condition now but every day I see her a little weaker and more incapable of any effort. Figs are particularly welcome, since they are no trouble to eat. So thank you, Sylvia'.[10]

Valentine's ordeal lasted another forty days, until November 9th. She was 63.

Dear Elizabeth

Valentine died yesterday morning—here, as she wished. She had been under morphia for two days and not conscious at all.

She wished her ashes to be buried in the churchyard at East Chaldon, and I think that will be agreed to.

I send my real sympathy.

Sylvia

Elizabeth did not—out of respect for Sylvia could not—attend the memorial service or the interment. To me, she referred to Valentine's cancer in a tone which conveyed bitter finality—similar to what I heard in her voice when she told me a quarter of a century later that her own lung cancer was 'terminal' with a similar decisive and bitter emphasis.

Elizabeth and Evelyn's yearly stays in Oxford continued into the 1970s, but for shorter periods. The Park Town Crescent house was sold, and they rented a nearby apartment, but as investment income dwindled and Evelyn's condition worsened, the Oxford stays that had meant so much to both were done. Four years after Evelyn died, Elizabeth made a last visit to the England she loved and where during the war she had felt she belonged. (If questioned at British Immigration, according to Evelyn, she acted as though England belonged to her.) I drove her to the airport and settled her in a wheelchair; in London, two male friends met her and over the succeeding two weeks took her on a round of visits. She was by then very lame and deaf; it was physically difficult but determination carried her through. It was, she told me later, amazing that it had happened, a happy time.

As she wished, she stayed on at The Patch; a housekeeper came in several days a week, Tony kept up the garden which still retained perennials planted by her grandmother over fifty years before. Jane Connery, in the apartment above the garage, at the bank where she worked kept her eye on the steadily dwindling investments that had to be raided regularly for daily expenses. Elizabeth fixed her own breakfasts, drinks and hot supper, drove to the market and pharmacy.

I began making notes after my visits to have a record of her knowledge of the ancestry we shared in colonial New England and New Amsterdam, and on the Dorset time, some new particulars were emerging. The most potentially interesting one occurred in October 1990, but I had not learned enough then to take advantage of it. I noted in my journal that I had been at The Patch for a lunch Elizabeth gave to two friends she hadn't seen for over 40 years. 'Here was a strange old people's party,' I reported. 'I couldn't tell what the flavor of it was. Betty's deafness means that she would have heard very little, and they may have been deaf too.' Bill, whose surname I didn't catch, was there with a wife and Steven Clark, 'a friend of Bill's, who is married but his wife lives in Bath and comes to and fro.' Elizabeth told me after that he was a young Quaker whom Sylvia had met in Spain working for the American Friends Service Committee. It was only later when I read the letters that I realized how frequently he was in Dorset in the 1930s and 1940s, and that Elizabeth had met him first at a Quaker conference near Wilmington. If only I had known a bit more about this visitor I might have been less puzzled by the gathering. Steven Clark was a living witness to 'S & V' as they had been in the late 1930s and to the young Elizabeth. I now know that at the time of the luncheon he was 77.

Another witness to those years was Janet Machen, Sylvia's niece. Elizabeth first met Janet as a child when she and Sylvia visited the family in Amersham; almost twenty years later at Sylvia's suggestion they shared a flat in Mecklenburgh Square in the fraught September of 1938; they made a short visit to Chaldon and stayed in Miss Green's cottage and paid a call on Theodore Powys as guided by Sylvia's instructions. Elizabeth paid her passage to New York in the summer of 1939, and, after Warren, shared the 'horrid little flat' with Janet on Perry Street, in Greenwich Village, and comforted her on her tearful departure from New York in wartime. They became friends for life. Valentine sent news of Janet's anxious search for a husband and her first marriage. I had met her when she and her two children visited in Oxford. I knew that Janet had divorced her first husband and married Martin Pollock (the Martin who was due for a meal in The Dairy House in early 1939 according to Elizabeth's shopping list; in 1940 when he was working for a social service organization she requested his help in finding work to allow her to return to England).

In 1995, the year following Elizabeth's death, I visited Janet and Martin in their farmhouse in Margaret Marsh in the northern part of Dorset. 'I knew Janet from her youthful photos,' I wrote, 'she is short, friendly, wrinkled face, with eyes in poor condition from glaucoma and cataracts. Her warmth and understanding are always evident in her speech.' We talked in the sunny garden. She said Sylvia was 'like an older sister to me'. She summed up the affair as 'one of some happiness, a brief few moments for Betty [Elizabeth] and for Valentine, and an extraordinary bond between Betty and Valentine, a great love, much grief, and for Sylvia jealousy.' Janet showed me a box full of little presents that Valentine gave Elizabeth and which the latter presented to her when she and Martin visited The Patch the year before. She thought they were 'the full extent of them', but I had found a dozen or so more when I cleared the house, small objects that Valentine's discerning eye had found on her countryside scours. A few days later I noted, 'A beer in the garden, supper here. Talk of the Powyses—[she had] the journal of the Powys Society out for me. I discover that in the late '20s and early '30s Betty Muntz was Valentine's lover—causing Katie great torment. It seems that Katie's passion for Valentine was never requited. Aphrodite reigned over Chaldon!' She told me what the letters implied, that Valentine and Evelyn had 'had a fling' in 1935 when Evelyn was in Chaldon to rescue her sister Anne who was enamored of Llewelyn Powys. It was Valentine who introduced Betty to Evelyn in New York in 1939, 'to deflect Betty from her'. The story grew.[12]

Janet took me to the annual meeting of the Powys Society assembled at Montacute, Somerset, where the father of the eleven children had been Rector. Under umbrellas next to a restored pond where the Powys children once swam, one of the members read from Llewelyn's poems. 'Llewelyn describes this pond as it was when there was a keeper for it, a maid to bring the cushions for the boats, parties and boating.' Here was another connection with that time.

In the car on the way back from the meeting, Janet talked 'non-stop'. Of Valentine: 'she was completely irresponsible and self-involved, had no sympathy or respect for others in those involvements, thought that she could do just as she liked and with no consequences.' Elizabeth's 'harsh bullying was a cause of trouble between them'. I thought of what

I had read in the diaries of Elizabeth telling Valentine, 'let's get down to the facts, put it all on the table' when trying to convince her to stay in America in 1939, not an approach likely to succeed. At Yeovil she pointed out the hotel where Sylvia stayed during the 1949 episode, 'a dreary "railroad" type'. Sylvia came down to visit Janet and the children several times during that stay and 'was serene', Janet told me, a contrast to the anguish in her diary at the time. Of the astonishing episode when Elizabeth left Evelyn for the trial joint habitation followed by the mediation by Kes Cole, Janet says it was a 'fantasy' on both Elizabeth and Valentine's parts.

Another witness I visited was Monica (Hemmings) Ring, born in Dorset, and a caller at the Civil Defense office where Valentine worked in 1943, leading to a lifelong friendship, one that came to include Elizabeth. Charles Ring, her husband, was an officer in the British Army and over his career had a number of postings abroad, including Washington DC and Nigeria. Monica's lively letters from abroad and later in rural Dorset in her widowhood were a delight, always shared with me. Carola, her daughter, was a godchild of Elizabeth, and also a faithful correspondent. Monica lived in the engagingly named Puddletown, not far from Dorchester. She had been a strong presence in my talks with Betty, who often shared her letters.

> Found Monica without much difficulty on the basis of the spare description 'cottage with a hole in it to the east of the church'. I heard the dogs barking, and Monica's tall, lean form appeared. She is in her eighties, a delightfully direct and informal person. I have not seen her for 30 years or so—and then only briefly ... About the publication of Sylvia's diaries, Monica says they should have been kept private. 'Sylvia and Valentine were very kind and thoughtful people, nothing at all like what is revealed in the diaries.' In Monica's view they ought not to have been published. About the letters I have, she asks, 'are you going to burn them? or censor the bad parts?' She met Valentine when they worked together in the TA office in Dorchester during the war. Valentine was interested in the people who came, not restricted to those with literary interests. About Valentine and Elizabeth she says,

'It wouldn't have worked at all. Elizabeth was sociable, had a gift
for making friends, sought out people to do so; Valentine was a
solitary. It wouldn't have done.'

She was certainly right about the incompatibility of Valentine and
Elizabeth, and right about the latter's sociability. The diaries and some
of the letters are painful, but I did not consider burning them.

On another day I visited silent witnesses, Chaldon and the downs.
'There is a partial air of neglect about the village,' I wrote of Chaldon,
last seen forty years before.

The triangular green or common has a pathetic tree growing
in its midst; the buildings on the way in look disused; there is a
collapsed building through fire; Apple Tree cottage where Betty
Muntz lived is for sale and looks shabby. At first look, then, and
perhaps for the best, much of it has not kept up or been leveled
by the times. Closer look reveals a number of cottages, including
Betty's studio, which have been cared for. The vicarage is well set
up now. I stopped at the church first. Evidence of care there in the
roses planted along the path. The building itself was much altered
in mid-19th century. On one wall was the Bethlehem scene done
by the students in the school under Betty's supervision during
the war: figures of horses, sheep, dogs, the stable made from
scraps of cloth; a charming primitive. In the churchyard are Betty
and André Bonamy, dead in the 1970s. It tore at my heart to think
of them, the kindly, twinkling André who tried to get me to ride
John Barleycorn better, and the sweet-tempered Betty who had
devoted her life to being an artist. The lettering she had done on
the grave of her sister, Hope, was particularly fine. Was she able
to do the lettering or most of it for the stone that marks Valentine
and Sylvia? One rectangular stone for both. 'Non ominis moriae' (if
I have it right). I shuddered at the thought of the discord that lay
beneath that single stone. It is certainly so that all will not die, as
their presences have been much with me this year.

Tomas, the cat who had passage on the *Aquitania,* whose life began on the streets of London, is buried beneath the apple tree which can be seen from the kitchen window at The Patch, a stone commemorates him. Sylvia was 76 when Valentine died in 1969. She grieved deeply, Harman recounts; she read through Valentine's journals, and letters, reliving, questioning, appraising what might have been and should have been. Valentine was at the center of her imagination as she went through the details of their life together, copiously recorded in their journals and letters. Susanna Pinney typed these and a narrative by Sylvia commenting and expanding on them. These were the basis for the collection edited by Pinney and published in 1998. *I'll Stand by You: The Letters of Sylvia Townsend Warner and Valentine Ackland with Narrative by Sylvia Townsend Warner.* Valentine's affair with Elizabeth is a major preoccupation, her resentment, indeed hatred, of Elizabeth is a recurrent theme. The title conveys the message, that it was her duty to stand by Valentine, to defend her from Elizabeth; her reappraisals told her where she had failed. The several years of warm mentorship 'in the priestly role' had turned to dust. She died in 1976 at the age of 83. Her ashes were placed next to those of Valentine's in the West Chaldon churchyard marked by the shared stone.

Harman's biography came out in 1989, the diaries she edited in 1993, and *I'll Stand By You* in 1998, all of which give what could be called the Elizabeth affair a prominent place.

Elizabeth was lame as well as deaf, but able to live on her own until her last illness. She had regular visitors whom she entertained with tea served in her strawberry-decorated cups and saucers, or they joined her for the bourbon which she continued to take generously resulting in sharper opinions and comments post-6pm. After a fall, she reluctantly wore an alarm that she could activate to alert her neighbor in case of need. She drove until she dented the car in a parking lot. Her finances dwindled steadily; the one-time rich woman had her house still, but the revenue from investments shrank as the bank sold securities for routine expenses. When the doctor told her that she had lung cancer and that it was not treatable, she asked me to instruct him that under no circumstances should she be taken to the hospital, that she wished to remain at home. With the essential help of her neighbor,

Jane Connery, hospice nurses cared for her in the last weeks when the only medication was a morphine drip. When I arrived to pay a call on what was a week before she died, I found her on the phone to her friend Vivien Greene in England. I overheard her say that she didn't think much of the doctor and was thinking of finding someone else. I don't remember what triggered the comment, but I recorded that she told me with a trace of amusement, 'I always wanted to be a boy.'

A few days after that remark she was semi-conscious. I had arranged to come by train to Fairfield to drive with Tibor and Wade to The Patch. When I arrived the call had come that Elizabeth had gone. I gave the news to Wade. He cried out, 'O no', in shock. A moment later his focus was elsewhere, and he asked several times where we were going. Elizabeth's body was on a hospital bed in that front room with the Craske seascape and the portrait of the two ladies in their Oxford house in halcyon days. The nurse told us that when she came on duty that afternoon she saw how weakened her patient was. She took Elizabeth by the hands and told her, 'Elizabeth you can go now.' And she did.

Elizabeth willed her body to Yale-New Haven Hospital; 'it will do some good having them look at the body of a very old person.'

The Memorial Service was in the Congregational Church with its white painted pews and walls and long, clear windows. Her name was added to Evelyn's on the stone in the Middlebury town cemetery, not in the plot Will White had established for his family in the Riverside Cemetery in Waterbury near where the Whites of previous generations were buried. She had not wished to embarrass Wade with a burial that would include Evelyn. It was December 1994. Elizabeth was 88.

The estate consisted of the house, its contents—some of the books and furniture quite valuable—and investments worth about $130,000. Elizabeth's financial assets that had served her and her many friends so well were all but gone. In a year or two she would have been forced to move from The Patch. She had wanted me to live in The Patch after her and had told me that she was willing it to me. During her final summer she asked me if I planned to move there as was her dream. As I was satisfied with my situation in the city and couldn't take on the additional cost and responsibility, I told her no.

Monday, January 02, 1995

The new year began without being noticed until mid-morning. I was at The Patch with Phyllis. We drove up New Year's eve morning (crisp and bright), arrived at about 10:30. It was Phyllis' idea to help and to get away from the city on New Year's. Her help was invaluable. The two days we spent broke the back of the task—there was so much done ... With nothing of the slightest value thrown out, we managed to fill several large bags and in the process cleared working space there ... Then a start on the Everest—the second floor study with the round table laden with papers, the drop leaf desk with its thick layer of dust and piles of papers. P. took one end of the room, I the desk and table ... When I got to the letters amid the dross of cards, those from England. Finally to a large drawer and there were some from Valentine Ackland (which I had thought were all destroyed) ... There were photographs—the evanescent color snapshots taken by her and by visitors in the last twenty years, and further back the authoritative black and white ... At the end of the day, Phyllis commented that it was like experiencing an autobiography. What is there has pieces of Betty's range of interests: a notebook containing a bibliography, one listing first aid procedures for her Red Cross work during the war, a passionate note from Valentine Ackland in a small wooden box, tender letters from her late in life, a tender letter from Evelyn from 1944 ... a demanding letter to a bank manager, a sizzling letter to my wretched, speech-deprived father who had gone to see grandmother Griggs in 1965 after my *petit mal* seizure at Columbia and evidently disturbed her in her 90s, fanciful cartoons drawn by Prentiss Taylor in 1935 on her departure for Europe that gave an inkling of her artistic interests and vivacious circle of friends in the those years, letters to do with the Russian War Relief effort locally, a clipping showing her collecting clothes for the cause in South Dakota, a letter to the Leahy Clinic asking for their help to treat Evelyn's alcoholism (stating that Evelyn would not discuss it with her), letters from researchers inquiring about the lives of Valentine Ackland and Sylvia Townsend Warner, photos of the passionate, tempestuous and willful young woman the lady who died only three weeks ago once was.

71. Elizabeth in the dining-room at The Patch, 1989. Craske's 'The Window' is above the mantel; her grandmother's portrait on the wall behind her.

She was gifted, emotionally and intellectually powerful, conflicted and difficult, a terrible temper, passionate likes and dislikes. A persistent strain: a strong emotional and moral empathy with what she liked in literature above all. Was she foremost a scholar-bibliographer-researcher, historian? Or a would-be poet, or a possible teacher of literature? All those involved her passions. She was also a hostess and *bon vivant*, in some ways a *grande dame* in her way of entertaining and holding onto that house; and a devoted and fiercely loyal friend to difficult characters like Helen Gardner, a nourisher of the young who sent Carola [daughter of Monica Ring] to university, made Alice Cole's parents [Kes (Bullock) Cole was her mother] see reason and permit her marriage. Poignant is the character and fate of Evelyn Holahan, who savored 'my friend's' strength and pursuit of what interested and moved her, but who suffered under her domination and felt the 'thumb' of her control and in part the alcoholism was a way to get out from under. Wade too, and I to a far lesser extent and balanced by that extraordinary loyalty, were given that treatment. The experience in that room yesterday and the day before was to be in the presence of a powerful life and the currents that were part of it. I admire her greatly, feel that my own life is pallid beside hers, and regret that so often in late years she remained bound up, not accessible and that I could not feel free and easy with her (as the earlier pages of this diary bear some sad witness). I come closer to her in death and memory than I did in life.

Endnotes

Where no source is given for factual information, it has been derived from Wikipedia and other public domain sources.

I. Like an astonished nervous dither bird

1   EWW Journal, 28 January 1929. Box 29A.

2   Pinney (ed.) 1998, 163.

3   William H White and his family are among the subjects in *More Lasting than Brass* (Judd 2006).

4   George Heard Hamilton (1910–2004), then a graduate student at Yale, was a classmate of Wade White at Yale. Hamilton's many letters to Elizabeth over four decades are in the EWW Papers at NY PL.

5   EWW Journal, 12 February 1929. Box 29A.

6   The play *The Kingdom of God* was performed at the Ethel Barrymore Theatre on Broadway, with Barrymore leading a large cast in the newly built theater named for her. Brooks Atkinson in *The New York Times* called it an 'impressionable drama with gleams of magic handiwork', 21 December 1928.

7   EWW Journal, 13 February 1929. Box 29A

8   EWW Journal, 29 February 1929.

9   STW to David Garnett, 12 March 1929, Garnett (ed.) 1994, 42.

10   STW to David Garnett, 12 March 1929, Garnett (ed.) 1994, 43.

11   EWW Journal, 1 August 1929. Box 29A.

12   EWW Journal, 11 September 1929. Box 29A.

13   This and subsequent quotations are from EWW Journal, 1 August 1929. Box 29A.

14   EWW Journal, 15 August 1929. Box 29A.

15   Harman 1989, 47–50; Stinton 1988, 1, 21ff.

16   I am indebted to Morinne Krissdottir for this attribution.

17   STW to David Garnett, 14 April 1925, Garnett (ed.) 1994, 19–21

18   http://www.powys-society.org/The%20Powys%20Society%20T.%20 F.%20Powys.htm. Accessed 13 October 2017.

19   Krissdottir 2007; Graves 1983; Krissdottir and Peers (eds.) 1998); Peltier 1999.

20   Stinton 1988, 160; 148 ff.

21   Krissdottir 2007, 118–121.

22   Stinton 1988, 120.

23   Quoted in Krissdottir 2007, 296.

24   Krissdottir, op cit.

25   Bingham 2008, 9–24.

26   Bingham 2008, 75.

27   Stinton 1988, 133.

28   Stinton 1988, 134.

29   STW quoted in Bingham 2008, 21.

30   Stinton 1988, 136.

31   EWW Journal, 15 January 1930, Box 29A.

32   EWW Journal, 1 November, 1930

33   EWW Journal, 26 November 1930.

34   EWW Journal, 26 February 1933. Two years later, she would consider accepting if Pierson proposed marriage. He became a prominent member of the Yale English Department and a historian of Yale College.

35   EWW Journal, 1 January 1934.

II. Entering into a dream

1   EWW Journal, 1 January 1935. Box 29A.

2   EWW Journal, 8 June 1935.

3   EWW Journal, 16 June 1935.

4   This and the immediately succeeding quotes, EWW Journal, 23 July 1935.

5   EWW Journal, 7 May 1936.

6   VA in West Chaldon to EWW 25 June 1936. Box 34.

7   VA in West Chaldon to EWW in Lincolnshire, 2 July 1936. Year assigned from reference to wedding. Box 34.

8   Bindon Abbey is a 12th-century Cistercian abbey on the downs a few miles east of Chaldon, now in ruins. Tess's house is a cottage in the village of Marnhull near Dorchester that Thomas Hardy may have used as the model for the house where Tess of the D'Urbervilles was born. Woodsford Castle, near Dorchester, is the remaining side of a massive 14th-century fortified manor house. Corfe Castle is a majestic ruin built by William the Conqueror in the Purbeck hills near the coast, destroyed by the Parliamentarian forces in the English Civil War. These were among the great sites of Dorset that Sylvia and Valentine wished to share with Elizabeth.

9   STW at West Chaldon to EWW at Breakneck, 14 November 1936, in Maxwell (ed.) 1988, 41–42. This is the only one of STW's letters to EWW to have been included in Maxwell's edition.

10   STW at West Chaldon to EWW at Breakneck, 25 December 1936. Box 29A.

11   VA at West Chaldon to EWW at Breakneck, 27 December 1936. Box 29A.

12   EWW Journal, 1 January 1937, Gilbertsville, NY.

III. The new breath of life blowing out of England

1   STW from the Gran Hotel Victoria, Madrid, to EWW at Breakneck, 6 March 1937. Ellipses as in original. Box 34.

2   Notes by EWW. Box 29A.

3   STW from West Chaldon to EWW at 107 Prospect Street, 1 April 1937. Box 35.

4   Elizabeth's newly acquired cat, given family names.

5   Rose Macaulay (1881–1958) was at this time a celebrated British novelist and columnist; she became best known for *The Towers of Trebizond* (1956).

6   STW from West Chaldon to EWW at 107 Prospect Street, 4 April 1937. Box 35.

7   Florence Keates, whose family would also stay with Sylvia for a while during the war as evacuees.

8   STW at Matlock, Derbyshire to EWW at Breakneck, 25 April 1937. Box 34.

9   Folder 1937, Box 30.

10   VA at West Chaldon to EWW c/o English-Speaking Union, London, 7 May 1937, Box 34.

11   Douglas McKee was a Yale friend and correspondent, then teaching English at a boarding school. Irwin Hoffman was a New York painter.

12   EWW Journal, 16, 17, 20 May 1937. Box 29A.

13   STW at West Chaldon to EWW at Breakneck, 14 May 1937. Box 34.

14   Steven Clark, frequently referred to in later letters, was one of the Clark family who owned C & J Clark, makers of Clarks Shoes, based in nearby Street, Somerset. In 1937 he was then 24 years old, seven years Elizabeth's junior. He had grown up in England, had been educated at King's College, Cambridge, and at Swarthmore in Pennsylvania. At the time of this letter he was in Wilmington working for Joseph Bancroft & Co, a family firm on his American mother's side. During the war he returned to England to Clarks. As Elizabeth reports shortly, she did meet him at a Quaker gathering near Wilmington.

15   VA at West Chaldon to EWW at 107 Prospect Street, 19 May [1937]. Box 34.

16 STW at West Chaldon to EWW at Breakneck, 21 May 1937. Box 34.

17 Ralph Bates (1899–2000) was an English-born writer deeply involved
    in the cause of the Loyalists in Spain, one of the organizers of the
    International Brigade and an active speaker on behalf of the Loyalist
    cause in the US. He had been briefly arrested in France for arms-
    smuggling, but had returned to Spain in February 1937. In Madrid
    he founded the International Brigade's newspaper, *The Volunteer
    for Liberty*. From that experience he wrote the book with that title.
    His best known work is *The Olive Field* (1936).

18 Jean Starr Untermeyer (1880–1970) was an American musician
    and poet who visited Sylvia and Valentine in Chaldon in the 1930s.

19 STW at West Chaldon to EWW, 16 June 1937. Box 34.

20 The case involved nine adolescent African-American teenagers
    accused of rape in Alabama in 1931. Three trials followed, with
    defense by the American Communist Party and Northern liberals.
    Charges were later dropped for some of the young men. Others
    were sentenced to 75 years, one to death—which he avoided
    by escaping and was later pardoned.

21 VA in West Chaldon to EWW. 17 June 1937 Box 34.

22 EWW Journal, 1 July 1937. Box 29A.

23 STW at West Chaldon to EWW at Breakneck, 2 August 1937. Box 34.

24 STW at Frome Vauchurch to EWW at Breakneck, 27 August 1937.
    Box 34.

25 Douglas Stewart (1913–1985), born in New Zealand, was at this time
    briefly and unsuccessfully seeking work as a journalist in England in
    the course of which he interviewed British writers. He left for Australia
    in 1938 and in the course of his life published 13 books of poetry and
    was an important literary editor. He came to be considered a major
    Australian poet.

26 VA at Frome Vauchurch to EWW at Breakneck, postcard,
    29 August 1937. Box 34.

27 Pre-metric British coinage was in pounds, shillings and pence, often
    referred to by their abbreviations of L (pounds, derived from the
    Latin for pound, *libra*), S (shillings) and D (the pennies, the d apparently
    derived from the Roman *denarius*). There is no connection with
    Lysergic acid diethylamide (LSD).

28   STW to David Garnett. 22 June 1932, Garnett (ed.) 1994, 51–52.
      Correspondence from John Craske and his wife, Laura Craske,
      exhibition materials, and related items are in Box 30b.

29   VA at Frome Vauchurch to EWW at Breakneck, 7 September 1937.
      Box 34.

30   Anna Louise Strong (1885–1970), American-born journalist then and
      later reported on Communist and USSR-inspired movements across the
      world. The book that Elizabeth sent may have been *Spain in Arms* (1937).

31   STW at Frome Vauchurch to EWW at Breakneck, 7 September 1937.
      Box 34.

32   EWW at Breakneck to VA at Frome Vauchurch, 12 September 1937,
      carbon copy, severely faded. Box 34.

33   Folder 1937. Box 30.

34   STW at Frome Vauchurch to EWW at Breakneck, 23 September 1937.
      Box 34.

35   VA at Frome Vauchurch to EWW at Breakneck, 24 September 1937.
      Box 34.

36   VA at Tythrop House, Kingsey, Bucks. to EWW at Breakneck,
      10 October 1937. Box 34.

37   A complete copy of *An American Herb Calendar* is in Box 48. Letters from
      Prentiss Taylor are in various locations in the EWW Papers.

38   EWW Journal, 20 October 1937. Box 29A.

39   VA at Frome Vauchurch, Maiden Newton to EWW at Breakneck,
      29 November 1937. Box 34.

40   Federico Garcia Lorca, the Spanish poet, was shot by Nationalist
      militia in August 1936. John Cornford, English poet and Communist,
      died in action near Cordoba in December 1936; Ralph Windsor Fox,
      British novelist, historian, member of the International Brigade,
      was killed in one of its first actions, December 1936.

41   STW at Frome Vauchurch to EWW at Breakneck, 2 December 1937.
      Box 34.

42 VA at Frome Vauchurch to EWW at 101 Prospect Street,
    29 December 1937. Box 34.

43 STW at Frome Vauchurch to EWW at 101 Prospect Street,
    29 December 1937. Box 34.

44 William Cobbett (1763–1835), English pamphleteer, farmer,
    and journalist, whose great achievement was the promotion
    of extended suffrage resulting in the Reform Act of 1832. He was
    consistently a liberal critic of authority. He was in the United States
    from 1892 to 1800; if he had settled there, as Sylvia implies, England
    would have lost a great reformer. Henry Addington, 1st Viscount
    Sidmouth (1757–1844) was a British statesman, and Prime Minister
    of the United Kingdom from 1801 to 1804, and Home Secretary
    1812–1818, responsible for repressive measures which Cobbett
    vigorously opposed and in succeeding years he opposed
    Catholic emancipation and parliamentary reform, both
    of which Cobbett advocated.

45 Clipping. Box 30A.

IV. Violent and ecstatic happiness

1 EWW at Breakneck to STW at Frome Vauchurch (carbon copy),
   21 June 1938. Box 31.

2 MWW at Breakneck to EWW, Lippmann article enclosed. 15 July 1938.
   Box 30.

3 STW at Frome Vauchurch to EWW at Breakneck, forwarded to
   Rockport, Mass., 12 July 1938. Box 31.

4 John & Edward Bumpus, Ltd., booksellers invoice to EWW,
   9 July and 31 July 1938. Box 31.

5 EWW on board SS *Bremen* to MWW at Breakneck, 13 August 1938.
   Box 20.

6 EWW on the SS *Bremen* to WHW at Breakneck, 15 August 1938.
   Box 30.

7 EWW at 2 Queens Gate, London SW7 to MWW at Breakneck,
   18 August 1938. Box 30.

8 STW at Frome Vauchurch to EWW c/o the Misses Milen,
   2 Queens's Gate, London, SW7, 20 August 1938. Box 31.

9 EWW at 2 Queen's Gate, London SW7, to MWW at Breakneck,
   22 August 1938. Box 30.

10 EWW notes, 18–31 August 1938. Box 30B.

11 Martin Pollock's second wife would be Sylvia's cousin Janet Machen;
    he would be her second husband.

12 EWW from 2 Queen's Gate, London SW7 to MWW at Breakneck,
    25 August 1938. Box 30.

13 STW at Frome Vauchurch to EWW c/o Machen c/o Ryecroft,
    4 Mecklenburgh Square, London WC1, 27 August 1938. Box 31.

14 Sylvia's mother was a Purefoy.

15 Elizabeth intended to research the historical uses of woad,
    Isatis tinctoria, the plant used as a source of blue dye.

16 EWW at 4 Mecklenburgh Square, London WC1 to MWW at Breakneck.
    Box 31.

17   EWW notes, 1–15 September 1938. Box 30B.

18   Nesta Knox, EWW's former Latin tutor.

19   MWW at Breakneck to EWW in England, 2 September 1938. Box 30.

20   EWW at Carlton Mansions Hotel, 2 Bedford Place, London WC1,
     6 September 1938. Box 30.

21   STW at Frome Vauchurch to EWW at Carlton Mansions, 2 Bedford Place,
     London WC1, 12 September 1938. Box 31.

22   EWW notes, 16–30 September. Box 30B.

23   EWW in the train en route to Maiden Newton to MWW at Breakneck,
     16 September 1938. Box 30.

24   John Robertson Scott (1866–1962), radical journalist, lived at Idbury Manor
     from where he edited *The Countryman*.

25   EWW at King's Arms Hotel, Amersham, to MWW at Breakneck,
     25 September 1938. Box 30.

26   21 September 1938 EWW at Winterton, Norfolk, Journal 145. Box 29A.

27   Henry Fuller was about to matriculate at Cambridge University;
     his father was travelling with him. They were friends of the White family
     from Connecticut.

28   Hitler raised new demands on France and Britain at a meeting in
     Bad Godesberg.

29   VA at Frome Vauchurch to EWW at Charlton Mansions, 2 Bedford Place,
     London WC1, 24 September 1938. Box 31.

30   Cable from VA to EWW in England, after 24 September 1938
     (date illegible). Box 31.

31   STW at Frome Vauchurch to EWW at Carlton Mansions, London,
     24 September 1938. Box 31.

32   Rafael Alberti (Rafael Alberti Merelo) (1902–1999), poet and supporter
     of the Spanish Republic. Maria Teresa Leon (Maria Teresa Leon Goyri)
     (1903–1988), poet, novelist, lifelong companion of Alberti; Jose Bergamin
     (1895–1983), poet.

33   Louis Aragon (1897–1982), French poet, novelist and editor, a long-time
     supporter of the Communist Party active in the Resistance in World War II.

34   EWW at King's Arms Hotel, Arnersham, to MWW at Breakneck,
     25 September 1938. Box 30.

35   STW at Frome Vauchurch to EWW at 2 Bedford Place, London, WC1,
     25 September 1938. Box 31.

36   Clarence Pickett, Executive Director of the American Friends Service
     Committee 1929–1950.

37   Richard Ford (1796–1858), English writer who published *Handbook
     for Travellers in Spain* in two volumes in 1846.

38   VA at Frome Vauchurch to EWW at Carlton Mansions, 2 Bedford Place,
     London WC1, 26 September 1938. Box 31.

39   The ARP, or Air Raid Precautions service, was set up during the
     prelude to the Second World War in Britain to protect civilians from
     the dangers of air-raids. They were responsible for civilian adherence
     to wartime regulations.

40   EWW at the Blue Boar, Cambridge to MWW at Breakneck,
     1 October 1938. Box 30.

41   STW at Frome Vauchurch to EWW at Carlton Gardens, 2 Bedford Place,
     London WC1 with EWW note to Janet Machen on reverse of envelope,
     30 September 1938. Box 31.

42   Chamberlain quoted Hotspur and Shakespeare from the plane door
     en route to Munich.

43   MWW at Breakneck to EWW in London, 30 September 1938. Box 30.

44   VA at Frome Vauchurch to EWW at Carlton Gardens, 2 Bedford Place,
     London WC1, 30 September 1938. Box 31.

45   C S Calverley, the Victorian-era translator.

46   STW at Frome Vauchurch to EWW at 2 Bedford Place, London WC1,
     1 October 1938. Box 31.

47   1–9 October EWW notes. Box 30B.

48   EWW at Carlton Gardens to MWW at Breakneck, 4 October 1938.
     Box 30.

49   STW postcard to EWW, at 2 Bedford Place, London, 5 October 1938.
     Box 51.

50 EWW at Carlton Gardens, London, to MWW at Breakneck,
    7 October 1938. Box 30.

51 STW at Frome Vauchurch to EWW Centre Quaker International,
    12 rue Guy de la Brosse, Paris 5e, 8 October 1938. Box 31.

52 VA at Frome Vauchurch to EWW at Centre Quaker International, Paris,
    8 October 1938. Box 31.

53 EWW at the Hotel Commodore, 12 Boulevard Haussmann, Paris,
    11 October 1938. Box 30. *Your Forces and How to Use Them* was
    by Christian D Larson (1912). Larson was a practitioner of the school
    of 'New Thought' that encouraged positive thinking and the release
    of positive and creative energies.

54 STW at Frome Vauchurch to EWW at the American Hospital, Neuilly,
    14 October 1938. Box 31

55 Henry More (1614–1687), English philosopher of the Cambridge
    Platonist School and a prolific writer of verse and prose.

56 Gagoulards were members of La Cagoule (The Cowl), a French Fascist,
    anti-Communist group.

57 Robert Arthur James Gascoyne-Cecil, 5th Marquess of Salisbury
    (1893–1972), known as Viscount Cranborne from 1903 to 1947,
    was Under-Secretary for Foreign Affairs from 1935 to 1938
    while Anthony Eden was Foreign Minister.

58 The Parc Buttes Chaumont in the 19e arrondissement in Paris
    has a high position overlooking the city. It was designed by
    Georges Eugene Haussmann (1803–1891).

59 EWW at Chennevières-sur-Marne, France to MWW at Breakneck,
    15 October 1938. Box 30. She had been staying with a friend.

60 MWW at Breakneck to EWW in England, 15 October 1938. Box 30.

61 MWW at Breakneck to EWW at The American Hospital,
    Neuilly-sur-Seine. Paris, 17 October 1938. Box 30.

62 EWW at The American Hospital, Neuilly-sur-Seine, Paris, to MWW
    at Breakneck, 19, 20 October 1938. Box 30.

63 VA at Frome Vauchurch to EWW at the American Hospital,
    Neuilly-sur-Seine, Paris, 19 October 1938. Box 31.

64 STW at Frome Vauchurch to EWW at the American Hospital Paris, 19 October 1938. Box 31.

65 Cable from STW at Maiden Newton to EWW American Hospital Neuilly-sur-Seine, Paris, 19 October 1938. Box 31.

66 STW at Frome Vauchurch to EWW in the American Hospital, Paris, 19 October 1938. Box 31.

67 Thomas Otway (1652–1685), English dramatist, best known for *Venice Preserv'd ,or A Plot Discovered* (1683).

68 For the 'White variety' of melancholia see sections on George Luther White, EWW's grandfather, in Judd 2009, vol. 1.

69 EWW at Frome Vauchurch, to MWW at Breakneck, 26 October 1938. Box 30.

70 MWW at Breakneck to EWW at Frome Vauchurch, 30 October 1938. Box 30.

71 EWW at Frome Vauchurch to MWW at Breakneck, 4 November 1938. Box 30.

72 MWW at Breakneck to EWW at Frome Vauchurch, 21 November 1938. Box 30.

73 EWW at Frome Vauchurch to MWW at Breakneck, 24 November 1938. Box 30.

74 Three poems by STW, one dedicated to EWW, November 1938. Box 31.

75 STW at Frome Vauchurch to MWW at Breakneck, 19 November 1938. Box 31.

76 STW to EWW on her 'flight', late 1938. Box 29A.

77 Box 31. None of these poems is printed in Bingham 2008.

78 MWW at Breakneck to EWW at Frome Vauchurch, 1 December 1938. Box 30.

79 Alexander Crane (1904–1953) was an artist specializing in watercolors. At this period he lived in Cheshire, Connecticut. He married in 1941 and lived the last years of his life in Hyannis, Mass.

80 Pinney (ed.) 1998, 166. Alexander Crane's letters from this period are in Box 31. Other letters from Alexander Crane are in Boxes 30B and 34.

81 EWW at Frome Vauchurch to MWW at Breakneck, December 1938. Box 30.

82 EWW at Frome Vauchurch to MWW at Breakneck, 9 December 1938. Box 30.

83 Scutt 1997.

84 Ibid, and in Judd 1997, 87–89.

85 Pitt 1992.

86 VA to EWW December 1938; EWW Journal 1 January 1939. Box 29A; VA 1949 reference, Pinney (ed.) 1998, 217.

87 Pinney (ed.) 1998, 164.

88 MWW at Breakneck to EWW at Frome Vauchurch, 12 December 1938. Box 30.

89 Cable from MWW at Breakneck to EWW at Frome Vauchurch, 15 December 1938. Box 30.

90 MWW at Breakneck to EWW at Frome Vauchurch, 17 December 1938. Box 30.

91 EWW at Frome Vauchurch to MWW at Breakneck, 25 December 1938. Box 30.

92 Pinney (ed.) 1998, 165.

93 STW in Frome Vauchurch to MWW at Breakneck, 25 December 1938. Box 31.

94 31 December 1938 Journal 146; note from Valentine, interleaved. Box 29A.

V. She is like the sea

1   Pinney (ed.) 1998, 164–65, Harman 1989, 177

2   EWW at Frome Vauchurch to MWW at Strawberry Hill camp, SC, 2 February 1939. Box 36.

3   MWW at the Strawberry Hill camp to EWW at Frome Vauchurch, 23 February 1939. Box 36.

4   EWW at Frome Vauchurch to MWW at Strawberry Hill camp, SC, 14 February 1939. Box 36.

5   Letters from Mrs B M Smith are in Boxes 30A, 37, 41, 43, 44.

6   Page from notebook kept by EWW at Chaldon. 2 March 1939. Box 36.

7   EWW at Chaldon 'No the heart does not break', 9 March 1939. Box 30A.

8   EWW poem 'Shall we blame Spring', March 1939. Box 30A.

9   Harman 1989, 178–79.

10   Pinney (ed.) 1998, 167. Ludwig Renn (the pen name of Arnold Friedrich Vieth von Golsseneau) was born in Germany to a Saxon noble family in 1889. A career officer in the German Army, he fought as a battalion commander in the First World War. During the German Revolution Renn refused to fire on striking workers. After leaving the army he studied law, political economy, history of art and Russian philology in Gottingen and Munich (1920–23) before working in the art trade in Dresden. After travelling in Europe, he settled in Vienna where he studied archaeology and East Asian history (1926–27). He became increasingly interested in politics and began reading the work of Karl Marx, Vladimir Lenin, and John Reed. Converted to socialism Renn returned home and in 1928 joined the German Communist Party (KPD). In 1928 the *Frankfurter Zeitung* began serializing his novel *War* [*Krieg*], based on his experiences during the First World War; it was published in book form in 1929. Renn also worked as co-editor of the left-wing magazine *Aufbruch*. Renn published his second novel, *Nachkrieg*, about the Spartakist Rising in 1930. He also lectured at the Marxist workers' school in Berlin. A member of the German Communist Party in 1928, he early became an opponent of Adolf Hitler and the Nazi Party. In 1932 he was arrested and charged with 'literary high treason'. After his release from prison in 1935, Renn moved to Switzerland. The following

year he joined the International Brigades in Spain attempting to protect the Popular Front government against the right-wing forces led by General Franco. He initially defended Madrid in the German expatriate Thälmann Battalion, as a leader. Later on in the war, he was chief of staff of the XI International Brigade. (A photo from the period shows him in uniform with Ernest Hemingway in Spain in 1936–37.) In 1937 he toured the United States in an attempt to raise funds for the Republican Army in the Spanish Civil War. In 1938 he was director of the officer school of the People's Army in Cambrils, Catalonia. He met Sylvia and Valentine on one of their two visits to Spain during its civil war. After Franco's victory, Renn escaped to France where as a stateless person he was interned for some months. He came to Dorset after his release in the spring of 1939. In May of that year he accompanied Sylvia, Valentine and Elizabeth on the *Aquitania* to New York. He settled in Mexico during the war where he became professor of European history at the University of Morelia. He remained active in politics and became president of the Latin American Committee for Free Germans. Renn also wrote extensively about his experiences during the Spanish Civil War. With the defeat of Nazi Germany in the Second World War Renn returned to Dresden where he became professor of anthropology. In 1948 he was appointed chairman of the Saxonia Culture Federation. He also served as president of the Academy of Arts (1969–75). Among the many languages he could write and speak was the international language Esperanto; he supported the international Esperanto movement. He died in Berlin 21 July 1979.

11   Pinney (ed.) 1998, 169.

12   EWW in East Chaldon to MWW at Strawberry Hill camp, SC, 17 April 1939. Box 36; 7 April 1938 to EWW at the Dairy House, Chaldon from C E Montague Pollard, National Joint Committee for Spanish Relief, London., Box 36; EWW personal reminiscence to PHJ.

13   Vernon Lee was the pseudonym of the British writer Violet Paget (1856–1935), a writer of supernatural fiction and an early follower of Walter Pater; she wrote over a dozen volumes of essays on art, music, and travel. Because of STW's knowledge of music, the book Elizabeth chose for her may have been *Music and Its Lovers* (1932).

14 STW at Frome Vauchurch to EWW at the Dairy House; Chaldon, 5 April 1939. Box 37.

15 Harman 1989, 179; Mulford 1988, 135.

16 STW at Frome Vauchurch to EWW at the Dairy House, 14 May 1939. Box 36.

17 Harman 1989, 179; 20 May 1939 Receipt for passage for one cat [Tomas], SS *Aquitania*, Cunard White Star Line. Box 36.

18 EWW reminiscences to PHJ, 20 October 1990.

19 PHJ recollection from talk with EVH, 1970s.

20 STW at West Chaldon to EVH at 224 Madison Avenue, NY, 14 May 1936. Box 29A.

21 STW at 24 West Chaldon, Dorset to EVH in New York, 23 July 1936. Box 29A.

22 EWW reminiscences to PHJ, 20 October 1990.

23 Harman 1989, 180. Reminiscences from H Wade White and Stuart E Judd to PHJ.

24 STW at 26 Jane Street, New York to EWW at Breakneck, 8 June 1939. Box 29A.

25 Pinney (ed.) 1998, 169.

26 Poem by VA, 'it is a Wednesday', before the 10th of June 1939; acrostic poem by VA 'dear st elizabeth', June 1939. Box 29A.

27 EWW poems, 'Now that delight is known'; 'When you came quietly', probably June 1939. Box 29A.

28 STW at Breakneck to EVH in New York City, 17 June 1939. Box 37.

29 VA at Breakneck to EVH in New York, 17 June 1939. Box 37.

30 STW at 26 Jane St., NYC to Paul Nordoff, 14 July 1939. Paul Nordoff Collection, Manuscripts and Archives Division, The New York Public Library.

31 Janet Machen at 29 Regent's Square, WC1 London, to EWW at Breakneck, 27 June 1939. Box 30B.

32 Harman 1989, 179; Ackland 1985, 134; Pinney (ed.) 1998, 169.

33 STW at 26 Jane Street, NYC to Paul Nordoff, 14 July 1939.
   Nordoff Collection NYPL.

34 Pinney (ed.) 1998, 170.

35 STW at the Kibbe house, Warren, Connecticut to EWW at Breakneck,
   18 July 1939. Box 37.

36 Pinney (ed.) 1998, 174; Harman 1989, 180.

37 EWW notes on the Nazi-Soviet Pact, August 1939. Box 36.

38 EWW in Warren, Conn. to MWW at Breakneck, 30 August 1939. Box 36.

39 11 October 1949, Harman (ed.) 1994, 148; Sylvia devotes five pages
   of her narrative in *I'll Stand by You* to the strains of the stay in Warren.
   169–174.

40 STW c/o Karl Erickson, Peto. NC to EWW at Breakneck,
   8 September 1939. Box 37.

41 The Wilcox graves were at East Berlin, Connecticut.

42 STW at the Hotel Latham, NYC to EWW at Breakneck, 19 September 1939.
   Box 37.

43 VA to EWW, note, Hotel Latham, NYC, September 1939. Box 43A.

44 Pinney (ed.) 1998, 176.

45 STW at the Hotel Latham, NYC to EWW at 42 Perry Street, NYC,
   3 October 1939. Box 37.

46 VA to EWW, New York, September 1939. Box 43A.

47 STW at Frome Vauchurch to EWW at Breakneck, 13 October 1938.
   Box 37.

48 STW at Frome Vauchurch to EVH at 40 Bank Street, NYC,
   13 October 1939. Box 37.

49 Parker (1852–1944) was a successful playwright, producer of historical
   pageants and a musician. Sir Edward Elgar (1857–1934), had been the
   leading British composer of his day.

50 London County Council.

51 STW postcard from Frome Vauchurch to EVH at 46 Bank Street,
   New York, 29 October 1939. Box 37.

52 VA at Frome Vauchurch to EWW at Apartment 4A, 42 Perry Street, NYC, 29 October 1939. Box 37.

53 Rogers Fruiterer and Florist, Dorchester to EWW at Breakneck, 18 November 1939. Box 37.

54 EWW reminiscence to PHJ, 20 October 1990.

55 Martin R. Pollock, 26 Great James St, London WC1 to EWW at 107 Prospect Street, Waterbury, 7 October 1939. Box 37. He was then expecting to receive a licence to practice medicine.

56 Philippa ('Katie') Powys in Chaldon to EWW at 42 Perry Street, NYC, 27 November 1939. Judd 1997, 97–98.

VI. Now and finally what love is and must be

1   STW at Frome Vauchurch to EWW at 42 Perry Street, NYC,
    1 January 1940. Box 40.

2   EWW Journal. Box 40 for this and following excerpts.

3   The drawing is now in the Sylvia Townsend Warner Room in the Dorset
    County Museum, presented to The Townsend Warner Archive at the
    Museum by PHJ in August 1998.

4   Phillip Kerr, Lord Lothian, British ambassador to the US, on
    11 December appealed for greater assistance from the US and implicitly
    conveyed the view that Britain was fighting America's war. Leslie Hore-
    Belisha, Secretary of State for War in the Chamberlain government, had
    been an advocate of conscription and preparedness. His resignation
    as interpreted by some as a gesture toward appeasement and a sign
    of lack of will in the government, as Elizabeth may have feared.

5   Katherine (Bullock) Cole, who lived at 96th Street and 5th Avenue.

6   Edwin Austin Abbey 1852–1911), American painter, subject of George
    Hamilton's Yale doctoral dissertation.

7   EWW notes for cable to VA, 17 January [1940]. Box 40.

8   STW at Frome Vauchurch to EVH in New York. 18 January 1940.
    Box 40.

9   Evelyn was to travel on assignment for her new job at the Benton
    & Bowles advertising agency.

10 Max Aitken, Lord Beaverbrook. (1879–1964), press lord, at that time
    publisher of the widely circulated *Daily Express,* later Minister of Aircraft
    Production under Churchill. John Reith (1889–1971), founder and
    Director of the British Broadcasting corporation 1927–1938 was
    then Minister of Information in the Chamberlain government.

11 Kotex were leading manufacturers of sanitary protection for women.

12 EWW note for cable to VA, undated but early 1940. Box 40.

13 EWW notes for cable to VA, 20 January 1940; EWW undated note
    for cable to VA, possibly 20 January. Box 40.

14   *The Tri-State Problems and the Tri-State Survey Committee* [1941] four
      page leaflet with return form for a donation to The Tri-State Advisory
      Committee, Inc., 130 Fifth Avenue, New York, NY. 'Elizabeth Wade White,
      Acting Secretary', Anne C. Couch, Research Adviser; includes lists of board
      members; within text 'in this war year of 1941'. Box 19. EWW notes on
      her work with Tri State, Box 40. Ref. to: *The American Mining Scene Catalog*,
      American-British Art Center, West 56th Street, New York, NY; includes
      lists of works in various genres and the artists. nd; notes made by EWW in
      connection with this show. Refs: US Department of Labor, Davison of Labor
      Standards, Washington DC, 'Conference on Health and Working Conditions
      in the Tri-State District, Joplin, Missouri April 25, 1940', mimeographed,
      43 pp.; Extensive notes by EWW on the Commission's work are found
      in Box 19.

15   John Robertson Scott at Idbury Manor to EWW at 42 Perry Street, NYC,
      25 January 1940. Box 40.

16   Draft for letter from EWW to STW ,early 1940 (January–March). Box 40.

17   EWW Journal, 1 February 1940. Box 40.

18   STW at Frome Vauchurch to EVH at 46 Bank Street, NYC, 28 February 1940.
      Box 40.

19   The main radio transmission for Ireland was located in Athlone on the
      Shannon River in its western portion, with a signal that could be heard
      through much of Europe.

20   EWW at 107 Prospect Street, Waterbury to US Passport Bureau, carbon,
      18 March 1940. Box 40.

21   Helen La Monte in Washington DC to EWW at 107 Prospect Street,
      Waterbury, 13 March 1940. Box 40.

22   These efforts are documented in materials are found in Box 40.

23   STW at Frome Vauchurch to EVH at 40 Bank Street, NYC, 29 March 1940.
      Box 40.

24   EWW poem, 'April in England, 1940', April 1940. Box 40.

25   Philippa ('Katie') Powys in East Chaldon to EWW at 42 Perry St., NYC,
      12 April 1940. Judd 1997, 100–101.

26 EVH (Biltmore Hotel, Providence, RI letterhead, from internal evidence from Rochester, NY) to EWW at the Mark Twain Hotel, St. Louis, 15 April 1940. Box 41.

27 VA at Frome Vauchurch to EWW at 42 Perry Street, NYC, 17 April 1940. Box 40.

28 STW at Frome Vauchurch to EWW at Breakneck. 12 June 1940. Box 40.

29 EWW approved for Red Cross, 19, 21 June 1940. Box 40.

30 EVH at 40 Bank St., NYC, to EWW at Breakneck sent Special Delivery, 14 July 1940. Box 40.

31 EVH in Naples, NY [postmark] to EWW at 221 East 46th Street, NYC, 3 August 1940. Box 40.

32 STW at The Mill, Winterton, Norfolk to EVH at 46 Bank Street, NYC, 18 July 1940. Box 40.

33 Wendell Willkie (1892–1944) was a 'dark horse' candidate who won the Republican nomination in 1940 to run against Franklin D. Roosevelt for President in the 1940 fall election. Charles Coughlin (1891–1979) was a Roman Catholic priest in a Michigan church who had a large audience for his regular weekly broadcasts; he was vehemently anti-Roosevelt, anti-Semitic and supportive of some of Hitler's policies.

34 Raymond Gram Swing (1887-1968), the broadcaster, strongly in favor of US intervention in the war.

35 VA at Winterton, Norfolk to EVH in NYC, 30 August 1940. Box 40.

36 EVH in New York (Benton & Bowles letterhead), carbon, to VA at Winterton, 9 September 1940. Box 40.

37 PHJ notes made 20 October 1990, 'Notes on the White family'. Box 34

38 EVH, unstamped Benton & Bowles envelope addressed 'Elizabeth', 23 December 1940. Box 40.

39 EWW at Breakneck to EVH in NYC, 26 December 1940. Box 43.

VII. A last meeting must happen one time

1 STW at Frome Vauchurch to EVH at 519 East 19th Street, NYC, 5 January 1941. Box 41.

2 Auxiliary Fire Service, created to support the regular London Fire Brigade.

3 VA at Frome Vauchurch to EWW at 519 East 19th Street, NYC, 8 May [1943]. Box 42. Dated 1943 from the reference to the book by Anna Seghers which arrived as noted in the 24 May letter.

4 This marriage did not take place.

5 Anna Seghers (1900–1983), German born Jewish writer, a Communist in the 1930s, author of a number of novels. In her last years she became a citizen of the GDR in East Germany, and died in East Berlin. The book did arrive as noted in VAs letter of 24 May 1943.

6 VA at Frome Vauchurch to EWW at 351 East 19th Street NYC, 20 May 1943. Box 41.

7 VA from Dorset Rural District Council, Civil Defence Office, Dorchester to EWW at 351 East 19th Street, NYC, 24 May 1943. Box 41

8 VA at the Civil Defence Office, Dorchester to EWW at 351 East 19th Street, NYC, 27 May 1943. Box 41.

9 *Le Crève-Coeur*, by Louis Aragon. Published in 1941, it chronicled France under the Nazi occupation.

10 The Women's Voluntary Service was to act as a support unit for the Air Raid Precautions (ARP) units, working with the civilian population.

11 VA at Frome Vauchurch to EWW at 351 East 19th Street, NYC, 31 May 1943. Box 41.

12 Telegram VA at Frome Vauchurch to EWW at 351 East 19th Street, New York City, 8 June 1943. Box 41.

13 VA at Frome Vauchurch to EWW at 351 East 19th Street, NYC, 20 July 1943. Box 41.

14 VA at Frome Vauchurch to EWW at 351 East 19th Street, NYC, 13 August 1943. Box 41.

15 Karen von Blixen-Finecke (1885–1962), also writing as Isak Dinesen. The book was probably *Winter's Tales*, published in 1942

16 Ascribed to December 1943 from ref. to 5 December in the letter and to Russian War Relief employment of EWW. Box 41.

17 STW at Frome Vauchurch to EWW, 16 September 1945. Box 44.

18 STW at Frome Vauchurch to EWW at The Patch, 10 January 1946. Box 44.

19 STW at Frome Vauchurch to EWW at The Patch, 29 December 1947. Box 44.

20 See EWW notes, correspondence, and other materials relating to the Progressive Party campaign in Box 43.

21 STW at Frome Vauchurch to EWW at The Patch, 24 January 1949. Box 43.

22 Mary (Wade) White was suffering from cancer.

23 STW at Frome Vauchurch to EWW at The Patch, 31 March 1948. Box 43

VIII. The flame rekindled and abated

1   Alyse Gregory at Chydyok, East Chaldon to EWW at the Antelope Hotel, Dorchester, 10 April 1949. Box 43.

2   Pinney (ed.) 1998, 216–17.

3   Harman 1989, 223.

4   Pinney (ed.) 1998, 217.

5   20 June 1949, Harman 1989, 223.

6   Pinney (ed.) 1998, 228.

7   Ackland 1985, 132.

8   Harman (ed.) 1994, 132.

9   28 April 1948, Will of Mary (Wade) White. Box 43.

10   Recollection by PHJ of Stuart E Judd's comments when the will was published.

11   Harman (ed.) 1994, 28 July 1949, 133.

12   Harman 1989, 225.

13   Pinney (ed.) 1998, 231; Harman 1989, 225.

14   VA at Frome Vauchurch to EWW at The Patch, 8 August 1949. Box 43A.

15   Joan (Ackland) Woolcombe was Valentine's older sister.

16   VA at Frome Vauchurch to STW in Devon, 27 July 1949, in Pinney (ed.) 1998, 251–255.

17   12 August 1949, Harman (ed.) 1994, 133.

18   12 August 1949, Harman (ed.) 1994, 133–34.

19   15 August 1949, Harman (ed.), 134.

20   18 August 1949, Harman (ed.) 1994, 134.

21   21 August 1949, Harman (ed.) 1994, 135.

22   22 August 1949, Harman (ed.) 1994, 135.

23   31 August, 1949, Harman (ed.) 1994, 136–37.

24 Douglas McKee at Gilbertsville, NY to EWW at The Patch, 29 August 1949. Box 43.

25 Katherine Bullock Cole at Tuxedo Park, N.Y. to EWW c/o VA, Frome Vauchurch, 12 September 1949, Box 43.

26 EVH at The Patch to EWW c/o Warner/Ackland, Frome Vauchurch, 1 September 1949. Box 43.

27 6 September 1949, Harman (ed.) 1994, 139.

28 VA at Frome Vauchurch to STW at the Pen Mill Hotel, Yeovil, 4 September 1949; Pinney (ed.) 1998, 245–47.

29 EVH at The Patch, Middlebury to EWW in England, carbon copy, 5 September 1949. Box 43.

30 EVH at the Hotel Algonquin, New York to EWW at Frome Vauchurch, 6 September 1949. Box 43.

31 In Peekskill, on the Hudson north of New York City there had been a violent riot at an outdoor concert by Paul Robeson, who had made statements that seemed to favor the Soviet Union. Evelyn and Elizabeth were fervent admirers of Robeson for his political views and as a singer and actor.

32 EVH at The Patch to EWW c/o Warner-Ackland, Frome Vauchurch, postcard, 9 September 1949. Box 43.

33 VA at Frome Vauchurch to STW at the Pen Mill Hotel, Yeovil, 13 September 1949; Pinney (ed.) 1998, 154–55.

34 12 September, Harman (ed.) 1994), 142.

35 14 September 1949, Harman (ed.) 1994, 142.

36 15 September 1949, Harman (ed.) 1994), 143.

37 EVH at The Patch to EWW c/o Warner-Ackland, Frome Vauchurch, carbon copy, 14 September 1949. Box 43.

38 VA at Frome Vauchurch to STW at the Pen Mill Hotel, Yeovil, 19 September 1949; Pinney (ed.) 1998, 158–60.

39 STW at the Pen Mill Hotel, Yeovil to VA at Frome Vauchurch, 21 September 1949; Pinney (ed.) 1998, 263.

40   Ruth Ackland at Winterton, Norfolk to EWW at Frome Vauchurch, 19 September 1949. Box 43.

41   16 September 1949, 5 September 1951, Harman (ed.) 1994, 143, 179.

42   18 September 1949, Harman (ed.) 1994, 144.

43   VA at Frome Vauchurch to STW at Pen Mill Hotel, Yeovil, 26 September 1949; Pinney (ed.) 1998, 269.

44   EVH at The Patch, Middlebury to EWW in England, carbon copy, 20 September 1949. Box 43.

45   The writer James Agee (1909–1955) is best known for *Let Us Now Praise Famous Men* with photographs by Walker Evans, the novel, *A Death in the Family,* posthumously given the Pulitzer Prize in 1958, film criticism and screenplays. He married Mia Fritsch in 1948, his third wife.

46   Douglas McKee at 22 Rue Boissonade, Paris to EWW c/o VA at Frome Vauchurch, 22 September 1949. Box 43.

47   Ruth Ackland in London to EWW 'with Miss V. Ackland', Queen's House, St. James's Court, SW1, 29 September 1949. Box 43.

48   29 September 1949, Harman (ed.) 1994, 145.

49   VA at Frome Vauchurch to EWW at The Patch, 2 October 1949. Box 43. Ellipsis in the original.

50   11 October 1949, Harman (ed.) 1994, 148.

51   16 October 1949, Harman (ed.) 1994, 149.

52   24 October 1949, Harman (ed.) 1994, 150.

53   18 November 1949, Harman (ed.) 1994, 151–52. Evelyn's letter of May has not been found; the more recent one is probably EVH's letter of 14 September 1949, above.

54   VA at Frome Vauchurch to STW, 21 November 1949, Pinney (ed.) 1998, 378.

55   30 December 1949, Harman (ed.) 1994, 152–53.

56   18 & 20 January 1950, Harman (ed.) 1994, 154–55.

57   Katherine (Bullock) Cole at the Hotel Vendome, Paris to EWW at The Patch, 20 January 1950. Box 43.

58   Katherine (Bullock) Cole at the Berkeley Hotel, London to EWW at The Patch, 25 January 1950. Box 43.

59   28 January 1950, Harman (ed.) 1994, 155.

60   Katherine (Bullock) Cole at the Berkeley Hotel, London to EWW at The Patch, 6 February 1950. Box 43.

61   21 February 1950, Harman (ed.) 1994, 158.

62   EVH at The Patch to EWW, c/o English-Speaking Union, London, carbon copy, 19 March 1950. Box 43.

63   23 March 1950, Harman (ed.) 1994, 163.

64   Harman 1989, 240

65   STW at Frome Vauchurch to Alyse Gregory at Chydyok, West Chaldon, 29 March 1950, in Maxwell (ed.) 1988, 117.

66   Correspondence on these arrangements from HWW is in Box 43.

67   EVH in Rochester to EWW at The Patch, 7 July 1950. Box 43.

Epilogue

1   These and subsequent quotations in this chapter from PHJ Journals, 1952, 1953, 1954. PHJ mss.

2   'Notes on the White family by PHJ, 1990–1994', Box 34.

3   PHJ visit to Claire Harman in Oxford; journal entry 4 July 1995.

4   The catalog, reviews, and sales records of Wade's work may be found in the box devoted to him at the Mattatuck Museum.

5   The originals are in Boxes 43A (1950s) and Box 45 (1960–69); scanned copies are available in three bound volumes numbering 568 pages in Box 45.

6   VA at Frome Vauchurch to EWW at Oxford, October [1952]. Box 43A.

7   Major Charles Ring of the British Army had been reassigned from Nigeria to the UK. His wife and daughter followed.

8   VA at Frome Vauchurch to EWW, 14 July 1969. Box 45.

9   VA at Frome Vauchurch to EWW, Middlebury, Conn. 17 September 1969, Box 45.

10   STW at Frome Vauchurch to EWW, 5 November 1969, Box 45.

11   STW at Frome Vauchurch to EWW, 10 November 1969, Box 45.

12   These and successive quotations from this 1995 visit, PHJ Journals.

Select bibliography

Archives and Manuscript Collections

Mattatuck Museum, Waterbury, Conn. Research Collection,
White Family Papers

Manuscripts and Archives Division, The New York Public Library,
Elizabeth Wade White papers

Peter Haring Judd Papers (privately held)

Genealogical and Historical Material on the White and Related Families

Peter Haring Judd, *The Hatch and Brood of Time: Five Phelps Families in the Atlantic World, 1720–1880* (Boston: Newbury Street Press, 1999).

——, *More Lasting than Brass: A Thread of Family from Revolutionary New York to Industrial Connecticut* (Boston: The Northeastern University Press and the Newbury Street Press, 2004).

——, *Genealogical and Biographical Notes: Haring-Herring, Clark, Denton, White, Griggs, Judd, and related families* (New York, by the author, Lulu.com, 2005).

——, *Ninety Years of Family Letters, 1850s–1930s: Haring, White, Griggs, Judd Families of New York and Waterbury,* Connecticut, 2 vols. (New York, by the author, Lulu.com, 2009).

——, *Four American Ancestries: White, Griggs, Cowles, Judd, including Haring, Phelps, Denison, Clark, Foote, Coley, Haight, Ayers, and related families,* 3 vols, (New York: by the compiler, Lulu.com. 2008).

Books and Articles

Ackland, Valentine, *For Sylvia: An Honest Account* (London: Chatto & Windus, 1985).

Bingham, Frances, ed., *Valentine Ackland: Journey from Winter. Selected Poems* (Manchester, England: Fyfield Books, 2008).

Blackburn, Julia, *Threads: The Delicate Life of John Craske* (London, Jonathan Cape, 2015).

Garnett, Richard, ed., *Sylvia and David: The Townsend Warner/Garnett Letters* (London: Sinclair Stevenson, 1994).

Graves, Richard Perceval, *The Brothers Powys* (London: Routledge & Kegan Paul, 1983).

Harman, Claire, *Sylvia Townsend Warner: A Biography* (London: Chatto & Windus, 1989).

Harman, Claire, ed., *The Diaries of Sylvia Townsend Warner* (London: Chatto & Windus, 1994).

Judd, Peter Haring, 'Letters from Katie Powys to Elizabeth Wade White, 1938-1939', *Powys Journal* 12 (1997), 77–81.

Krissdottir, Morine, *Descents of Memory: The Life of John Cowper Powys* (New York, Woodstock and London: Overlook Duckworth, Peter Mayer Publishers, Inc. 2007).

Krissdottir, Morine, and Roger Peers, eds., *The Dorset Year: the Diary of John Cowper Powys June 1934–July 1935* (The Powys Press, 1998).

Maxwell, William, ed. *Letters: Sylvia Townsend Warner,* (New York: The Viking Press, 1988).

Mulford, Wendy, *This Narrow Place: Sylvia Townsend Warner and Valentine Ackland: Life, Letters and Politics, 1930–1951.* (London: Pandora, 1988).

Pinney, Susanna, ed., *I'll Stand by You: The Letters of Sylvia Townsend Warner and Valentine Ackland with Narrative by Sylvia Townsend Warner* (London: Pimlico, Random House, 1998).

Pitt, Angela, 'Passions that Disturb: The Diaries of Katie Powys', 7–27, *The Powys Journal* 2 (1992), 23.

Scutt, Theodora, 'Katie', *The Powys Journal* 7 (1997): 87.

Stinton, Judith, *Chaldon Herring: The Powys Circle in a Dorset Village* (Woodbridge, Suffolk: The Boydell Press, 1988).

Peltier, Jacqueline, *Alyse Gregory: A Woman at Her Window* (London: Cecil Woolf, 1999).

White, Elizabeth Wade, *Anne Bradstreet: The Tenth Muse* (New York and London: Oxford University Press, 1971).

Index

A

Abercrombie & Fitch   279, 280

Ackland, Ruth   30, 70, 208, 215, 263, 265, 295, 297, 313, 314, 319, 365, 367, 379, 425, 426

Ackland, Valentine *passim*; see also the Dorset Sappho

  For Sylvia   3, 29, 351, 428

  Letters and Notes

  — to EVH 17 June 1939   229

  — to EVH 30 August 1940   300

  — to EWW 25 June 1936   41

  — to EWW 2 July 1936   42

  — to EWW 27 December 1936   46

  — to EWW 7 May 1937   60

  — to EWW 19 May 1937   66

  — to EWW 17 June 1937   75

  — to EWW 29 August 1937   87

  — to EWW 7 September 1937   89

  — to EWW 24 September 1937   102

  — to EWW 17 October 1937   108

  — to EWW 29 November 1937   111

  — to EWW 29 December 1937   120

  — to EWW 24 September 1938   150

  — to EWW 26 September 1938   159

  — to EWW 30 September 1939   167

  — to EWW 8 October 1938   174

  — to EWW 19 October 1938   181

  — to EWW 31 December 1938   208

  — to EWW September 1939   244, 246

  — to EWW 29 October 1939   254

  — to EWW 17 April 1940   286

  — to EWW 8 May 1943   309

  — to EWW 20 May 1943   311

  — to EWW 24 May 1943   313

  — to EWW 27 May 1943   314

  — to EWW 31 May 1943   320

  — to EWW 20 July 1943   321

  — to EWW 13 August 1943   329

— to EWW 8 August 1949   354
— to EWW 2 October 1949   368
— to EWW October 1952   390
— to EWW 17 September 1969   393
Poems
— 'dear st elizabeth'   226
— 'it is a Wednesday'   225
— 'Moving across the field'   79
— 'O very brightly in the distance'   197
— 'Scarlet the cockcrow'   196
Acorn Inn, Evershot   348
Addington, Henry (Viscount Sidmouth)   123, 408
AFS (Auxiliary Fire Service)   308
AFSC (American Friends Service Committee)   97, 98, 151, 176, 180
Agee, James   220, 366, 425
Alcaya, Eduardo Ruiz, Sr y Sra   211, 215–17
Aldeburgh   89
Alden, John   367
Algonquin Hotel   360, 424
Alianza de Intelectuales   152
Alice in Wonderland   290
America First movement   294
American Civil Liberties Union   73, 268
American Friends Service Committee, see AFSC
American Hospital, Paris   181, 190, 412, 413
American stock market crash   33
American Writers' League   69
Amersham   19, 20, 33, 154, 155, 386, 395, 410
Amulree Hotel, by Dunkeld, Perthshire   390
An American Herb Calendar   109, 118, 408
Anderson, Redwood   315
Anson, Rev. Canon   354
Apple Tree Cottage   5, 398
Aragon, Louis   151, 153, 172, 214, 220, 329, 411, 422
Arden, Delaware   110
Argentine Valley   9
ARP (Air Raid Precaution)   160, 162, 315, 411
Assisi   68
Association Internationale des Ecrivains pour la Défense de la Culture   58
astrolabe   19, 386
Athlone radio   278, 420

B

Bad Godesberg conference   410

Bailalailou   176

Bal Tabarin   59

Banbury   145

Basque children's homes and camps   90, 92, 104, 105, 110, 113, 142

Bassett, George (Curly)   227, 233

Bates, Ralph   69, 71, 72, 406

Battle of Britain   295

Bavaria   128

BBC (British Broadcasting Corporation)   271, 272, 299, 306, 346

Beethoven, Ludwig von   277

Benchley, Robert   218

Benicassim   157

Benton & Bowles   249, 301, 419, 421, 422

Benzedrine   365

Beowulf   267

Bergamin, Jose   152, 411

Berkshire   153

Berlioz, Hector   179

   Harold in Italy   380

Bess, Demaree   211

Beston, Thomas   85

Beth Car   22, 32, 45

Biarritz   291

Bible, The   23, 261, 272

Bilbao   74, 76, 114

Bindon Abbey   43, 405

Bingham, Frances   3, 29, 413

Birmingham   144, 163, 311

Blackwall Tunnel   6

Blake, William   1

Blicking   147

Blitz, The   263, 308, 313

Blixen-Finecke, Karen von, see Dinesen, Isak

Blois   59

Bloomingdale's   243

Bloomsbury   143

Blue Boar, Cambridge   411

Bonamy, André   398

Boston, Massachusetts   367

Bournemouth   60, 276

Bradstreet, Anne   17, 34, 39, 40, 44, 46, 57, 63, 100, 118, 134, 135, 141, 173, 190,
    198, 207, 354, 376, 379, 381, 383, 384
Bradstreet, Simeon Mercy   85
Breakneck Hill   15, 16, 97, 100, 126, 225, 228, 229, 336
British Communist Party   40
British Museum   137, 138, 139, 143
Britten, Benjamin   89, 330
Bronte, Charlotte   168
Bronx Zoo   277
Brooks, Van Wyck   44
Browning, Robert   328
Brown's Hotel   19
Buckingham Palace   161, 163, 164
Buck, Percy   13
Bumpus Books   134, 161, 409
Burton, Robert   231
Bury St Edmunds   147

C

Café Anglais   161
Calamity Jane   357, 358
California   310
Calverley, C S   168, 411
Cambridge   163, 169, 170, 178, 283, 406, 410, 411, 412
Canton   103, 144
Carlton Mansions   139, 142, 162, 410, 411, 412
Catalonia   104, 416
Cather, Willa   134
cats, see Thomas, Tomas and Towzer
Cattistock   168
Catullus   168
Centrale Sanitaire Internationale   173
Cezanne, Paul   265
Chaldon (includes Chaldon Herring, East Chaldon, West Chaldon)   1, 3, 5, 9, 21,
    22, 23, 25–33, 38, 39, 41, 44, 46, 54, 56, 57, 60, 61, 64, 66, 69, 71, 80, 81, 83, 86,
    87, 102, 106, 140, 141, 143, 169, 174, 199, 211, 212, 217–19, 248, 261, 266, 394,
    395, 396, 398, 399
Chaldon Herring, see Chaldon
Chamberlain, Neville   125, 129, 143, 145, 154, 161, 162, 164, 167, 169, 170, 170,
    210, 289, 306, 411, 419, 420
Charlbury Road flat, Oxford   380
Charles I   344

Chartres   59

Chase, Helga   367

Cherokee, Kansas   274

Cheshire Cheese, The   137, 138, 161, 162

Cheshire, Connecticut   36, 198, 414

Chesil Beach   25

China   97, 101, 144, 166, 178, 306

Chipping Norton   145

Chiswick   19

Cholelith   334

Christ Church Meadow, Oxford   39

Churchill, Winston   289, 299, 347, 420

Chydyok   9, 25–27, 29, 38, 199, 348, 423, 426

cigarettes   160

C & J Clark Co, see Clarks

Clark, Steven   64, 67, 68, 72, 73, 90, 93, 87, 105, 116, 131, 309, 329, 331, 395, 406

Clarks   406

Clarkson, Gwen and Hugh   142

Cobbett, William   123, 408–09

Cochran, C B   59

Cobh   249

Cole, Alice   402

Cole, Katherine (Bullock) [Kes]   110, 267, 356, 372–75, 397, 419, 424, 426

Collis Browne   160

Communism   1, 40, 61, 63, 69, 80, 115, 168, 220, 232, 239, 310, 352, 353, 387, 407, 408, 411, 412, 415, 422

Connecticut   1, 4, 6, 13, 15, 89, 98, 99, 110, 126, 198, 210, 217, 232–37, 266, 337, 338, 343, 344, 379, 388, 410, 414, 418

Connery, Jane   394, 400

Corfe Castle   43, 405

Cornford, John   114, 408

Coronation (1937)   50, 54, 56–60

Coughlin, Father Charles   298, 421

Cranborne, Viscount   179, 412

Crane, Alexander   198, 414

Craske, John and Laura   9, 86–89, 91, 118, 120, 127, 128, 130, 144, 147, 153, 177, 265, 299, 341, 385, 400, 402, 407

Cresset Press   55

Crowthers   19, 386

Cummings, Jane   128, 162

Cunard Lines   4, 29, 269, 283, 417

Cunard, Nancy   336

Czechoslovakia   129, 142, 154, 166, 178, 353

D

Daily Worker, The   179, 189
Dairy House, The   211–15, 395, 416, 417
Daisy the dog   356, 357, 360, 362, 374
Daladier, Édouard   161
Denmark   285
Devon   160, 342, 424
Dewey, Thomas E   360
Dexedrine   365
Dick, Sheldon   274, 279
Dinesen, Isak   329, 423
Dobson, Sylvia   113
Donne, John   23, 246, 381
Dorchester   9, 73, 101, 168, 171, 190, 248, 261, 289, 305, 308, 348, 350, 397,
    405, 419
Dorset   1, 3, 5–10, 21, 23, 30, 32, 38, 65, 67, 71, 79, 89, 97, 99, 110, 123, 125, 126,
    128, 129, 144, 145, 156, 179, 200, 202–06, 210, 213, 217, 232, 261, 295, 303,
    348, 374, 376, 389, 395–97, 405, 416, 419
Dorset Sappho, the   362–63
Draper, Muriel   38
Duncan, Winifred   311, 312, 326
Dunkirk   289, 299, 341

E

East Anglia   141
East Berlin, Connecticut   418
East Chaldon, see Chaldon
East Dereham   120
East Lulworth   21
Eden, Anthony   179, 412
Edinburgh   348
Eeling   139
Egdon Heath   25
Egypt   179, 383
Elgar, Edward   250, 418
Eliot, T S   375, 381
Ellis, Havelock   218
Emerson, Ralph Waldo   44
Emrich, Dr   118
English-Speaking Union   60, 138, 406, 426

Evett, Mr and Mrs Ned   138–39

F

Fairfield, Connecticut   388, 400
Faulkner, William   68
Field, Rachel   134
Fifth Column   301
Five Marys, near Chaldon   21, 25
Flying Dutchman, The   176
Fogg Art Museum   388
Folkestone-Boulogne ferry   59, 171
Ford, Richard   158, 411
Foster, Bo   318
Fotheringhay Castle   170
Fox, Ralph   114, 115
France   43, 71, 130, 134, 136, 141, 143, 161, 174, 188, 210, 214, 239, 242, 289,
    290, 339, 348, 406, 410, 412, 416, 422
Franco, Francisco   40, 50, 53, 129, 214, 416
Frankfort Manor   120
Frascati   161
de Freitas, Geoffrey and Helen   139, 141, 142, 161, 171, 268
French without Tears   171
Friends, see AFSC and Quakers
Frisch, Mia   220
Frome, river   40, 85, 98, 205
Frome Vauchurch   5, 65, 83, 84, 87, 89, 92, 97, 101, 102, 108, 111, 116, 120, 121,
    125, 126, 130, 136, 139, 143, 145, 150, 152, 156, 159, 164, 167, 171, 174, 176,
    181, 184–206, 210, 214, 216, 243, 249, 254, 263, 264, 269, 276, 280, 289, 290,
    305, 309, 334, 339–42, 344, 350, 354–59, 361, 365, 368, 372, 373, 387, 389,
    390, 392
Frost, Robert   233
Fuller, Henry and father   149, 155, 156, 161, 162, 169, 171, 176, 177, 410

G

Gagoulards   178, 412
Gallup   268
Gardner, Dame Helen   381, 384, 395, 402
Garnett, David   18, 21, 22, 31, 403, 404, 407
Gascoyne-Cecil, Robert Arthur James, 4th Marquess of Salisbury,
    see Cranborne
George Washington Bridge   343

Germans   103, 242, 289, 312, 416
Germany   33, 53, 142, 161, 211, 239, 240, 257, 289, 415, 416, 422
Gilbertsville, New York   47, 405, 424
Glasgow   311
Gloucester, Massachusetts   36, 49, 367, 389
Gluck, Christoph Willibald   380
Gone with the Wind   266
Gorgas, Betty and Leon   117
Goyri, Maria Teresa Léon   411
Gray, Dr   194, 334, 335
Greece   383, 384
Greenaway, Kate   86, 248
Greene, Vivien   400
Greenwich Village   217, 220, 242, 244, 261, 395
Gregory, Alyse   26–29, 32, 217, 327, 348, 350, 361, 376, 389, 423, 426
    Dial, The   28
Griggs, Caroline Haring (White)   401
Gunther's   137, 138
Guy's Hospital   393

H

Hamilton, George Heard   18, 59, 61, 267, 268, 367, 403, 419
Handel, George Frederic   329
Hardy, Thomas   405
Harman, Claire   3, 8, 21, 210, 214, 233, 353, 376, 387, 388, 390, 399
Harriard   141
Harrods   269
Harrow School   13
Hartzler, Levi   170, 176
Harvard University   36, 388
Harworth   94
Haussmann, Georges-Eugène   412
Hay-Adams House   273
Hearst, William Randolph   228
Hemingway, Ernest   68, 416
Henry V   60, 161–63
Herald Tribune, The   129, 181
Herkovits, Melvin J   220
Hillman, Ernest   59
Hitler, Adolf   129, 145, 159, 161, 167, 210, 237, 239, 261, 285, 410, 415, 421
Hodann, Max   118
Hoffman, Irwin   61, 406

Holahan, Anne   29, 217, 253, 385, 396

Holahan, Elizabeth   376–77

Holahan, Evelyn V   2, 3, 6 29, 217–20, 227, 228, 229, 242, 249, 254, 263, 269, 272, 275, 276, 279, 280, 286, 292, 294, 295, 300, 301, 303, 305, 311, 316–18, 321, 333, 336, 337, 339, 342, 348, 349, 350, 352, 352, 355, 356, 357, 359–62, 364, 365, 367, 371, 373–82, 384, 385, 388, 389, 390, 392, 394, 396, 400–402

Letters and notes

— to EWW 23 December 1940   303

— to EWW 1 September 1949   357

— to EWW 5 September 1949   359

— to EWW 6 September 1949   360

— to EWW 14 September 1949   362

— to EWW 20 September 1949   366

— to EWW 19 March 1950   374

— to EWW 7 July 1950   376

— to VA 9 September 1940   301

Hollywood Anti-Nazi League   220

Home Guard   315

Hopkins, Gerard Manley   157

Hopper, Edward   265

Horace   167, 168

Hore-Belisha, Leslie   267, 419

Horlicks   156, 157

Hortus Floridus   55

Hotel Biltmore   13, 134, 421

Hotel Commodore   176, 412

Hotel Crillon   59

Hotel Latham   242–45, 418

Hotel Piccadilly   149

Hotel Plaza   18, 64, 266, 267

Hotel Plaza Athenée   59

Hotel Splendide   291

Hotel Waylin   18, 134

Hotspur   143, 164, 178, 179, 411

Huebsch, Ben   139, 243, 274

Huntingdon   170

Huntington   145

Hunt, Marion   375

Hyde Park   295

I

Idbury   145, 410, 420

Idlewild Airport   356
Indiana   263
International Brigade   53, 81, 158, 214, 406, 408, 416
Inverness Terrace   19
Ireland   278, 340, 420
Isle of Portland   25
Isle of Purbeck   307, 405
Italy   53, 179, 340, 379, 380

J

Jane Street   220, 221, 231, 417
Jasper County, Missouri   274
Jervoise, Thomas   141
Johnson, Mary Cowper   24
Johnson, Samuel   343
Joplin, Missouri   274, 286, 290, 420

K

Keates, Florence   68, 169, 248, 251, 252, 407
Keats, John   329
Kent   6, 138
Kentucky   263
Kenya   28
Kereces, Tibor   388
Keynes, John Maynard   282, 283
Kibbe family and house   233–36, 242, 243, 418
King's Arms, Amersham   154, 410, 411
King's Arms, Oxford   380
Knopf, Alfred A   22
Knox, Captain and Nesta   142, 410
Kunitz, Stanley   123

L

La Guardia, Fiorello   276
Lamb, The   170
La Monte, Helen   279, 420
de Lancey, Darragh   35, 61
Lawrence, Sir William   159
Lee, Vernon   134, 215, 416
Le Havre   59
Lehman, Herbert   305

Leighton, Claire   18
Liddon, Mrs   133
Lippmann, Walter   129, 130
Little Horsley   142
Long Milford   147
Lorca, Federico Garcia   105, 114, 115, 408
Low Countries   289
Lowestoft   147
Loyalist Spain   125, 126, 134, 176

M

Macaulay, Rose   55, 405
Machen, Arthur   19, 20, 139, 154, 343
Machen family   9, 33, 134, 386, 410
Machen, Janet   42, 113 136–38, 149, 154, 155, 161, 191, 213, 231, 235, 237, 238,
   261, 267 303, 389, 395, 409, 411, 417
Machen, Purefoy   19, 134, 154, 343
MacLeish, Archibald   18, 223
Madras   342
Madrid   40, 50–52
Magdalene College, Cambridge   163
Maillards, New York   134
Malmesbury   42–43, 57, 72, 99, 145
de la Mare, Walter   134, 231
Marnhull   391, 405
Martin, Mary   359
Marxism   54, 74, 78, 132, 221, 415
Massachusetts   34, 36, 44, 130
Mattatuck Historical Society   89, 268, 388
Maxims, Paris   59
McKee, Douglas   47, 356, 367, 406, 424, 425
Mecklenburgh Square   136, 139, 140, 395
Men and Dust   274, 279
Mexico   128, 130, 131, 312, 416
Middlebury, Connecticut   126, 229, 233, 255, 336, 374, 381, 382, 386, 400
Ministry of Information   271, 272
Minnesota   305, 321
Miss Green's cottage, Chaldon   31, 32, 395
Missouri   263, 274, 286, 420
Moline, Roger   339
Molotov-Ribbentrop Pact, see Nazi-Soviet Pact
Montacute   24, 396

More, Henry   178, 412

Moses, Robert   295

Mosley, Sir Oswald   329

Moxon, Granny   46

Mozart, Wolfgang Amadeus   356, 380

Munich   6, 125, 143, 161, 167, 176, 179, 181, 211, 411

Muntz, Elizabeth   5, 9, 23, 20, 24, 30, 31, 33, 264, 266, 327, 396, 398

Murphy, John F X   360, 362, 367

N

National Association for the Advancement of Colored People (NAACP)   93

Narvik   285

National Committee for People's Rights   274

National Executive Committee of the American League against War
   and Fascism   74

Naushon Island, Massachusetts   36

Nazi-Soviet Pact   239, 418

Neligan, Bishop   354

Neruda, Pablo   80

Nesbit, E   54

New Deal   33, 34, 211, 232, 263

New Haven, Connecticut   35, 36, 129, 167, 267, 267, 400

New Masses   219

New Milford, Connecticut   234

New School for Social Research   220

New York   1, 2, 4, 6, 13, 16, 18, 26, 28, 29, 34, 36, 56, 64, 67, 69, 74, 98, 110, 122,
   128, 130, 134, 210, 216, 217, 220, 225, 231, 232, 234, 242, 243, 245, 253, 261,
   263, 266, 269, 277, 294, 303, 305, 333, 343, 356, 360, 383, 386, 388, 395, 396,
   406, 416, 420, 425
   7th Avenue subway   276

New Yorker, The   56, 122, 130, 131, 218, 274, 278, 340

New Zealand   86, 407

Nigeria   397, 427

Nordoff, Paul   220, 231, 233, 237, 331

Norfolk   6, 9, 30, 32, 87, 88, 89, 91, 119, 120, 125, 136, 141, 143, 145, 147, 153,
   155, 241, 263, 295, 297, 300, 341, 379, 385

Northamptonshire   145

North Dakota   305

Northrop, Ruth   374

Norway   285

Norwich   147, 341, 348

Novello, Ivor   161, 162

O

Old Vic, The   60
Olivier, Laurence   60
Osler, Mrs   138, 142, 169
Ottawa, Oklahoma   274
Otway, Thomas   189, 413
Oxford   4, 5, 38, 39, 89, 104, 142, 348, 376, 379, 380–86, 390, 394, 395, 400; see
    also Charlbury Road flat; Christ Church Meadow; Park Town Crescent, Oxford

P

Paget, Violet, see Lee, Vernon
Pallach, 'Comrade'   117, 174
Palladium   149, 161
Parc Buttes Chaumont, Paris   179, 412
Paris 50, 56, 57, 59, 74, 93, 125, 134, 143, 151, 153, 169–72, 174, 176, 178–82,
    184, 185, 189, 193, 246, 289, 290, 348, 350, 367, 372, 374, 412, 413, 425, 426
Parker, Emily   161, 170
Parker, Louis Napoleon   250, 418
Parkinson's 'London Gillyflower'   129
Park Town Crescent, Oxford   381, 382, 390, 394
Paston Letters, The   150
Patch, The   266, 318, 336–38, 340, 342, 343, 352, 356, 359, 365, 376, 379, 382,
    384, 385–87, 394–96, 399, 400–02
Peekskill, New York   360, 361, 425
Pen Mill Hotel, Yeovil   356, 357, 424, 425
Pennsylvania   310, 406
Perry Street   244, 261, 290, 303, 395, 418–20
Petch, Barbara   252
Peterborough   163, 170
Peto, North Carolina   241, 418
Pickett, Clarence   157, 169, 170, 411
Pierson, George   35, 36, 404
Plato   6, 178, 370, 412
Plush   72, 99, 100, 109
Plymouth   157
Poland   210, 239, 278
Poles   278
Pollock, Janet, see Machen, Janet
Pollock, Martin   139, 216, 261, 395, 409, 419
poppadamus [poppadoms]   204
Port-Bou, France   117

Powys, C F   24
Powys family   29, 33, 38, 389, 396
Powys, Gertrude   25–27
Powys, John Cowper   25, 86
Powys, Llewelyn   22, 26, 28, 29, 39, 217, 396
Powys, Mary Cowper (Johnson)   24
Powys, Philippa (Katie)   23–28, 30, 33, 38, 201, 211, 213, 261, 266, 285, 327, 384,
   396, 419, 421
   The Blackthorn Winter   26
   Driftwood and Other Poems   26
   letter to EWW 27 November   1939 261, 419
   letter to EWW 12 April 1940   285, 421
Powys, Theodora (Susie / Susan)   22, 47
Powys, Theodore   3, 5, 21-25, 29, 32, 38, 41, 43, 45–47, 140, 268, 395
   An Interpretation of Genesis   21
   Soliloquies of a Hermit   21
   The Left Leg   21, 22
Powys, Violet   22, 23, 47, 85, 140, 268
Powys, William   27, 28, 199
Progressive Party   339, 353, 423
Prunier's   59, 137, 138, 141, 149
Public Records Office   138, 142
Puddletown   397
Purefoy family   140; see also Machen, Purefoy
Purefoy, George   141
Puritans   17, 194, 387

Q

Quaglino's   59, 60
Quakers   97, 110, 117, 118, 129, 134, 143, 157, 159, 169–71, 176, 395, 406, 412;
   see also AFSC
Queen's Gate, Kensington   135, 409

R

Rats' Barn   27, 60, 127, 199, 201, 209, 266
Read, Herbert   267
Red Cross   43, 294, 297, 305, 340, 401, 421
Reigate   139, 141
Reith, John   271, 272, 420
Renn, Ludwig   132, 211, 214, 215, 217, 269, 283, 415
Reynolds, Stephen   24

Rhode Island   15
Richardson, Stanley   152
Rilke, Rainer Maria   47
Ring, Carola   390, 397, 402
Ring, Charles   331, 390, 397, 427
Ring, Monica (Hemmings)   309, 316, 318, 325, 327, 330, 333, 342, 343, 346,
     390, 397, 402
Riverside Cemetery, Waterbury   400
Roberts, Clyde   170
Robeson, Paul   360, 425
Rochester, New York   217, 376
Rogers Florists, Dorchester   261, 340, 419
Rogers, Mrs   138, 149, 241, 248
Rohde, Miss   139, 141
Roosevelt, Franklin Delano   33, 145, 210, 267, 421
Rossetti, Dante Gabriel   15
Rousseau, Jean-Jacques
     Le Doaunier   87
Russia   53, 84, 115, 238, 281; see also Soviet Union
Russian War Relief   305, 318, 321, 335, 353, 357, 401, 423

S

Sacre Coeur   179
Sailor's Return, The   5, 31, 32, 60
Salisbury   4, 370, 390–2
Salisbury, Lord, see Cranborne, Viscount
Sapieha   278
Saturday Evening Post, The   211
Savoy Hotel   30, 60
Scapa Flow   279
Scilly Islanders   306
Scott, John Robertson   145, 267, 274, 410
     The Countryman   274, 279, 410
Scottsboro Boys, The   73, 93, 94
Scott, Sir Walter   251
Seghers, Anna   310, 313, 422
Service Special des Jeunes   339
Shadwick, travel agent   149, 156, 161, 171
Shelley, Percy Bysshe   58
Shipley, R C   279
Silchester   390
Simpsons-in-the-Strand   137, 138

Sir John Soane's Museum   138
Skilton, John   59
Skinner, Mr   228
Smith, G   138
Smith, Mr and Mrs   211, 248, 285, 415
Snell, Sara   137
Snow White   204
Soap for Spain Fund   50, 52, 81, 89, 92, 93, 160, 173
Society of British Herbalists   141
Socorro Rojo   112, 121
Somerset   24, 141, 396, 406
Southampton   60, 138, 156, 157, 159, 162, 188, 189, 217, 250
South Carolina   15, 18, 34, 210
South Dakota   357, 401
Soviet Union   40, 239, 279, 305, 352, 425; see also Russia
Spain   1, 40, 43, 46, 50, 52, 53, 56, 58, 66, 73, 82–84, 97, 100, 101, 103–07, 112, 114–18, 123, 125, 126, 129, 130, 134, 135, 137, 143, 149, 150–52, 154, 157, 158, 160, 161, 166, 169–76, 178, 180, 181, 189, 208, 210, 214, 239, 344, 395, 406, 407, 416
Spanish Armada   5
Spanish Civil War   1, 6, 416
Spanish Republic   52, 106, 107, 215, 346, 411, 416
SS *Aquitania*   217, 220, 234, 246, 247, 399, 416, 417
SS *Bremen*   60, 63, 64, 75, 80, 100, 134, 162, 232, 356, 409
SS *Europa*   128, 134, 162
SS *Mauretania*   231
SS *Normandie*   59
SS *Queen Mary*   156, 163, 218, 219
Stalin, Joseph   239, 352, 353
Steam Boat Springs, Colorado   270
Steinbeck, John
    Of Mice and Men   68, 70
Stewart, Donald Ogden   220
Stewart, Douglas   86
Stinton, Judith   27, 30
St Paul, Minnesota   321
Stratford-on-Avon   8, 42
Street   157, 159, 406
Strong, Anna Louise   84, 90, 407
Stuart, Francis   134
Sturminster Newton   391
Swarthmore, Pennsylvania   406
Swift, Jonathan   103

T

Tathman, C   139
Taylor, Prentiss   36, 39, 109, 110, 130, 401, 408
Thame   142
Thames, the   6, 308
Third American Writers' Conference   216, 220
Thomas (cat)   43, 45, 54, 55, 57, 65, 71, 75, 85, 100, 102, 105, 128, 153, 188, 205, 248, 343, 368
Thomas, Edward   115
Thomson, Miss   170
Three Trees, North Dakota   270
Tilney, Bradford   161
The Times Literary Supplement   3
The Times   179, 251
Tobias and Sara   368, 369
Tolmin, Stephen (Tommy)   21
Tomas (cat)   217, 234, 241, 265, 267, 340, 342, 343, 345, 356, 357, 360, 362, 374, 376, 392, 399, 417
Torquay   345
Towcester   145
Towzer (cat)   57, 67, 85
Traherne, Thomas   150, 151
Trinity House   306
Tri-State Commission   263, 273, 274, 279, 290, 294, 420
    Living, Working, and Health Conditions in the Tri-State Mining Area   274
Troilus and Cressida   170
Truman administration   339
Tudor Church Music   13
Tythrop House   107, 108, 111, 115, 408

U

University City, Madrid   121
Untermeyer, Jean Starr   69, 406
US Department of Labor   263, 274, 420
US Department of State   274
US Passport Bureau   279, 420
USSR, see Soviet Union

V

Valencia   50, 82, 118, 180, 215
Vale of the White Horse   151
van der Pass, Crispin   55
Vatican, the   50
Vergil   168
Vermont   272, 280
Vesuvius   295
Victoria the Great   137, 138
Viking Press   140, 218, 236
Virgil, see Vergil

W

Waddell, Helen   268
Wade, Martha (Starkwether)   336
Walden   120, 123
Wallace, Henry A   339, 344, 346, 353
Walsh, Dr   268
Ward, F J (bookseller)   150, 368
Warner, Sylvia Townsend, *passim*
    After the Death of Don Juan   133, 137, 139, 158
    A Garland of Straw   333
    I'll Stand by You   3, 348, 399, 418
    Lolly Willowes   13, 129
    Mr Fortune's Maggot   13
    The True Heart   18
    Summer Will Show   219
    Letters and notes
    — to EVH 14 May 1936   218
    — to EVH 23 July 1936   219
    — to EVH 17 June 1939   228
    — to EVH 13 October 1939   249
    — to EVH 29 October 1939   254
    — to EVH 18 January 1940   269
    — to EVH 28 February 1940   276
    — to EVH 29 March 1940   280
    — to EVH 18 July 1940   295
    — to EVH 5 January 1941   305
    — to EWW 25 December 1936   44
    — to EWW 6 March 1937   50
    — to EWW l April 1937   54

— to EWW 4 April 1937   56
— to EWW 25 April 1937   58
— to EWW 14 May 1937   64
— to EWW 21 May 1937   69
— to EWW 16 June 1937   71
— to EWW 2 August 1937   81
— to EWW 27 August 1937   83
— to EWW 7 September 1937   92
— to EWW 23 September 1937   101
— to EWW 2 December 1937   116
— to EWW 29 December 1937   121
— to EWW 12 July 1938   130
— to EWW 20 August 1938   136
— to EWW 27 August 1938   139
— to EWW 12 September 1938   143
— to EWW 24 September 1938   152
— to EWW 25 September 1938   156
— to EWW 30 September 1938   164
— to EWW 1 October 1938   169
— to EWW 5 October 1938   171
— to EWW 8 October 1938   171
— to EWW 14 October 1938   176
— to EWW 19 October 1938   185, 188
— to EWW 20 October 1938   189
— to EWW 5 April 1939   215
— to EWW 14 May 1939   216
— to EWW 8 June 1939   221
— to EWW 18 July 1939   234
— to EWW 8 September 1939   241
— to EWW 19 September 1939   243
— to EWW 3 October 1939   245
— to EWW 13 October 1939   247
— to EWW January 1940   264
— to EWW 12 June 1940   290
— to EWW December 1943   324
— to EWW 16 September 1945   339
— to EWW 10 January 1946   341
— to EWW 29 December 1947   342
— to EWW 24 January 1948   344
— to EWW 31 March 1948   345
— to EWW 10 November 1969   394
— to MWW 19 November 1938   193
— to MWW 26 December 1938   206

Poems
— 'And now it is that I'   192
— 'Sometimes a Christ'   193
Warren, Connecticut   233–35, 239, 240, 243, 331, 332, 365, 370, 395, 418;
see also Kibbe House
Washington, DC   137, 221, 273, 274, 279, 397, 420
Waterbury, Connecticut   13, 15–17, 34, 50, 58, 61, 73, 81, 89, 96–98, 101, 102,
105, 117, 118, 156, 268, 294, 305, 336, 346, 352, 375, 388, 400
Waterloo Station   141
Watson Galleries   228
Webb, Beatrice and Sydney   310
Wells-next-the-sea   175
West Chaldon, see Chaldon
Westminster Abbey   56, 161, 162
Westminster Bridge   162
Weston and Hardin   140
Westover School   15, 16, 33, 279, 381
Weymouth   310, 334
White, Elizabeth Wade
Anne Bradstreet, The Tenth Muse   40, 63, 100, 135, 141, 190, 198, 207, 354,
376, 379, 381, 383, 384
Letters and notes
— on the Nazi-Soviet Pact, August1939   239
— talk on Spanish Civil War relief   52
— to EVH 26 December 1940   303
— to MWW 18 August 1938   135
— to MWW 22 August 1938   139
— to MWW 25 September 1938   154
— to MWW 1 October 1938   161
— to MWW 4 October 1938   170
— to MWW 11 October 1938   176
— to MWW 15 October 1938   180
— to MWW 26 October 1938   189
— to MWW 25 December 1938   204
— to STW 21 June 1938   126
— to STW early 1940   274
— to VA 12 September 1937   97
— to VA 9 March 1939   213
— to VA February 1940   273
Poems
— 'April in England'   284
— 'Now that delight is known'   227

— 'September 1939'   240
— 'Shall we blame Spring'   213
— 'The old year's youngest fire'   124
White, Henry Wade ('Wade')   7, 14, 17, 47, 59, 64, 134, 135, 143, 167, 192, 220, 222, 266, 267, 268, 313, 352, 356, 367, 376, 380, 383, 384, 386, 387, 389, 400, 402, 403, 417, 427
American Precisionist style   17, 388
White & Holahan Books   336
White, Mary (Wade)   15, 129, 130, 134, 142, 143, 145, 154, 167, 176, 181, 189, 193, 197–99, 203, 204, 206, 210, 220, 222, 225, 232, 266, 336, 338, 348, 351–53, 367, 376, 385, 386, 402, 423
Letters and notes
— to EWW 15 October 1938   181
— to EWW 17 October 1938   181
— to EWW 30 October 1938   190
— to EWW 21 November 1938   190
— to EWW 1 December 1938   197
— to EWW 12 December 1938   203
— to EWW 15 December 1938   203
— to EWW 17 December 1938   203
— to EWW 23 February 1939   210
White, William Henry   15, 16, 19, 33, 34, 63, 119, 135, 143, 155, 156, 166, 167, 203, 220, 222, 225, 266, 338, 353, 356, 357, 359, 362, 366, 385, 386, 400, 403
Whitman, Walt   118, 213
Wilcox family graves   418
Wilhelm Meister   215
Willkie, Wendell   298, 421
Wilmington, Delaware   64, 395, 406
Winfrith Heath   21
Winterton   30, 143–47, 185, 197, 206, 208, 210, 215, 220, 232, 263, 235, 295, 300, 313, 314, 322, 389, 410, 421, 425
woad (Isatis tinctoria)   141, 207, 410
Women's Land Army   261
Woodlawn Trustees   64
Woodsford Castle   43, 405
Woolcombe, Joan (Ackland)   355, 424
Wool   60, 141
Working Women's College   177
Wren churches   306, 307
Writer's Association, The   55
WVS, Women's Voluntary Service   319

Y

Yale College   17, 34, 35, 36, 47, 59, 268, 400, 403, 404, 406, 419
Yang, Shelley   144
Yarmouth   147
Yeovil   348, 356, 365, 397, 424, 425
YMCA   307

About the author

Peter Haring Judd graduated from Harvard College AB *cum laude* in 1954; he served two years in the US Army as an enlisted man in Staff communications at the Pentagon. He earned a PhD from the Department of Political Science, Columbia University in 1970, with the dissertation, British Perspectives on the United States, 1840–1860.

He was with the Corporate and Environmental Planning Department of Northeast Utilities in Connecticut for twenty years, with numerous writing assignments and latterly planning a system-wide energy conservation initiative. In 1983 he was appointed Assistant Commissioner, Energy Conservation Division, in the Department of Housing Preservation and Development (HPD) in New York City. He retired from New York City service in 1991.

His *The Hatch and Brood of Time: Five Phelps Families* in *the North Atlantic World, 1730–1880* (1999) received the Year 2000 award for family history from the Connecticut Society of Genealogists and from the American Society of Genealogists, the Donald Lines Jacobus Award, the leading award in the field. His *More Lasting than Brass: a Thread of Family from Revolutionary New York to Industrial Connecticut* (2004) received the Grand Prize in genealogy from the Connecticut Society. In 2008 he published a three-volume account of the direct paternal and maternal ancestries of his four grandparents, *Four American Ancestries: White, Griggs, Cowles, Judd ... and related families*. His two-volume compilation of family letters, *Affection: Ninety Years of Family Letters, 1850s–1930s: Haring, White, Griggs, Judd Families of New York and Waterbury, Connecticut* (2008), received the Connecticut Society's Literary Awards Prize in Family History. In March 2008 The Association of Professional Genealogists Quarterly published his article, 'Adding Muscle and Sinew: Spicing Up a Family Narrative'. He is a professional actor, performing regularly in New York's smaller theaters. He lives on Manhattan's Upper West Side and is active in numerous cultural organizations.

www.peterhjudd.com